# REFLECTIONS
## OF A
# NEOCONSERVATIVE

# REFLECTIONS OF A NEOCONSERVATIVE

*Looking Back, Looking Ahead*

## Irving Kristol

Basic Books, Inc., Publishers

NEW YORK

Library of Congress Cataloging in Publication Data

Kristol, Irving.
  Reflections of a neoconservative.

  Includes index.
  1.  Conservatism—Addresses, essays, lectures.
2.  Political science—Addresses, essays, lectures.
3.  Economics—Addresses, essays, lectures.   4.   World
politics—1945–          —Addresses, essays, lectures.
I.  Title.
H33.K73   1983        320.5′2        83–70763
ISBN 0–465–06872–3

For

Gertrude Himmelfarb Kristol,

my wife and intellectual companion

of four decades

*Everything that passes for politics today will be unmasked as religion tomorrow.*

—KIERKEGAARD


*Everything begins with the mystical and ends in the political.*

—PÉGUY

# CONTENTS

# Contents

## V

## NEOCONSERVATISM AND FOREIGN POLICY

## VI

## RELIGION AND THE JEWS

# INTRODUCTION

It was the socialist critic Michael Harrington who first applied the term "neoconservative" to those who, like myself, had begun to move away from a liberalism that had lost its moral and political bearings. It is hardly surprising that I should have acquired a new political identity in this way. The key ideological terms of modern political debate have all been either invented or popularized by the Left—"liberal," "conservative," and "reactionary," "socialist" and "capitalist," "Left" and "Right" themselves—so that it is extremely difficult for those on the non-Left to come up with an adequate self-definition. They would have to invent a wholly new political vocabulary. The sensible course, therefore, is to take your label, claim it as your own, and run with it.

Every now and then, to be sure, someone who is not of the Left will declare that all these ideological categories are outmoded, and the time has come to proceed with the business of politics in some kind of pragmatic, nonideological way. But such declarations are as if written on water. They usually represent little more than an effort, in a spirit of resignation, to ratify the views of the more moderate Left as a new consensus and orthodoxy on which public policy will be based. That effort always fails. The policies of the moderate Left invariably turn out to have germinating within themselves contradictions that lead to crises in economic policy, social policy, foreign policy. And as the moderate Left comes into discredit, the more militant and extreme Left once again regains the commanding heights of ideological authority.

To be sure, the Right also revives and quickens to life under such circumstances. It may even win elections or, in nonparliamentary regimes, seize power through a military coup. But these tend to represent little more than temporary interregna. For it is characteristic of the Right—has been characteristic for well over a century and a half now—that it neither convincingly claims ideological authority nor even feels the need to make such a claim. And, in the modern world, a non-ideological politics is a politics disarmed.

It has been so since the American and French revolutions, which ushered in the ideological era of politics. This politics is ideological in the sense that it consists of political beliefs that are oriented in a melioristic way—a "progressive" way, as one says—toward the future. It is impossible for any set of political beliefs in the modern era to engage popular sentiments without such a basic orientation. In this sense, all modern societies of whatever kind conceive themselves to be progressive. The rare exception, an overtly "reactionary," backward-looking regime, is correctly perceived to be an absurd and transient, and usually nasty, anachronism.

The reason modern politics is so essentially ideological is that modern reality—economic, social, technological, intellectual, political—will not have it otherwise. Only in a static society can politics conform to its traditional premodern ideal: "tending to the arrangements of society" (in Michael Oakeshott's phrase) in a sober and prudent way, so as to achieve domestic tranquillity, while conforming to traditional notions of just, official behavior. But in a world of scientific-technological innovation and economic growth, with all its transformations of economic and social reality as well as the accompanying changes of values and habits, politics must of necessity assume another guise. It must be committed to shaping the future with at least as much energy as to preserving a traditional attachment to the past.

But there are different political modes of progressiveness with radically different political implications. In the modern world there are two such modes: the one arising from the French-Continental Enlightenment, the other from the Anglo-Scottish Enlightenment. The two overlap, of course; they were both, after all, aspects of that great intellectual and spiritual movement we call the Enlightenment, a movement that created the preconditions of modernity itself. The differences, however, are even more significant, and are exemplified in the two different revolutions they gave birth to, the French and the American, and in the two modern political traditions they defined.

It was in the relation of politics to economics, and of politics to religion, that these two traditions most starkly differentiated themselves. The French Revolution promised not only liberty, fraternity, equality, but "happiness" itself. It was logical, therefore, that the nineteenth-century heirs to this tradition should affirm that the state, in the hands of the "right men" and following the "correct" policies, could solve, through central planning, the economic problems of society—the problem of poverty simultaneously with the problem of economic inequality, the problem of vigorous economic growth simultaneously with a "fair" distribution of economic goods. For this to come to pass, the government had to manage the economy while reforming the minds of its people so that economic incentives were displaced by "social" incentives as spurs to economic growth. The germs of twentieth-century totalitarianism, whether self-declared Left or Right, were activated by that grandiose, indeed utopian, commitment.

In contrast, the Anglo-Scottish Enlightenment produced an Adam Smith and a James Madison rather than a Robespierre or a Saint-Simon. The aim was not to minimize or abolish self-interest as a goad to economic and political activity but instead to channel that self-interest into the disciplinary context of the marketplace for goods, and into that simulacrum of a "marketplace" for influence and ideas known as representative government. The assumption was that as men improved their material condition through economic activity, and as they gained experience in self-government, they would become more "civil," more enlightened, more gentle and humane in their relations with one another.

Moreover, the Anglo-Scottish Enlightenment further assumed that the increase of affluence would bring with it a strengthening of those traditional moral values hitherto associated with church and synagogue. These values might become more secular, less theological, in the ways they were perceived, felt, or interpreted, but they would still have the power to "civilize" the individuals in the new, liberal community. It was this respectfulness toward moral beliefs as part of a spiritual heritage that allowed Edmund Burke, generally regarded as the founder of modern conservatism, to be a friend and admirer of Adam Smith. The Continental Enlightenment, on the other hand, with its far more ambitious aims, could rest content with nothing less than a true "transvaluation of values," with traditional religions discarded into "the dustbin of history," and with the new history of a new era discovering, immanent within its own progressive unfolding, new and appropriate values. Its temper therefore inclined toward a gnostic hostility to a world it had never created but had merely been born into, and an antinomian contempt for merely established institutions and codes of conduct from which it sought "liberation."

Over these past two centuries it is the legacy of the French-Continental Enlightenment that has come to dominate the political culture of the modern world. It has done so either brutally, in the Soviet Union most notably, but also in the several dozen self-declared "Marxist" regimes established since World War II; or hesitantly, as in "social-democratic" polities; or insidiously, with the infusion of "Left" (i.e., gnostic-antinomian) ideas, attitudes, and sentiments into liberal societies. This last has been the American experience. The liberal impulse in the United States has moved decidedly leftward in the past fifty years, while what is called "conservatism" is, among economists and in the business community, little more than a nostalgia for the nineteenth-century version of liberalism. (Among intellectuals the nostalgia usually reaches further back into the centuries.)

It is within this new constellation of ideological forces that neoconservatism emerged as an intellectual tendency in the late 1960s and 1970s. What is "neo" ("new") about this conservatism is that it is resolutely free of nostalgia. It, too, claims the future—and it is this claim, more than anything else, that drives its critics on the Left into something approaching a frenzy of denunciation. Those critics feel not at all uncomfortable coping with the economic conservatism of a Milton Friedman, the social conservatism of a Friedrich Hayek, the cultural conservatism of a Russell Kirk, or the philosophical and political conservatism of a Leo Strauss. They regard these as pockets of resistance, either to be cleaned up when time permits or simply left to wither on the vine. But neoconservatism has the kind of ideological self-consciousness and self-assurance—most of its original spokesmen, after all, had migrated from the Left—and even ideological boldness which has hitherto been regarded as the legitimate (indeed exclusive) property of the Left.

It must be emphasized that much of the intellectual substance of neoconservatism—to the degree, at least, that this has been defined so far—derives from these other conservative tendencies. From Milton Friedman, neoconservatism has learned to appreciate the virtues of a market economy as the engine of economic growth. From Friedrich Hayek it has learned to appreciate the important truth that social institutions are the product of human action but rarely of human design. From the cultural conservatives and the political philosopher Leo Strauss it has learned to appreciate the significance of precapitalist moral and philosophical traditions.

In this regard, neoconservatism is a syncretistic intellectual movement. But it aims at more than syncretism; it seeks a new synthesis. For aside from what it has inherited from preexisting conservative outlooks, it has its own distinctive inclinations. In economic and social policy, it feels no lingering hostility to the welfare state, nor does it accept it resignedly, as a necessary evil. Instead it seeks not to dismantle the welfare state in the name of free-market economics but rather to reshape it so as to attach to it the *conservative* predispositions of the people. This reshaping will presumably take the form of trying to rid the welfare state of its paternalistic orientation, imposed on it by Left-liberalism, and making it over into the kind of "social insurance state" that provides the social and economic security a modern citizenry demands while minimizing governmental intrusion into individual liberties. Limited government, as neoconservatives see it, is not in opposition to energetic government. The two can be and ought to be natural corollaries of one another.

As with domestic policy, so with foreign policy. Neoconservatism is not merely patriotic—that goes without saying—but also nationalist. Patriotism springs from love of the nation's past; nationalism arises out of hope for the nation's future, distinctive greatness. Nationalism in our time is probably the most powerful of political emotions. The extreme Left knows this, which is why, when it is in power, it immediately attaches nationalism to its ideological aspirations. The moderate Left, the social-democratic Left, is so preoccupied with its domestic agenda that it is instinctively antinationalist, and this is a profound source of its weakness. Traditional conservatism, in our century at least, will blow the patriotic bugles at appropriate occasions, but it is far less interested in foreign policy than in economics. Neoconservatives believe—as does the Left—that politics always takes some degree of priority over economics, and that in foreign policy this is most especially true. They therefore believe that the goals of American foreign policy must go well beyond a narrow, too literal definition of "national security." It is the national interest of a world power, as this is defined by a sense of national destiny, that American foreign policy is about, not a myopic national security.

I have said that neoconservatism accepts without qualm the inevitable priority of politics over economics. It is this that gives it its contemporaneity of spirit, and makes the Left so extraordinarily anxious about a "movement"—not more than an intellectual tendency really—that is, in strictly political terms, only moderately influential. But it is also this fixing of priorities that creates tensions between neoconservatism and what one may call establishment conservatism as represented by the Republican party. It brings neoconservatives into frequent disagreements with conservative economists, most of whom are loath, perhaps as a consequence of a *déformation professionelle,* to give politics priority over "correct" economics. It also brings neoconservatives into frequent disagreement with the business community, especially the corporate community, which tends to be apolitical (in the larger sense of the term) when it is not antipolitical. And, inevitably, this means that neoconservatives will often find themselves at odds with the cast of mind represented by established conservative politicians.

It has been remarked, by some of the critics as well as some of the advocates of neoconservatism, that there appears to be a "populist" temper to the neoconservative impulse. Though the term is unfortunate, there is a kind of truth behind the statement. Any ideology that gives politics a priority over economics is bound to have a populist hue, since most ordinary people—in this day and age at least, and perhaps always—see things in that same order. The "conservatism" of neoconservatism leads naturally to an insistence on standards of excellence and virtue; it is anything but populist in that respect, and indeed would seem to be what we have come to call "elitist." (This is most obvious in its attitude toward education and public morals.) But the "neo" in neoconservatism is its insistence that the American people have always had an instinctive deference toward such standards, and that the American democracy has never been egalitarian in this sense. Economic and cultural egalitarianism—as distinct from the social and legal egalitarianism essential to a viable democracy—has been a passion of the intellectual class, never of the people. This is another way of saying that the American people remain profoundly bourgeois, in their populism as in so many other respects.

Because this populism is bourgeois, the American people are simultaneously individualistic and communal in their outlook. They really do believe there is such a thing as the "public interest"—a *res publica* that is something more than the summation of individual interests. In this they depart from the individualist-utilitarian model of nineteenth-century liberalism that has been preserved within conventional twentieth-century conservatism. But they do not believe this public interest can be rationally defined, at a moment in time, by any kind of expert or consortium of experts, and they definitely do not believe that, in peacetime at any rate, it receives its incarnation in the federal government in Washington. Rather they believe it to emerge from the process of self-government in all relevant institutions—government at all levels, but also local school boards, religious congregations, professional organizations, trade unions, trade associations, organized charities, organized enthusiasm for almost any imaginable activity. It is in institutions such as these that American individualism and its bourgeois populism find their most congenial expression.

And it is the spirit of bourgeois populism, until recently so inarticulate, that neoconservatism seeks to define, refine, and represent. To put it in somewhat grandiose terms: Neoconservatism aims to infuse American bourgeois orthodoxy with a new self-conscious intellectual vigor, while dispelling the feverish mélange of gnostic humors that, for more than a century now, has suffused our political beliefs and has tended to convert them into political religions. Our intellectuals may feel "alienated" from the orthodoxy represented by "the American way of life"; they may feel homeless and hopeless in the world this way of life has created. The American people, in their overwhelming majority, do not feel so alienated, homeless, or hopeless. It is the self-imposed assignment of neoconservatism to explain to the American people why they are right, and to the intellectuals why they are wrong.

The essays in this book, written at various times and for different occasions, have been collected with an eye to explaining my own evolution from a youthful socialism toward a more mature—I should like to think!—neoconservatism, and also to give as clear a sense as possible of what the intellectual and political substance of neoconservatism, as I interpret it, is today. My interpretation, of course, is not authoritative. Other neoconservatives may disagree with this emphasis or that—we are in no way a coherent, organized movement—but I should be surprised if those disagreements were more than marginal.

In order to give a more precise historical perspective on this evolution, I have included, in addition to two autobiographical memoirs, three essays on Judaism written some three decades ago. These essays reveal a strong inclination to religious neoorthodoxy—in theory if not in observance—at a time when I casually assumed myself to be a liberal in politics. Some of the more astute readers of these essays at the time warned me that they emitted nonliberal premonitions. They turned out, of course, to be absolutely right.

I have also reprinted some essays from my first book, *On the Democratic Idea in America* (1972), because the book itself is out of print and because they help round out the neoconservative point of view as it has evolved over time.

I have reprinted all of the essays as originally written and published, despite the fact that I would surely say some things differently today, and might not even say some things at all. But I do presume to think that the quest over the years for a neoconservative point of view is at least as interesting as the point of view that I have finally come to hold today. Becoming a neoconservative has, for me, been a most engaging process of self-education, and I should like to believe that there are men and women who might wish to share this process with me.

New York, New York
February 1983

# I

# IN THE
# BEGINNING . . .

# 1

# *Memoirs of*
# *a Trotskyist*

Nᴏᴛ ʟᴏɴɢ ᴀɢᴏ, I passed through the Loeb Student Center, at New York University's Washington Square campus. It is a modern and luxurious building—to my eyes, definitely "posh"—with comfortable sofas and chairs, ample space and light and all those little amenities that correspond to our middle-class notions of "gracious living." On that particular day, the main lounge was half-empty; a few students were slumped in armchairs, reading or dozing, while here and there groups of two or three were chatting over cups of coffee. As I stood there gazing with wonder at the opulence of it all, and with puzzlement at the languor of it all, I was prompted once again to remember the physical squalor and mental energy of Alcove No. 1 at CCNY [City College of New York].

Such memories had been provoked more than once during the turbulent 1960s. Anyone who had been a student radical in the 1930s was bound to be moved to compare his own experiences (or the recollections of his own experiences) with the rebellions he observed a generation later. The danger of such an exercise, in the heat of the tumult, is the natural temptation toward the fogy's lament: "Why can't they be as we were?" In truth, that is a legitimate question—if it is meant seriously as a question, and not merely as a reproach.

Perhaps now that the wave of student radicalism has subsided, to be succeeded (temporarily at least) by a kind of sullen resignation, one can put those memories to paper without seeming patronizing or self-serving. The student radicalism of the 1930s was indeed different from that of the 1960s, and different in ways that tell us something important, I think, about what happened to American society (and to the rebels against that society) in the intervening decades. And if the comparison is to the advantage of the earlier radicalism—as I admit right off it will be—it is because, in my opinion, the United States in the 1930s was in many ways a healthier (if materially far less prosperous) society than it has become, so that rebellion was healthier, too.

I was graduated from City College in the spring of 1940, and the honor I most prized was the fact that I was a member in good standing of the Young People's Socialist League (Fourth International). This organization was commonly, and correctly, designated as Trotskyist (not "Trotskyite," which was a term used only by the official Communists, or "Stalinists" as we called them, of the day). I have not set foot on the City College campus since my commencement. The present president of the college, Robert Marshak, has amiably urged me to come and see the place again—it is very different but still recognizable, he says. I have promised to go, but somehow I think I may never find the time.

It is not that my memories of CCNY are disagreeable. On the contrary: When I think back to those years, it is with a kind of nostalgia. It was at that place, and in that time, that I met the young men—there were no women at the uptown campus then—who became my lifelong friends. The education I got was pretty good, even if most of it was acquired outside the classroom. My personal life was no messier or more troubled than any adolescent's. True, I was poor—but so was everyone else, and I was by no means the poorest. True, too, it was not fun commuting by subway for more than an hour each way from and to Brooklyn, where I lived. But the memory of poverty and those tedious subway rides has faded with time, whereas what I now recollect most vividly is the incredible vivacity with which we all confronted the dismal 1930s.

Is it then perhaps my radical past, now so firmly disowned, that bothers me and makes CCNY unhallowed ground? I think not. I have no regret about that episode in my life. Joining a radical movement when one is young is very much like falling in love when one is young. The girl may turn out to be rotten, but the experience of love is so valuable it can never be entirely undone by the ultimate disenchantment.

But my feelings toward those radical days are even more positive than this kind of general reflection suggests. For the truth is that being a young radical was not simply part of my college experience; it was practically the whole of it. If I left City College with a better education than did many students at other and supposedly better colleges, it was because my involvement in radical politics put me in touch with people and ideas that prompted me to read and think and argue with a furious energy. This was not a typical experience—I am talking about a relatively small group of students, a particular kind of student radical. Going to City College meant, for me, being a member of this group. It was a privileged experience, and I know of no one who participated in it who does not look back upon it with some such sentiment.

So why have I never returned to visit the place? Perhaps because I know it is impossible. *That* place no longer exists. It has vanished with the time of which it was so integral a part. Whatever is now happening at City College, I doubt that I am likely to comprehend, much less enjoy, it. For what I have seen of student radicalism on various campuses over the past dozen years baffles and bothers me. It seems to be more a psychological than a truly political phenomenon. There is a desperate quest for self-identity, an evident and acute involvement of one's political beliefs with all kinds of personal anxieties and neuroses, a consequent cheerlessness and truculence.

The changing connotation of the term "alienated" tells us much. At City College in the 1930s we were familiar enough with the word and the idea behind it. But for us it was a sociological category and referred to the condition of the working class. We were not alienated. By virtue of being radical intellectuals, we had "transcended" alienation (to use another Marxist term). We experienced our radicalism as a privilege of rank, not as a burden imposed by a malignant fate. It would never have occurred to us to denounce anyone or anything as "elitist." The elite was us—the "happy few" who had been chosen by History to guide our fellow creatures toward a secular redemption.

Alcove No. 1 was located in the City College lunchroom, a vast ground-floor space which even we, who came from slums or near-slums, judged to be an especially slummy and smelly place. There was a small semicircular counter where one could buy franks or milk or coffee. I suppose they also sold some sandwiches, but I certainly never bought one, and I do not remember anyone else ever committing such an act of unmitigated profligacy. The less poor among us purchased a frank or two; the rest brought their lunches from home—hard-boiled egg sandwiches, cream-cheese sandwiches, peanut-butter sandwiches, once in a while even a chicken sandwich—and there was always a bit of sandwich swapping to enliven one's diet. There was also some sandwich scrounging by those who were *really* poor; one asked and gave without shame or reservation.

The center of the lunchroom, taking up most of the space, consisted of chest-high, wooden tables under a low, artificial ceiling. There, most of the students ate their lunches, standing up. (I looked upon this as being reasonable, since at Boys' High, in Brooklyn, we had had the same arrangement. To this day I find it as natural to eat a sandwich standing up as sitting down.) Around this central area there was a fairly wide and high-ceilinged aisle; and bordering the aisle, under large windows with small panes of glass that kept out as much light as they let in, were the alcoves—semicircular (or were they rectangular?), each with a bench fitted along the wall and a low, long refectory table in the middle. The first alcove on the right, as you entered the lunchroom, was Alcove No. 1, and this soon became most of what City College meant to me. It was there one ate lunch, played Ping-Pong (sometimes with a net, sometimes without), passed the time of day between and after classes, argued incessantly, and generally devoted oneself to solving the ultimate problems of the human race. The penultimate problems we figured could be left for our declining years, after we had graduated.

I would guess that, in all, there were more than a dozen alcoves, and just how rights of possession had been historically established was as obscure as the origins of the social contract itself. Once established, however, they endured, and in a manner typical of New York's "melting pot," each religious, ethnic, cultural, and political group had its own little alcove. There was a Catholic alcove, the "turf" of the Newman Society, a Zionist alcove, an Orthodox Jewish alcove; there was a black alcove for the handful of blacks then at CCNY, an alcove for members of the athletic teams, and so forth. But the only alcoves that mattered to me were No. 1 and No. 2, the alcoves of the anti-Stalinist Left and pro-Stalinist Left, respectively. It was between these two alcoves that the war of the worlds was fought, over the faceless bodies of the mass of students, whom we tried desperately to manipulate into "the right position" but about whom, to tell the truth, we knew little and cared less.

City College was known at the time as a "radical" institution, and in an era when most college students identified themselves as Republicans the ascription was not incorrect. If there were any Republicans at City—and there must have been some—I never met them, or even heard of their existence. Most of the students, from Jewish working-class or lower-middle-class backgrounds with a socialist tint, were spontaneously sympathetic to the New Deal and F.D.R. The really left-wing groups, though larger than elsewhere, were a distinct minority. Alcove No. 2, by far the most populous of the "political" alcoves, could rarely mobilize more than four hundred or five hundred out of a total enrollment of perhaps twenty thousand students for a protest rally, or "action"; we in Alcove No. 1 numbered about thirty "regulars" and were lucky to get an audience of fifty to one hundred for one of ours. But then, as now, student government and student politics were a minority affair, and what the passive majority thought really did not matter. What "happened" on campus was determined by *them*—the denizens of Alcove No. 2—or *us*. In truth, very little did happen; but at the time what did seemed terribly important. During my first three years, *they* controlled the college newspaper; in my last year, we got control. It was a glorious victory, and I do think that we went on to publish a slightly less mendacious newspaper—but I have not even a vague remembrance of what we were slightly less mendacious about.

I shall not say much about Alcove No. 2—the home of the pro-Stalinist Left—but, Lord, how dreary a bunch they seemed to be! I thought then, with a sectarian snobbery that comes so easily to young radicals, that they really did not and never would amount to much. And I must say—at the risk of being accused of smugness—that in all these intervening decades, only two names from Alcove No. 2 have come to my attention. One is now a scientist at a major university. The other was Julius Rosenberg.

I do believe their dreariness was a fact, and that this dreariness in turn had something to do with the political outlook they took it upon themselves to espouse. These were young college students who, out of sympathy with Communism as officially established in the Soviet Union, had publicly to justify the Moscow trials and the bloody purge of old Bolsheviks; had publicly to accept the self-glorification of Joseph Stalin as an exemplar of Communist virtue and wisdom; had publicly to deny that there were concentration camps in the Soviet Union, and so forth, and so forth. Moreover, since this was the period of the popular front, they had for the time to repudiate (by way of reinterpretation) most of the Marxist-Leninist teachings on which their movement was ostensibly founded.

Though I had no trouble understanding how a young man at that time could have joined the Young Communist League, or one of its "fronts," I did find it hard to imagine how he stayed there. Not everyone did stay, of course; many of the members of Alcove No. 1 had had their first political experience with a Stalinist group and had left in disillusionment. But those who did stay on for any length of time—well, it had to have deleterious effects on their quality of mind. After all, members of the congregation of Alcove No. 2 were actually forbidden, under pain of ostracism and exile, to enter into conversation or even argument with any member of Alcove No. 1! This prohibition was dutifully obeyed, and such mindless obedience could not fail to have its costs.

Which brings me to Alcove No. 1, where pure intellect—a certain kind of intellect, anyway—reigned unchallenged.

Alcove No. 1 was the place you went to if you wanted to be radical *and* have a theory as to the proper kind of radical you should be. When I say "theory," I mean that in the largest sense. We in Alcove No. 1 were terribly concerned with being "right" in politics, economics, sociology, philosophy, history, anthropology, and so forth. It was essential to be right in all of these fields of knowledge, lest a bit of information from one should casually collide with a theoretical edifice and bring the whole structure tumbling down. So all the little grouplets that joined together to make Alcove No. 1 their home were always in keen competition to come up with startling bits of information—or, better yet, obscure and disorienting quotations from Marx or Engels or Lenin or Trotsky—that would create intellectual trouble for the rest of the company.

The Trotskyists, with perhaps a dozen members, were one of the largest grouplets and unquestionably the most feverishly articulate. Almost as numerous, though considerably less noisy, were the Socialists, or "the Norman Thomas Socialists" as one called them, to distinguish them from other kinds of socialists. Among these other kinds, none of which ever had more than two or three representatives in Alcove No. 1, were the Social Democrats (or "right-wing socialists") who actually voted for F.D.R., and the "revolutionary socialists" who belonged to one or another "splinter group"—the Ohlerites, the Marlinites, the Fieldites, the Lovestonites, and the who-can-remember-what-other-ites —which, finding itself in "principled disagreement" with every other sect, had its own little publication (usually called a "theoretical organ") and its own special prescription for achieving *real* socialism. In addition, and finally, there were a handful of "independents"—exasperating left-wing individualists who either could not bring themselves to join any group or else insisted on joining them all in succession. What held this crazy conglomeration together was, quite simply, the powerful presence of Alcove No. 2, and, beyond that, the looming shadow of Stalinism with its threat of so irrevocably debasing the socialist ideal as to rob humanity of what we were certain was its last, best hope.

Obviously, in such a milieu certain intellectual qualities tended to be emphasized at the expense of others. We were strongly inclined to celebrate the analytical powers of mind rather than the creative, and we paid more heed to public philosophies than to private ones. It cannot be an accident that so many graduates of Alcove No. 1 went on to become professors of social science; in a sense, what Alcove No. 1 provided was a peculiarly intense undergraduate education in what is now called social science but which we then called (more accurately, I sometimes think) political ideology. Nor can it be an accident that none of the graduates of Alcove No. 1—none who were there in my time, anyway—subsequently achieved any kind of distinction in creative writing or the arts; in that ideological hothouse, the personal vision and the personal accent withered for lack of nourishment.

So I do not want to be misunderstood as claiming superlative merits for Alcove No. 1 as an educational milieu. On the other hand, it *was* an authentic educational milieu. And this, I suppose, is why so many went on to become professors—getting paid, as it were, for continuing to be interested in the things they had always been interested in.

In some respects the quintessential representative of this milieu was Seymour Martin Lipset, now professor of sociology and political science at Stanford—a kind of intellectual bumblebee, whose function it was to spread the pollen of ideological doubt and political consternation over all Alcove No. 1's flowering ideologies. Irving Howe, in contrast, was a pillar of ideological rectitude. Thin, gangling, intense, always a little distant, his fingers incessantly and nervously twisting a cowlick as he enunciated sharp and authoritative opinions, Irving was the Trotskyist leader and "theoretician." In the years since, he has gone on to become a famous literary critic and a professor of literature at the City University. But he has remained politically *engagé*, though slowly moving "right" from Trotskyism to democratic socialism (as represented in his journal, *Dissent*). Since I have abandoned my socialist beliefs altogether, I feel that I am still ahead of him politically.

Daniel Bell, now professor of sociology at Harvard, was at the opposite pole from Irving. He was that rarity of the 1930s: an honest-to-goodness social-democratic intellectual who believed in "a mixed economy," a two-party system based on the British model, and other liberal heresies. His evident skepticism toward all our ideologies would ordinarily have disqualified him from membership in Alcove No. 1. But he had an immense intellectual curiosity, a kind of amused fondness for sectarian dialectics, knew his radical texts as thoroughly as the most learned among us, and enjoyed "a good theoretical discussion" the way some enjoy a Turkish bath—so we counted him in. Over the years, his political views have probably changed less than those of the rest of us, with the result that, whereas his former classmates used to criticize him from the Left, they now criticize him from all points of the ideological compass.

Others who later found, to their pleasant surprise, that what they had been doing in Alcove No. 1 was what the academic world would come to recognize and generously reward as "social science" were Nathan Glazer (Harvard), Philip Selznick (Berkeley), Peter Rossi (Johns Hopkins), Morroe Berger (Princeton), I. Milton Sacks (Brandeis), Lawrence Krader and Bernard Bellush (City University), Seymour Melman (Columbia), Melvin J. Lasky (now editor of *Encounter*)—and others who may be just as pleased not to read their names in this context.

Bellush, a calm, and obstinately moderate socialist of the Norman Thomas persuasion, was a most unlikely candidate to serve as a central symbol of student radicalism, and yet at one point he did. During an anti-ROTC [Reserve Officers' Training Corps] demonstration, Bernie was arrested for punching a police officer. The ensuing trial was a field day for us, as we "mobilized" the student body to attend protest rallies ("Cops off the campus!"), pack the courtroom, and so forth. Bernie was acquitted, and it was a moment of triumph. I must confess, however, that to this day I cannot honestly say whether or not he actually did punch that police officer; with typical radical disingenuousness, we studiously avoided asking either him or ourselves that question. Strange as it may sound to today's radical student, we really would have been disturbed had he been guilty as charged. At the very least, we would have been plunged into an endless debate on the finer points of "revolutionary morality." With the experience of Stalinism constantly in mind, we were extremely sensitive to the possibility that radical means could corrupt radical ends.

I certainly do not mean to suggest that membership in Alcove No. 1 was any kind of prerequisite for subsequent academic distinction. Kenneth Arrow, for instance, now a Nobel Prize-winning professor of economics at Harvard, and David Landes, now professor of history at Harvard, were contemporaries of mine at City who kept their distance from Alcove No. 1 and found other useful things (like studying) to do with their time. Nevertheless, it does seem clear to me that there was an academic impulse at work in Alcove No. 1, even if none of us understood its shaping force at the time. I mention this simply to emphasize the connection which was then possible—in many instances, probable—between student radicalism and intellectual vitality, a connection which seems to have been attenuated over the succeeding years.

Alcove No. 1 was, as I have said, where our real college education took place. Being a professor at City in those days was not a very attractive job. True, you had tenure and this counted for much in the 1930s. But you taught fifteen hours a week, had no private office, no faculty club, no library where you could do research; you commuted to the campus by subway, and, if you were a younger faculty member, your pay amounted to little more than pocket money. As a result, the very best professors left, if they could.

The Depression made it more difficult for many to do this, and the students benefited from their misfortune. But the fact remains that, for the bright, inquiring student, City College was a pretty dull educational place. The student who came seeking an intellectual community, in which the life of the mind was strenuously lived, had to create such a community and such a life for himself.

That an authentic educational process could exist outside of such a political community I discovered, to my amazement, at the University of Chicago, a couple of years after I left City. My wife had a graduate fellowship in history there, and I hung around the campus as a "nonstudent" for the better part of a year, working part-time as a freight handler on the Illinois Central while waiting for my draft records to be transferred from New York. I still see that year as through a golden haze—and I have never met a Chicago alumnus of that period who does not see it likewise. Under the powerful leadership of Robert M. Hutchins and Mortimer J. Adler, undergraduate education at Chicago centered on reading "great books," thinking about them, arguing about them. And the students did read, did think, did argue passionately. True, Chicago also had its share of young anti-Stalinist radicals who constituted a counterpart—much more literary, much less political—to Alcove No. 1. (Saul Bellow, Isaac Rosenfeld, Oscar Tarcov, H. J. Kaplan, and Leslie Fiedler were members of that group.) But the point is that, at Chicago, you did not *have* to be political to lead a vigorous intellectual life and be a member of an authentic intellectual community.

Though the specifically political radicalism of Alcove No. 1 was conventional and coarse enough, what gave it its special quality was the fact that it was intertwined with an intense interest in, and deference to, the "highbrow" in culture, philosophy, and the arts. The two most influential journals in Alcove No. 1 were the *New International* and *Partisan Review.* The first was the Trotskyist theoretical organ and, confined by dogma though it certainly was, it was also full of a Marxist scholasticism that was as rigorous and learned, in its way, as the Jesuit scholasticism it so strikingly paralleled. Its contributors—Trotsky himself, Max Schachtman, James Burnham, Dwight Macdonald, C. L. R.

James—were Marxist intellectuals. There were many important things one could not learn from reading the *New International;* but one most emphatically did learn how to read an intellectual discourse and several of us learned how to write one.

*Partisan Review,* the journal of the anti-Stalinist, left-wing, cultural avant-garde, was an intimidating presence in Alcove No. 1. Even simply to understand it seemed a goal beyond reach. I would read each article at least twice, in a state of awe and exasperation—excited to see such elegance of style and profundity of mind, depressed at the realization that a commoner like myself could never expect to rise into that intellectual aristocracy, an aristocracy that included Lionel Trilling, Philip Rahv, William Phillips, Sidney Hook, Mary McCarthy, Paul Goodman, Clement Greenberg, Harold Rosenberg, Meyer Schapiro, and F. W. Dupee. I have recently had occasion to reread some of these issues of *Partisan Review* and, though I now see limitations then not visible to me, I also must affirm that it was a most remarkable magazine. The particular mission it set itself—to reconcile a socialist humanism with an individualistic "modernism" in the arts (the latter frequently being, in the 1930s, associated with "reactionary" political attitudes)—established a dialectic of challenge and response that released the finest creative energies. The effort at reconciliation eventually failed, in a quite unpredictable way, as the emerging "counterculture" gradually abolished the category of the highbrow altogether. But it was a bold, imaginative effort, and *Partisan Review* in its heyday was unquestionably one of the finest American cultural periodicals ever published—perhaps even the very finest.

In addition, there were the frequent debates which we attended. The term "debate" as used today really does not do them justice. To begin with, they ignored all conventional time limits. A speaker like Max Schachtman, the Trotskyist leader, or Gus Tyler of the Socialist party, could argue at a high pitch of moral and intellectual and rhetorical intensity for two, three, even four hours. (Since the Stalinists refused to debate with other left-wing groups, we were always debating among ourselves.) When, in 1940, the Trotskyists split into two factions, it was after a debate among four speakers that continued for two whole days. (The most succinct presentation, by James Burnham, lasted only two hours, and caused many of those present to question his "seriousness.") And, incredible as it may seem, the quality of the presentations was in all respects up to the quantity. They were—within the limits imposed by their socialist preconceptions—learned, witty, articulate, intellectually rigorous. I have never since seen or heard their equal, and, as a learning experience for college students, they were beyond comparison.

So far as I can see, universities today are not significantly better or worse than they were in the 1930s; they are not—as they were not—intellectual communities. But the rebellion against the "merely academic" has tended to take the form of a secession from the life of the mind altogether.

The radicalism of the 1930s was decidedly an adult movement, in which young people were permitted to participate. We young Trotskyists were as numerous as the adult party, but we unquestioningly accepted the authority of the latter. In contrast, the radicalism of the 1960s was a generational movement, bereft of adult models and adult guidance. It is not easy to understand just how this came about, but one thing is certain: The radicals of the 1960s were what they were because American society and American culture—which means we, the adults—permitted them (sometimes encouraged them) to grow up to be what they were. It is not, as some think, that we failed to impose our adult *beliefs* upon our children. That would be an absurd enterprise. What we failed to do is to transmit adult *values* to them—values affecting the way one holds beliefs, which would have encouraged them to take their own and others' beliefs seriously, and to think coherently about them. And precisely because we adults encouraged our twenty-year-old children to be "kids," their rebellion so often resembled a bewildering and self-destructive tantrum.

As to why American adults failed their children in this way—well, since some of my best friends are now social scientists, I will leave that for them to figure out.

1977

13

# 2

# Memoirs of a "Cold Warrior"

Russell Lynes, authority on what is highbrow and lowbrow, in and out, recently wrote: "The new chic status symbol of the highbrow is to have been unknowingly on the CIA [Central Intelligence Agency] payroll." Well, perhaps; but I am not so sure. I have the feeling that, of late, I have not been really chic at all.

I have been getting that feeling because an awful lot of people—including some old (now former) friends—keep assuring me that the *Zeitgeist* has passed me by. I am a dropout from history, they murmur, and probably beyond the reach of retraining and rehabilitation. For I was a creature of the 1940s and 1950s, an anticommunist liberal, a political organism that is deemed to have suffered permanent damage from overexposure to the subzero climate of the cold war. In contrast, the "new breed" of the 1960s is genetically wholesome, intellectually incorruptible, and securely possessed of the knowledge that "anticommunism" has never been anything but an elaborate con game on behalf of the power structure.

About this new breed itself, I shall have a few things to say. But first of all, I must recount the inside story of my involvement with the

CIA. It is not a particularly interesting story, I hasten to warn. On the other hand, that fact in itself is interesting in a way. For it suggests that the ever-increasing appetite for political melodrama, in our time, is easily outstripping the supply. The truth about the cold war, when finally exposed to historical scrutiny, is—in my opinion—not likely to be so very different from the conventional memories which we "cold warriors" carry around in our heads.

I was co-founder (with Stephen Spender) of *Encounter* magazine, in London, in 1953, and remained co-editor until 1958. The magazine was sponsored by the Congress for Cultural Freedom, a liberal anticommunist organization with headquarters in Paris. Had I known what has since been revealed, that both the congress and *Encounter* were subsidized by the CIA, I would not have taken the job. Not, I hasten to add, because I disapproved of the CIA or even of secret subsidies (at certain times, in certain places, under certain conditions, for specific and limited purposes). Aside from the fact that the CIA, as a secret agency, seems to be staffed to an extraordinary extent by incorrigible blabbermouths, I have no more reason to despise it than, say, the Post Office. (Both are indispensable, both are exasperatingly inept.) No, I would have refused to go for two reasons: First, because I was (and am) exceedingly jealous of my reputation as an independent writer and thinker. Second, because, while in the Army during World War II, I had taken a solemn oath to myself that I would never, never again work as a functionary in a large organization, and especially not for the U.S. government. It is an oath I have so far kept inviolate—except for those five years when I was unwittingly on the CIA payroll.

But how could I have been so unwitting? Were there no signs of the CIA presence? Were there not, during my time, rumors of secret governmental subventions? Why did I not believe them?

Rumors there were, but they were not particularly credible. Most of these rumors issued from sources—left-wing, anti-American or both—that would have been happy to circulate them, true or not, and one discounted them in advance. Besides, as against such rumors there was the *fact* of the Farfield Foundation, our ostensible sponsor, which subsidized *Encounter* via a grant to the Congress for Cultural Freedom.

The Farfield Foundation was no shadowy or ghostly entity. Its president, Julius (Junky) Fleischmann—whose millions derived from yeast, gin, and other profitable commodities—would float over to London every now and then, on his yacht, and Spender would give a "London literary party" for him. There, he would be introduced as "the patron" of *Encounter,* and he would acknowledge the introduction with a gracious modesty that seemed very becoming, and was—we now know—even more becoming than it seemed.

On several occasions, both Spender and I questioned him about the rumors. He repudiated them indignantly, and said that if anyone dared to print the barest hint of such a libel, he would promptly institute legal proceedings. In the event, of course, they did, and he did not.

Mind you, I really bear no animosity toward Junky, and I doubt that Spender does, either. I am sure he was moved by patriotic motives, and it is even possible that *some* of the money came from his own pocket. (Like many such conduits, the Farfield Foundation was a mixture of bona fide philanthropy and CIA dollars.) Moreover, Junky himself unquestionably did, like so many millionaires, have a genuine passion for "Culture" and for culture heroes. I am sure he meant me no harm, though he ended by doing me no good. The only amends I believe he owes any of us is, perhaps, to reimburse Spender for those liquor bills of yesteryear.

There were other reasons, too, why we never could take those rumors seriously. To begin with, there was the editorial freedom that was granted by the congress to its various magazines—*Encounter* in London, *Tempo Presente* in Italy, *Preuves* in Paris. The editors of *Tempo Presente* were Ignazio Silone and Nicola Chiaramonte—two men whose notorious and prickly independence of spirit intimidates even their friends. If I were running the CIA, I would be scared silly of entrusting them with *anything.* Even now, the mere imagining of it makes me retrospectively nervous, on behalf of the CIA.

In the case of *Encounter,* I can testify that the idea of any secret editorial wire-pulling by the CIA was not only unthinkable, it was literally impossible: Spender and I made our editorial decisions in London, and there just was not anyone around to look over our shoulders while we did so. The congress had no office or representative in London. The only person who came close to filling this description was Malcolm Muggeridge, who was then—among many other things—president of the British Committee for Cultural Freedom, an offshoot of the congress.

I would have drinks with Malcolm maybe twice a year, and our conversations would be about Muggeridge, not *Encounter*—especially they would be about the particular journalistic scandal Malcolm was at that moment busily creating. I do not recall a single discussion that touched on so solemn a matter as *Encounter*'s editorial policy. To tell the truth, I do not recall a single one of those conversations with Malcolm that could even be called sober.

Prior to going to *Encounter,* I had been managing editor of *Commentary,* then (and still) sponsored by the American Jewish Committee. The relations of the editors of *Encounter* to the congress were in all respects comparable to those of the editors of *Commentary* to the Committee. In both cases, we had been hired because our views (including, of course, our political views) and talents were congenial to the sponsoring organization. We could always be fired, were our services unsatisfactory. Aside from that, our editorial freedom was complete.

To be sure, the American Jewish Committee would occasionally let it be known to the editors of *Commentary* that it might have less difficulty in fund-raising if the editors were a bit more solicitous of rabbinical opinion. Similarly, the Congress would let it occasionally be known that its work abroad would be made easier, and its overseas program would be strengthened, if *Encounter* found some Indian or Egyptian or Ghanaian writers to publish. In both cases, such gentle interventions were not entirely ignored; an independent editor need not be a prima donna. Spender and I did make an extra effort to publish Asian and African writers. The returns on this effort were, I fear, minimal.

But of anything resembling political censorship of *Encounter* by its sponsors, there was no trace. I may have been, technically, a "dupe" of the CIA; *Encounter* was not. Perhaps it will be said that my own frequently expressed political opinions were so clearly "safe," from the CIA's point of view, that censorship was superfluous. Maybe so.* On the other hand, it is not quite so simple as that, as the following incident will illustrate:

In 1955, Spender and I—for reasons I no longer recollect, and may never have comprehended—found that we were, as they say, "getting on each other's nerves." (We have, since this time, become good friends.) Stephen decided to do something about it—that is, replace me with a new American editor. He enlisted the support of Muggeridge *and* of the executive secretary of the Congress for Cultural Freedom—who had a "witting" connection with the CIA, as he has since candidly admitted. At the very last moment, when my bags were packed and my boat tickets purchased, this seditious (from my point of view) movement petered out, as the result of interventions on my behalf by British and American friends. The man who was to have replaced me was Dwight Macdonald!†

Could the CIA really have "endorsed" *him*? Dwight has spent a

---

*Not long ago, I learned from an unimpeachable source that the CIA did contemplate approaching me to become a "witting" agent—but that, when the agency ran a security check on me, I failed to come up with a passing grade. So there are advantages to having been a young radical: It protects one against undesirable solicitations.

†Indeed, as a result of the preliminary commitment that had been made to him, he did join the staff of *Encounter* for a year, as an associate editor.

fruitful life and a distinguished career purposefully being a security risk to just about everyone and everything within reach of his typewriter. If the agency had ever tried to run a check on him, the computers would have gone mad with anxiety. So what did the CIA have in mind?

I do not know. It could be that, most of the time, the CIA never had very much in its mind. Or possibly, someone, someday, will tell us the CIA's side of the story. From some recently published tidbits, one gathers that, during the McCarthy period, the CIA gathered unto itself a group of dispossessed liberals who, unable to shape the overseas public policy of the U.S. government, set out to shape its private policy. The ironies implicit in this situation are too numerous to count, and they should make a fascinating narrative for the lucky historian who first gets his hands on the agency's files. (Given the agency's adeptness at secrecy, these files will doubtless soon be auctioned off as government surplus property.) But, back in the early 1950s, one knew nothing about these shenanigans. Eisenhower was president, Dulles was secretary of state, and the idea that such an administration would secretly come to the support of the likes of me or Dwight Macdonald or Ignazio Silone or Bertrand Russell (then chairman of the Congress!) was too ridiculous to contemplate.

That is the way it was. In retrospect, of course, it is bound to look different. Apparently, it looks different now even to some people who lived through the events and participated in them. One writer, who was my house guest in London, and who has more recently been busy "exposing" the CIA in *Ramparts*, reports in his autobiography that he enjoyed my hospitality despite our political differences; I wonder why he forgot to mention those differences at the time. Another house guest, now a prominent figure in book publishing (and, in the 1950s, a member in good standing of the American Committee for Cultural Freedom), reports in the *New York Review of Books* that moral and intellectual corruption was rife among our crowd; at the time, he seemed to be rather enjoying the company he kept.

I am old enough, and hardened enough, not to be wounded (or even surprised) by this sort of thing. People change their views and, inevitably, rewrite their autobiographies—sometimes with no awareness of duplicity.

What does irritate me is the prevalence of the snide remarks about "an underground gravy train," "official limousines," "travel in style," and so on. I enjoy high living as much as the next man, and I suppose that if the Farfield Foundation (i.e., the CIA) had offered me a limousine, I might have thought it a very useful article. But it did not. The CIA may have been the last of the big spenders in other areas, but back in those days it was generally assumed by everyone (including, apparently, the CIA) that being an intellectual was not a way to make money.

My average annual salary during my five years at *Encounter* was $9,500. One could then live well in London on such a salary, and we did, so I am not complaining. Nor did I mind that my family and I flew tourist class, on the two home leaves that were granted me in those five years. Never having flown first class in my life, I did not know what I was missing. It does bother me, however, that all these $25,000-a-year men should now pontificate (at 10 cents or more a word) about the "corruption" that is supposed to have prevailed in the 1950s. (*Encounter*, incidentally, paid its contributors 3 cents a word.)

This notion of an intellectual class living high off the hog is, of course, part and parcel of a larger vision: of an intellectual class that was elevated into membership in the "ruling elite," the Establishment, in order to render service in the conduct of the cold war. The idea that, in the late 1940s and early 1950s, there was a mass *trahison des clercs* by the liberal anticommunist intellectuals—a treason suitably rewarded with money, honors, and privileges of all kinds—is by now so widespread on the college campus that I despair of correcting it. Still, for the record, I'd like to attempt a reminder of what it was really like to be a liberal anticommunist in those days.

To begin with, it meant having practically no influence at all outside the hermetic universe of New York literary politics. The supposed connection between, say, the liberal intellectuals in New York and the political powers in Washington is wholly mythical.

When I left this country to join *Encounter*, I had been for five years an editor—in the end, managing editor—of *Commentary*, which was then the leading liberal anticommunist publication. My writings in *Commentary* had attracted a certain measure of attention. Yet I had never in my life been to Washington, D.C.; I had never seen a congressman or senator or high government official in the flesh; no agency of the American government had ever asked me for my opinion on *anything*.

My influence in the nation at large was of the same magnitude. I had never been invited by any foundation, to any conference, anywhere; I had never received a foundation grant (still have not, for that matter); I had never been invited to speak on any college campus; I had never been asked to write for such publications as *Harpers*, the *Atlantic Monthly*, the *New York Times Magazine*; I had never been asked even to review a book by anyone except the *New Leader* (another liberal anticommunist publication, of limited circulation, which paid no authors' fees). It is perhaps understandable, therefore, that I had no idea I was effecting a merger with the Establishment (*that* term did not even exist then) or the "power elite" (a term just beginning to get currency when I left for England). In those days, my moment of most intimate contact with the national purpose and national power came when I was introduced to Arthur Schlesinger, Jr., who had actually written a Book-of-the-Month-Club selection and was reported to know some very important people in the Democratic party.

Nor was my case a singular one. All of those who constituted the liberal anticommunist intellectual community in New York—and it could hardly have been said to exist elsewhere—had a similar experience. Many of these became very famous and distinguished people: Diana and Lionel Trilling, Daniel Bell, Mary McCarthy, the editors of *Partisan Review,* Dwight Macdonald, Leslie Fiedler, Sidney Hook, Nathan Glazer. But in the first decade after World War II, their fame and their distinction were limited to—and their talents appreciated by—a very small circle indeed. They wrote mainly for one another, not out of cliquishness but because no one else seemed much interested. Washington was a million light-years away, and one could no more influence it than one could influence the drift of the galaxies.

This state of affairs was in no way remarkable, or exceptional, or temporary. For close to two decades, liberal anticommunism was a minority movement among intellectuals. It had been so in the 1930s; it was still so in the 1940s; it was only a little less so in the 1950s. I do not mean, and emphatically do not wish to be taken to mean, that a majority—or even a significant proportion—of American liberals or American intellectuals were *pro* communist. They were not. They were, in the useful phrase invented, I think, by Sidney Hook, "anti-anticommunist."

What the phrase signifies is an aversion to the "excesses" of communism coupled with a profound reluctance to be unnecessarily nasty about communism per se. For instance, an anti-anticommunist would certainly be willing to censure the Soviet Government for imprisoning rabbis and priests. But, being an "enlightened" and "progressive" person, he would not be particularly bothered by the fact that this government insisted that the tenets of "atheism" be officially taught in the schools, and that criticism of them not be permitted anywhere. Similarly, he might protest against the imprisonment of writers who violated the code of "Socialist realism." But the mass extermination of middle-class peasants ("kulaks") left him cold; these people were tainted with the profit motive and were therefore expendable.

I am sure we all know many such people. They have been with us a long while now—long enough to breed a generation of young men and women on our campuses to whom even the parents' anti-anticommunism is just another version of anticommunism.

One frequently hears it said, these days, in a completely matter-of-fact way, that liberal anticommunists during the 1950s were "obsessed" by the specter of communism. I find this an eccentric way of putting it. It touches the truth only to the extent that liberal anticommunists believed that the Soviet regime was contemptible, not only in what it specifically did, but in what it generally was—that is, Communist. (I still believe it.) Nevertheless, there would not have been a cold war, for us or anyone, if this regime had not been engaged in a worldwide campaign of ideological belligerency against liberal nations, liberal values, and liberal institutions. And it is worth recalling that, together with this ideological belligerency, there went a great deal of vulgar, brutal, material terror.

There was nothing "spectral" about Communist activities during that period; they were as substantial as they were alarming. In the Soviet Union itself, an insane tyrant was busy relentlessly and senselessly persecuting the Russian people, dispatching them by the tens of thousands to concentration camps, arranging monstrous "show trials" at which children recited prefabricated indictments of their parents, silencing any writer or artist who showed a glimmer of originality, imposing a conformity of thought and opinion (even of rhetoric) to a degree unsurpassed in all of European history. Throughout Soviet-occupied Eastern Europe this same political paranoia became the established orthodoxy. And in Western Europe there existed large, well-organized Communist parties with the expressed intention of dragging their fellow citizens down this very same road.

Strangely enough, sections of the intellectual community in this country and in Europe were disinclined to believe their eyes. Incorrigibly optimistic about any regime that called itself "socialist" or "progressive," these people insisted that reports of Stalinist terror were either mendacious or exaggerated. Among the more sophisticated and "philosophical" of these intellectuals there emerged ingenious apologies for the "historical necessity" of every brutish act a Communist regime could perpetrate. (See the writings of Jean-Paul Sartre at this time.) This current of opinion—procommunist or anti-anticommunist—was powerful, influential, obdurate. We who were liberal anticommunists found our work depressing and unrewarding. There appeared to be no way to persuade our fellow intellectuals of truths that seemed to us then, as now, self-evident.

We never did persuade them. Khrushchev did that, with his famous "secret speech," in which he said about Stalinism everything that anticommunists had been saying for years. Did this vindicate anticommunism? Not at all. Those who had previously denied the existence of a Stalinist terror in Russia and East Europe now accepted the half-hearted repudiation of this terror as evidence that the Soviet regime was "evolving" toward a truer, higher, more humane version of Communism. This peculiar dialectic has continued ever since. Repeatedly, each new group of Communist leaders has denounced the crimes of its predecessors. Just as repeatedly, every such denunciation is taken as redounding to the credit of Communism itself.

Still, by the mid-1950s the "thaw" was under way, and liberal anticommunists had reason to think that history had taken a turn for the better. The Hungarian revolution of 1956 was a setback, but only a temporary one. I know that we at *Encounter,* and the other intellectuals associated with the Congress for Cultural Freedom, were as eager as anyone to "build bridges" to the East. So far from being obsessed with anticommunism, we too were fascinated with the potential for "liberalization" that seemed to have been released. We foresaw the "polycentric" impulse among the various national Communist parties, but we never imagined that "revisionism" in Asia and Latin America could take the reactionary forms it has assumed in, say, China and Cuba. We had Tito in mind, not Mao.

In those middle years of the 1950s, I had many occasions to meet East European intellectuals at meetings—formal and informal—in London, Paris, and elsewhere. There was never the slightest problem of "communication." Indeed, I cannot even recall having any serious political arguments with them. One simply assumed, at the outset, that the Communist system, as it had developed in Russia, was politically reprehensible and economically absurd. These intellectuals from the East were, of course, "Socialists"—but their main interest was in combining Socialism with political and even economic liberalism. *This* kind of Socialist one had always been at ease with. After all, among the contributors to *Encounter* had been Hugh Gaitskell, Denis Healey, Roy Jenkins, Anthony Crosland, and others of their persuasion in the Labor party.

The Russians, to be sure, were different. Not many Russian intellectuals were then permitted to visit the West—though, occasionally, some party functionaries were baptized "intellectuals" for the purpose of showing up at some conference or other. But over these past years, even this has changed. One does have the opportunity to meet and chat with real Russian intellectuals, either abroad or (more often) in Russia—and *they* have no particular complaints against the kind of liberal anticommunism that was represented by *Encounter* or me. Indeed, most of them strike me as being liberal anticommunist Communists. It is not an easy political philosophy to define or make sense of. But, then, neither are most of the political philosophies in the West.

What it comes down to is this: *My* cold war—the struggle against Stalinist terror in Russia, and against a neo-Stalinist, totalitarian, international movement—is largely over. True, the Soviet Union is a great power whose interests often conflict with those of the United States; this can make life dangerous and depressing (as in the recent Middle East conflict), but it is no kind of special problem for intellectuals. True, too, Russia remains an authoritarian and repressive regime. But, then, it always has been.

The main thing, from my point of view, is that what used to be called "Communism" in Europe in the 1950s has spent most of its ideological force;* the international Communist movement has lost its monolithic character and structure; the Soviet Union no longer seems much interested in setting up "front" organizations of intellectuals or others; the intellectuals themselves in Russia and East Europe are engaged in courageous "confrontations" with their own regimes, and while they have my blessings, I do not see that they need or want my help.

These intellectuals may call themselves, and believe themselves to be, Communists. But they clearly want no cold war with me, and I reciprocate their sentiments. We still have important disagreements, but I really have little doubt that, if I were to spend an evening now with a representative group of Russian and East European intellectuals, we should talk mainly about the "new breed" of radicals who have sprouted up all over the world, and we would surely agree that they represent a threat to "our" civilization—even, perhaps, to "our" way of life.

The Russian writers I have met find the contents of *Encounter* (now under private ownership) far more to their taste than the neo-Castroism of the *New York Review of Books.* The ideological heroes of the New Left—Herbert Marcuse, Frantz Fanon, Régis Debray—evoke no response among the intellectuals of Communist Europe, and you find no blown-up photos of Che Guevara in the faculty offices of Moscow University. A Western "progressive" like Conor Cruise O'Brien might think that the persecution of Soviet intellectuals is, paradoxically, a sign that the Soviet regime is more elevated than our own, because *there* the

*A leading Polish Marxist philosopher who spent some weeks at Oxford was asked how he liked it. He responded with enthusiasm: "It's a marvelous place! Absolutely marvelous! Here you find people who are actually willing to talk about Marxism!" I can vouch for the truth of this anecdote.

authorities take ideas very seriously. A Russian intellectual finds this "sophisticated" proposition simply perverse, as indeed it is.

So I find it more than a little odd that I—and others like me—should be denounced as an obsessive anticommunist and an incorrigible cold warrior. But, then, I must admit that I find many things odd about the new radicalism in American intellectual and literary circles. I am confused by middle-aged radicals who insist, in one and the same breath, that the present distribution of income is horribly inequitable and that you cannot live decently in New York on less than $50,000 a year. I am bewildered by a highbrow left-wing magazine which proudly advertises that it is "cliquish" and "snobbish." I do not comprehend the merger that seems to have taken place between the literary Left and café society, or the calm assumption that writers are and ought to be "celebrities." I do not understand the view—becoming ever more popular—that mental illness in our decadent society is a positive sign of health, and that schizophrenics are in closer touch with ultimate reality than the rest of us. I do not think homosexuality is normal; I distrust drugs, and I do not find pornography all that readable.

No: Russell Lynes notwithstanding, and despite my unwitting connection with the CIA, I am not chic at all. Not in this country, not today. And there is still a sense, I suppose, in which I can fairly be called a cold warrior. What I mean is: I believe in individual liberty and representative democracy; I prefer a modified form of capitalism to any other proposed economic system; I am certain Castro is no good model for Latin American progress; I consider Maoism as detestable as fascism and not easily distinguishable from it; I do not see that the underdeveloped countries of the Third World represent any kind of wave of the future, and Che Guevara is not my idea of Robin Hood. But this is a new and different kind of cold war, in another time, for the most part in other places, and involving different ideologies. Looking back on the cold war of the 1950s against Stalinism, I can at moments feel positively nostalgic for the relatively forthright way it posed unambiguous moral issues. No amount of revisionist rewriting will affect my view of these moral proprieties. It was, by every canon I recognize, a just war, and I am pleased to have had a small part in it.

1968

# II

# THE CULTURE OF
# DEMOCRATIC
# CAPITALISM

# 3

# The Adversary
# Culture of
# Intellectuals

NO SOONER did the late Lionel Trilling coin the phrase "adversary culture" than it became part of the common vocabulary. This is because it so neatly summed up a phenomenon that all of us, vaguely or acutely, had observed. It is hardly to be denied that the culture that educates us—the patterns of perception and thought our children absorb in their schools, at every level—is unfriendly (at the least) to the commercial civilization, the bourgeois civilization, within which most of us live and work. When we send our sons and daughters to college, we may expect that by the time they are graduated they are likely to have a lower opinion of our social and economic order than when they entered. We know this from opinion poll data; we know it from our own experience.

We are so used to this fact of our lives, we take it so for granted, that we fail to realize how extraordinary it is. Has there ever been, in all of recorded history, a civilization whose culture was at odds with the values and ideals of that civilization itself? It is not uncommon that a culture will be critical of the civilization that sustains it—and always critical of the failure of this civilization to realize perfectly the ideals that it claims as inspiration. Such criticism is implicit or explicit in Aristophanes and Euripides, Dante and Shakespeare. But to take an adversary posture toward the ideals themselves? That is unprecedented. A few writers and thinkers of a heretical bent, dispersed at the margins of the culture, might do so. But culture as a whole has always been assigned the task of, and invariably accepted responsibility for, sustaining and celebrating those values. Indeed, it is a premise of modern sociological and anthropological theory that it is the essence of culture to be "functional" in this way.

Yet ours is not. The more "cultivated" a person is in our society, the more disaffected and malcontent he is likely to be—a disaffection, moreover, directed not only at the actuality of our society but at the ideality as well. Indeed, the ideality may be more strenuously opposed than the actuality. It was, I think, Oscar Wilde who observed that, while he rather liked the average American, he found the ideal American contemptible. Our contemporary culture is considerably less tolerant of actuality than was Oscar Wilde. But there is little doubt that if it had to choose between the two, it would prefer the actual to the ideal.

The average "less cultivated" American, of course, feels no great uneasiness with either the actual or the ideal. This explains why the Marxist vision of a radicalized working class erupting into rebellion against capitalist society has turned out to be so erroneous. Radicalism, in our day, finds more fertile ground among the college-educated than among the high-school graduates, the former having experienced more exposure to some kind of adversary culture, the latter—until recently, at least—having its own kind of "popular" culture that is more accommodating to the bourgeois world that working people inhabit. But this very disjunction of those two cultures is itself a unique phenomenon of the bourgeois era, and represents, as we shall see, a response to the emergence, in the nineteenth century, of an "avant-garde," which laid the basis for our adversary culture.

Bourgeois society is without a doubt the most prosaic of all possible societies. It is prosaic in the literal sense. The novel written in prose, dealing with the (only somewhat) extraordinary adventures of ordinary people, is its original and characteristic art form, replacing the epic poem, the lyric poem, the poetic drama, the religious hymn. These latter were appropriate to societies formally and officially committed to transcendent ideals of excellence—ideals that could be realized only by those few of exceptional nobility of character—or to transcendent visions of the universe wherein human existence on earth is accorded only a provisional significance. But bourgeois society is uninterested in such transcendence, which at best it tolerates as a private affair, a matter for individual taste and individual consumption, as it were. It is prosaic, not only in form, but in essence. It is a society organized for the convenience and comfort of common men and common women, not for the production of heroic, memorable figures. It is a society interested in making the best of this world, not in any kind of transfiguration, whether through tragedy or piety.

Because this society proposes to make the best of this world, for the benefit of ordinary men and women, it roots itself in the most worldly and common of human motivations: self-interest. It assumes that, though only a few are capable of pursuing excellence, everyone is capable of recognizing and pursuing his own self-interest. This "democratic" assumption about the equal potential of human nature, in this limited respect, in turn justifies a market economy in which each individual defines his own well-being, and illegitimates all the paternalistic economic theories of previous eras. One should emphasize, however, that the pursuit of excellence by the few—whether defined in religious, moral, or intellectual terms—is neither prohibited nor inhibited. Such an activity is merely interpreted as a special form of self-interest, which may be freely pursued but can claim no official status. Bourgeois society also assumes that the average individual's conception of his own self-interest will be sufficiently "enlightened"—that is, sufficiently far-sighted and prudent—to permit other human passions (the desire for community, the sense of human sympathy, the moral conscience, etc.) to find expression, albeit always in a voluntarist form.

It is characteristic of a bourgeois culture, when it exists in concord with bourgeois principles, that we are permitted to take "happy endings" seriously (". . . and they lived happily ever after"). From classical antiquity through the Renaissance, happy endings—worldly happy endings—were consigned to the genre of Comedy. "Serious" art focused on a meaningful death, in the context of heroism in battle, passion in love, ambition in politics, or piety in religion. Such high seriousness ran counter to the bourgeois grain, which perceived human fulfillment—human authenticity, if you will—in terms of becoming a good citizen, a good husband, a good provider. It is, in contrast to both pre-bourgeois and postbourgeois *Weltanschauungen,* a *domestic* conception of the universe and of man's place therein.

This bourgeois ideal is much closer to the Old Testament than to the New—which is, perhaps, why Jews have felt more at home in the bourgeois world than in any other. That God created this world and affirmed its goodness; that men ought confidently to be fruitful and multiply; that work (including that kind of work we call commerce) is elevating rather than demeaning; that the impulse to "better one's condition" (to use a favorite phrase of Adam Smith's) is good because natural—these beliefs were almost perfectly congruent with the world view of postexilic Judaism. In this world view, there was no trace of aristocratic bias: Everyman was no allegorical figure but, literally, every common person.

So it is not surprising that the bourgeois world view—placing the needs and desires of ordinary men and women at its center—was (and still is) also popular among the common people.* Nor is it surprising that, almost from the beginning, it was an unstable world view, evoking active contempt in a minority, and a pervasive disquiet among those who, more successful than others in having bettered their condition, had the leisure to wonder if life did not, perhaps, have more interesting and remote possibilities to offer.

The emergence of romanticism in the middle of the eighteenth century provided an early warning signal that, within the middle class itself, a kind of nonbourgeois spiritual impulse was at work. Not antibourgeois; not yet. For romanticism—with its celebration of noble savages, *Weltschmerz,* passionate love, aristocratic heroes and heroines, savage terrors confronted with haughty boldness and courage—was mainly an escapist aesthetic mode as distinct from a rebellious one. It provided a kind of counterculture that was, on the whole, safely insulated from bourgeois reality, and could even be tolerated (though always uneasily) as a temporary therapeutic distraction from the serious business of living. A clear sign of this self-limitation of the romantic impulse was the degree to which it was generated, and consumed, by a particular section of the middle class: women.

One of the less happy consequences of the women's liberation movement of the past couple of decades is the distorted view it has encouraged of the history of women under capitalism. This history is interpreted in terms of repression—sexual repression above all. That repression was real enough, of course; but it is absurd to regard it as nothing but an expression of masculine possessiveness, even vindictiveness. Sexual repression—and that whole code of feminine conduct we have come to call Victorian—was imposed and enforced by women, not men (who stand to gain very little if *all* women are chaste). And women insisted on this code because, while sexually repressive, it was also liberating in all sorts of other ways. Specifically, it liberated women, ide-

---

*This generalization, skimming over differences in national traditions and religious cultures (especially Protestant vs. Catholic cultures), is obviously an oversimplification. But it is only an oversimplification, not a distortion.

ally if not always actually, from their previous condition as sex objects or work objects. To put it another way: All women were now elevated to the aristocratic status of *ladies,* entitled to a formal deference, respect, consideration. (Even today, some of those habits survive, if weakly—taking off one's hat when greeting a female acquaintance, standing up when a woman enters the room, etc.) The "wench," as had been portrayed in Shakespeare's plays, was not dead. She was still very much to be found in the working and lower classes. But her condition was not immutable; she, too, could become a lady—through marriage, education, or sheer force of will.

The price for this remarkable elevation of women's status was sexual self-restraint and self-denial, which made them, in a sense, owners of valuable (if intangible) property. It is reasonable to think that this change in actual sexual mores had something to do with the rise of romanticism, with its strong erotic component, in literature—the return of the repressed, as Freud was later to call it. For most of those who purchased romantic novels, or borrowed them (for a fee) from the newly established circulating libraries, were women. Indeed they still are, even today, two centuries later, though the romantic novel is now an exclusively popular art form, which flourishes outside the world of "serious" writing.

This extraordinary and ironical transformation of the novel from a prosaic art form—a tradition that reached its apogee in Jane Austen—to something radically different was itself a bourgeois accomplishment. It was made possible by the growing affluence of the middle classes that provided not only the purchasing power but also the leisure and the solitude ("a room of one's own"). This last point is worth especial notice.

It is a peculiarity of the novel that, unlike all previous art forms, it gains rather than loses from becoming a private experience. Though novels were still occasionally read aloud all during the romantic era, they need not be and gradually ceased to be. Whereas Shakespeare or Racine is most "enchanting" as part of a public experience—on a stage, in daylight—the novel gains its greatest power over us when we "consume" it (or it consumes us) in silence and privacy. Reading a novel then becomes something like surrendering oneself to an especially powerful daydream. The bourgeois ethos, oriented toward prosaic actualities, strongly disapproves of such day dreaming (which is why, even today, a businessman will prefer not to be known as an avid reader of novels, and few in fact are). But bourgeois women very soon discovered that living simultaneously in the two worlds of nonbourgeois "romance" and bourgeois "reality" was superior to living in either one.

*31*

The men and women who wrote such novels (or poems—one thinks of Byron) were not, however, simply responding to a market incentive. Writers and artists may have originally been receptive to a bourgeois society because of the far greater individual freedoms that it offered them; and because, too, they could not help but be exhilarated by the heightened vitality and quickened vivacity of a capitalist order with its emphasis on progress, economic growth, and liberation from age-old constraints. But, very quickly, disillusionment and dissent set in, and the urge to escape became compelling.

From the point of view of artists and of those whom we have come to call "intellectuals"—a category itself created by bourgeois society, which converted philosophers into *philosophes* engaged in the task of critical enlightenment—there were three great flaws in the new order of things.

First of all, it threatened to be very boring. Though the idea of ennui did not become a prominent theme in literature until the nineteenth century, there can be little doubt that the experience is considerably older than its literary expression. One can say this with some confidence because, throughout history, artists and writers have been so candidly contemptuous of commercial activity between consenting adults, regarding it as an activity that tends to coarsen and trivialize the human spirit. And since bourgeois society was above all else a commercial society—the first in all of recorded history in which the commercial ethos was sovereign over all others—their exasperation was bound to be all the more acute. Later on, the term "philistinism" would emerge to encapsulate the object of this sentiment.

Second, though a commercial society may offer artists and writers all sorts of desirable things—freedom of expression especially, popularity and affluence occasionally—it did (and does) deprive them of the status that they naturally feel themselves entitled to. Artists and writers and thinkers always have taken themselves to be Very Important People, and they are outraged by a society that merely tolerates them, no matter how generously. Bertolt Brecht was once asked how he could justify his Communist loyalties when his plays could neither be published nor performed in the USSR, while his royalties in the West made him a wealthy man. His quick rejoinder was: "Well, there at least they take me seriously!" Artists and intellectuals are always more respectful of a regime that takes their work and ideas "seriously." To be placed at a far distance from social and political power is, for such people, a deprivation.

Third, a commercial society, a society whose civilization is shaped by market transactions, is always likely to reflect the appetites and preferences of common men and women. Each may not have much money, but there are so many of them that their tastes are decisive. Artists and intellectuals see this as an inversion of the natural order of things, since it gives "vulgarity" the power to dominate where and when it can. By their very nature "elitists" (as one now says), they believe that a civilization should be shaped by an *aristoi* to which they will be organically attached, no matter how perilously. The consumerist and environmentalist movements of our own day reflect this aristocratic impulse, albeit in a distorted way: Because the democratic idea is the only legitimating political idea of our era, it is claimed that the market does not truly reflect people's preferences, which are deformed by the power of advertising. A minority, however, is presumed to have the education and the will to avoid such deformation. And this minority then claims the paternalist authority to represent "the people" in some more authentic sense. It is this minority which is so appalled by America's "automobile civilization," in which everyone owns a car, while it is not appalled at all by the fact that in the Soviet Union only a privileged few are able to do so.

In sum, intellectuals and artists will be (as they have been) restive in a bourgeois-capitalist society. The popularity of romanticism in the century after 1750 testifies to this fact, as the artists led an "inner emigration" of the spirit—which, however, left the actual world unchanged. But not all such restiveness found refuge in escapism. Rebellion was an alternative route, as the emergence of various socialist philosophies and movements early in the nineteenth century demonstrated.

Socialism (of whatever kind) is a romantic passion that operates within a rationalist framework. It aims to construct a human community in which *everyone* places the common good—as defined, necessarily, by an intellectual and moral elite—before his own individual interests and appetites. The intention was not new—there is not a religion in the world that has failed to preach and expound it. What was new was the belief that such self-denial could be realized, not through a voluntary circumscription of individual appetites (as Rousseau had, for example, argued in his *Social Contract*) but even while the aggregate of human appetites was being increasingly satisfied by ever-growing material prosperity. What Marx called "utopian" socialism was frequently defined by the notion that human appetites were insatiable, and that a self-limitation on such appetites was a precondition for a socialist community. The trouble with this notion, from a political point of view, was that it was not likely to appeal to more than a small minority of men and women at any one time. Marxian "scientific" socialism, in contrast, promised to remove this conflict between actual and potentially ideal human nature by creating an economy of such abundance that appetite as a social force would, as it were, wither away.

Behind this promise, of course, was the profound belief that modern science—including the social sciences, and especially including scientific economics—would gradually but ineluctably provide humanity with modes of control over nature (and human nature, too) that would permit the modern world radically to transcend all those limitations of the human condition previously taken to be "natural." The trouble with implementing this belief, however, was that the majority of men and women were no more capable of comprehending a "science of society," and of developing a "consciousness" appropriate to it, than they were of practicing austere self-denial. A socialist elite, therefore, was indispensable to mobilize the masses for their own ultimate self-transformation. And the techniques of such mobilization would themselves of necessity be scientific—what moralists would call "Machiavellian"—in that they had to treat the masses as objects of manipulation so that eventually they would achieve a condition where they could properly be subjects of their own history making.

Michael Polanyi has described this "dynamic coupling" of a romantic moral passion with a ruthlessly scientific conception of man, his world, and his history as a case of "moral inversion." That is to say, it is the moral passion that legitimates the claims of scientific socialism to absolute truth, while it is the objective necessities that legitimate every possible form of political immorality. Such a dynamic coupling characterized, in the past, only certain religious movements. In the nineteenth and twentieth centuries, it became the property of secular political movements that sought the universal regeneration of mankind in the here and now.

The appeal of any such movement to intellectuals is clear enough. As intellectuals, they are qualified candidates for membership in the elite that leads such movements, and they can thus give free expression to their natural impulse for authority and power. They can do so, moreover, within an ideological context, which reassures them that, any superficial evidence to the contrary notwithstanding, they are disinterestedly serving the "true" interests of the people.

But the reality principle—*la force des choses*—will, in the end, always prevail over utopian passions. The fate of intellectuals under socialism is disillusionment, dissent, exile, silence. In politics, means determine ends, and socialism everywhere finds its incarnation in coercive bureaucracies that are contemptuously dismissive of the ideals that presumably legitimize them, even while establishing these ideals as a petrified orthodoxy. The most interesting fact of contemporary intellectual life is the utter incapacity of so-called socialist countries to produce socialist intellectuals—or even, for that matter, to tolerate socialist intellectuals. If you want to meet active socialist intellectuals, you can go to Oxford or Berkeley or Paris or Rome. There is no point in going to Moscow or Peking or Belgrade or Bucharest or Havana. Socialism today is a dead end for the very intellectuals who have played so significant a role in moving the modern world down that street.

In addition to that romantic-rationalist rebellion we call socialism, there is another mode of "alienation" and rebellion that may be, in the longer run, more important. This is romantic antirationalism, which takes a cultural rather than political form. It is this movement specifically that Trilling had in mind when he referred to the adversary culture.

Taking its inspiration from literary romanticism, this rebellion first created a new kind of "inner emigration"—physical as well as spiritual—in the form of "bohemia." In Paris, in the 1820s and 1830s, there formed enclaves of (mostly) young people who displayed *in nuce* all the symptoms of the counterculture of the 1960s. Drugs, sexual promiscuity, long hair for men and short hair for women, working-class dress (the "jeans" of the day), a high suicide rate—anything and everything that would separate them from the bourgeois order. The one striking difference between this bohemia and its heirs of a century and a quarter later is that to claim membership in bohemia one had to be (or pretend to be) a producer of "art," while in the 1960s to be a consumer was sufficient. For this transition to occur, the attitudes and values of bohemia had to permeate a vast area of bourgeois society itself. The engine and vehicle of this transition was the "modernist" movement in the arts, which in the century after 1850 gradually displaced the traditional, the established, the "academic."

The history and meaning of this movement are amply described and brilliantly analyzed by Daniel Bell in his *The Cultural Contradictions of Capitalism* (1976). Suffice it to say here that modernism in the arts can best be understood as a quasi-religious rebellion against bourgeois sobriety, rather than simply as a series of aesthetic innovations. The very structure of this movement bears a striking resemblance to that of the various gnostic-heretical sects within Judaism and Christianity. There is an "elect"—the artists themselves—who possess the esoteric and redeeming knowledge *(gnosis);* then there are the "critics," whose task it is to convey this gnosis, as a vehicle of conversion, to potential adherents to the movement. And then there is the outer layer of "sympathizers" and "fellow travelers"—mainly bourgeois "consumers" of the modernist arts—who help popularize and legitimate the movement within the wider realms of public opinion.

One can even press the analogy further. It is striking, for instance, that modernist movements in the arts no longer claim to create "beauty" but to reveal the "truth" about humanity in its present condition. Beauty is defined by an aesthetic tradition that finds expression in the public's "taste." But the modern artist rejects the sovereignty of public taste, since truth can never be a matter of taste. This truth always involves an indictment of the existing order of things, while holding out the promise, for those whose sensibilities have been suitably reformed, of a redemption of the spirit (now called "the self"). Moreover, the artist himself now becomes the central figure in the artistic enterprise—he is the hero of his own work, the sacrificial redeemer of us all, the only person capable of that transcendence that gives a liberating meaning to our lives. The artist—painter, poet, novelist, composer—who lives to a ripe old age of contentment with fame and fortune strikes us as having abandoned, if not betrayed, his "mission." We think it more appropriate that artists should die young and tormented. The extraordinarily high suicide rate among modern artists would have baffled our ancestors, who assumed that the artist—like any other *secular* person—aimed to achieve recognition and prosperity in this world.

Our ancestors would have been baffled, too, by the enormous importance of critics and of criticism in modern culture. It is fascinating to pick up a standard anthology in the history of literary criticism and to observe that, prior to 1800, there is very little that we would designate as literary criticism, as distinct from philosophical tracts on aesthetics. Shakespeare had no contemporary critics to explain his plays to the audience; nor did the Greek tragedians, nor Dante, Racine, and so forth. Yet we desperately feel the need of critics to understand, not only the modern artist, but, by retrospective reevaluation, all artists. The reason for this odd state of affairs is that we are looking for something in these artists—a redeeming knowledge of ourselves and our human condition—which in previous eras was felt to lie elsewhere, in religious traditions especially.

The modernist movement in the arts gathered momentum slowly, and the first visible sign of its success was the gradual acceptance of the fact that bourgeois society had within it two cultures: the "avant-garde" culture of modernism, and the "popular culture" of the majority. The self-designation of modernism as avant-garde is itself illuminating. The term is of military origin, and means not, as we are now inclined to think, merely the latest in cultural or intellectual fashion, but the foremost assault troops in a military attack. It was a term popularized by Saint-Simon to describe the role of his utopian-socialist sect vis-à-vis the bourgeois order, and was then taken over by modernist innovators in the arts. The avant-garde is, and always has been, fully self-conscious of its hostile intentions toward the bourgeois world. Until 1914, such hostility was as likely to move intellectuals and artists toward the romantic Right as toward the romantic Left. But Right or Left, the hostility was intransigent. This is, as has been noted, a cultural phenomenon without historical precedent.

And so is the popular culture of the bourgeois era, though here again we are so familiar with the phenomenon that we fail to perceive its originality. It is hard to think of a single historical instance where a society presents us with two cultures, a "high" and a "low," whose values are in opposition to one another. We are certainly familiar with the fact that any culture has its more sophisticated and its more popular aspects, differentiated by the level of education needed to move from the one to the other. But the values embodied in these two aspects were basically homogeneous: The sophisticated expression did not *shock* the popular, nor did the popular incite feelings of revulsion among the sophisticated. Indeed, it was taken as a mark of true artistic greatness for a writer or artist to encompass both aspects of his culture. The Greek tragedies were performed before all the citizens of Athens; Dante's *Divine Comedy* was read aloud in the squares of Florence to a large and motley assemblage; and Shakespeare's plays were enacted before a similarly mixed audience.

The popular culture of the bourgeois era, after 1870 or so, tended to be a culture that educated people despised, or tolerated contemptuously. The age of Richardson, Jane Austen, Walter Scott, and Dickens—an age in which excellence and popularity needed not to contradict one another, in which the distinction between "highbrow" and "lowbrow" made no sense—was over. The spiritual energy that made for artistic excellence was absorbed by the modernist, highbrow movement, while popular culture degenerated into a banal reiteration—almost purely commercial in intent—of "wholesome" bourgeois themes.

In this popular literature of romance and adventure, the "happy ending" not only survived but became a standard cliché. The occasional unhappy ending, involving a sinful action (e.g., adultery) as its effectual cause, always concluded on a note of repentance, and was the occasion for a cathartic "good cry." In "serious" works of literature in the twentieth century, of course, the happy ending is under an almost total prohibition. It is also worth making mention of the fact that popular literature remained very much a commodity consumed by women, whose commitments to the bourgeois order (a "domestic" order, remember) has always been stronger than men's. This is why the women's liberation movement of the past two decades, which is so powerfully moving the female sensibility in an antibourgeois direction, is such a significant cultural event.

In the last century, the modernist movement in the arts made constant progress at the expense of the popular. It was, after all, the only serious art available to young men and women who were inclined to address themselves to solemn questions about the meaning of life (or "the meaning of it all"). The contemporaneous evolution of liberal capitalism itself encouraged modernism in its quest for moral and spiritual hegemony. It did this in three ways.

First, the increasing affluence that capitalism provided to so many individuals made it possible for them (or, more often, for their children) to relax their energetic pursuit of money, and of the goods that money can buy, in favor of an attention to those nonmaterial goods that used to be called "the higher things in life." The antibourgeois arts in the twentieth century soon came to be quite generously financed by restless, uneasy, and vaguely discontented bourgeois money.

Second, that spirit of worldly rationalism so characteristic of a commercial society and its business civilization (and so well described by Max Weber and Joseph Schumpeter) had the effect of delegitimizing all merely traditional beliefs, tasks, and attitudes. The "new," constructed by design or out of the passion of a moment, came to seem inherently superior to the old and established, this latter having emerged "blindly" out of the interaction of generations. This mode of thinking vindicated the socialist ideal of a planned society. But it also vindicated an anarchic, antinomian, "expressionist" impulse in matters cultural and spiritual.

Third, the tremendous expansion—especially after World War II—of postsecondary education provided a powerful institutional milieu for modernist tastes and attitudes among the mass of both teachers and students. Lionel Trilling, in *Beyond Culture,* poignantly describes the spiritual vitality with which this process began in the humanities—the professors were "liberated" to teach the books that most profoundly moved and interested them—and the vulgarized version of modernism that soon became the mass counterculture among their students who, as consumers, converted it into a pseudo-bohemian life-style.

Simultaneously, and more obviously, in the social sciences, the antibourgeois socialist traditions were absorbed as a matter of course, with "the study of society" coming quickly and surely to mean the management of social change by an elite who understood the verities of social structure and social trends. Economics, as the science of making the best choices in a hard world of inevitable scarcity, resisted for a long while; but the Keynesian revolution—with its promise of permanent prosperity through government management of fiscal and monetary policy—eventually brought much of the economics profession in line with the other social sciences.

So utopian rationalism and utopian romanticism have, between them, established their hegemony as adversary cultures over the modern consciousness and the modern sensibility.

But, inevitably, such victories are accompanied by failure and disillusionment. As socialist reality disappoints, socialist thought fragments into heterogeneous conflicting sects, all of them trying to keep the utopian spark alive while devising explanations for the squalid nature of socialist reality. One is reminded of the experience of Christianity in the first and second centuries, but with this crucial difference: Christianity, as a religion of transcendence, of *other-worldly* hope, of faith not belief, was not really utopian, and the Church Fathers were able to transform the Christian rebellion against the ancient world into a new, vital Christian orthodoxy, teaching its adherents how to live virtuously, that is, how to seek human fulfillment in this world even while waiting for their eventual migration into a better one. Socialism, lacking this transcendent dimension, is purely and simply trapped in this world, whose realities are for it nothing more than an endless series of frustrations. It is no accident, as the Marxists would say, that there is no credible doctrine of "socialist virtue"—a doctrine informing individuals how actually to live "in authenticity" as distinct from empty rhetoric about "autonomous self-fulfillment"—in any nation (and there are so many!) now calling itself socialist. It is paradoxically true that other-worldly religions are more capable of providing authoritative guidance for life in this world than are secular religions.

The utopian romanticism that is the impulse behind modernism in the arts is in a not dissimilar situation. It differs in that it seeks transcendence—all of twentieth-century art is such a quest—but it seeks such transcendence within the secular self. This endeavor can generate that peculiar spiritual intensity that characterizes the antibourgeois culture of our bourgeois era, but in the end it is mired in self-contradiction.

The deeper one explores into the self, without any transcendental frame of reference, the clearer it becomes that nothing is there. One can then, of course, try to construct a metaphysics of nothingness as an absolute truth of the human condition. But this, too, is self-contradictory: If nothingness is the ultimate reality, those somethings called books, or poems, or paintings, or music are mere evasions of truth rather than expressions of it. Suicide is the only appropriate response to this vision of reality (as Dostoevski saw long ago) and in the twentieth century it has in fact become the fate of many of our artists: self-sacrificial martyrs to a hopeless metaphysical enterprise. Those who stop short of this ultimate gesture experience that *tedium vitae,* already mentioned, which has made the "boringness" of human life a recurrent theme, since Baudelaire at least, among our artists.

This modern association of culture and culture heroes with self-annihilation and ennui has no parallel in human history. We are so familiar with it that most of us think of it as natural. It is, in truth, unnatural and cannot endure. Philosophy may, with some justice, be regarded as a preparation for dying, as Plato said—but he assumed that there would never be more than a handful of philosophers at any time. The arts, in contrast, have always been life-affirming, even when dealing with the theme of death. It is only when the arts usurp the role of religion, but without the transcendence that assures us of the meaning of apparent meaninglessness, that we reach our present absurd (and *absurdiste*) condition.

Moreover, though utopian rationalism and utopian romanticism are both hostile to bourgeois society, they turn out to be, in the longer run, equally hostile to one another.

In all socialist nations, of whatever kind, modernism in the arts is repressed—for, as we have seen, this modernism breeds a spirit of nihilism and antinomianism that is subversive of *any* established order. But this repression is never entirely effective, because the pseudo-orthodoxies of socialism can offer no satisfying spiritual alternatives. It turns out that a reading of Franz Kafka can alienate from socialist reality just as easily as from bourgeois reality, and there is no socialist Richardson or Fielding or Jane Austen or Dickens to provide an original equipoise. Who are the "classic" socialist authors or artists worthy of the name? There are none. And so young people in socialist lands naturally turn either to the high modernist culture of the twentieth century or to its debased, popularized version in the counterculture. Picasso and Kafka, blue jeans and rock and roll may yet turn out to be the major internal enemies of socialist bureaucracies, uniting intellectuals and the young in an incorrigible hostility to the status quo. Not only do socialism and modernism end up in blind alleys—their blind alleys are pointed in radically different directions.

Meanwhile, liberal capitalism survives and staggers on. It survives because the market economics of capitalism does work—does promote economic growth and permit the individual to better his condition while enjoying an unprecedented degree of individual freedom. But there is something joyless, even somnambulistic, about this survival.

For it was the Judeo-Christian tradition which, as it were, acted as the Old Testament to the new evangel of liberal, individualistic capitalism—which supplied it with a moral code for the individual to live by, and which also enabled the free individual to find a transcendental meaning in life, to cope joyfully or sadly with all the *rites de passage* that define the human condition. Just as a victorious Christianity needed the Old Testament in its canon because the Ten Commandments were there—along with the assurance that God created the world *"and it was good,"* and along, too, with its corollary that it made sense to be fruitful and multiply on this earth—so liberal capitalism needed the Judeo-Christian tradition to inform it authoritatively about the use and abuse of the individual's newly won freedom. But the adversary culture, in both its utopian-rationalist and utopian-romantic aspects, turns this Judeo-Christian tradition into a mere anachronism. And the churches, now themselves a species of voluntary private enterprise, bereft of all public support and sanction, are increasingly ineffectual in coping with its antagonists.

Is it possible to restore the spiritual base of bourgeois society to something approaching a healthy condition?

One is tempted to answer no, it is not possible to turn back the clock of history. But this answer itself derives from the romantic-rationalist conception of history, as elaborated by Saint-Simon and Hegel and Marx. In fact, human history, read in a certain way, can be seen as full of critical moments when human beings deliberately turned the clock back. The Reformation, properly understood, was just such a moment, and so was the codification of the Talmud in postexile Judaism. What we call the "new" in intellectual and spiritual history is often nothing more than a novel way of turning the clock back. The history of science and technology is a cumulative history, in which new ways of seeing and doing effectively displace old ones. But the histories of religion and culture are not at all cumulative in this way, which is why one cannot study religion and culture without studying their histories, while scientists need not study the history of science to understand what they are up to.

So the possibility is open to us—but, for better or worse, it is not the only possibility. All we can say with some certainty, at this time, is that the future of liberal capitalism may be more significantly shaped by the ideas now germinating in the mind of some young, unknown philosopher or theologian than by any vagaries in annual GNP statistics. Those statistics are not unimportant, but to think they are all-important is to indulge in the silly kind of capitalist idolatry that is subversive of capitalism itself. It is the ethos of capitalism that is in gross disrepair, not the economics of capitalism—which is, indeed, its saving grace. But salvation through this grace alone will not suffice.

1979

# 4

# Pornography, Obscenity, and the Case for Censorship

Being frustrated is disagreeable, but the real disasters in life begin when you get what you want. For almost a century now, a great many intelligent, well-meaning, and articulate people—of a kind generally called liberal or intellectual, or both—have argued eloquently against any kind of censorship of art and/or entertainment. And within the past ten years, the courts and the legislatures of most Western nations have found these arguments persuasive—so persuasive that hardly a man is now alive who clearly remembers what the answers to these arguments were. Today, in the United States and other democracies, censorship has to all intents and purposes ceased to exist.

Is there a sense of triumphant exhilaration in the land? Hardly. There is, on the contrary, a rapidly growing unease and disquiet. Somehow, things have not worked out as they were supposed to, and many notable civil libertarians have gone on record as saying this was not what they meant at all. They wanted a world in which *Desire under the*

*Elms* could be produced, or *Ulysses* published, without interference by philistine busybodies holding public office. They have got that, of course; but they have also got a world in which homosexual rape takes place on the stage, in which the public flocks during lunch hours to witness varieties of professional fornication, in which Times Square has become little more than a hideous market for the sale and distribution of printed filth that panders to all known (and some fanciful) sexual perversions.

But disagreeable as this may be, does it really matter? Might not our unease and disquiet be merely a cultural hangover—a "hang-up," as they say? What reason is there to think that anyone was ever corrupted by a book?

This last question, oddly enough, is asked by the very same people who seem convinced that advertisements in magazines or displays of violence on television do indeed have the power to corrupt. It is also asked, incredibly enough and in all sincerity, by people—for example, university professors and schoolteachers—whose very lives provide all the answers one could want. After all, if you believe that no one was ever corrupted by a book, you have also to believe that no one was ever improved by a book (or a play or a movie). You have to believe, in other words, that all art is morally trivial and that, consequently, all education is morally irrelevant. No one, not even a university professor, really believes that.

To be sure, it is extremely difficult, as social scientists tell us, to trace the effects of any single book (or play or movie) on an individual reader or any class of readers. But we all know, and social scientists know it too, that the ways in which we use our minds and imaginations do shape our characters and help define us as persons. That those who certainly know this are nevertheless moved to deny it merely indicates how a dogmatic resistance to the idea of censorship can—like most dogmatism—result in a mindless insistence on the absurd.

I have used these harsh terms—"dogmatism" and "mindless"—advisedly. I might also have added "hypocritical." For the plain fact is that none of us is a complete civil libertarian. We all believe that there is some point at which the public authorities ought to step in to limit the "self-expression" of an individual or a group, even where this might be seriously intended as a form of artistic expression, and even where the artistic transaction is between consenting adults. A playwright or theatrical director might, in this crazy world of ours, find someone willing to commit suicide on the stage, as called for by the script. We would not allow that—any more than we would permit scenes of real physical torture on the stage, even if the victim were a willing masochist. And

I know of no one, no matter how free in spirit, who argues that we ought to permit gladiatorial contests in Yankee Stadium, similar to those once performed in the Colosseum at Rome—even if only consenting adults were involved.

The basic point that emerges is one that Walter Berns has powerfully argued: No society can be utterly indifferent to the ways its citizens publicly entertain themselves.* Bearbaiting and cockfighting are prohibited only in part out of compassion for the suffering animals; the main reason they were abolished was because it was felt that they debased and brutalized the citizenry who flocked to witness such spectacles. And the question we face with regard to pornography and obscenity is whether, now that they have such strong legal protection from the Supreme Court, they can or will brutalize and debase our citizenry. We are, after all, not dealing with one passing incident—one book, or one play, or one movie. We are dealing with a general tendency that is suffusing our entire culture.

I say pornography *and* obscenity because, though they have different dictionary definitions and are frequently distinguishable as "artistic" genres, they are nevertheless in the end identical in effect. Pornography is not objectionable simply because it arouses sexual desire or lust or prurience in the mind of the reader or spectator; this is a silly Victorian notion. A great many nonpornographic works—including some parts of the Bible—excite sexual desire very successfully. What is distinctive about pornography is that, in the words of D. H. Lawrence, it attempts "to do dirt on [sex] . . . [It is an] insult to a vital human relationship."

In other words, pornography differs from erotic art in that its whole purpose is to treat human beings obscenely, to deprive human beings of their specifically human dimension. That is what obscenity is all about. It is light years removed from any kind of carefree sensuality—there is no continuum between Fielding's *Tom Jones* and the Marquis de Sade's *Justine.* These works have quite opposite intentions. To quote Susan Sontag: "What pornographic literature does is precisely to drive a wedge between one's existence as a full human being and one's existence as a sexual being—while in ordinary life a healthy person is one who prevents such a gap from opening up." This definition occurs in an essay *defending* pornography—Miss Sontag is a candid as well as gifted critic—so the definition, which I accept, is neither tendentious nor censorious.

*This is as good a place as any to express my profound indebtedness to Walter's Berns's superb essay "Pornography vs. Democracy," in the Winter 1971 issue of *The Public Interest.*

Along these same lines, one can point out—as C. S. Lewis pointed out some years back—that it is no accident that in the history of all literatures obscene words, the so-called four-letter words, have always been the vocabulary of farce or vituperation. The reason is clear; they reduce men and women to some of their mere bodily functions—they reduce man to his animal component, and such a reduction is an essential purpose of farce or vituperation.

Similarly, Lewis also suggested that it is not an accident that we have no offhand, colloquial, neutral terms—not in any Western European language at any rate—for our most private parts. The words we do use are either (1) nursery terms, (2) archaisms, (3) scientific terms, or (4) a term from the gutter (i.e., a demeaning term). Here I think the genius of language is telling us something important about man. It is telling us that man is an animal with a difference: He has a unique sense of privacy, and a unique capacity for shame when this privacy is violated. Our "private parts" are indeed private, and not merely because convention prescribes it. This particular convention is indigenous to the human race. In practically all primitive tribes, men and women cover their private parts; and in practically all primitive tribes, men and women do not copulate in public.

It may well be that Western society, in the latter half of the twentieth century, is experiencing a drastic change in sexual mores and sexual relationships. We have had many such "sexual revolutions" in the past—the bourgeois family and bourgeois ideas of sexual propriety were themselves established in the course of a revolution against eighteenth-century "licentiousness"—and we shall doubtless have others in the future. It is, however, highly improbable (to put it mildly) that what we are witnessing is the Final Revolution which will make sexual relations utterly unproblematic, permit us to dispense with any kind of ordered relationships between the sexes, and allow us freely to redefine the human condition. And so long as humanity has not reached that utopia, obscenity will remain a problem.

One of the reasons it will remain a problem is that obscenity is not merely about sex, any more than science fiction is about science. Science fiction, as every student of the genre knows, is a peculiar vision of power: What it is really about is politics. And obscenity is a peculiar vision of humanity: What it is really about is ethics and metaphysics.

Imagine a man—a well-known man, much in the public eye—in a hospital ward, dying an agonizing death. He is not in control of his bodily functions, so that his bladder and his bowels empty themselves of their own accord. His consciousness is overwhelmed and extinguished by pain, so that he cannot communicate with us, nor we with him. Now, it would be, technically, the easiest thing in the world to put a television camera in his hospital room and let the whole world witness this spectacle. We do not do it—at least we do not do it as yet—because we regard this as an *obscene* invasion of privacy. And what would make the spectacle obscene is that we would be witnessing the extinguishing of humanity in a human animal.

Incidentally, in the past our humanitarian crusaders against capital punishment understood this point very well. The abolitionist literature goes into great physical detail about what happens to a man when he is hanged or electrocuted or gassed. And their argument was—and is—that what happens is shockingly obscene, and that no civilized society should be responsible for perpetrating such obscenities, particularly since in the nature of the case there must be spectators to ascertain that this horror was indeed being perpetrated in fulfillment of the law.

Sex—like death—is an activity that is both animal and human. There are human sentiments and human ideals involved in this animal activity. But when sex is public, the viewer does not see—cannot see—the sentiments and the ideals. He can only see the animal coupling. And that is why, when men and women make love, as we say, they prefer to be alone—because it is only when you are alone that you can make love, as distinct from merely copulating in an animal and casual way. And that, too, is why those who are voyeurs, if they are not irredeemably sick, also feel ashamed at what they are witnessing. When sex is a public spectacle, a human relationship has been debased into a mere animal connection.

It is also worth noting that this making of sex into an obscenity is not a mutual and equal transaction but rather an act of exploitation by one of the partners—the male partner. I do not wish to get into the complicated question as to what, if any, are the essential differences—as distinct from conventional and cultural differences—between male and female. I do not claim to know the answer to that. But I do know—and I take it as a sign that has meaning—that pornography is, and always has been, a man's work; that women rarely write pornography; and that women tend to be indifferent consumers of pornography.* My own guess, by way of explanation, is that a woman's sexual experience is ordinarily more suffused with human emotion than is man's, that men are more easily satisfied with autoerotic activities, and that men can therefore more easily take a more "technocratic" view of sex and its pleasures. Perhaps this is not correct. But whatever the explanation,

---

*There are, of course, a few exceptions. *L'Histoire d'O,* for instance, was written by a woman. It is unquestionably the most *melancholy* work of pornography ever written. And its theme is precisely the dehumanization accomplished by obscenity.

there can be no question that pornography is a form of "sexism," as the women's liberation movement calls it, and that the instinct of women's liberation has been unerring in perceiving that when pornography is perpetrated, it is perpetrated against them, as part of a conspiracy to deprive them of their full humanity.

But even if all this is granted, it might be said—and doubtless will be said—that I really ought not to be unduly concerned. Free competition in the cultural marketplace—it is argued by people who have never otherwise had a kind word to say for laissez-faire—will automatically dispose of the problem. The present fad for pornography and obscenity, it will be asserted, is just that, a fad. It will spend itself in the course of time; people will get bored with it, will be able to take it or leave it alone in a casual way, in a "mature way," and, in sum, I am being unnecessarily distressed about the whole business. The *New York Times,* in an editorial, concludes hopefully in this vein.

> In the end . . . the insensate pursuit of the urge to shock, carried from one excess to a more abysmal one, is bound to achieve its own antidote in total boredom. When there is no lower depth to descend to, ennui will erase the problem.

I would like to be able to go along with this line of reasoning, but I cannot. I think it is false, and for two reasons, the first psychological, the second political.

The basic psychological fact about pornography and obscenity is that it appeals to and provokes a kind of sexual regression. The sexual pleasure one gets from pornography and obscenity is autoerotic and infantile; put bluntly, it is a masturbatory exercise of the imagination, when it is not masturbation pure and simple. Now, people who masturbate do not get bored with masturbation, just as sadists do not get bored with sadism, and voyeurs do not get bored with voyeurism.

In other words, infantile sexuality is not only a permanent temptation for the adolescent or even the adult—it can quite easily become a permanent, self-reinforcing neurosis. It is because of an awareness of this possibility of regression toward the infantile condition, a regression which is always open to us, that all the codes of sexual conduct ever devised by the human race take such a dim view of autoerotic activities and try to discourage autoerotic fantasies. Masturbation is indeed a perfectly natural autoerotic activity, as so many sexologists blandly assure us today. And it is precisely because it is so perfectly natural that it can be so dangerous to the mature or maturing person, if it is not controlled or sublimated in some way. That is the true meaning of Portnoy's complaint. Portnoy, you will recall, grows up to be a man who is incapable of having an adult sexual relationship with a woman; his sexuality remains fixed in an infantile mode, the prisoner of his autoerotic fantasies. Inevitably, Portnoy comes to think, in a perfectly *infantile* way, that it was all his mother's fault.

It is true that, in our time, some quite brilliant minds have come to the conclusion that a reversion to infantile sexuality is the ultimate mission and secret destiny of the human race. I am thinking in particular of Norman O. Brown, for whose writings I have the deepest respect. One of the reasons I respect them so deeply is that Mr. Brown is a serious thinker who is unafraid to face up to the radical consequences of his radical theories. Thus, Mr. Brown knows and says that for his kind of salvation to be achieved, humanity must annul the civilization it has created—not merely the civilization we have today, but all civilization—so as to be able to make the long descent backward into animal innocence.

And that is the point. What is at stake is civilization and humanity, nothing less. The idea that "everything is permitted," as Nietzsche put it, rests on the premise of nihilism and has nihilistic implications. I will not pretend that the case against nihilism and for civilization is an easy one to make. We are here confronting the most fundamental of philosophical questions, on the deepest levels. In short, the matter of pornography and obscenity is not a trivial one, and only superficial minds can take a bland and untroubled view of it.

In this connection, I must also point out, those who are primarily against censorship on liberal grounds tell us not to take pornography or obscenity seriously, while those who are for pornography and obscenity on radical grounds take it very seriously indeed. I believe the radicals—writers like Susan Sontag, Herbert Marcuse, Norman O. Brown, and even Jerry Rubin—are right, and the liberals are wrong. I also believe that those young radicals at Berkeley, some seven years ago, who provoked a major confrontation over the public use of obscene words, showed a brilliant political instinct. And once Mark Rudd could publicly ascribe to the president of Columbia a notoriously obscene relationship to his mother, without provoking any kind of reaction, the SDS [Students for a Democratic Society] had already won the day. The occupation of Columbia's buildings merely ratified their victory. Men who show themselves unwilling to defend civilization against nihilism are not going to be either resolute or effective in defending the university against anything.

I am already touching upon a political aspect of pornography when I suggest that it is inherently and purposefully subversive of civilization and its institutions. But there is another and more specifically political aspect, which has to do with the relationship of pornography and/or obscenity to democracy, and especially to the quality of public life on which democratic government ultimately rests.

Though the phrase "the quality of life" trips easily from so many lips these days, it tends to be one of those clichés with many trivial meanings and no large, serious one. Sometimes it merely refers to such externals as the enjoyment of cleaner air, cleaner water, cleaner streets. At other times it refers to the merely private enjoyment of music, painting, or literature. Rarely does it have anything to do with the way the citizen in a democracy views himself—his obligations, his intentions, his ultimate self-definition.

Instead, what I would call the "managerial" conception of democracy is the predominant opinion among political scientists, sociologists, and economists, and has, through the untiring efforts of these scholars, become the conventional journalistic opinion as well. The root idea behind this managerial conception is that democracy is a "political system" (as they say) which can be adequately defined in terms of—can be fully reduced to—its mechanical arrangements. Democracy is then seen as a set of rules and procedures, and *nothing but* a set of rules and procedures, whereby majority rule and minority rights are reconciled into a state of equilibrium. If everyone follows these rules and procedures, then a democracy is in working order. I think this is a fair description of the democratic idea that currently prevails in academia. One can also fairly say that it is now the liberal idea of democracy par excellence.

I cannot help but feel that there is something ridiculous about being this kind of a democrat, and I must further confess to having a sneaking sympathy for those of our young radicals who also find it ridiculous. The absurdity is the absurdity of idolatry—of taking the symbolic for the real, the means for the end. The purpose of democracy cannot possibly be the endless functioning of its own political machinery. The purpose of any political regime is to achieve some version of the good life and the good society. It is not at all difficult to imagine a perfectly functioning democracy which answers all questions except one—namely, why should anyone of intelligence and spirit care a fig for it?

There is, however, an older idea of democracy—one which was fairly common until about the beginning of this century—for which the conception of the quality of public life is absolutely crucial. This idea starts from the proposition that democracy is a form of self-government, and that if you want it to be a meritorious polity, you have to care about what kind of people govern it. Indeed, it puts the matter more strongly and declares that if you want self-government, you are only entitled to it if that "self" is worthy of governing. There is no inherent right to self-government if it means that such government is vicious, mean, squalid, and debased. Only a dogmatist and a fanatic, an idolater of democratic machinery, could approve of self-government under such conditions.

And because the desirability of self-government depends on the character of the people who govern, the older idea of democracy was very solicitous of the condition of this character. It was solicitous of the individual self, and felt an obligation to educate it into what used to be called "republican virtue." And it was solicitous of that collective self which we call public opinion and which, in a democracy, governs us collectively. Perhaps in some respects it was nervously oversolicitous—that would not be surprising. But the main thing is that it cared, cared not merely about the machinery of democracy but about the quality of life that this machinery might generate.

And because it cared, this older idea of democracy had no problem in principle with pornography and/or obscenity. It censored them—and it did so with a perfect clarity of mind and a perfectly clear conscience. It was not about to permit people capriciously to corrupt themselves. Or, to put it more precisely: In this version of democracy, the people took some care not to let themselves be governed by the more infantile and irrational parts of themselves.

I have, it may be noticed, uttered that dreadful word censorship. And I am not about to back away from it. If you think pornography and/or obscenity is a serious problem, you have to be for censorship. I will go even further and say that if you want to prevent pornography and/or obscenity from becoming a problem, you have to be for censorship. And lest there be any misunderstanding as to what I am saying, I will put it as bluntly as possible: If you care for the quality of life in our American democracy, then you have to be for censorship.

But can a liberal be for censorship? Unless one assumes that being a liberal *must* mean being indifferent to the quality of American life, then the answer has to be yes, a liberal can be for censorship—but he ought to favor a liberal form of censorship.

Is that a contradiction in terms? I do not think so. We have no problem in contrasting *repressive* laws governing alcohol and drugs and tobacco with laws *regulating* (i.e., discouraging the sale of) alcohol and drugs and tobacco. Laws encouraging temperance are not the same thing as laws that have as their goal prohibition or abolition. We have not made the smoking of cigarettes a criminal offense. We have, however, and with good liberal conscience, prohibited cigarette advertising on television, and may yet, again with good liberal conscience, prohibit it in newspapers and magazines. The idea of restricting individual free-dom, in a liberal way, is not at all unfamiliar to us.

I therefore see no reason why we should not be able to distinguish repressive censorship from liberal censorship of the written and spoken word. In Britain, until a few years ago, you could perform almost any play you wished, but certain plays, judged to be obscene, had to be per-formed in private theatrical clubs, which were deemed to have a "seri-ous" interest in theater. In the United States, all of us who grew up using public libraries are familiar with the circumstances under which certain books could be circulated only to adults, while still other books had to be read in the library reading room, under the librarian's skeptical eye. In both cases, a small minority that was willing to make a serious effort to see an obscene play or read an obscene book could do so. But the impact of obscenity was circumscribed and the quality of public life was only marginally affected.*

I am not saying it is easy in practice to sustain a distinction between liberal and repressive censorship, especially in the public realm of a de-mocracy, where popular opinion is so vulnerable to demagoguery. Moreover, an acceptable system of liberal censorship is likely to be ex-ceedingly difficult to devise in the United States today, because our edu-cated classes, upon whose judgment a liberal censorship must rest, are so convinced that there is no such thing as a problem of obscenity, or even that there is no such thing as obscenity at all. But, to counterbal-ance this, there is the further, fortunate truth that the tolerable margin for error is quite large, and single mistakes or single injustices are not all that important.

This possibility of error, of course, occasions much distress among artists and academics. It is a fact, one that cannot and should not be denied, that any system of censorship is bound, upon occasion, to treat unjustly a particular work of art—to find pornography where there is only gentle eroticism, to find obscenity where none really exists, or to find both where its existence ought to be tolerated because it serves a larger moral purpose. Though most works of art are not obscene, and though most obscenity has nothing to do with art, there are some few works of art that are, at least in part, pornographic and/or obscene. There are also some few works of art that are in the special category of the comic-ironic "bawdy" (Boccaccio, Rabelais). It is such works of

---

*It is fairly predictable that someone is going to object that this point of view is "elitist"—that, under a system of liberal censorship, the rich will have privileged access to pornography and obscenity. Yes, of course, they will—just as, at present, the rich have privileged access to heroin if they want it. But one would have to be an egalitarian maniac to object to this state of affairs on the grounds of equality.

art that are likely to suffer at the hands of the censor. That is the price one has to be prepared to pay for censorship—even liberal censorship.

But just how high is this price? If you believe, as so many artists seem to believe today, that art is the only sacrosanct activity in our profane and vulgar world—that any man who designates himself an artist thereby acquires a sacred office—then obviously censorship is an intolerable form of sacrilege. But for those of us who do not subscribe to this religion of art, the costs of censorship do not seem so high at all.

If you look at the history of American or English literature, there is precious little damage you can point to as a consequence of the censorship that prevailed throughout most of that history. Very few works of literature—of real literary merit, I mean—ever were suppressed; and those that were, were not suppressed for long. Nor have I noticed, now that censorship of the written word has to all intents and purposes ceased in this country, that hitherto suppressed or repressed masterpieces are flooding the market. Yes, we can now read *Fanny Hill* and the Marquis de Sade. Or, to be more exact, we can now openly purchase them, since many people were able to read them even though they were publicly banned, which is as it should be under a liberal censorship. So how much have literature and the arts gained from the fact that we can all now buy them over the counter, that, indeed, we are all now encouraged to buy them over the counter? They have not gained much that I can see.

And one might also ask a question that is almost never raised: How much has literature lost from the fact that everything is now permitted? It has lost quite a bit, I should say. In a free market, Gresham's Law can work for books or theater as efficiently as it does for coinage—driving out the good, establishing the debased. The cultural market in the United States today is being preempted by dirty books, dirty movies, dirty theater. A pornographic novel has a far better chance of being published today than a nonpornographic one, and quite a few pretty good novels are not being published at all simply because they are not pornographic, and are therefore less likely to sell. Our cultural condition has not improved as a result of the new freedom. American cultural life was not much to brag about twenty years ago; today one feels ashamed for it.

Just one last point, which I dare not leave untouched. If we start censoring pornography or obscenity, shall we not inevitably end up censoring political opinion? A lot of people seem to think this would be the case—which only shows the power of doctrinaire thinking over reality. We had censorship of pornography and obscenity for 150 years, until almost yesterday, and I am not aware that freedom of opinion in this country was in any way diminished as a consequence of this fact. Fortunately for those of us who are liberal, freedom is not indivisible. If it were, the case for liberalism would be indistinguishable from the case for anarchy; and they are two very different things.

But I must repeat and emphasize: What kinds of laws we pass governing pornography and obscenity, what kind of censorship—or, since we are still a federal nation, what kinds of censorship—we institute in our various localities may indeed be difficult matters to cope with; nevertheless the real issue is one of principle. I myself subscribe to a liberal view of the enforcement problem: I think that pornography should be illegal *and* available to anyone who wants it so badly as to make a pretty strenuous effort to get it. We have lived with under-the-counter pornography for centuries now, in a fairly comfortable way. But the issue of principle, of whether it should be over or under the counter, has to be settled before we can reflect on the advantages and disadvantages of alternative modes of censorship. I think the settlement we are living under now, in which obscenity and democracy are regarded as equals, is wrong; I believe it is inherently unstable; I think it will, in the long run, be incompatible with any authentic concern for the quality of life in our democracy.

1971

# 5

# *Urban Civilization and Its Discontents*

IT IS in the nature of democratic countries that, sooner or later, all serious controversy—whether it be political, social, or economic—will involve an appeal to the democratic principle as the supreme arbiter of the rights and the wrongs of the affair. One might begin by invoking the idea of justice, or liberty, or equity, or natural rights; but in the end what is unjust or illiberal or unnatural—or even what is simply "un-American"—will be defined in terms of what is most properly democratic. It follows, therefore, that to the extent to which our idea of democracy is vague or unrealistic or self-contradictory, we shall be less able to resolve the issues that divide us.

I do not mean, of course, that a neat and precise and generally accepted definition of democracy will in and of itself automatically pacify the body politic and avoid bitter conflicts of interests and values. There is no magic in ideas, even when we superstitiously attribute a quasi-divine authority to them. But ideas do give shape to our senti-

Adapted from the inaugural lecture as Henry Luce Professor of Urban Values, New York University, April 1970.

ments, our consciences, and our moral energies. And a muddled idea can, in time, give birth to some fairly grotesque political realities. One has only to recall that, for nearly a century after the formation of the American republic, it was widely accepted that our idea of democracy for all was compatible with a condition of slavery for some, to realize that this is no mere abstract possibility. And the fact that it required a bloody civil war to establish what the authentic intentions of our democracy were would indicate that—as in certain older theological controversies that disrupted the real world of Christendom—the precise meaning of the democratic dogma can have the most material bearing upon the kind of society we live in and the ways in which we live in it.

At the moment, for example, we are all of us much exercised about the quality of life in our American urban civilization. I have no intention, at this time, of analyzing the numerous problems which make up what we familiarly call the "crisis of our cities." Instead, I should like to focus on the apparent incapacity of our democratic and urban civilization to come to grips with these problems. In other words, if it is proper to say that we experience the crisis of our cities, it is equally proper to say that we *are* the urban crisis. And what I want to suggest further is that one of the main reasons we are so problematic to ourselves is the fact that we are creating a democratic, urban civilization while stubbornly refusing to think clearly about the relation of urbanity to democracy.

In this respect, we are far removed indeed from the founding fathers of this republic, who thought deeply about this relationship—but in a way so uncongenial to us that we find it most difficult to take their thinking seriously. We even find it difficult to study their thinking fairly. Thus, in the many books that have appeared in recent years surveying the history of the American city and of American attitudes toward the city, we usually find a discussion of the "agrarian bias" of the founding fathers. More often than not, this is taken quite simply to mean that their opinions were an unreflective expression of their rural condition: a provincial prejudice, familiar enough—the antagonism of country to town is no new thing—and understandable enough in human terms, but now to be regarded as rather quaint and entirely unilluminating. I think that this approach is not only an obstacle to our understanding the American past; it also represents a lost opportunity for us to take our bearings in the present.

To take such a bearing, we ought to begin with an appreciation of the fact that the ideas of the founding fathers did not, in their sum, amount to an agrarian *bias* so much as an antiurban *philosophy;* which is to say, the founding fathers had reasons for thinking as they did, and until we consider these reasons and come to terms with them, we are more likely to be living testimony to the validity of their apprehensions than to the presumed anachronistic character of these apprehensions.

The founding fathers saw democracy in America as resting upon two major pillars. The first, whose principles and rationale are so superbly set forth in *The Federalist Papers,* was the "new science of government" which made popular government possible in a large and heterogeneous republic. This new science designed a machinery of self-government that has to be considered as one of the most remarkable political inventions of Western man. The machinery is by now familiar to us; representative and limited government, separation of powers; majority rule but refined so that it had to express the will of various majorities elected in various ways; a diffusion of political and economic power which would thwart the intentions of any single-minded faction no matter how large and influential, and so on and so forth. The basic idea behind all these arrangements was that the pursuit of self-interest was the most reliable of human motivations on which to build a political system—but this pursuit had to be, to use one of their favorite phrases, the pursuit of self-interest "rightly understood," and such right understanding needed the benevolent, corrective checks and balances of the new political machinery to achieve decent self-definition—that is, to converge at a point of commonweal.

The second pillar envisaged by the founding fathers was of a spiritual order—and the fact that most of us today prefer to call it "psychological" rather than spiritual would have been taken by them as itself a clear sign of urban decadence. To designate this pillar they used such phrases as "republican morality" or "civic virtue," but what they had constantly in mind was the willingness of the good democratic citizen, on critical occasions, to transcend the habitual pursuit of self-interest and devote himself directly and disinterestedly to the common good. In times of war, of course, republican morality took the form of patriotism—no one, after all, has ever been able to demonstrate that it is to a man's self-interest to die for his country. In times of peace, republican morality might take the form of agreeing to hold public office; since the founding fathers assumed that the holders of such office would be men of property, to whom the pleasures of private life were readily available, and since they further thought of political ambition as a form of human distemper, they could candidly look upon public service as a burden as well as an honor. But whatever the occasion, such a capacity for disinterested action seemed to them—as even today, it still seems to some—a necessary complement to the pursuit of self-interest rightly understood.

Now, given these ideas on how popular government in America could survive and prosper, it is only natural that the founding fathers should have taken a suspicious view of big cities and should have wondered whether, in the end, they could be compatible with a free and popular government. In this suspicion and wonder they were anything but original. The entire literature of classical political philosophy—from Plato, Aristotle, and Cicero on to Montesquieu—exhibits a similar skepticism, to put it mildly, concerning the quality of life that people lead in big cities, and expresses doubt whether the habits of mind generated there—what we might call the urban mentality: irreverent, speculative, pleasure-loving, self-serving, belligerent toward all conventional pieties—are compatible with republican survival. Nor, it should be observed, did the real, historical world present much reassurance, by way of contrary evidence. The big cities that the founding fathers knew or read about all displayed in luxuriant abundance the very vices they wished above all to avoid in the new nation they were constructing. From imperial Rome to imperial London and Paris, the big city was the locus of powerful, illiberal, and undemocratic government, inhabited by people who were either too wretched and depraved to be free, democratic citizens, or by ambitious, self-seeking men to whom the ideals of popular government were utterly alien and even repugnant.

That *small* cities could be soberly and democratically governed, the founding fathers understood well enough—Geneva and Athens and the towns of New England testified to that. That medium-sized cities could sustain a modified and partial form of popular government, based on a deferential citizenry and a patrician elite, they also knew—the histories of republican Rome and Venice were very familiar to them, and their own Boston or Philadelphia offered them living instances of this general truth. But the wisdom of the ages had reached an unequivocal conclusion, in which they concurred, about large, populous, cosmopolitan cities: The anonymous creatures massed in such a place, clawing one another in a sordid scramble for survival, advantage, or specious distinction, their frantic lives reflecting no piety toward nature, God, or the political order—such people were not of the stuff of which a free-standing, self-governing republic could be created. Or, to put this point in a more philosophical way, which would have been immediately comprehensible to our ancestors even if it sounds a little strange to us: If self-government, as an ideal to be respected, means the willingness of people to permit their baser selves to be directed by their better selves, then this precondition of self-government is least likely to be discovered among the turbulent and impassioned masses of big cities.

*58*

Today, in the second half of the twentieth century, this theory of the founding fathers is being put to the test, and I do not see how anyone can be blithely sanguine about the ultimate conclusions that will be drawn. Our most obvious difficulty is that we have so many big cities and seem so persistently inept in devising a satisfactory machinery of self-government in them—swinging wildly from the corrupt rule of political machines to abortive experiments in decentralized, direct democracy, with a slovenly bureaucracy providing the barest minimum of stability in between. This is indeed a sore perplexity to us; and no clear solution seems visible even to the most thoughtful among us—witness the uncertainty among our political scientists whether our major cities should evolve into supercities, almost little states, or whether they would be better off dissolving into mini-cities, almost small towns. Twenty years ago the first prospect seemed the more enchanting; today it is the second; tomorrow the winds of doctrine might once again suddenly reverse themselves. Our ideas about our cities are as unsettled and as uneasy as the cities themselves.

But this obvious difficulty is only the smaller part of the challenge posed us. Though we are indeed becoming ever more "a nation of cities," we are *not*—despite a contrary impression created by the news media—on our way to becoming a nation of very big cities. The proportion of our population in cities of over one million has been drifting downward for several decades now, and this proportion is, in the decades ahead, more likely to decline further than it is to increase. Many of the traditional functions of the great metropolis are being radically decentralized, both by technological and by sociological innovation. Air travel has already robbed the metropolis of its role as a transportation hub for people; air freight is gradually doing the same thing for goods. And just think of the extraordinary way in which our cultural community—our writers and artists and sculptors and musicians and dramatists—has, with recent years, been dispersed among the university campuses of the nation. A city like New York is more and more becoming a showplace for the work of creative artists, rather than a milieu in which they live. Even bohemia, that most urban of cultural phenomena, has been transplanted to and around the university campus.

It is conceivable, therefore, that, though our major cities keep floundering in a sea of troubles, the nation as a whole will not be profoundly affected. And what so many people now proclaim to be an imminent apocalypse may yet turn out to be not much more than—though it is also not much less than—a change of life for our older cities. Even the most critical problem which today confronts these cities—the problem of black Americans living in the squalid isolation of their ghettos—may yet reveal to posterity a very different meaning from the despairing significance we ascribe to it today. For these are the citizens who, if we are lucky, might infuse these cities with a new vigor and a new purpose. It is hard to see who else can accomplish this—it is hard even to see who else would care enough to try. As a white New Yorker, born and bred, I am bound to have confused feelings about such a course of events. But I should like to think I am a sufficiently objective student of the city not to see as a crisis what may merely be a personal problem of adaptation to historical change.

But I digress: Because I am a man who has lived all his life in big, old cities, I am inevitably more keenly interested in them than, as a student of the contemporary city, I perhaps ought to be. The overwhelming majority of my fellow Americans clearly prefer to live elsewhere, and this preference is by now an established feature of American life, for better or worse. If we are a nation of cities, we are also becoming to an ever greater degree a nation of relatively small and middle-sized cities. These are the growing centers of American life—especially if we count as "small cities," as we should, those scattered university campuses which support populations of 30,000 or more. It is quite true that these new cities are not spread uniformly over the land but tend to cluster in what we call "metropolitan areas." This fact has led some observers to conclude hastily that such settlements have only a transient, juridical existence—that they ought properly to be regarded as part of an incipient "megalopolis," in the process of coalescing. This is almost surely an illusion—or, if one prefers, a nightmare. Though a great many urban sociologists and urban journalists seem to be convinced that Americans in large numbers would really prefer to live in the central city and are being forced out of their cities by one external cause or another, the evidence is quite plainly to the contrary. People leave the big cities, or refuse to come to them, because they positively prefer the kinds of lives they can lead in smaller suburban townships or cities of modest size; and these people are not going to become citizens of any kind of megalopolis. Indeed, though most central cities are now aware of their ghetto populations only as a source of trouble and calamity, one can predict with considerable confidence that ten years from now these same central cities will be fighting tooth-and-nail to hold on to these populations, as they too begin to experience the attractions of urban life outside our major urban centers.

And here, I think, we have at last come to what I would consider the heart of the matter. For the overwhelming fact of American life today, whether this life be lived in a central city or a suburb or a small city—or even in those rural areas where something like a third of our population still resides—is that it is *life in an urban civilization.* In terms of the *quality* of American life, the United States is now one vast metropolis. Cities are nothing new; the problems of cities are nothing new; but an urban civilization is very new indeed, and the problems of an urban civilization are without precedent in human history.

When I say that our urban civilization is something radically new, I am obviously not unmindful of the historical fact that, in a profound sense, just about every civilization we have known has been urban in origin and character. Civilization, both the high and the low of it, is something that has always been bred in cities—which is why all romantic rebels against civilization, in the past as in our own time, so vehemently repudiate the "artificiality" and "superficiality" and "inhumanity" of city life. But the city and its civilization have always been one thing, while the rest of the nation and its way of life have been another. Between these two things there has always existed a high degree of tension—on the whole a creative tension, though it has sometimes found release in exceedingly ugly moments. Between urban life in the city and provincial life outside the city there has always been a gulf of mistrust, suspicion, and contempt. Yet it is not too far-fetched to say that each was an indispensable antibody for the other's healthy existence. Life in the city could, for example, be careless of conventional morality, and even have an experimental attitude toward all moral rules, precisely because of the reassuring certainty that, throughout the rest of the nation, there prevailed a heavy dullness and conformity. This dullness and conformity reassured the city man, even as he mocked it, that his moral experiments were in the nature of singular explorations with no necessary collective consequences. Similarly, the sovereignty of conventional morality outside the city was sustained by reason of the fact that those who would rebel against it simply emigrated to the urban center. In addition, the rigid character of this traditional morality was made more tolerable to the provincial citizenry because of the known and inevitable fact that, in most cases, urban experiments in freedom were not equally or altogether successful for the individual who was presumptuous enough to engage in them. And when they did succeed—when they resulted in artistic creativity or political distinction—the provincial nation participated, at no cost to itself, in the glory.

Now, this provincial nation has been liquidated. To anyone like myself who watches old movies on television—and by old movies I mean no more than fifteen or twenty years old—the most striking impression is of a world that belongs to another era. These movies have farmers' daughters—honest-to-goodness farmers' daughters, with all that this implies for the sophisticated urban imagination; they have happy, neighborly suburban families who smugly and snugly pass the evening watching themselves on television; they have prim school-marms and prissy schoolmistresses; they have absentminded professors who do not know the difference between a foundation garment and a foundation grant; they have hicks who run gas stations and cops who drop in for apple pie; they have children who address their fathers as "sir"; they have virginal college maidens and hardly any graduate students at all; they have wildly efficient and fanatically loyal secretaries—in short, they have a race of people who only yesterday were the average and the typical, and who have so suddenly become, in their laughable unreality, a species of "camp."

What has happened, clearly, is that provincial America—that America which at least paid lip service to, if it did not live by, the traditional republican morality; that America which, whether on the farm or in suburb or small town, thought it important to preserve the appearance of a life lived according to the prescriptions of an older agrarian virtue and piety; that America which was calmly philistine and so very, very solid in its certainties—that America is now part and parcel of urban civilization. The causes of this transformation are so obvious as to need no elaboration; one can simply refer in passing to the advent of the mass media and of mass higher education, and there is not much more that needs to be said. The ultimate consequences of this transformation, however, are anything but obvious. We know what happens—both for good and bad; and it is ineluctably for both good and bad—when an urban center liberates the energies—both for creation and destruction; and it is ineluctably for both—of provincial émigrés; what happens constitutes the history of urban civilization. But we do not know what happens, for the sufficient reason that it has never happened before, when an urban civilization becomes a mass phenomenon, when the culture of the city becomes everyman's culture, and when urban habits of mind and modes of living become the common mentality and way of life for everyone.

If the founding fathers were worried about the effects of a few large cities upon the American capacity for self-government, what—one wonders—would they make of our new condition? One is reasonably certain they would regard it as an utterly impossible state of affairs. And whether they would be correct in this regard is something that it will be up to us to determine. Certainly the history of American cities, during this past century and a half, does not permit us to dismiss their fears as either irrational or anachronistic. Though these cities have made America great, and though a city like New York can be said—especially in these last years, when it has become a world cultural capital—to have made America glorious, it does not follow, as we so naturally might think, that they have strengthened the fundaments of American democracy. Greatness and glory are things the human race has always prized highly, but we ought not to forget that the political philosophers of democracy have always looked upon them with distrust, as virtues appropriate to empires rather than to self-governing republics, and have emphasized moral earnestness and intellectual sobriety as elements that are most wanted in a democracy.

We can, perhaps, have a better appreciation of the problem we have created for ourselves if we start from the proposition—which sounds like a tautology but has far-reaching implications—that in a democracy the people are the ruling class. This does not mean, of course, that the people as a whole run the affairs of state or that the people's will finds prompt expression in the decisions of government. Even in a society which is officially an aristocracy, the ruling class never has that kind of instant power and instant authority. Indeed, one suspects that a government which was *so* responsible would barely have the capacity to govern at all—and one knows for certain that, were such a government to exist, it could be manned only by servile mediocrities who set no value upon their own opinions or judgment. No, when one says that in a democracy the people are the ruling class, one means that the character of the government and the destiny of the nation are in the longer run determined by the character of the people rather than of any particular class of people.

I know that we are today unaccustomed to thinking in terms such as these, and that the very phrase "the character of the people" has an odd ring to it. In part, this is because American political theory, as it has evolved into American political science, has tended to conceive of democracy exclusively in terms of procedural and mechanical arrangements—in terms of self-interested individuals who rightly understand that it is to their own interest to follow the "rules of the game." This idea goes back to the founding fathers, as has been said—but taken by itself, and divorced from the idea of republican morality, it leads to a self-destructive paradox, as some political scientists have recently come to realize. For when everyone follows the rules of the game, it can then be demonstrated—with all the rigor of a mathematical theorem—that it is to the self-interest of individuals or of organized factions *not* to follow the rules of the game, but simply to take advantage of the fact that the others do. That there are such individuals and factions, only too willing to draw this logical inference, and to act upon it, current American events vividly remind us. And political science, being "value-free," as they say, cannot come up with any persuasive arguments as to why they should not act this way.

Another reason why we cannot seriously contemplate this question of "the character of the people" is that, in the generations which succeeded that of the founding fathers, it came to be believed that this character was not something formed by individual efforts at moral self-definition, but rather that the popular character was inherently good enough—not perfect perhaps, but good enough—so as not to require self-scrutiny. What we may call the transcendental-populist religion of democracy superseded an original political philosophy of democracy. This religion has now so strong a hold that mention of the very idea of a "corrupt people," a common idea in classical political philosophy, is taken as evidence of a nasty antidemocratic bias upon the part of the thinker who would dare entertain it. If things go wrong in our democracy, the persons we are least likely to blame are ourselves. Instead, we seek out the influence of wicked "vested interests," malign "outside agitators," or arrogant "Establishments."

I am not asserting that the American people, at this moment, are a corrupt people—though it worries me that they are so blandly free from self-doubt about this possibility. What I am saying is that they are more and more behaving in a way that would have alarmed the founding fathers even as it would have astonished them. To put it bluntly, they are more and more behaving like a collection of mobs.

The term "mob" entered the language in the latter part of the eighteenth century and was used to describe the new population of the new industrial cities that were then emerging. This population was not only a population uprooted from its villages; it was also *déraciné* with regard to traditional pieties, whether religious, moral, or political. It was a population which felt itself—as in truth it largely was—the victim of external forces, in no way responsible for its own fate, and therefore indifferent to its own character. It was a population which, in its political dependency, could be exploited by unscrupulous profiteers; it was a population which, in its political isolation, could be exploited by zealous demagogues; it was a population which, in its moral bewilderment, could be exploited by wild mystagogues; it was a population whose potential did not go much beyond riotous destructiveness.

It was because the founding fathers did not see how such a population could be capable of self-government that they took so dim a view of large cities. The mob, as it was then to be seen in London and Paris, and even incipiently in New York or Boston, seemed to them the very antithesis of a democratic citizenry: a citizenry self-reliant, self-determining, and at least firmly touched by, if not thoroughly infused with, republican morality. It takes a transcendental-populist faith of truly enormous dimensions to find in this attitude a mere agrarian bias. The founding fathers were philosophic men, of no such populist faith, and they had no qualms about insisting that popular government was sustained by "a people" as distinct from a mob.

The history of all modern industrial societies is the story of the gradual transformation of original urban mobs into a people, even as their numbers increased manyfold. The secret behind this transformation was not faith but economics—and especially the economics of technological innovation. If it did not occur to the founding fathers that such a transformation was likely or even possible, this was because they could have no intimation of the fantastic economic growth that the coming century and a half would experience. It was not, indeed, until the turn of this century that thinking men began to be shaken loose from their Malthusian spectacles and to be able to see things as they really were. Even so intelligent and liberal a thinker as E. L. Godkin, in several decades of writing for the *Nation,* could not disabuse himself of the notion that the lower urban classes were doomed to exist as something like a permanent mob by the iron laws of Malthusian doctrine. The politics of such a mob, obviously, could only be the politics of expropriation as against the bourgeois politics of participation.

Well, it worked out differently and better. As productivity increased, the urban mob became an urban citizenry—and, more recently, a suburban citizenry, mimicking in an urban context various aspects of that agrarian life-style which was once thought to be of such political significance. The "bourgeoisification" of society was *the* great event of modern history. Where once we had the bourgeois confronting the masses, we now have bourgeois masses—a fact which has been a source of concern to revolutionary romantics and romantic revolutionaries, both of whom have expectations for the masses which far outrun the bourgeois condition. Even many cautious liberals have been taken aback at the ease with which this society was breeding bourgeois men and women, and a small library of literature was published between 1945 and 1965 that complained of the "homogenization" of American society, of its passionless and conformist quality, of the oppressive weight of consensus, and of the disinclination to conflict and dissent.

That library is now gathering dust, along with the voluminous literature on the iron law of wages. For something very odd and unexpected has, in the past decade, been happening to the bourgeois masses who inhabit our new urban civilization. Though bourgeois in condition and life-style, they have become less bourgeois in ethos, and strikingly more moblike in action. Perhaps this has something to do with a change in the economic character of our bourgeois civilization. Many critics have noted the shift from a producer's ethic (the so-called Protestant ethic) to a consumer's ethic, and go on to affirm that a bourgeois society of widespread affluence is in its essence radically different from a bourgeois society where scarcity automatically imposes a rigorous discipline of its own. This explanation is all the more plausible in that it echoes, in an academic way, the wisdom of the ages as to the corrupting effects of material prosperity upon the social order. The fact that these consequences come as so great a surprise to us—that, having created the kind of affluent society we deliberately aimed at, and having constructed the kind of "progressive" urban civilization we always wanted, that, having done all this, we have also created an unanticipated problem for ourselves—this fact is but a sign of our impoverished political imagination.

The ways in which various strata of our citizenry—from the relatively poor to the relatively affluent—are beginning to behave like a bourgeois urban mob are familiar to anyone who reads his newspaper, and I do not propose to elaborate upon them. The interesting consideration is the extent to which a mob is not simply a physical presence but also, and above everything else, a state of mind. It is, to be precise, that state of mind which lacks all those qualities that, in the opinion of the founding fathers, added up to republican morality: steadiness of character, deliberativeness of mind, and a mild predisposition to subordinate one's own special interests to the public interest. Since the founding fathers could not envisage a nation of bourgeoisie—a nation of urbanized, prosperous, and strongly acquisitive citizens—they located republican morality in the agrarian sector of American life. We, in this century, have relocated it in the suburban and small-city sector of American life—our contemporary version of America's "grass roots." And it now appears that our anticipations may be treated as roughly by history as were those of the founding fathers.

The causes for this dismaying reversal of expectations are only now being explored by our social critics. Lionel Trilling, especially, has pointed out how the avant-garde, antibourgeois, elite culture—what he calls "the adversary culture"—of our bourgeois society has been gradually incorporated into our conventional school curriculum and, with the spread of mass higher education, has begun to shape the popular culture of our urbanized masses. This is an ambiguous process toward which one can only have ambiguous feelings. No one, after all, can sincerely mourn the passing of the *Saturday Evening Post* and of that superficial, provincial, and, above all, philistine popular culture it so smugly affirmed. This culture may have contributed to political stability, but it also represented a spiritual torpor that, in the end, could only be self-defeating because it was so thin in its sense of humanity. On the other hand, there is something positively absurd in the spectacle of prosperous suburban fathers flocking to see—and evidently enjoying—*The Graduate*, or of prosperous, chic, suburban mothers unconcernedly humming "Mrs. Robinson" to themselves as they cheerfully drive off to do their duties as den mothers. This peculiar schizophrenia, suffusing itself through the bourgeois masses of our urban society, may be fun while it lasts; but one may reasonably suppose that, sooner or later, people will decide they would rather not die laughing at themselves, and that some violent convulsions will ensue.

Why the very best art of bourgeois society—the work of our most gifted poets, painters, novelists, and dramatists—should have, and should have had from the very first days of the romantic movement, such an animus against its own bourgeois world is a question one can only speculate on. Presumably it has something to do with the diminished role that disinterested social values, or transcendent religious values, play in a society governed by the principle of self-interest, even perhaps self-interest rightly understood, but most especially self-interest that makes no effort at self-understanding or self-discipline. But if one can only speculate about the deeper causes of our present disorders, no subtle speculation is needed to see that a democratic-urban civilization which is empty of democratic-urban values is almost surely a civilization in trouble. The symptoms of this trouble plague us every day and in just about every way. If I dwell upon one such symptom, it is only because this one in particular strikes me as so perfectly signifying our inability—it may even be our unwillingness—to comprehend the role of republican morality in a democratic-urban civilization. I refer to the problems of drugs.

Now, I have no interest in venturing into the swamp of controversy that surrounds this topic in the conventional terms in which it is publicly discussed. I do not think it so important to ascertain which drugs are medically bad for you, or just how bad each one is. I think the problem of drugs would be just as serious even if it were determined that marijuana, or amphetamines, or LSD were medically harmless; or if some biochemist were to come up with a way to make these drugs—or even a drug like heroin—medically harmless. What makes a drug a truly serious problem is less its medical aspect than its social purpose. Cigarettes are bad for you, but cigarette smoking poses no kind of threat to our society or to our civilization. Alcohol is likely to cause more harm than good to the average person, but the cocktail party is no threat to our society or our civilization. On the other hand, it is well to recollect that a century ago all social critics agreed that alcohol *was* such a threat, because it was being consumed by the new urban working class in such a way—not only to such a degree, but in such a way—as to demoralize this class and prevent its assimilation into bourgeois, democratic society.

And here we have arrived at the nub of the question as I see it. What counts is *why* drugs or intoxicants are taken, not whether they are. What counts is the meaning and moral status of the action, not its physiological dimensions. Alcohol ceased to be a public issue in this country when social drinking, for purposes of conviviality, succeeded gin-swilling, whose aim was to get out of this world as rapidly as possible. With drugs, the reverse process has taken place. Drug addiction is not itself a new thing; the doctor who would take an occasional shot of morphine so as to be able to keep functioning, the elderly lady who relied upon an opium-laced patent medicine to keep her on her rounds of civic and familial activities—these are familiar enough figures in our past. But today drug taking has become a mass habit—among our young masses especially—whose purpose is to secede from our society and our civilization; and such a declaration requires a moral answer, not a medical one.

Though the prohibition movement is now very censoriously treated by our American historians, one thing must be said for it: It not only knew the gin mills were medically bad—anyone could see that—it also knew *why* it was bad for a citizen to destroy himself in this way. It had *reasons* to offer, reasons that had to do with the importance of republican morality for those citizens of a self-governing nation —which is to say: The movement for prohibition had a good conscience, both social and moral. Today, in dismal contrast, even those, and they are certainly an overwhelming majority, who believe that the drug habit is bad seem incapable of giving the reasons why. I mean the real reasons why, which have to do with the reasons why it is desirable to function as an autonomous and self-reliant citizen in our urban, democratic society, rather than to drift through life in a pleasant but enervating haze. The moral code for all civilizations must, at one time or another, be prepared to face the ultimate subversive question: "Why not?" Our civilization is now facing that very question in the form of the drug problem, and, apparently, it can only respond with tedious, and in the end ineffectual, medical reports.

It is this startling absence of values that represents the authentic urban crisis of our democratic, urban nation. The fact that the word "urbanity" applies both to a condition of urban things and a state of urban mind may be an accident of philology, but if so it is a happy accident, for it reminds us of the interdependence of mind and thing. That same interdependence is to be found in the word "democracy," referring as it does simultaneously to a political system and to the spirit—the idea—that animates this system. The challenge to our urban democracy is to evolve a set of values and a conception of democracy that can function as the equivalent of the republican morality of yesteryear. This is our fundamental urban problem. Or, in the immortal words of Pogo: "I have seen the enemy and they is us."

1970

# III

# THE POLITICAL
# PHILOSOPHY OF
# NEOCONSERVATISM

# 6

# Confessions of a True, Self-Confessed— Perhaps the Only— "Neoconservative"

I T has long been a cliché of liberal discourse that what this country needs is a truly intelligent and sophisticated conservatism to replace the rather primitive, philistine, and often racist conservatism that our history is only too familiar with. This new and desirable conservatism should have a philosophic and literary dimension which would rectify the occasional excesses of liberal ideology. It should even have a nebulous but definitely genteel political dimension, since it is likely that we shall always, at intervals, need a brief interregnum of conservative government whose function it is to consolidate and ratify liberal reforms. The ideal conservative president, from this liberal point of view, would be a Dwight Eisenhower who read Lionel Trilling instead of paperback Westerns, who listened to chamber music instead of playing golf—but who would be, in all other respects, as inert as the real President Eisenhower in fact was.

What we absolutely do *not* need or want, from this liberal perspective, is a conservatism with strong ideas of its own about economic policy, social policy, or foreign policy—especially if these ideas can pass academic muster and survive intellectual debate. Such a conservatism might actually affect public policy, even become a shaping force in American politics, and this is simply impermissible. The very possibility of such a conservatism is a specter that haunts the liberal imagination and can propel it into frenzies of exorcism.

It is because the liberal intellectual community—and particularly the liberal-Left intellectual community, which is not quite the same thing, if almost the same thing—sees "neoconservatism" as representing such an awful possibility that it is so terribly agitated about it. Note: It is *they*, not us, who are excited. It is even they who gave us our name in the first place (specifically, it was Michael Harrington). *We* don't go around talking about neoconservatism. Indeed, such supposed representatives of this "movement" as Daniel Bell, Daniel Patrick Moynihan, Nathan Glazer, Norman Podhoretz, Aaron Wildavsky, Samuel Huntington, Roger Starr, Seymour Martin Lipset, and James Q. Wilson all shy away from the designation—some of them quite violently. Others, such as Robert Nisbet and Edward Banfield, call themselves "conservatives," without benefit of qualification. I myself have accepted the term, perhaps because, having been named Irving, I am relatively indifferent to baptismal caprice. But I may be the only living and self-confessed neoconservative, at large or in captivity.

It was to be expected, therefore, that the first book on neoconservatism would be written by one of *them*, not by one of *us*. Peter Steinfels is a Left-liberal journalist, a "democratic socialist" apparently, and his book, *The Neoconservatives: The Men Who Are Changing America's Politics* (Simon & Schuster, 1979), is a polemic disguised as a report and "fair" commentary. The pretense is even more annoying than the polemic, which takes the form of interspersing summaries of our presumed views with constant reminders—lest the reader be contaminated—of just how far short these fall from wholesome "progressive" opinion. (There is also the insinuation that neoconservatism is really a profit-making enterprise disguised as intellectual work.) This rhetorical strategy makes for a long but tedious book, the reading of which is a wearying experience. It is as if Mr. Steinfels, morally opposed to capital punishment, had decided to nag neoconservatism to death.

I do not wish to suggest that the book is without merit. There is, for instance, an excellent couple of sentences on page 4:

## Confessions of a True, Self-Confessed "Neoconservative"

> Political thought—in the United States today—is moving steadily in two directions. There are those, like democratic socialists, who feel they must reach beyond contemporary liberalism in order to fulfil its promises. And there are those, like the neoconservatives, who feel they must reach beyond contemporary liberalism to preserve its heritage.

That is very well put—though it would be more correct to talk not of the promises *of* liberalism, but of the promises generated *by* and grafted *onto* liberalism in the course of this century. Democratic socialism can be seen as the fulfillment of liberalism only in a Hegelian sense—that is, it absorbs, transcends, and nullifies it, all at the same time. Neoconservatism, on the other hand, is indeed "reformationist" as Mr. Steinfels suggests. It tries to "reach beyond" contemporary liberalism in the way that all reformations, religious or political, do—by a return to the original sources of liberal vision and liberal energy so as to correct the warped version of liberalism that is today's orthodoxy.

Another way of defining these two antithetical tendencies is to say that the one is modern-utopian, the other classical-realist in temper and intellectual inclination. Nothing reveals this more clearly than Mr. Steinfels's accusation against neoconservatism that it is committed to "stability as the prerequisite for justice rather than the other way around." I do not know of a single political philosopher, from Plato to Tocqueville, or any of the founding fathers (always excepting an occasional wayward remark by Jefferson), who would have thought such a commitment anything but obviously sensible. To demand "justice" as a precondition for political or social stability is to make a demand on this world which the world has ever refused to concede. Mr. Steinfels, who is a Catholic intellectual—he is executive editor of *Commonweal*—has, in his passion for "justice now," forgotten everything he may once have learned from reading St. Augustine or St. Thomas.

It should be clear by now that I do think there really is such a thing as neoconservatism—but it is most misleading to think of it as any kind of "movement." It holds no meetings, has no organizational form, has no specific programmatic goals, and when two neoconservatives meet they are more likely to argue with one another than to confer or conspire. But it is there, nevertheless—an impulse that ripples through the intellectual world; a "persuasion," to use a nice old-fashioned term; a mode of thought (but not quite a school of thought).

What are its distinctive features? I shall list them as I see them—but to say that this listing is unofficial would be the understatement of the decade.

1. Neoconservatism is a current of thought emerging out of the academic-intellectual world and provoked by disillusionment with con-

temporary liberalism. Its relation to the business community—the traditional source of American conservatism—is loose and uneasy, though
not necessarily unfriendly.

2. Unlike previous such currents of thought—for example, the
Southern Agrarians or the Transcendentalists of the nineteenth century—neoconservatism is antiromantic in substance and temperament.
Indeed, it regards political romanticism—and its twin, political utopianism—of any kind as one of the plagues of our age. This is but another
way of saying it is a philosophical-political impulse rather than a liter-
ary-political impulse. Or, to put it still another way: Its approach to the
world is more "rabbinic" than "prophetic."

3. The philosophical roots of neoconservatism are to be found
mainly in classical—that is, premodern, preideological—political philosophy. Here the teaching and writing of the late Leo Strauss (never
mentioned by Mr. Steinfels) are of importance, though many neoconservatives find him somewhat too wary of modernity. Neoconservatives
are admiring of Aristotle, respectful of Locke, distrustful of Rousseau.

4. The attitude of neoconservatives to bourgeois society and the
bourgeois ethos is one of detached attachment. In the spirit of Tocqueville, neoconservatives do not think that liberal-democratic capitalism
is the best of all imaginable worlds—only the best, under the circumstances, of all possible worlds. This *modest* enthusiasm distinguishes neoconservatism from the Old Right and the New Right—both of which
are exceedingly suspicious of it.

5. Neoconservatism is inclined to the belief that a predominantly
market economy—just how "predominant" is a matter for some disagreement—is a necessary if not sufficient precondition for a liberal society. (Daniel Bell, as the theoretician for what may be called our
"social-democratic wing," would presumably take issue with this judgment.) It also sees a market economy as favorable to economic growth.

6. Neoconservatives believe in the importance of economic growth,
not out of any enthusiasm for the material goods of this world, but because they see economic growth as indispensable for social and political
stability. It is the prospect of economic growth that has made it possible
to think—against the grain of premodern political thought—of democracy as a viable and enduring sociopolitical system.

7. Neoconservatives, though respecting the market as an economic
mechanism, are not libertarian in the sense, say, that Milton Friedman
and Friedrich A. von Hayek are. A conservative welfare state—what
once was called a "social insurance" state—is perfectly consistent with
the neoconservative perspective. So is a state that takes a degree of responsibility for helping to shape the preferences that the people exercise

in a free market—to "elevate" them, if you will. Neoconservatives, moreover, believe that it is natural for people to *want* their preferences to be elevated. The current version of liberalism, which prescribes massive government intervention in the marketplace but an absolute laissez-faire attitude toward manners and morals, strikes neoconservatives as representing a bizarre inversion of priorities.

8. Neoconservatives look upon family and religion as indispensable pillars of a decent society. Indeed, they have a special fondness for all of those intermediate institutions of a liberal society which reconcile the need for community with the desire for liberty.

Karl Marx once wrote that the human race would eventually face the choice between socialism and barbarism. Well, we have seen enough of socialism in our time to realize that, in actuality as distinct from ideality, it can offer neither stability nor justice, and that in many of its versions it seems perfectly compatible with barbarism. So most neoconservatives believe that the last, best hope of humanity at this time is an intellectually and morally reinvigorated liberal capitalism.

I could go on but I had better not. I suspect that too many of my neoconservative friends will already have taken exception to one or another thing I have said. For this is an intellectual current full of all sorts of little knotty whirlpools, each being agitated by some problem in political, social, or economic theory that needs further exploration, further thought. And that, I think, is what makes neoconservatism so interesting—the fact that it is as concerned with the questions it cannot yet satisfactorily answer as with those it thinks contemporary liberalism has answered incorrectly.

1979

# 7

# *The American Revolution*

## *as a*

## *Successful Revolution*

A S we approach the bicentennial of the American Revolution, we find ourselves in a paradoxical and embarrassing situation. A celebration of some kind certainly seems to be in order, but the urge to celebrate is not exactly overwhelming. Though many will doubtless ascribe this mood to various dispiriting events of the recent past or to an acute public consciousness of present problems, I think this would be a superficial judgment. The truth is that, for several decades now, there has been a noticeable loss of popular interest in the Revolution, both as a historical event and as a political symbol. The idea and very word, "revolution," are in good repute today; the American Revolution is not. We are willing enough, on occasion, to pick up an isolated phrase from the Declaration of Independence, or a fine declamation from a founding father—Jefferson, usually—and use these to point up the shortcomings of American society as it now exists. Which is to say, we seem to be prompt to declare that the Revolution was a success only when it permits us to assert glibly that we have subsequently failed it. But this easy exercise in self-indictment, though useful in some respects, is on the whole a callow affair. It does not tell us, for instance, whether there is an important connection between that successful Revolution and our subsequent delinquencies. It merely uses the Revolution for rhetorical-political purposes, making no serious effort at either understanding it or understanding ourselves. One even gets the impression that many of us regard ourselves as too sophisticated to take the Revolution seriously—that we see it as one of those naive events of our distant childhood which we have since long outgrown but which we are dutifully reminded of, at certain moments of commemoration, by insistent relatives who are less liberated from the past than we are.

I think I can make this point most emphatically by asking the simple question: What ever happened to George Washington? He used to be a Very Important Person—indeed, *the* most important person in our history. Our history books used to describe him, quite simply, as the "Father of his Country" and in the popular mind he was a larger-than-life figure to whom piety and reverence were naturally due. In the past fifty years, however, this figure has been radically diminished in size and virtually emptied of substance. In part, one supposes, this is because piety is a sentiment we seem less and less capable of, most especially piety toward fathers. We are arrogant and condescending toward all ancestors because we are so convinced we understand them better than they understood themselves—whereas piety assumes that they still understand us better than we understand ourselves. Reverence, too, is a sentiment which we, in our presumption, find somewhat unnatural. Woodrow Wilson, like most Progressives of his time, complained about the "blind worship" of the Constitution by the American people. No such complaint is likely to be heard today. We debate whether or not we should obey the laws of the land, whereas for George Washington—and Lincoln too, who in his lifetime reasserted this point most eloquently—obedience to law was not enough: They thought that Americans, as citizens of a self-governing polity, ought to have *reverence* for their laws. Behind this belief, of course, was the premise that the collective wisdom incarnated in our laws, and especially in the fundamental law of the Constitution, understood us better than any one of us could ever hope to understand it. Having separated ourselves from our historic traditions and no longer recognizing the power inherent in tradition itself, we find this traditional point of view close to incomprehensible.

Equally incomprehensible to us is the idea that George Washington was the central figure in a real, honest-to-God revolution—the first significant revolution of the modern era and one which can lay claim to being the only truly successful revolution, on a large scale, in the past two centuries. In his own lifetime, no one doubted that he was the central figure of that revolution. Subsequent generations did not dispute the fact and our textbooks, until about a quarter of a century ago, took it for granted, albeit in an ever more routine and unconvincing way. We today, in contrast, find it hard to take George Washington seriously as a successful revolutionary. He just does not fit our conception of what a revolutionary leader is supposed to be like. It is a conception that easily encompasses Robespierre, Lenin, Mao Tse-tung, or Fidel Castro—but can one stretch it to include a gentleman (and a gentleman he most certainly was) like George Washington? And so we tend to escape from that dilemma by deciding that what we call the American Revolution was not an authentic revolution at all, but rather some kind of pseudorevolution, which is why it could be led by so unrevolutionary a character as George Washington.

Hannah Arendt, in her very profound book *On Revolution,* to which I am much indebted, has written:

> Revolutionary political thought in the nineteenth and twentieth centuries has proceeded as though there never had occurred a revolution in the New World and as though there never had been any American notions and experiences in the realm of politics and government worth thinking about.

It is certainly indisputable that the world, when it contemplates the events of 1776 and after, is inclined to see the American Revolution as a French Revolution that never quite came off, whereas the founding fathers thought they had cause to regard the French Revolution as an American Revolution that had failed. Indeed, the differing estimates of these two revolutions are definitive of one's political philosophy in the modern world: There are two conflicting conceptions of politics, in relation to the human condition, which are symbolized by these two revolutions. There is no question that the French Revolution is, in some crucial sense, the more "modern" of the two. There is a question, however, as to whether this is a good or bad thing.

It is noteworthy that, up until about fifteen years ago, most American historians of this century tended to look at the American Revolution through non-American eyes. They saw it as essentially an abortive and incomplete revolution, in comparison with the French model. But more recently, historians have become much more respectful toward the American Revolution, and the work of Bernard Bailyn, Edmund S. Morgan, Caroline Robbins, Gordon S. Wood, and others is revealing to us once again what the Founding Fathers had, in their day, insisted was the case: that the American Revolution was an extremely *interesting* event, rich in implication for any serious student of politics. These historians have rediscovered for us the intellectual dimensions of the American Revolution, and it is fair to say that we are now in a position to appreciate just how extraordinarily self-conscious and reflective a revolution it was.

All revolutions unleash tides of passion, and the American Revolution was no exception. But it *was* exceptional in the degree to which it was able to subordinate these passions to serious and nuanced thinking about fundamental problems of political philosophy. The pamphlets, sermons, and newspaper essays of the revolutionary period—only now being reprinted and carefully studied—were extraordinarily "academic," in the best sense of that term. Which is to say, they were learned and thoughtful and generally sober in tone. This was a revolution infused by *mind* to a degree never approximated since, and perhaps never approximated before. By mind, not by dogma. The most fascinating aspect of the American Revolution is the severe way it kept questioning itself about the meaning of what it was doing. Enthusiasm there certainly was—a revolution is impossible without enthusiasm—but this enthusiasm was tempered by doubt, introspection, anxiety, skepticism. This may strike us as a very strange state of mind in which to make a revolution; and yet it is evidently the right state of mind for making a successful revolution. That we should have any difficulty in seeing this tells us something about the immaturity of our own political imagination, an immaturity not at all incompatible with what we take to be sophistication.

Just a few weeks ago, one of our most prominent statesmen remarked to an informal group of political scientists that he had been reading *The Federalist Papers* and he was astonished to see how candidly our founding fathers could talk about the frailties of human nature and the necessity for a political system to take such frailties into account. It was not possible, he went on to observe, for anyone active in American politics today to speak publicly in this way: He would be accused of an imperfect democratic faith in the common man. Well, the founding fathers for the most part, and most of the time, subscribed to such an "imperfect" faith. They understood that republican self-government could not exist if humanity did not possess—at some moments, and to a fair degree—the traditional "republican virtues" of self-control, self-reliance, and a disinterested concern for the public good. They also understood that these virtues did not exist everywhere, at all times, and that there was no guarantee of their "natural" preponderance. James Madison put it this way:

As there is a degree of depravity in mankind which requires a certain degree of circumspection and distrust; so there are other qualities in human nature which justify a certain portion of esteem and confidence. Republican government presupposes the existence of these qualities in a higher degree than any other form.

Despite the fact that Christian traditions are still strong in this country, it is hard to imagine any public figure casually admitting, as Madison did in his matter-of-fact way, that "there is a degree of depravity in mankind," which statesmen must take into account. We have become unaccustomed to such candid and unflattering talk about ourselves—which is, I suppose, only another way of saying that we now think democratic demagoguery to be the only proper rhetorical mode of address as between government and people in a republic. The idea, so familiar to the Puritans and still very much alive during our revolutionary era, that a community of individual sinners could, under certain special conditions, constitute a good community—just as a congregation of individual sinners could constitute a good church—is no longer entirely comprehensible to us. We are therefore negligent about the complicated ways in which this transformation takes place and uncomprehending as to the constant, rigorous attentiveness necessary for it to take place at all.

The founders thought that self-government was a chancy and demanding enterprise and that successful government in a republic was a most difficult business. We, in contrast, believe that republican self-government is an easy affair, that it need only be instituted for it to work on its own, and that when such government falters it must be as a consequence of personal incompetence or malfeasance by elected officials. Perhaps nothing reveals better than these different perspectives the intellectual distance we have traveled from the era of the Revolution. We like to think we have "progressed" along this distance. The approaching bicentennial is an appropriate occasion for us to contemplate the possibility that such "progress," should it continue, might yet be fatal to the American polity.

In what sense can the American Revolution be called a successful revolution? And if we agree that it was successful, why was it successful? These questions cannot be disentangled, the "that" and the "why" comprising together one's basic (if implicit) explanation of the term, "successful revolution." These questions are also anything but academic. Indeed I believe that, as one explores them, one finds oneself constrained to challenge a great many preconceptions, not only about the

The American Revolution as a Successful Revolution

nature of revolution but about the nature of politics itself, which most of us today take for granted.

To begin at the beginning: The American Revolution was successful in that those who led it were able, in later years, to look back in tranquillity at what they had wrought and to say that it was good. This was a revolution which, unlike all subsequent revolutions, did not devour its children: The men who made the revolution were the men who went on to create the new political order, who then held the highest elected positions in this order, and who all died in bed. Not very romantic, perhaps. Indeed positively prosaic. But it is this very prosaic quality of the American Revolution that testifies to its success. It is the pathos and poignancy of unsuccessful revolutions which excite the poetic temperament; statesmanship which successfully accomplishes its business is a subject more fit for prose. Alone among the revolutions of modernity, the American Revolution did not give rise to the pathetic and poignant myth of "the revolution betrayed." It spawned no literature of disillusionment; it left behind no grand hopes frustrated, no grand expectations unsatisfied, no grand illusions shattered. Indeed, in one important respect the American Revolution was so successful as to be almost self-defeating: It turned the attention of thinking men away from politics, which now seemed utterly unproblematic, so that political theory lost its vigor, and even the political thought of the founding fathers was not seriously studied. This intellectual sloth, engendered by success, rendered us incompetent to explain this successful revolution to the world, and even to ourselves. The American political tradition became an inarticulate tradition: It worked so well we did not bother to inquire why it worked, and we are therefore intellectually disarmed before those moments when it suddenly seems not to be working so well after all.

The American Revolution was also successful in another important respect: It was a mild and relatively bloodless revolution. A war was fought, to be sure, and soldiers died in that war. But the rules of civilized warfare, as then established, were for the most part quite scrupulously observed by both sides: There was none of the butchery which we have come to accept as a natural concomitant of revolutionary warfare. More important, there was practically none of the off-battlefield savagery which we now assume to be inevitable in revolutions. There were no revolutionary tribunals dispensing "revolutionary justice"; there was no reign of terror; there were no bloodthirsty proclamations by the Continental Congress. Tories were dispossessed of their property, to be sure, and many were rudely hustled off into exile; but so far as I have been able to determine, not a single Tory was executed for harboring counter-revolutionary opinions. Nor, in the years after the Revolution, were Tories persecuted to any significant degree (at least by today's standards) or their children discriminated against at all. As Tocqueville later remarked, with only a little exaggeration, the Revolution "contracted no alliance with the turbulent passions of anarchy, but its course was marked, on the contrary, by a love of order and law."

A law-and-order revolution? What kind of revolution is that, we ask ourselves? To which many will reply that it could not have been much of a revolution after all—at best a shadow of the real thing, which is always turbulent and bloody and shattering of body and soul. Well, the American Revolution was not that kind of revolution at all, and the possibility we have to consider is that it was successful precisely because it was not that kind of revolution—that it is we rather than the American revolutionaries who have an erroneous conception of what a revolution is.

Dr. Arendt makes an important distinction between "rebellion" and "revolution." By her criteria the French and Russian revolutions should more properly be called "rebellions," whereas only the American Revolution is worthy of the name. A rebellion, in her terms, is a meta-political event, emerging out of a radical dissatisfaction with the human condition as experienced by the mass of the people, demanding instant "liberation" from this condition, an immediate transformation of all social and economic circumstance, a prompt achievement of an altogether "better life" in an altogether "better world." The spirit of rebellion is a spirit of desperation—a desperate rejection of whatever exists, a desperate aspiration toward some kind of utopia. A rebellion is more a sociological event than a political action. It is governed by a blind momentum which sweeps everything before it, and its so-called leaders are in fact its captives, and ultimately its victims. The modern world knows many such rebellions, and all end up as one version or another of "a revolution betrayed." The so-called betrayal is, in fact, nothing but the necessary conclusion of a rebellion. Since its impossible intentions are unrealizable and since its intense desperation will not be satisfied with anything less than impossible intentions, the end result is always a regime which pretends to embody these intentions and which enforces such false pretensions by terror.

A revolution, in contrast, is a political phenomenon. It aims to revise and reorder the political arrangements of a society, and is therefore the work of the political ego rather than of the political id. A revolution is a practical exercise in political philosophy, not an existential spasm of the social organism. It requires an attentive prudence, a careful calculation of means and ends, a spirit of sobriety—the kind of spirit exemplified by that calm, legalistic document, the Declaration of Independence. All this is but another way of saying that a successful revolution cannot be governed by the spirit of the mob. Mobs and mob actions there will always be in a revolution, but if this revolution is not to degenerate into a rebellion, mob actions must be marginal to the central political drama. It may sound paradoxical but it nevertheless seems to be the case that only a self-disciplined people can dare undertake so radical a political enterprise as a revolution. This is almost like saying that a successful revolution must be accomplished by a people who want it but do not desperately need it—which was, indeed, the American condition in 1776. One may even put the case more strongly: A successful revolution is best accomplished by a people who do not really want it at all, but find themselves reluctantly making it. The American Revolution was exactly such a reluctant revolution.

The present-day student of revolutions will look in vain for any familiar kind of "revolutionary situation" in the American colonies prior to 1776. The American people at that moment were the most prosperous in the world and lived under the freest institutions to be found anywhere in the world. They knew this well enough and boasted of it often enough. Their quarrel with the British crown was, in its origins, merely over the scope of colonial self-government, and hardly anyone saw any good reason why this quarrel should erupt into a war of independence. It was only after the war got under way that the American people decided that this was a good opportunity to make a revolution as well—that is, to establish a republican form of government.

Republican and quasi-republican traditions had always been powerful in the colonies, which were populated to such a large degree by religious dissenters who were sympathetic to the ideas incorporated in Cromwell's Commonwealth. Moreover, American political institutions from the very beginning were close to republican in fact, especially those of the Puritan communities of New England. Still, it is instructive to note that the word *republic* does not appear in the Declaration of Independence. Not that there was any real thought of reinstituting a monarchy in the New World: No one took such a prospect seriously. It was simply that, reluctant and cautious revolutionaries as they were, the Founding Fathers saw no need to press matters further than they had to, at that particular moment. To put it bluntly: They did not want events to get out of hand and saw no good reason to provoke more popular turbulence than was absolutely necessary.

One does not want to make the American Revolution an even more prosaic affair than it was. This was a revolution—a real one—and it was infused with a spirit of excitement and innovation. After all, what the American Revolution, once it got under way, was trying to do was no small thing. It was nothing less than the establishment, for the first time since ancient Rome, of a large republican nation, and the idea of reestablishing under modern conditions the glory that had been Rome's could hardly fail to be intoxicating. This Revolution did indeed have grand, even millennial, expectations as to the future role of this new nation in both the political imagination and political history of the human race. But certain things have to be said about these large expectations, if we are to see them in proper perspective.

The main thing to be said is that the millenarian tradition in America long antedates the Revolution and is not intertwined with the idea of revolution itself. It was the pilgrim fathers, not the founding fathers, who first announced that this was God's country, that the American people had a divine mission to accomplish, that this people had been "chosen" to create some kind of model community for the rest of mankind. This belief was already so firmly established by the time of the Revolution that it was part and parcel of our political orthodoxy, serving to legitimate an existing "American way of life" and most of the institutions associated with that way of life. It was a radical belief, in the sense of being bold and challenging and because this new "way of life" was so strikingly different from the lives that common people were then living in Europe. It was *not* a revolutionary belief. Crèvecoeur's famous paean of praise to "this new man, the American," was written well before the Revolution; and Crèvecoeur, in fact, opposed the American Revolution as foolish and unnecessary.

To this traditional millenarianism, the Revolution added the hope that the establishment of republican institutions would inaugurate a new and happier political era for all mankind. This hope was frequently expressed enthusiastically, in a kind of messianic rhetoric, but the men of the Revolution—most of them, most of the time—did not permit themselves to become bewitched by that rhetoric. Thus, though they certainly saw republic as "the wave of the future," both Jefferson and Adams in the 1780s agreed that the French people were still too "depraved," as they so elegantly put it, to undertake an experiment in self-government. Self-government, as they understood it, presupposed a certain way of life, and this in turn presupposed certain qualities on the part of the citizenry—qualities then designated as "republican virtues"—that would make self-government possible.

Similarly, though one can find a great many publicists during the Revolution who insisted that, with the severance of ties from Britain, the colonies had reverted to a Lockean "state of nature" and were now free to make a new beginning for all mankind and to create a new political order that would mark a new stage in human history—though such assertions were popular enough, it would be a mistake to take them too seriously. The fact is that Americans had encountered their "state of nature" generations earlier and had made their "social compact" at that time. The primordial American social contract was signed and sealed on the *Mayflower*—literally signed and sealed. The subsequent presence of all those signatures appended to the Declaration of Independence, beginning with John Hancock's, are but an echo of the original covenant.

To perceive the true purposes of the American Revolution, it is wise to ignore some of the more grandiloquent declamations of the moment—Tom Paine, an English radical who never really understood America, is especially worth ignoring—and to look at the kinds of political activity the Revolution unleashed. This activity took the form of constitution making, above all. In the months and years immediately following the Declaration of Independence, all of our states drew up constitutions. These constitutions are terribly interesting in three respects. First, they involved relatively few basic changes in existing political institutions and almost no change at all in legal, social, or economic institutions; they were, for the most part, merely revisions of the preexisting charters. Secondly, most of the changes that were instituted had the evident aim of weakening the power of government, especially of the executive; it was these changes—and especially the strict separation of powers—that dismayed Turgot, Condorcet, and the other French *philosophes,* who understood revolution as an expression of the people's will-to-power rather than as an attempt to circumscribe political authority. Thirdly, in no case did any of these state constitutions tamper with the traditional system of local self-government. Indeed they could not, since it was this traditional system of local self-government which created and legitimized the constitutional conventions themselves.

In short, the Revolution reshaped our political institutions in such a way as to make them more responsive to popular opinion and less capable of encroaching upon the personal liberties of the citizen—liberties which long antedated the new constitutions and which in no way could be regarded as the creation or consequence of revolution. Which is to say that the purpose of this Revolution was to bring our political institutions into a more perfect correspondence with an actual American way of life which no one even dreamed of challenging. This "restructuring," as we would now call it—because it put the possibility of republican self-government once again on the political agenda of Western civilization—was terribly exciting to Europeans as well as

Americans. But for the Americans involved in this historic task, it was also terribly frightening. It is fair to say that no other revolution in modern history made such relatively modest innovations with such an acute sense of anxiety. The Founding Fathers were well aware that if republicanism over the centuries had become such a rare form of government, there must be good reasons for it. Republican government, they realized, must be an exceedingly difficult regime to maintain—that is, it must have grave inherent problems. And so they were constantly scurrying to their libraries, ransacking classical and contemporary political authors, trying to discover why republics fail, and endeavoring to construct a "new political science" relevant to American conditions which would give this new republic a fair chance of succeeding. That new political science was eventually to be embodied in *The Federalist*—the only original work of political theory ever produced by a revolution and composed by successful revolutionaries. And the fact that very few of us have ever felt the need seriously to study *The Federalist* and that Europeans—or in our own day, Asians and Africans—have barely heard of it tells us how inadequately we understand the American Revolution, and how distant the real American Revolution has become from the idea of revolution by which we moderns are now possessed.

This idea of revolution, as the world understands it today, is what Dr. Arendt calls rebellion. It involves a passionate rejection of the status quo—its institutions and the way of life associated with these institutions. It rejects everything that exists because it wishes to create everything anew—a new social order, a new set of economic arrangements, a new political entity, a new kind of human being. It aims to solve not merely the political problem of the particular political community, at that particular moment, but every other problem that vexes humanity. Its spirit is the spirit of undiluted, enthusiastic, free-floating messianism: It will be satisfied with nothing less than a radical transformation of the human condition. It is an idea and a movement which is both meta-political and subpolitical—above and below politics—because it finds the political realm itself too confining for its ambitions. Meta-politically, it is essentially a religious phenomenon, seized with the perennial promise of redemption. Subpolitically, it is an expression of the modern technological mentality, confident of its power to control and direct all human processes as we have learned to control and direct the processes of nature. Inevitably, its swollen pride and fanatical temper lead to tragic failure. But precisely because of this pride and this fanaticism, failure leads only to partial and temporary disillusionment. When this kind of revolution is "betrayed"—which is to say, when the consequences of revolution lose all congruence with its original purpose—the true revolutionary believer will still look forward to a second coming of the authentic and unbetrayable revolution.

The French Revolution was the kind of modern revolution I have been describing; the American Revolution was not. It is because of this, one supposes, that the French Revolution has captured the imagination of other peoples—has become indeed the model of "real" revolution—in a way that the American Revolution has not been able to do. The French Revolution promised not only a reformation of France's political institutions, but far more than that. It promised, for instance—as practically all revolutions have promised since—the abolition of poverty. The American Revolution promised no such thing, in part because poverty was not such a troublesome issue in this country, but also—one is certain—because the leaders of this revolution understood what their contemporary, Adam Smith, understood and what we today have some difficulty in understanding: namely, that poverty is abolished by economic growth, not by economic redistribution—there is never enough to distribute—and that rebellions, by creating instability and uncertainty, have mischievous consequences for economic growth. Similarly, the French Revolution promised a condition of "happiness" to its citizens under the new regime, whereas the American Revolution promised merely to permit the individual to engage in the "pursuit of happiness."

It should not be surprising, therefore, that in the war of ideologies which has engulfed the twentieth century, the United States is at a disadvantage. This disadvantage does not flow from any weakness on our part. It is not, as some say, because we have forgotten our revolutionary heritage and therefore have nothing to say to a discontented and turbulent world. We have, indeed, much to say, only it is not what our contemporaries want to hear. It is not even what we ourselves want to hear, and in *that* sense it may be correct to claim we have forgotten our revolutionary heritage. Our revolutionary message—which is a message not of the Revolution itself but of the American political tradition from the *Mayflower* to the Declaration of Independence to the Constitution—is that a self-disciplined people *can* create a political community in which an ordered liberty will promote both economic prosperity and political participation. To the teeming masses of other nations, the American political tradition says: To enjoy the fruits of self-government, you must first cease being "masses" and become a "people," attached to a common way of life, sharing common values, and existing in a condition of mutual trust and sympathy as between individuals and even social classes. It is a distinctly odd kind of "revolutionary" message, by twentieth-century criteria—so odd that it seems not revolutionary at all, and yet so revolutionary that it seems utterly utopian. What the twentieth century wants to hear is the grand things that a new government will do for the people who put their trust in it. What the American political tradition says is that the major function of government is, in Professor Oakeshott's phrase, to "tend to the arrangements of society," and that free people do not make a covenant or social contract with their government, or with the leaders of any "movement," but among themselves.

In the end, what informs the American political tradition is a proposition and a premise. The proposition is that the best national government is, to use a phrase the founding fathers were fond of, "mild government." The premise is that you can only achieve mild government if you have a solid bedrock of local self-government, so that the responsibilities of national government are limited in scope. And a corollary of this premise is that such a bedrock of local self-government can only be achieved by a people who—through the shaping influence of religion, education, and their own daily experience—are capable of governing themselves in those small and petty matters which are the stuff of local politics.

Does this conception of politics have any relevance to the conditions in which people live today in large areas of the world—the so-called underdeveloped areas, especially? We are inclined, I think, to answer instinctively in the negative, but that answer may itself be a modern ideological prejudice. We take it for granted that if a people live in comparative poverty, they are necessarily incapable of the kind of self-discipline and sobriety that makes for effective self-government in their particular communities. Mind you, I am not talking about starving people, who are in a prepolitical condition and whose problem is to get a strong and effective government of almost any kind. I am talking about *comparatively* poor people. And our current low estimate of the political capabilities of such people is an ideological assumption, not an objective fact. Many of our frontier communities, at the time of the Revolution and for decades afterward, were poor by any standards. Yet this poverty was not, for the most part, inconsistent with active self-government. There have been communities in Europe, too, which were very poor—not actually starving, of course, but simply very poor—yet were authentic political communities. The popular musical *Fiddler on the Roof* gave us a picture of such a community. It is always better not to be so poor, but poverty need not be a pathological condition, and political pathology is not an inevitable consequence of poverty, just as political pathology is not inevitably abolished by prosperity. Poor people can cope with their poverty in many different ways. They are people, not sociological creatures, and in the end they will cope as their moral and political convictions tell them to cope. These convictions, in turn, will be formed by the expectations that their community addresses to them—expectations which they freely convert into obligations.

In *The Brothers Karamazov,* Dostoevski says that the spirit of the Antichrist, in its modern incarnation, will flaunt the banner, "First feed people, and *then* ask of them virtue." This has, in an amended form, indeed become the cardinal and utterly conventional thesis of modern politics. The amended form reads: "First make people prosperous, and then ask of them virtue." Whatever reservations one might have about Dostoevski's original thesis, this revised version is, in the perspective of the Judeo-Christian tradition, unquestionably a blasphemy. It is also, in the perspective of the American political tradition, a malicious and inherently self-defeating doctrine—self-defeating because those who proclaim it obviously have lost all sense of what virtue, religious or political, means. Nevertheless, practically all of us today find it an inherently plausible doctrine, a staple of our political discourse. This being the case, it is only natural that we ourselves should have such difficulty understanding the American political tradition, and that when we expend it to the world, we distort it in all sorts of ways which will make it more palatable to the prejudices of the modern political mentality.

It would not be fair to conclude that the American political tradition is flawless, and that it is only we, its heirs, who are to blame for the many problems our society is grappling with—and so ineptly. The American Revolution was a successful revolution, but there is no such thing, either in one's personal life or in a nation's history, as unambiguous success. The legacy of the American Revolution and of the entire political tradition associated with it is problematic in all sorts of ways. Strangely enough, we have such an imperfect understanding of this tradition that, even as we vulgarize it or question it or disregard it, we rarely address ourselves to its problematic quality.

The major problematic aspect of this tradition has to do with the relationship of the "citizen" to the "common man." And the difficulties we have in defining this relationship are best illustrated by the fact that, though we have been a representative democracy for two centuries now, we have never developed an adequate theory of representation. More precisely we have developed *two* contradictory theories of representation, both of which can claim legitimacy within the American political tradition and both of which were enunciated, often by the same people, during the Revolution. The one sees the public official as a common man who has a mandate to reflect the opinions of the majority; the other sees the public official as a somewhat uncommon man—a more-than-common man, if you will—who, because of his talents and character, is able to take a larger view of the "public interest" than the voters who elected him or the voters who failed to defeat him. One might say that the first is a "democratic" view of the legislator, the second a "republican" view. The American political tradition has always had a kind of double vision on this whole problem, which in turn makes for a bewildering moral confusion. Half the time we regard our politicians as, in the nature of things, probably corrupt and certainly untrustworthy; the other half of the time, we denounce them for failing to be models of integrity and rectitude. Indeed, we have a profession—journalism—which seems committed to both of these contradictory propositions. But politicians are pretty much like the rest of us and tend to become the kinds of people they are expected to be. The absence of clear and distinct expectations has meant that public morality in this country has never been, and is not, anything we can be proud of.

In a way, the ambiguity in our theory of representation points to a much deeper ambiguity in that system of self-government which emerged from the Revolution and the Constitutional Convention. That system has been perceptively titled, by Professor Martin Diamond, "a democratic republic." Now, we tend to think of these terms as near-synonyms, but in fact they differ significantly in their political connotations. Just how significant the difference is becomes clear if we realize that the America which emerged from the Revolution and the Constitutional Convention was the first democratic republic in history. The political philosophers of that time could study the history of republics and they could study the history of democracies, but there was no opportunity for them to study both together. When the founding fathers declared that they had devised a new kind of political entity based on a new science of politics, they were not vainly boasting or deceiving themselves. It is we, their political descendants, who tend to be unaware of the novelty of the American political enterprise, and of the risks and ambiguities inherent in that novelty. We simplify and vulgarize and distort, because we have lost the sense of how bold and innovative the Founding Fathers were, and of how problematic—necessarily problematic—is the system of government, and the society, which they established. Witness the fact that, incredibly enough, at our major universities it is almost impossible to find a course, graduate or undergraduate, devoted to *The Federalist*.

What is the difference between a democracy and a republic? In a democracy, the will of the people is supreme. In a republic, it is not the will of the people but the rational consensus of the people—a rational consensus which is implicit in the term consent—which governs the people. That is to say, in a democracy, popular passion may rule—*may*, though it need not—but in a republic, popular passion is regarded as unfit to rule, and precautions are taken to see that it is subdued rather than sovereign. In a democracy all politicians are, to some degree, demagogues: They appeal to people's prejudices and passions, they incite their expectations by making reckless promises, they endeavor to ingratiate themselves with the electorate in every possible way. In a republic, there are not supposed to be such politicians, only statesmen—sober, unglamorous, thoughtful men who are engaged in a kind of perpetual conversation with the citizenry. In a republic, a fair degree of equality and prosperity are important goals, but it is liberty that is given priority as the proper end of government. In a democracy, these priorities are reversed: The status of men and women as consumers of economic goods is taken to be more significant than their status as participants in the creation of political goods. A republic is what we would call "moralistic" in its approach to both public and private affairs; a democracy is more easygoing, more "permissive" as we now say, even more cynical.

The founding fathers perceived that their new nation was too large, too heterogeneous, too dynamic, too mobile for it to govern itself successfully along strict republican principles. And they had no desire at all to see it governed along strict democratic principles, since they did not have that much faith in the kinds of common men likely to be produced by such a nation. So they created a new form of "popular government," to use one of their favorite terms, that incorporated both republican and democratic principles, in a complicated and ingenious way. This system has lasted for two centuries, which means it has worked very well indeed. But in the course of that time, we have progressively forgotten what kind of system it is and *why* it works as well as it does. Every now and then, for instance, we furiously debate the question of whether or not the Supreme Court is meeting its obligations as a democratic institution. The question reveals a startling ignorance of our political tradition. The Supreme Court is not—and was never supposed to be—a democratic institution; it is a republican institution which counterbalances the activities of our various democratic institutions. Yet I have discovered that when you say this to college students, they do not understand the distinction and even have difficulty thinking about it.

So it would seem that today, two hundred years after the American Revolution, we are in a sense victims of its success. The political tradition out of which it issued and the political order it helped to create are imperfectly comprehended by us. What is worse, we are not fully aware of this imperfect comprehension and are frequently smug in our convenient misunderstandings. The American Revolution certainly merits celebration. But it would be reassuring if a part of that celebration were to consist, not merely of pious clichés, but of a serious and sustained effort to achieve a deeper and more widespread understanding of just what it is we are celebrating.

1976

# 8

# *American Historians and the Democratic Idea*

$A$LTHOUGH it is hardly a secret, I had better affirm it explicitly right at the outset: I am no kind of historian. I am a journalist, at best a man of letters, and I am keenly aware that, as Voltaire observed, a man of letters resembles a flying fish: "If he raises himself up a little, the birds devour him; if he dives, the fish eat him up." I take this to mean that insofar as I refer to general ideas, I shall be devoured by the scholarly eagles, and that insofar as I refer to particular details, I shall be eaten alive by the scholarly sharks. On the other hand, it is in the nature of a flying fish that he cannot for too long skim nervously along the surface. That suits neither his instincts nor his appetite. So, in what follows, I shall be at the historian's mercy, without really expecting any from him.

As a matter of fact the only reason I feel justified in proposing these thoughts to a scholarly public is that some years ago I set out to write a book. The book was supposed to deal with the present state of the democratic idea in America and with the way in which the ambiguities surrounding this idea have been the cause of many of our contemporary social and political problems. For obvious reasons, some background reading in American history seemed like a useful preparatory exercise. Well, that exercise turned out to be more strenuous and less satisfying than I anticipated. To my dismay, I discovered that, far from providing me with any convenient, ready-made historical perspective on the fate of the democratic idea in America, most American historians simply offered me further and quite unwelcome evidence of, first, how confused this idea has been during most of America's history and, second, how confused American historians themselves have been about this idea. It is not that American historians are notably reticent about what has happened to democracy in America. They obviously have a great deal to say. But they appear to have given so very little thought to the various meanings that the idea of democracy might have. Perhaps it ought not to have surprised me that American historians, like other Americans, have so little aptitude for, or interest in, what is essentially a problem of political philosophy. But I confess that it did.

Let me give a couple of examples of what I have in mind. If one were to ask, "What is the most effectively conservative piece of legislation passed by the federal government in this century?" the answer, I submit, is both obvious and incontestable. It is the Nineteenth Amendment, extending the suffrage to women. The voting habits of the American population are something we know a great deal about, and there is just no question but that women, to the extent that they do more than duplicate their husbands' votes, are to be found disproportionately in the conservative wing of the electorate. Yet in all our history books the Nineteenth Amendment is regarded as a progressive and liberal action, not at all as a conservative one. This strikes me as being a curious state of affairs and suggests that there is something odd about the way in which Americans go about writing their history.

Another example. If one were to ask, "What is the most effectively conservative piece of legislation passed by state legislatures in this century?" the answer—which I again submit is both obvious and incontestable—is the popular referendum. There must be hundreds of American historians alive today who, in their respective localities, have seen some of their most cherished and most liberal ideas—school integration, for instance, or less restrictive zoning laws—buried in a referendum. Yet when they enter their classrooms, or write their books, all this is forgotten or ignored. Almost invariably they regard the advent of the popular referendum as a victory for both democracy and liberalism. They are very upset when you point out that this seems not to be the case. And they get utterly bewildered if you dare to suggest that based on certain other conceptions of democracy or liberty one need not regard it as a victory for either.

It is clear that something is at work here that is not to be explained by the ordinary canons of historical scholarship. What is involved, it seems to me, is an ideology so powerful as to represent a kind of religious faith. Indeed, we can fairly call this ideology "the democratic faith," since this term is frequently and approvingly used by members of the congregation themselves. Because it is an authentic faith, it is a very complicated and conglomerate affair. But I believe one can say two truthful and simple things about it.

First of all, it evidently cares much more about ascertaining the source and origin of political power than it does about analyzing the existential consequences of this power. Which is to say, like all faiths it places much more emphasis on men's "good" intentions—in this case, men's democratic intentions—than on whatever may follow from these intentions. And, of course, like all faiths it ends up grappling with the problem of evil—with the existence of disorder, and decay, and injustice, which ought not to exist in a society constructed on democratic principles, but which patently do. This problem itself is usually resolved in the traditional religious way—that is, by assuming that it flows from the conspiracy of wicked demiurges ("vested interests," in American jargon) or the undue influence of "alien" ideas that frustrate the perfection we are entitled to.

Second, and this is but a corollary of my first point, what we are dealing with is obviously *not* a political philosophy. The only reason I go to the trouble of pointing this out is that once upon a time, in this country, the question of democracy *was* a matter for political philosophy, rather than for faith. And the way in which a democratic political philosophy was gradually and inexorably transformed into a democratic faith seems to me to be perhaps the most important problem in American intellectual—and ultimately political—history. In this transformation, American historians have played a significant role—although, being themselves for the most part men of good democratic faith, they have been so busy playing this role that they have rarely got around to explaining it to us, or to themselves.

The difference between a democratic faith and a democratic political philosophy is basically this: Whereas a faith may be attentive to the *problems* of democracy, it has great difficulty perceiving or thinking about the *problematics* of democracy. By "problematics" I mean those kinds of problems that flow from, that are inherent in, that are generated by democracy itself. These problematics change their hue with time and circumstance: The founding fathers would have been as bewildered by the

current status of the popular referendum as are our progressive historians. But what makes them problematics rather than problems is that
they are organically connected with the political system of democracy
itself rather than with any external or adventitious factors.

It really is quite extraordinary how the majority of American historians have, until quite recently, determinedly refused to pay attention
to any thinker, or any book, that treated democracy as problematic. Although our historians frequently quote from this source, and much effort has been made to determine who wrote which paper, it is a fact
that no American historian has ever written a book on *The Federalist Papers.* (As a further matter of fact, *no one* in America—historian, political
scientist, jurist, or whatever—ever published a book on *The Federalist*
until a few years ago, when a Swiss immigrant scholar rather clumsily
broke the ice.) Men like E. L. Godkin, Herbert Croly, Paul Elmer More,
even Tocqueville, have interested American historians mainly as
"source material"—hardly anyone goes to them to *learn* anything about
American democracy. And it is certainly no accident that our very greatest historian, Henry Adams, who did indeed understand the problematics of democracy, is a "loner," with no historical school or even a
noteworthy disciple to carry on in his tradition. As Richard Hofstadter
pointed out, there are plenty of Turnerites and Beardites and, of course,
Marxists among American historians, but there are no Adamsites or
Tocquevillians.

In this respect, the contrast between American historians and the
men who created this democracy is a striking one. Although none of
the founding fathers can be called a political philosopher, most of them
were widely read in political philosophy and had given serious thought
to the traditional problems of political philosophy. One of these traditional problems was the problematic character of democracies. The
founding fathers were aware that, in centuries past, democracy—in the
sense of the unfettered rule of the *demos,* of the majority—had been one
of the least stable and not always the most admirable of political regimes. And this awareness—shared by practically all educated men of
the time—caused them to devise a system that was more democratic
than the "mixed regimes" that most political philosophers approved of,
yet that also possessed at least some of the virtues thought to be associated with a mixed regime. Such virtues pertained not to the *origins* of
government but to its *ends.* In short, the founding fathers sought to establish a "popular government" that could be stable, just, free; where
there was security of person and property; and whose public leaders
would claim legitimacy not only because they were elected officials but
also because their character and behavior approximated some accepted

models of excellence. The fact that they used the term "popular government" rather than "democracy" is an accident of historical semantics. They were partisans of self-government—of government by the people—who deliberately and with a bold, creative genius "rigged" the machinery of the system so that this government would be one of which they, as thoughtful and civilized men, could be proud.

In establishing such a popular government, the founding fathers were certainly under the impression that they were expressing a faith in the common man. But they were sober and worldly men, and they were not about to hand out blank checks to anyone, even if he was a common man. They thought that political institutions had something to do with the shaping of common men, and they took the question, *"What kind of common man does our popular government produce?"* to be as crucial a consideration as any other. They took it for granted that democracy was capable of bringing evil into the world, and they wanted a system of government that made this as unlikely as possible, and that was provided with as strong an inclination toward self-correction as was possible. And I should guess that they would have regarded as a fair test of their labors the degree to which common men in America could rise to the prospect of choosing uncommon men, speaking for uncommon ideals, as worthy of exercising authority over them.

The founding fathers, then, established what they thought to be—and what the world then unanimously thought to be—a democratic process for the American people. But they looked beyond this democratic process to the spirit—the ideal intent—that might animate it. This conception is very nicely expressed in words that Matthew Arnold a century later directed toward his American audiences:

> The difficulty for democracy is, how to find and keep high ideals. The individuals who compose it are, the bulk of them, persons who need to follow an ideal, not to set one; and one ideal of goodness, high feeling, and fine culture, which an aristocracy once supplied to them, they lose by the very fact of ceasing to be a lower order and becoming a democracy. Nations are not truly great solely because the individuals composing them are numerous, free, and active; but they are great when these numbers, this freedom, and this activity are employed in the service of an ideal higher than that of an ordinary man, taken by himself.

These words doubtless sound anachronistic to the ears of those who have in their lifetime heard a president of the United States declare that he would disarm the ideological opponents of democracy by distributing the Sears, Roebuck catalog among them. But such words would not have sounded strange to the founding fathers, many of whom had occasion to say much the same thing. Between the political philosophy of the founding fathers and the ideology of the Sears, Roebuck catalog, there stretches the fascinating—and still largely untold—story of what happened to the democratic idea in America.

In the writing of our first major historian, George Bancroft, one can already see a clear premonition of things to come. His was a muted and rather covert operation: The Jacksonians, of whom Bancroft was one, were not eager to emphasize any ideological or philosophical differences they might have had with the founding fathers, whose memory was still revered among the electorate. Nevertheless, what was involved in Bancroft's work was a giant step toward the redefinition of the democratic idea. It is striking that in his voluminous writings Bancroft paid hardly any attention—gave only passing notice—to *The Federalist*. Indeed, in his *History of the Formation of the Constitution* he pretty much denied that the founding fathers had any serious political ideas in their heads at all. "The men who framed it [the Constitution] followed the lead of no theoretical writer of their own or preceding times. . . . They wrought from the elements which were at hand, and shaped them to meet the new experiences which had arisen." It was important for Bancroft to assert this, because he did not want to seem to be taking issue with the founding fathers in articulating his belief that "the common judgment in taste, politics, and religion is the highest authority on earth, and the nearest possible approach to an infallible decision." Bancroft's strategy was to defend Jacksonian democracy as a restoration of the original republic in the face of an "aristocratic" conspiracy. It was only if, as Bancroft claimed, the founding fathers had no political ideas that his own political ideas could be represented as the natural extension of their work. In fact, and of course, Bancroft's notion of popular infallibility was utterly alien to the founding fathers, and had been explicitly rejected by them.

It was, then, within less than half a century of the founding of the republic that this major revolution in American thought took place, that an original political *philosophy* of democracy was replaced with a religious *faith* in democracy. The sources of this revolution—in theology, in literature, and in politics itself—are not at all mysterious, although they have usually been studied in quite other connections. And the impact of this revolution on American politics and American thought is no mystery, either. Still, the men who were involved in it were usually careful to play down its revolutionary character, and preferred to say—some in all sincerity, others with a seeming sincerity that I find suspect—that all they were doing was to draw some natural inferences from the heritage bequeathed to them by the founding fathers.

The nature of this new democratic faith was perhaps most candidly expressed, in political terms, by George Sidney Camp in his book *Democracy* (1841). Camp claimed that his book was the first defense of democracy as the best form of government for all people, in all places, at all times, ever to be written in the United States. So far as I know, he is absolutely justified in this claim. No man who ever studied political philosophy, and seriously contemplated the problems of governing men, had ever said such a thing; certainly none among the founding fathers ever did. But Camp could and did say it because he and his contemporaries had abolished political philosophy, to all intents and purposes, and replaced it with a transcendental faith in the common man. The quality of this transcendental faith can be exemplified by quotations from dozens of writers of the time, of which the following—from the senior Henry James, in 1852—is not untypical:

> Democracy is not so much a new form of political life as a dissolution and disorganization of old forms. It is simply a resolution of government into the hands of the people, a taking down of that which has before existed, and a recommitment of it to its original sources.

In this mass endeavor at redefining the democratic idea, historians after Bancroft were much less involved than poets, publicists, and men of letters. On the contrary: American historians of the nineteenth century were distinctly more Whiggish and neo-Federalist in their ideological complexion than other classes of writers. Most of them were born in Whiggish households, were engaged in such Whiggish occupations as university education and the law, and had connections with the genteel Brahmin culture of New England and New York. One can understand, therefore, why they were not easy converts to the new transcendental faith of democracy. What is less easy to understand is how most of them—always excepting Adams—managed to dodge any kind of direct confrontation with the transformation of American democracy that was occurring before their very eyes. Perhaps they were intimidated by popular opinion; perhaps, as patriotic Americans, they were reluctant to look too hard and too closely at this matter; perhaps they really did believe that, although the democratic faith clearly represented a departure from the political philosophy of the founding fathers, nevertheless this was a temporary phenomenon, and that ultimately there would be an amiable convergence. Whatever the explanation, however, it is the case that the bulk of nineteenth-century American historiography has about it a curious evasiveness, what one may even call a lack of relevance. (In the case of someone like Parkman, who was perhaps the most gifted of his generation, it is not too harsh to use the term "escapism.") That this is more than a personal impression on my part is indicated by the fact that American historians of today have little occasion to refer back to these predecessors—and, indeed, most of their writings are out of print.

Such was the situation until the advent of Turner and Beard—at which point, of course, everything changed. Now, for the first time, the historical profession—the official guardians of our civic traditions—made explicit to the American mind what had conveniently been hitherto implicit in American life: the repudiation of the political philosophy of the founding fathers. The shock of recognition that this effected upon the American public was profound and unwelcome.

In browsing through the literature generated by "the Turner thesis" and "the Beard thesis," I am impressed by the way in which most twentieth-century historians have managed to convert an important ideological debate into a matter of academic opinion. Much of this literature centers around the question of whether Turner and Beard were right or wrong in the inferences they drew from their evidence. Only rarely will a historian poke around the premises on which Turner and Beard established their historical writings. Yet it is these premises that are the most interesting and important aspects of their work.

In Turner's writings, the various things he has to say about the frontier are of no great significance compared with the way he uses the term "democracy." After all, no one has ever doubted that the frontier experience had an impact on the American character, that this impact was in the direction of egalitarianism, and that this egalitarianism in turn has had repercussions in all areas of American life. The exact degree of the egalitarian tilt that the frontier, as compared with other influences, did exercise is an issue that may be—and has been—debated. But Turner would hardly have created such a fuss, he would hardly be the major historian he is, if all he had done was to call attention in a somewhat exaggerated fashion to the influence of the frontier. To appreciate Turner's importance, I would argue, one has to see him not so much as a historian as an ideologue; and to understand his work fully, one should regard it as being primarily an ideological enterprise.

The point of this enterprise is indeed to be found in Turner's famous dictum that American democracy was born on the frontier—but that point is not to be found where we have customarily looked at it. Turner was not saying anything terribly novel about the frontier, but he *was* saying something new and important about the way we should use the term "democracy." In effect, he was redefining the democratic idea for the historical profession along lines that had already become familiar outside this profession. He was saying that by democracy we ought to mean the Jacksonian-egalitarian-populist transcendental faith in the common man, and he was further explicitly stating that this was something different from, and antithetical to, the kind of democratic political philosophy that the founding fathers believed in. Turner made Americans aware that the conventional republican pieties, which used the word "democracy" as little more than a synonym for "American," were, to say the least, ambiguous. And he offered to young historians the exciting prospect of rewriting American history in the light of a democratic faith.

To get a clear notion of what Turner really did, it is useful to turn to an earlier essay on the relation of the frontier to American democracy. I refer to the essay by E. L. Godkin entitled "Aristocratic Opinions of Democracy," which was published in 1865. The fact that this essay is not much read, and only infrequently referred to, even by historians of American democracy, indicates with what success Turner achieved his true intention—which was, precisely, to make essays like Godkin's as unread and unremembered as possible, even by historians of American democracy.

Godkin's essay is a thoughtful rejoinder to what he took to be Tocqueville's excessively pessimistic views of the prospects for American democracy. Whether or not Godkin was correct in his interpretation of Tocqueville is here beside the point. In any case, Godkin—who regarded himself as a perfectly good American democrat—was dismayed by what he took to be Tocqueville's assertion that the many virtues of American democracy were incompatible with a high degree of civilization, an elevated culture, and a noble conception of public life. He conceded that these were not yet to be found in America, but attributed their absence to the special material circumstances of American history—*and especially to the continual, pervasive influence of the frontier.* Although Godkin had many kind words for the frontier, he did allow that it was the aggressive, self-seeking individualism, the public disorderliness, the philistine materialism of the American frontier that prevented American democracy from achieving a more splendid destiny. And he held out the hope that, as the influence of the frontier inevitably declined, the quality of American civilization and of American public life would markedly improve.

Now, it is clear that Godkin's idea of democracy was not Turner's—was, indeed, very much at odds with Turner's. It was what we would today designate as a neo-Federalist idea, which regarded egalitarianism as not only an attribute of democracy but also a problem for it, which was very much concerned with seeing to it that the American democracy was deferential to certain high republican ideals—and, of course, to those republican institutions and those "best men" that represented these ideals. Turner never refuted Godkin; Turner—even in his later years, when his feelings about the frontier were mixed—never really tried to come to terms with Godkin; he never really argued, in a serious way, with anyone whose conception of democracy differed from his own. He simply did what all successful ideologues do when they establish a new orthodoxy; he ignored, and persuaded everyone else to ignore, the very existence of these different views—and where this was impossible, he blandly excluded these views from the spectrum of democratic opinion, relocating them on another spectrum vaguely called "aristocratic."

I shall not discuss Charles A. Beard in any detail, since his originality, like Turner's, lay in persuading the historical profession to accept the new ideological redefinition of the democratic idea. Aside from imputing crudely self-interested motives to the founders—a bit of malice that was not really crucial to his argument—Beard, so far as I can see, ended up with the aggressive assertion that the founding fathers were not Jacksonian democrats and were men of only partial democratic faith. He was right, of course. The really interesting question is *why* they were not, and whether perhaps they might have had good reason for being what they were. It was not until the end of his life that Beard addressed himself to this question, and in the course of answering it he tacitly abandoned his original thesis. But, by this time, American historians had naturally ceased being interested in Beard.

Nor shall I say anything more about the "progressive" school of historical scholarship that has been the dominant orthodoxy of these past six decades. I am sure I have made it sufficiently clear that, whatever the merits—and they are often considerable—of particular progressive historians, their work seems to me crucially deficient by virtue of their *simpliste* conception of democracy. I find too much theodicy in their writings, and too little political philosophy. I have learned much from them—but only rarely have I learned what they set out to teach me.

As one might expect, I am far more sympathetic to the work of the so-called revisionists—such men as Richard Hofstadter, Marvin Meyers, Stanley Elkins, and others—who have perceived that the democratic faith of progressive historiography does not really square with the facts of our democratic history. These are the historians of my lifetime whom I find most instructive and most "relevant." And yet in the end I have to conclude that even they are curiously unsatisfying. They trouble me because they are, precisely, revisionists in their attitude and perspective. That is to say, they are excellent in pointing out the shortcomings of the standard, progressive account of such historical phenomena as Jacksonianism, abolitionism, populism. But it is never clear to me what they would put in its place—or whether, indeed, they really want to go so far as to put anything new in its place. They seem to see their task as primarily corrective, and while their corrections strike me as persuasive and pertinent, such revisionism leaves me with the feeling that many important things—perhaps even the most important things—remain to be said.

It is true that a few scholars, sometimes counted very loosely among the revisionists, *have* offered such a perspective and general statement. But this only reinforces my uneasiness. Thus, in reacting against the notion that American history can be seen as one long conflict between those of true democratic faith and an ever-incipient "aristocratic" reaction, Daniel Boorstin has emphasized—quite correctly, in my view—the "consensus" in political attitudes that most Americans have, throughout their history, subscribed to. For him, the relative immunity of our society to ideological speculation is a fortunate circumstance, and he quotes with approval Edmund Burke: "The bulk of mankind on their part are not excessively curious concerning any theories, whilst they are really happy; and one sure symptom of an ill-conducted state is the propensity of the people to resort to them." Now I happen to agree with both Burke and Boorstin on the truth of this proposition. I dislike ideologically turbulent societies because they have a tendency to barbarize men who may previously have been at least modestly civilized, and to primitivize ideas that may previously have been at least modestly fine and complex. But I would go on to note that Boorstin is reading Burke carelessly, and that Burke does not mean what Boorstin seems to think he does. Burke, in this quotation, was talking about "the bulk of mankind" and "the people." He was *not* talking about political philosophers or historians or scholars—he was, after all, one himself. Burke thought it was a disaster when political philosophies became popular ideologies. But he never meant to suggest that truly thoughtful men should not engage in political philosophy, and one can hardly doubt that he valued political philosophy and political philosophers very highly. Burke could not have had a high regard for a society where *no one* was engaging in the serious study of politics—a study that was, for him, one of the noblest of human enterprises. In short, I do not think Burke, were he alive today, would regard the history of American democracy with quite the same satisfaction that Boorstin does. He might even be somewhat appalled at the enduring *mindlessness* of this democracy.

Professor Louis Hartz has also a new and general interpretation of American history. But there is an interesting difference between Hartz and Boorstin. Where Boorstin emphasizes the *non*-ideological character of American democracy, Hartz emphasizes its *uni*-ideological character. He, too, stresses the extent to which American political opinion has represented an enduring consensus, but this time it is around an idea, and does not merely reflect, as in Boorstin, a "pragmatic" adaptation to life on the American continent. The idea—the American liberal-democratic idea—is compounded of a few Lockean dogmas. And the history of American thought is little more than the changes rung—the permutations and combinations—within this idea.

Anyone who is even reasonably familiar with European history over these past two centuries cannot doubt the validity of this thesis—cannot doubt that, in comparison with Europe, America has had a remarkable homogeneity of ideology. But what is truly astonishing is that Hartz, after demonstrating the dominion of Lockean ideology, proceeds to insist that ideology itself is of no importance anyway. "The system of democracy," he tells us, "works by virtue of certain processes which its theory never describes, to which, indeed, its theory is actually hostile." This process involves "group coercion, crowd psychology, and economic power"; out of the push and pull of conflicting interests, there emerges an equilibrium that represents a kind of gross public interest. If and when we examine the ideology of this democratic process, and find it faulty or deficient, this is a crisis of democracy's image, not of its reality—a mere "agony of the mind rather than of the real world."

I must say that I was taken aback when Hartz, who is an intellectual historian of considerable talent and insight, led me to this conclusion. Only in America, I thought, could a historian of ideas—whose major work reveals the very great influence that a particular version of the democratic idea has had upon our history—end up with the assertion that political mind has no dominion over political matter. That the statement is false on the basis of Hartz's own work bothers me less than the fact that it is false in general—I honestly do not see how any intelligent man with even the slightest bit of worldly experience could entertain this belief. The political ideas that men have *always* help to shape the political reality they live in—and this is so whether these be habitual opinions, tacit convictions, or explicit ideologies. It is ideas that establish and define in men's minds the categories of the politically possible and the politically impossible, the desirable and the undesirable, the tolerable and the intolerable. And what is more ultimately real, politically, than the structure of man's political imagination? Hartz's own book reveals that there is nothing more real; and his book will survive the rather bewildering lessons he has managed to learn from it.

Reading Boorstin and Hartz, one comes away with the strong impression that America has been a very lucky country. I do not doubt this for a moment. But unless one is willing to claim that this luck is a sign of an enduring Divine benevolence—unless one believes that Americans are indeed sons of the Covenant, a chosen people—it is very difficult to argue from the fact of luck to the notion that democracy in America is a *good* form of government, or that we have more than an expediential commitment to this form of government. And while, as I have said, I recognize America's good luck, I really cannot believe that Americans are a historically unique and chosen people. I am myself a Jew and an American, and with all due respect to the Deity, I think the odds are prohibitive that He would have gone out of His way to choose me twice over.

Lucky we have been, but perhaps our luck is beginning to run out. I believe that all of us are well aware that the areas of American life that are becoming unstable and problematic are increasing in numbers and size every day. Yet our initial response—and it usually remains our final response—is to echo Al Smith: "All the ills of democracy can be cured by more democracy." But is this really true? Is it true of our mass media, of our political party system, of our foreign policy, of our crisis in race relations? Is it not possible that many of the ills of our democracy can be traced to this democracy itself—or, more exactly, to this democracy's conception of itself? And how are we even to contemplate this possibility if our historians seem so unaware of it?

It appears to me that there is a great deal of work still to be done in American history. To begin with, one would like to know *why* the political philosophy of the founding fathers was so ruthlessly unmanned by American history. Was it the result of inherent flaws in that political philosophy itself? Was it a failure of statesmanship? Was it a consequence of external developments that were unpredictable and uncontrollable? These questions have hardly been asked, let alone answered. And the reason they have not been asked is, first of all, the dominance of the progressive historian, who sees American history in terms of an ineluctable and providential "Rise of the Common Man," and, second, that even the revisionists shy away from raising the basic issues of political philosophy that are involved.

I should like to think that I am as good a democrat as the average historian, with as genuine an affection for the common man. But unlike the "consensus historians," I do not see that the condition of American democracy is such as automatically to call forth my love and honor, although I respect it enough to offer it my obedience. And unlike the so-called conflict historians, I get no relief in discovering as many instances as possible of civil strife and mob disorder. Both of these schools of thought, it seems to me, perceive the common man—the one in his potential for merely self-centered activity, the other in his exclusive potential for resisting authority—in terms that remind me of Ortega's definition of the "mass man": the individual who is not capable of assuming responsibility for self-limitation, for a kind of self-definition that is both generous and self-respecting. Interestingly enough, Ortega's definition of the mass man is identical with Plato's definition of the tyrant. Which in turn suggests that the idea of the tyranny of the majority—whether it be an essentially mindless, self-seeking majority or a simply rancorous one—is capable of more general application than has hitherto been thought to be the case. And this, in its turn, leads me to wonder whether American historians themselves have not too frequently, and all too willingly, fallen victim to what is ultimately a tyrannical vulgarization of the democratic idea.

1970

# 9

# *The Emergence of Two Republican Parties*

$S$INCE the 1980 election we have witnessed many thoughtful discussions of whether it was a "critical" election—that is, whether it represented one of those basic party realignments, the dethronement of an established majority party by its opposition, which appear to occur about every thirty years. Interesting as these discussions have been, they miss an important point: The really basic political changes in a modern democracy invariably involve changes *within* parties which, over the longer term, alter the very meaning of a party alignment.

It is often said that the election of Franklin D. Roosevelt and his first steps toward the welfare state assured the hegemony of the Democratic party in the decades to follow. This is true in a sense, but it overlooks the fact that the Democrats in those decades energetically evolved into a very different party from the one that elected Roosevelt. Had there not been such an evolution, it is doubtful there would have been electoral hegemony.

The Democratic party of 1932–36, like all modern political parties, had its "liberal" and "conservative" wings, represented respectively by the Northern urban "machines" and the Southern agrarian populists. The tension between these wings was such that the party could be described as an uneasy and unstable coalition that could hardly look forward to being a relatively secure majority. Nevertheless, that is what it became. How did it happen?

The usual explanation is that various economic, demographic, and cultural changes gradually ensured the dominance of the liberal Northern wing over the conservative South. But this ignores the fact that the liberalism that eventually conquered the party was not at all the liberalism of the Northern, urban machines, but rather a liberalism that destroyed those machines in the very process of coming to power.

It was a liberalism that provided a whole new army of party activists, recruited new constituencies, produced new leadership at all levels, created whole new agendas for public attention and concern. During 1936–72, this new liberalism "tore the party apart" with factional strife, as the party establishment kept complaining. But it was a creative factionalism, for it also infused the party with new political and intellectual energy, and it did this by making the Democratic party *interesting,* the place where the action was. It is not surprising, then, that U.S. political history since the New Deal is mainly the history of the Democratic party, with the Republicans providing a series of running footnotes.

Since 1972, however, this new wave *is* the establishment, and signs of inertia and decay are visible. The younger leaders of the Democrats are mere replicas of yesteryear's leaders, and the party has become largely reactive, promising simply a restoration to the better times of an earlier era. In short, it is becoming boring—as boring as the Republican party has been for more than half a century.

The question is whether the Republicans, after the election of 1980, are on the move, whether there are new creative energies at work. It is a most difficult question. The major difficulty centers on Ronald Reagan. Does he really *want* to move the party forward, even at the cost of intraparty tension, or even dissension? Above all, is he a political leader or merely another conventional Republican president?

Not since Theodore Roosevelt has the Republican party shown the faintest comprehension of the nature of presidential leadership in a modern democracy. It has failed to understand that the idea of limited government is not contradictory to the idea of energetic government or (what comes to the same thing) responsive government.

Theodore Roosevelt correctly perceived that the sudden emergence of giant corporations ("the trusts") ran against the American grain of his day, for such concentrations of private power seemed to most Americans incongruent with the individualistic version of "free enterprise" so long familiar to them. He acted with dispatch and vigor—not always wisely, but he did act.

In contrast, the Republican party ever since World War I has been ignoring its constituencies, actual or potential, and narrowing its vision. It has won elections, but often only in reaction to Democratic incompetence or outright misgovernment. Each victorious election since 1932 has been a mere interregnum, a holding pattern of activity. Presidents Eisenhower, Nixon (in his first term, that is) and Ford were good presidents by conventional standards, and historians are already beginning to speak more benignly about them. But they did nothing to rejuvenate or even strengthen their party, or to alter the drift of politics. It is no wonder that Democrats have come to regard themselves as the natural, preordained, governing party, and behave with such irresponsible, petulant fury when in opposition.

The Republican party as we know it came into being in the 1920s. It was then that the GOP defined itself proudly as the "businesslike" party—expressing the ethos of the business community, especially the corporate community. In that decade a best-selling book by a Republican advertising executive explains that Jesus Christ could be best understood and appreciated as the greatest salesman ever. Political leadership came to be wholly equated with prudent, astute management of the affairs of state. So-called country-club Republicans—at the highest level Bohemia Grove Republicans—became a dominant element.

Fortunately, party loyalties die hard in a democracy, and the Republican party did retain enough strength in white Anglo-Saxon Protestant rural and small-town communities, and among small businessmen, to be viable. It was a gradually dwindling strength, however, as many in these areas found Democratic energy more attractive than Republican inertia. Meanwhile, Catholics, Jews, "ethnics" of all kinds, blacks and the rapidly increasing (in both numbers and influence) academic-intellectual-media communities took up residence in the Democratic party.

The election of 1980, for the first time, provided signs that a new Republican party might be emerging. Ronald Reagan was anything but a typical Republican candidate, and never earned the favor of the Republican establishment—not even of the corporate community, which definitely preferred a John Connolly or a George Bush. He came "out of the West," riding a horse, not a golf cart, speaking in the kind of nationalist-populist tonalities not heard since Teddy Roosevelt, appealing to large sections of the working class, to the increasingly numerous religious fundamentalists, and even to the growing if still small number of conservative and neoconservative intellectuals. His posture was forward-looking, his accent was on economic growth rather than on economic sobriety. All those Republicans with the hearts and souls of accountants—the traditional ideological core of the party—were nervous, even dismayed.

They need not have been. There are, it turns out—perhaps there always have been—two Ronald Reagans. The presidential Ronald Reagan is quite different from the campaigning Ronald Reagan. Not altogether different, it must be said in all fairness, but disquietingly different to an unexpected degree. Only at the United Nations, with Jeane Kirkpatrick, does one see the kind of spiritedness one had hoped for in the administration as a whole; as a result, she is easily the most popular figure in the cabinet. David Stockman, who promised to be another untypical Republican, has been inexplicably transformed into a conventional guardian of the federal budget—an important job, but one others could have performed as well. Most of the rest of the high officials in this administration would have felt perfectly at home working for Nixon and Ford, as many in fact did.

Mr. Reagan himself seems content, most of the time, to assume the role of chief executive officer, the topmost manager of a managerial-Republican administration. Every now and then he shows a flash of the Ronald Reagan that might have been but these intermittent flashes are quickly dimmed. The influence of conservative Republican economists—talented men who equate the political imagination with a dangerous concupiscence—remains strong. So does the influence of the established Republican leaders in the Senate, for whom aversion to risk is the cardinal rule of conservative politics. So the administration bumbles along in foreign policy, in social policy, in economic policy, resembling more and more the caricature of Republicans in liberal cartoons.

It is not that mistakes, as some complain, are made too often. An administration that provides energetic leadership will always make its fair share of mistakes—but will leave those mistakes behind it, to be contemplated by historians. On the other hand, an administration that lies dead in the water will accumulate its errors like barnacles.

So was the critical election of 1980 merely a mirage? One would have to concede the likelihood of this were it not for the presence in the House of several dozen new, younger congressmen, and in the Senate of a handful of new Republican senators, who are becoming increasingly frustrated, increasingly restive, increasingly active. They are post–New Deal Republicans who have far less regard for Herbert Hoover than for Teddy Roosevelt.

## The Emergence of Two Republican Parties

One might recall that in 1933 the Democratic House and Senate had no greater number of such representatives who turned out to be architects of the party's future. They prevailed in the end by being determined, factional, and "divisive." The Republican party has always regarded with horror such unmannerly conduct from its members. It is just possible, however, that the new "model" Republicanism these younger Republicans represent will, in the years ahead, break the Republican mold. If they do, 1980 will in truth have been a critical election.

1983

# 10

# *Socialism:*
# *An Obituary*
# *for an Idea*

THE most important political event of the twentieth century is not the crisis of capitalism but the death of socialism. It is an event of immense significance. For with the passing of the socialist ideal there is removed from the political horizon the one alternative to capitalism that was rooted in the Judeo-Christian tradition and in the Western civilization which emerged from that tradition. Now, to ever-greater degree, anti-capitalism is becoming synonymous with one form or another of barbarism and tyranny. And since capitalism, after two hundred or so years, is bound to endure crisis and breed disaffection, it is nothing short of a tragedy that anticapitalist dissent should now be liberated from a socialist tradition which—one sees it clearly in perspective—had the function of civilizing dissent, a function it was able to perform because it implicitly shared so many crucial values with the liberal capitalism it opposed.

Today, we live in a world with an ever-increasing number of people who call themselves socialists, an ever-increasing number of political regimes that call themselves socialist, but where the socialist ideal itself has been voided of all meaning, and frequently of all humane substance as well. It must be emphasized that this is not a question of the institutional reality diverging markedly from the original, inspiring ideal—as the Christian Church, let us say, diverged from the original vision of the Gospels. That kind of wayward development is natural and inevitable, if always dismaying—ideals pay a large price for their incarnation. In the case of contemporary socialism, however, the ideal itself has ceased to be of any interest to anyone—it has not been adapted to reality but contemptuously repudiated by it.

True, there is a dwindling band of socialist fideists who keep insisting that we must not judge socialism by any of its works. The Soviet Union, they tell us, is not "socialist" at all; nor is China, or Yugoslavia, or Cuba, or Hungary, or all those other "people's democracies." Neither, of course, are such regimes as exist in Peru or Syria or Zaire, whose claims to socialist legitimacy are not to be taken seriously. As for Western countries with social-democratic governments, such as Britain or Sweden—well, they get a passing grade for "effort" but it seems that they are insufficiently resolute or intelligent to bring "true" socialism about.

This is all quite ridiculous, of course. Socialism is what socialism does. The plaintive lament of the purist that socialism (or capitalism, or Christianity) has "never really been tried" is simply the expression of petulance and obstinacy on the part of ideologues who, convinced that they have a more profound understanding than anyone else of the world and its history, now find that they have been living a huge self-deception. People who persist in calling themselves socialist, while decrying the three-quarters of the world that has proclaimed itself socialist, and who can find a socialist country nowhere but in their imaginings—such people are anachronisms. As such they do serve a purpose: They help the historian and scholar understand what socialists used to think socialism was all about. One could discover that from reading books, to be sure, but it is sometimes enlightening to interview an actual survivor.

The absolute contradiction between the socialist reality today and the original socialist ideal is most perfectly revealed by the utter refusal of socialist collectivities even to think seriously about that ideal. Perhaps the most extraordinary fact of twentieth-century intellectual history is that all thinking about socialism takes place in nonsocialist countries. In this respect, one can again see the fallacy in the analogy—so frequently and glibly made—between contemporary socialism and early Christianity. The Church certainly did deviate from the original teachings of Jesus and his apostles, and did transform these teachings into a theology suitable for an institutional religion. But these deviations and transformations, this development of Christian doctrine, were the work of the Church Fathers, whose powerful minds can fascinate us even today. In the case of contemporary socialism, there are no Church Fathers—only heretics, outside the reach of established orthodoxies, developing doctrines for which socialist authority has no use at all. Not a single interesting work on Marxism—not even an authoritative biography of Karl Marx!—has issued from the Soviet Union in its sixty years of existence. If you want to study Marxism, with Marxist intellectuals, you go to Paris, or Rome, or London, or some American university campus. There are no intellectual hegiras to Moscow, Peking, or Havana. Moreover, the works of Western Marxist thinkers—and some are indeed impressive—are suppressed in socialist lands. Sartre's Marxist writings have never been published in Russia, just as Brecht's plays have never been produced there, and just as Picasso's paintings have never been exhibited there. Socialism, apparently, is one of those ideals which, when breathed upon by reality, suffers immediate petrifaction. Which is why all those who remain loyal to this ideal will always end up bewailing another "revolution betrayed."

The inevitable question is: What was the weakness at the heart of this ideal that made it so vulnerable to reality? But in an obituary, it is indelicate to begin with the deceased's flaws of mind and character. It is more appropriate to take cognizance of, and pay one's respects to, his positive qualities. And the socialist ideal was, in many respects, an admirable one. More than that: It was a *necessary* ideal, offering elements that were wanting in capitalist society—elements indispensable for the preservation, not to say perfection, of our humanity.

The basic defects of a liberal-capitalist society have been obscured from us by the socialist critique itself—or, to be more precise, by the versions of this critique which ultimately became the intellectual orthodoxy of the socialist movements. The original sources of socialist dissent are best discovered by going back to the original socialists: the so-called utopian socialists, as distinguished from the later "scientific" socialists. Reading them, one finds that socialism derives its spiritual energy from a profound dissatisfaction, not with one or another aspect of liberal modernity, but with that modernity itself. Indeed, the original socialist criticism of the bourgeois world is, to a remarkable degree, a secular version of the indictment which the "reactionary" Catholic Church was then continually making, though to a world increasingly deaf to Christian tonalities.

The essential point of this indictment was that *liberty was not enough.*

A society founded solely on "individual rights" was a society that ultimately deprived men of those virtues which could only exist in a *political community* which is something other than a "society." Among these virtues are a sense of distributive justice, a fund of shared moral values, and a common vision of the good life sufficiently attractive and powerful to transcend the knowledge that each individual's life ends only in death. Capitalist society itself—as projected, say, in the writings of John Locke and Adam Smith—was negligent of such virtues. It did not reject them and in no way scorned them, but simply assumed that the individual would be able to cope with this matter as he did with his other "private" affairs. This assumption, in turn, was possible only because the founders of capitalism took it for granted that the moral and spiritual heritage of Judaism and Christianity was unassailable, and that the new individualism of bourgeois society would not "liberate" the individual from this tradition. It might free him from a particular theology, or a particular church; but he would "naturally" rediscover for himself, within himself, those values previously associated with that theology or church. This was very much a Protestant conception of the relation between men and the values by which they lived and died. It survived so long as traditional religious habits of mind survived in the individualist, secularized society of bourgeois capitalism. Which is to say, for many generations capitalism was able to live off the accumulated moral and spiritual capital of the past. But with each generation that capital stock was noticeably depleted, had to be stretched ever thinner to meet the exigencies of life. Bankruptcy was inevitable, and we have seen it come in our own time, as a spirit of nihilism has dismissed not only the answers derived from tradition but the very meaningfulness of the questions to which tradition provided the answers. A "good life" has thus come to signify a satisfactory "life-style"—just another commodity that capitalism, in its affluence and generosity, makes available in a thousand assorted varieties, to suit a thousand tastes.

Socialism can be seen, in retrospect, to have been a kind of rebellion against the possibilities of nihilism inherent in the bourgeois Protestant principle—an effort, within the framework of modernity, to reconstruct a political community that would withstand the corruptions of modernity itself. To call it a "secular religion" is not far off the mark, and most of the original "utopian" socialists would have found nothing arguable in this ascription. The Saint-Simonians, as we know, very consciously set out to establish a post-Christian religion that preserved the best of Christianity as they understood it. All the utopian-socialist communities had a religious core—at the very least a "religion of humanity" into whose values young people were indoctrinated. To challenge or criticize those values, and the way of life associated with them, was to risk immediate expulsion. In our own time, the Israeli kibbutz can remind us of what a socialist community, in the original sense, was supposed to be like.

This utopian socialism was not really utopian at all. Indeed, it is the only kind of socialism that has ever worked. The trouble is that it can only work under certain very restricted conditions. (1) The people who set out to create a socialist community must sincerely subscribe to socialist beliefs. (2) They must be satisfied with a *small* community—otherwise there will be division of labor, bureaucracy, social classes, in short a "society" rather than a community. And (3) they must be fairly indifferent to material goods, so that a *voluntary* equality will easily prevail. In circumstances such as these, socialist communities "work," in the sense of continuing to exist and continuing to hold on to the loyalties of a new generation as well as those of the founding members. They work most effectively, as historians of socialism are fond of pointing out, when the religious core is strongest, because then the shared values are most successfully affirmed and reaffirmed. It is no accident, after all, that the Greek *polis*—the model of political community—neither believed in nor practiced religious toleration, to say nothing of religious pluralism.

But this kind of socialism has always been marginal to socialist history, which had much larger ambitions. The "scientific socialism" of Marx and his followers—whether they defined themselves as "orthodox" Marxists, "neo"-Marxists, "revisionist" Marxists, or whatever—aimed to transform all of society, and quickly. It derided the idea of slowly converting people to a belief in socialism, until these people formed a majority. Similarly, it contemptuously rejected the notion of creating model socialist communities within the womb of capitalist society—as, say, the early Christians created their own exemplary communities throughout the Roman empire. Though the moral and spiritual impetus toward socialism may have been derived—and is still largely derived—from a profound sense of the inadequacy of modernity to satisfy the yearnings for political community, postutopian socialism itself has become a modernist political doctrine. This is true of both the Communist and social-democratic versions of scientific socialism, each of which, in its own way, takes a "managerial" and manipulative approach to politics, and tries to create a new political community through the actions of government upon an unenlightened and recalcitrant populace.

The crucial difference between scientific socialism and utopian socialism lay in the attitude toward economic growth and material prosperity. The utopians were not much interested in affluence, as we have come to understand that term—that is, an ever-increasing amount and variety of consumers' goods made available to an ever-increasing proportion of the population. They were by no means Spartan in their conception of a good community. They *did* expect to abolish poverty and to achieve a decent degree of material comfort, which would be equally shared. But their conception of a "decent" standard of living was, by twentieth-century standards, quite modest. This modesty was a matter of principle: Being community-oriented rather than individual-oriented, utopian socialism saw no merit in the constant excitation of individual appetites, which would inevitably place severe strains on the bonds of community. The main function of the socialist community, as they conceived it, was to produce a socialist type of individual—a person who had transcended the vulgar, materialistic, and divisive acquisitiveness that characterized the capitalist type of individual. Here again, the Israeli kibbutz gives us an insight into the utopian intention. The kibbutz aims to satisfy all the basic economic needs of the community, and even to achieve a pleasing level of comfort for its membership. But "affluence," in the sense of widespread individual possession of such "luxuries" as automobiles, television sets, hi-fi radios and record players, freezers and refrigerators, travel abroad, and so forth, is solemnly regarded as a political threat, to be coped with cautiously and prudently.

Scientific socialism, in contrast, denounced capitalism for failing to produce the society of abundance made possible by modern technology, and mocked at utopian socialism for wishing to curb "needs" rather than satisfying them copiously. This approach made it possible for scientific socialism to become the basis of a mass movement, since it pandered so explicitly to the mass appetites excited—but also, to some degree, at any particular moment, frustrated—by capitalism. The political mass movements that had socialist goals then divided into two kinds: those which thought a liberal parliamentary democracy should be preserved within a socialist community, and those which thought this both unrealistic and undesirable. In the twentieth century, both these movements succeeded in establishing themselves as the governments of major nations. And in all such instances the end result has been frustration and disillusionment.

In the case of totalitarian socialism—that current of socialist thought for which Lenin stands to Marx as St. Paul did to Jesus—the frustration has been absolute and definitive. Central economic planning of a rigorous kind has demonstrated a radical incapacity to cope with a complex industrialized economy and urbanized society. Obviously, the central planners can do certain things—that is, build steel mills or dams or armament factories. But the Pharaohs of ancient Egypt could boast of comparable achievements—there is nothing socialist about the ability of an all-powerful state to get certain things done. What the central planners of the Soviet Union clearly cannot do is to create an "affluent" society in which its citizens would have a standard of living on the level of that of Western Europe and America. The immense bureaucracy involved in such planning simply cannot compete with the free market as an efficient mechanism for allocating resources, nor is bureaucratic caution able to substitute for entrepreneurial risk-taking as a mechanism of innovation and economic growth.

Yet a Western standard of affluence is precisely what the Soviet citizens want. These citizens were never socialists in any meaningful sense of that term, nor have sixty years of Communist rule succeeded in making them such. In the earlier decades of the Soviet regime there was a lot of windy talk about "the new Soviet man" who would emerge from "the Soviet experiment." One hears little such prattle today, even from official Soviet sources. Soviet Communism is a pseudoreligion, and the Soviet government is a pseudotheocracy, which, even after decades of coercion and terror, has been pitifully unable to effect any kind of mass conversion to socialist beliefs. As has been noted, there are no socialist intellectuals in the Soviet Union—only an increasing number of antisocialist intellectuals. The effort to create a socialist society that would be more prosperous, more "affluent," than a capitalist one, while creating a socialist citizenry through unremitting *force majeure,* has been a disastrous failure. "Managerial" socialism has turned out to be far more utopian than utopian socialism.

The same destiny has awaited the non-Leninist, social-democratic version of managerial socialism. Where one can claim success for it, it is a success that is a kind of failure in socialist terms. Such is the case of Sweden, after decades of social-democratic government. It has been a prosperous country, with a healthy economy and a stable society—but its economy and society can be fairly described as "mixed," that is, half private capitalism, half state capitalism. Those Swedes who still think of themselves as socialists are intensely dissatisfied with this state of affairs, and are constantly urging the government toward greater state control and a more egalitarian distribution of income. Since the Swedish Social Democrats are still officially committed to the socialist ideal, they find it impossible to resist this ideological pressure. The drift is unremittingly toward the Left, and will remain so, as long as the Social Democrats are in office. The consequences for the Swedish economy are entirely predictable: slower economic growth, higher inflation, lower productivity—all amidst increasing popular discontent. That discontent will not be calmed by a more punitive and egalitarian tax system. Egalitarianism, in Sweden, does not reflect any sincere personal commitment on the part of the Swedish people to the ideal of equality. It is, rather, a strategy whereby organized labor on the one hand and the state bureaucracy on the other receive an ever-increasing share of the national income and of political power. This appetite will not be appeased by a more equal distribution of income or wealth. The demand for "more"—not for "more equal" but for "more"—will feed upon itself, until an economic, and eventually political, crisis will either create an authoritarian regime that copes with discontent by repressing it or provokes a reversion to a more liberal-capitalist economic order.

In a sense, Great Britain represents Sweden's socialist future. Though Britain's movement toward socialism came much later than Sweden's, and though some of the more conservative British socialists still talk as if a Swedish condition were the ultimate ideal they are striving for, the British impulse has been more powerful, less controllable, less deferential toward economic realities. There has been more nationalization of industry in Britain, the trade unions are far more belligerent, the Left socialists—the ideological fanatics who redouble their socialist efforts as the socialist ends fade into unreality—are more influential. The consequences for the British economy have been disastrous —Britain now vies with Italy for the title "the sick man of Europe"—and there have been no discernible compensating improvements in the British social and political order. No one even seriously claims that the British people are in any sense "happier" as a result of their socialist experiences. Indeed, all the objective indices of social pathology—crime, juvenile delinquency, corruption, ethnic dissent, emigration, and so forth—show steady increases.

It is hard to believe that Britain will simply continue on this downward course. The British love of liberty is still strong, the British liberal political tradition still possesses a large degree of popular acceptance, the British people as a whole are still more reliant on common sense than they are enamored of political fantasies. It is reasonable to expect that the Labour government will be succeeded by a Conservative government, and the British experience with socialism will be followed by a "reactionary" affirmation of the principles of liberal capitalism. But then the issue will be posed anew: What can a liberal-capitalist society do to inoculate itself against a resurgence of anticapitalist dissent?

We now know part of that answer. One of the things that can be done is to design all measures of "social welfare" so as to maintain the largest degree of individual choice. The demand for a "welfare state" is, on the part of the majority of the people, a demand for a greater minimum of political community, for more "social justice" (i.e., distributive justice), than capitalism, in its pristine, individualistic form, can provide. It is not at all a demand for socialism or anything like it. Nor is it really a demand for intrusive government by a powerful and ubiquitous bureaucracy—though that is how socialists and neosocialists prefer to interpret it. Practically all of the truly popular and widespread support for a welfare state would be satisfied by a mixture of voluntary and compulsory insurance schemes—old-age insurance, disability insurance, unemployment insurance, medical insurance—that are reasonably (if not perfectly) compatible with a liberal-capitalist society. Over the past quarter century, a host of conservative and neoconservative economists and social critics have showed us how such mechanisms could and would work, and their intellectual victory over earlier "Fabian" conceptions of social reform has been decisive. The problem, at the moment, is to persuade the business community and the conservative (i.e., antisocialist) political parties of their practicality. Not an easy mission, but not in principle an intractable one.

Other problems indigenous to a liberal-capitalist society are still virgin territory so far as constructive theory is concerned. What, for instance, shall we do about the government of those most peculiar capitalist institutions, the large corporations—bureaucratic (and, in a sense, "collectivist") versions of capitalist enterprise that Adam Smith would surely have detested? And, even more important, what can a liberal-capitalist society do about the decline of religious beliefs and traditional values—a decline organically rooted in liberal capitalism's conception of this realm as an essentially "private affair" neither needing nor meriting public sanction? These and other questions will continue to make any "counterreformation" on the part of liberal capitalism an exceedingly fragile enterprise. But they will have to be answered if the death of socialism is not simply to mean a general disintegration into political pseudosocialist forms whose only common element is a repudiation, in the name of "equality," of individual liberty as a prime political value.

As Cardinal Newman once observed, it is not too hard to show the flaws in any system of thought, religious or political, but an erroneous idea can be expelled from the mind only by the active presence of another idea. The dead idea of socialism is now putrifying both the world's mind and the world's body. It has to be removed and buried—with appropriate honors if that will help. Ironically, only liberal capitalism can perform that funereal task.

1976

# 11

## Machiavelli and the Profanation of Politics

THE *Secretum Secretorum* is a brief treatise attributed to Roger Bacon that had great currency during the later Middle Ages, in various "editions" and under various forms of the title *De Regimine Principum* as well as its own. It presents itself as a letter of advice from Aristotle to his student, Alexander of Macedon, who was having trouble ruling the Persians he had just conquered. In the course of this letter, Aristotle says that a king should put God's law before his own; avoid the sin of pride from which all other sins flow; converse with wise men; help the poor and needy; flee from lechery and lust; never break his oath; enjoy music while remaining of grave countenance; and so forth, and so forth. By far the most interesting thing about the *Secretum Secretorum* for the modern reader is its title. What, one wonders, is the secret?

The answer appears to be, quite simply, that there is none. Not really. All the title signifies is that the art of good government is something so rare, something which so few men ever discover, that it can be considered a hidden treasure. I have said "the art of good government"—the art of *self*-government would have been more precise. For the whole vast medieval and early modern literature concerned with *De regimine principum, De officio regis, De institutione principum,* and so on— Professor Allen Gilbert's *Machiavelli's 'Prince' and its Forerunners* gives us an idea of the number and scope of such works—intends primarily to instruct rulers on how to govern *themselves.* This is, under any conditions and for any man, the most difficult task in the world. It is especially difficult for a man who, like the prince, is surrounded by the temptations that go with wealth, power, and an atmosphere of servile flattery. In most cases, of course, since princes are only human, the effort is bound to fail. Such failures are not described in this highly moralistic literature, in part doubtless for fear of undermining the authority of government itself, but mainly for fear of setting a bad example.

The fact that this political literature was so little "sociological," so blandly mindless of economics, administration, even the military arts, obviously reflects to some extent the simple conditions of medieval life and medieval society. But only to some extent. If it is true that what the king did was less important than what kind of king he was; and if this in turn was less important than the fact that he was, indisputably, the rightful king—nevertheless, he had much to learn about his world that these guides never attempted to teach. Their self-limitation and, to our eyes, curious modesty appears to derive from their assumption that whereas morals, involving as it does a knowledge of the good, may be improved through exhortation and instruction, wise government is a practical activity that cannot be divorced from specific circumstances and which therefore can only be "learned" through the experience of ruling.

"Political science" in the medieval sense meant the description of obligations; it gave no further practical advice for it did not claim any special practical wisdom. It did not deny the existence of such wisdom; it simply denied that philosophers, as against statesmen, possessed it. It is one thing to say a king should be merciful; it is quite another to say that he should spare the life of a particular conspirator—for who can foresee whether such an individual act of mercy might not mean the ruin of the commonwealth and general misery? Providence, of course, knew the answer. But Providence was inscrutable, as much to philosophers as to anyone else. Only prophets could read the future; and all (including the Church) agreed that the age of prophecy was over. For a philosopher to attempt to judge human action by its consequences, instead of its concord with the moral law, was to claim a superhuman ability to foresee the general and ultimate results of specific actions. It was as a denial of this human ability that the Ten Commandments, and the moral code associated with it, were proclaimed as authoritative. And it was because he believed that men did not—and in the nature of things could not—have such power that St. Thomas said flatly: *"Eventus sequens non facit actum malum qui erat bonus, nec bonum qui erat malus."*

It is against such a background that one can appreciate the revolution in political theory that Niccolò Machiavelli accomplished. To be sure, the older order of thought did not vanish overnight. The year in which *The Prince* was probably finished was also the year of two such popular works as Erasmus's *Education of a Christian Prince,* an eloquent homily, and Thomas More's *Utopia.* This latter was in the classical rather than in the medieval tradition, but these had more in common with each other than with the modern mode. More's Utopia was located, not in the future, but out of time entirely; it posed an ideal and criticized reality in its name—but it did not suggest that reality could be transformed into ideality through political action. It was a purely normative exercise. Within the book itself, More inserts a dialogue on what role philosophers can play in politics (he had just been offered a post by Henry VIII), and concludes that, at best, he can by his counsel prevent some evil from being done. This was hardly what we would today call utopian doctrine. And, in the event, More's own martyrdom was to reveal that even this "at best" was an elusive possibility.

The homiletic tradition, then, continued after Machiavelli. Indeed, one finds innumerable specimens of the genre in the sixteenth and seventeenth centuries. But one also finds that, under the influence of "Machiavellianism," this genre is either being converted into, or tinged with, something new in political philosophy. This "something new" lies not merely in the fact that Machiavelli stands the tradition upon its head. He does do that. Whereas it had claimed moral authority and disclaimed political knowledge, he repudiates the established moral authority and asserts a kind of knowledge that the tradition did not recognize. Yet there had been Christian sects which insisted that the moral law had to be abrogated so as to prepare the way for the Second Coming; and there had been sects, too, which felt that, as a result of some secret communion with either God or the devil, they had been supplied with "the key" to man's temporal destinies. Machiavelli is no Christian heretic; he is the first of the post-Christian philosophers.

Post-Christian, not pre-Christian. Since Machiavelli lived during the Renaissance and, like all Renaissance writers, continually referred to Greek and Roman authors as his authorities, one is inevitably tempted to see in his thought a resurgent paganism. But a careful reading makes it obvious that Machiavelli uses his classical "authorities" in an arbitrary—and often downright cynical—manner. Moreover, the very spirit that pervades Machiavelli is markedly different from that which finds expression in, say, Thucydides or Tacitus. The classical writers, like Machiavelli, had no conception of Providence, believed that men were the toys of chance and necessity, and admitted that the universe was blind to human values—but they also asserted (or, at the very least, implied) that man could be superior to his fate insofar as he faced it with nobility of character, courage, and grace. Their writings breathe a *pietas* before the cosmic condition of the race; whereas Machiavelli writes with the sardonic iciness of inhuman fate itself. He is the first of the nihilists, not the last of the pagans.

This is not to suggest that he was devoid of human feeling. His passionate Italian patriotism was, for instance, doubtless genuine enough. So was the streak of sadism (no other word will do) that runs through his work, from his very first opuscule to his last. But these sentiments, though they have an important effect on the literary quality of his work, and help explain both its popularity in Italy and its notoriety everywhere, are subsidiary to his main purpose. This purpose, as announced in *The Prince,* is to describe "the way things really are" *(la verità effettuale della cosa)* rather than—as the medieval theorists had done—the "imagination" of it. "For many have pictured republics and principalities which in fact have never been known or seen, because how one lives is so far distant from how one ought to live, that he who neglects what is done for what ought to be done, sooner effects his ruin than his preservation."

But what, a modern reader is bound to ask, was so shocking about that? What, moreover, is "nihilistic" about it? Is it not a sensible attitude—indeed a "scientific" attitude?

These questions are best answered by another question: What in our own time is so shocking about de Sade? We know that the kinds of sexual activities he describes do exist and play an important role in men's lives. Lust, adultery, sodomy, pederasty, and all the various sexual aberrations have always been with us; and there is no question that they are necessary to the "happiness" of a large class of people. Yet in no country of the world may de Sade's books circulate freely. Our society seems to believe that unrestricted knowledge of these subjects constitutes pornography. It insists that, if they are to be discussed at all, it must either be in an esoteric manner (in medical textbooks) or within a moral framework that makes it clear one is treating of an evil, not merely a human phenomenon. And, for de Sade, there is no natural and prescriptive moral framework in sex, just as there is none in politics for Machiavelli.

Pornography may be defined as a kind of knowledge which has an inherent tendency to corrupt and deprave our imaginations. The twentieth century formally recognizes that pornography, as such, does exist; but it also feels committed to the contradictory thesis that knowledge per se is good and "enlightening." This is but another way of saying that the twentieth century is experiencing a crisis of values—not simply a conflict between values, but a crisis in the very idea of value. For if one allows that knowledge in and of itself may be the supreme value, one must go on to say that the knowledge of evil is as valuable as the knowledge of good, from which it flows that a man who is engaged in adding to our knowledge of evil is as virtuous as a man engaged in adding to our knowledge of good—in short, that the difference between evil and good is at most a matter of habitual terminology. This is, precisely, nihilism.

One cannot appreciate the new *frisson* that Machiavelli gave to his age without realizing that he appeared to his contemporaries as a kind of political pornographer. "I hold there is no sin but ignorance," Marlowe has him say in one of his plays. The ascription was entirely apt. For the message of Machiavelli was really nothing more than the message of pornographers everywhere and at all times: that there is no such thing as pornography. Nothing that Machiavelli said about affairs of state was really novel to his readers. They knew—everyone had always known—that politics is a dirty business; that a ruler may better secure his power by slaughtering innocents, breaking his solemn oaths, betraying his friends, than by not doing so. But they also knew, or had thought, or had said, that such a ruler would suffer the torments of hell for eternity. Where Machiavelli was original was first, in brazenly announcing these truths, and second, in implying as strongly as he could (he dared not be candid on this subject, for it would have cost him his head) that wicked princes did not rot in hell for the sufficient reason that no such place existed.

These two aspects of Machiavelli's originality were most intimately connected, and necessarily so. Had he accepted Christian morality and the prospect of divine judgment, he would never have wanted to break the traditional silence on the awful things men do in their lust for power; he would have been fearful of depraving the imagination of men, especially of princes, and of incurring responsibility for their damnation. Had he even accepted the moral code of the Graeco-Roman writers (who did not believe in divine judgment either) he would at least have indicated how awful these things were, no matter how inevitable in the course of human affairs. But instead he declared that an honest and enlightened man had no right to regard them as awful at all. They were inherent in the nature of things; and with the nature of things only fools and sentimentalists would quarrel. The classical writers knew that the rule of tyrants was an intrinsic possibility of human politics—one that was bound to find realization under certain circumstances that made tyranny the only alternative to chaos or foreign domination. They might "justify" tyranny; but without ever denying that it was tyranny. Machiavelli, in contrast, wrote a book of advice to aspiring tyrants in which the word "tyranny" simply does not appear.

There is in Machiavelli a deliberate, if sometimes artful debasement of political virtues. One of the secrets of his sparkling style is the playful way he gravely uses the conventional rhetoric in order to mock its conventional character. Thus, in his eulogy of Castruccio Castracani he writes solemnly: "He was just to his subjects, faithless to foreigners, and he never sought to conquer by force when he could do so by fraud." Such examples can be multiplied a hundredfold. His constant use of the term *virtù* to mean that which characterizes the virtuoso is perhaps his outstanding pun (e.g., Agathocles "accompanied his infamies with so much *virtù* that he rose to be praetor of Syracuse"). In the course of undermining the traditional political virtues, he also takes the opportunity—wherever possible—to show contempt for the established religion. He can do so under the guise of "interpreting" biblical history in his *Discourses*, as when he solemnly praises Moses and King David for their cruelty and ruthlessness; or he can do so more openly in a "technical" work like the *Art of War*, where he blames Christianity for the decline of martial prowess in Italy.

But the most candid statement of "Machiavellianism" is in his *Florentine History*. It is put into the mouth of "one of the boldest and most experienced" of the plebeian leaders during the revolt of 1378; but there can be no doubt that it is Machiavelli himself who is speaking from the heart:

> If we had now to decide whether we should take up arms, burn and pillage the houses of the citizens, and rob the churches, I should be the first among you to suggest caution, and perhaps to approve of your preference for humble poverty rather than risking all on the chance of a gain. But as you have already had recourse to arms, and have committed much havoc, it appears to me the point you have now to consider is, not how shall we desist from this destruction, but how we shall commit more in order to secure ourselves. . . . It is necessary to commit new offences by multiplying the plunderings and burnings and redoubling the disturbances . . . because, where small faults are chastised, great crimes are rewarded. . . . It grieves me to hear that some of you repent for consciences' sake of what you have already done and wish to go no further with us. If this be true you are not the sort of men I thought you were, for neither conscience nor shame

ought to have any influence upon you. Remember that those men who conquer never incur any reproach. . . . If you watch the ways of men, you will see that those who obtain great wealth and power do so either by force or fraud, and having got them they conceal under some honest name the foulness of their deeds. Whilst those who through lack of wisdom, or from simplicity, do not employ these methods are always stifled in slavery or poverty. Faithful slaves always remain slaves, and good men are always poor men. Men will never escape from slavery unless they are unfaithful and bold, nor from poverty unless they are rapacious and fraudulent, because both God and Nature have placed the fortunes of men in such a position that they are reached rather by robbery than industry, and by evil rather than by honest skill.

This is strong medicine indeed, and it was precisely as a kind of strong medicine that Machiavelli was first apologetically presented to the world. When his *Prince* was posthumously published in 1532, the printer, Bernardo di Giunta, dedicated it to Monsignor Giovanni Gaddi, asking to be protected from those critics "who do not realize that whatever teaches of herbs and medicines, must also teach of poisons—only thus can we know how to identify them." This medical metaphor has been fairly popular with writers on Machiavelli ever since (e.g., Ranke and Macaulay). It testifies to a recognition that Machiavelli *can* be a dangerous teacher; but it also claims that he may be a useful one.

Useful for what? To this question, there have been many answers, and a summary of them would be nothing short of a history of Machiavelli's influence on modern thought—it might be nothing short of a history of modern thought itself. But four of these answers are most prominent and most popular.

1. *The historical-scholarly answer.* The scholarship on Machiavelli and his times has been voluminous, technically superb, and almost invariably misleading. The bulk of this work has been done by Germans and Italians, and in both these countries the growing interest in Machiavelli was concurrent with efforts to form a united nation. For a century and a half after *The Prince* appeared, the commentators on Machiavelli—whether friendly or hostile—paid not the slightest attention to the final chapter, with its exhortation to free Italy from the barbarians. It was Herder who first saw in this the key to Machiavelli's thought, and who set the tone for modern scholarship. The tendency of this scholarship is to admire Machiavelli as one of the ideological founders of the modern national state, and it has seen in his seeming amorality a gesture of desperate patriotism and bitter pathos, suitable to his corrupt epoch. British scholars (usually Italophile) have also been inclined to follow this interpretation. This explains how it is that Macaulay came to say of Machiavelli's *oeuvre* that "we are acquainted with few writings which

exhibit so much elevation of sentiment, so pure and warm a zeal for the public good, or so just a view of the duties and rights of citizens," or that in our own day T. S. Eliot could assert, "such a view of life as Machiavelli's implies a state of the soul which may be called a state of innocence."

Now, Machiavelli was certainly an Italian patriot. But (as Professor Leo Strauss has demonstrated, in what is by far the best book on Machiavelli yet written) he was a patriot of a special kind. "I love my country more than my soul," he wrote to Guicciardini; and that he was sincere may be gathered from those scattered remarks in the *Discourses* where he emphasizes that, when a nation's interests are involved, no considerations of justice, legality, or propriety ought to affect our judgment. Whether one finds this laudable or not will, of course, depend on the relative estimates one places upon one's fatherland and one's soul. Very few of the scholars who admire Machiavelli are explicit on this point. A few, following Friederich Meinecke, concede resignedly that it is the ineluctable nature of political life to lead patriotic souls to perdition; though after the German experience of the past thirty years, one may expect to hear less of this. But, in any event, the basic trend of conventional Machiavelli scholarship is to suggest to the student that if a man cares dearly for his country, it does not much matter what else he cares for.

2. *The* raison d'état *answer.* It is reported that Mussolini kept a copy of *The Prince* on his night table. For all the good it did him, he was following an old tradition that goes back to the sixteenth and seventeenth centuries, when kings and ministers surreptitiously read Machiavelli or pale imitations of him in order to glean the esoteric and dreadful wisdom of *raison d'état.* (After Machiavelli was condemned by the Church, they may have shifted to Tacitus, who during that period was taken to be a proto-Machiavellian.) For with the rise of the absolute monarchies, there was a need for a theory of the state. The previous political theory, not of the state but of society—the theory of the Christian commonwealth, in which kingship was a well-defined office—had been rendered archaic; and into the vacuum thus created there rushed the esoteric doctrine of "reason of state." What this doctrine came down to was that (1) it was perfectly legitimate for a king to extend or secure his power and dominion by any and every means, that is, to act like a tyrant; and (2) his subjects must be left in ignorance of this truth lest it undermine their pious subservience to what passed for "duly constituted" authority—the king had to be hypocritical as well as unscrupulous.

This whole historical episode, during which the fashion of dabbling in *raison d'état* was the rage of courtiers, ministers, confessors, and paramours, has not yet been adequately told. The few ponderous German studies of it, properly humble before something that has the air of *Realpolitik,* completely miss its farcical aspect. For the "rules" of *raison d'état* are very similar to—they are sometimes identical with—the familiar household proverbs that can be quoted to suit any purpose. ("Look before you leap," and "He who hesitates is lost," etc.) Machiavelli is full of general rules and prescriptions—all of which conflict with one another, and some of which, as Professor Butterfield has shown, are patently contradicted by the evidence he marshals for their support. Such a state of affairs is unavoidable, since generalizations of this order have no purchase upon experience. When a king should murder his defeated enemies, and when he should treat them leniently, is not something that can be decided *a priori*—it is difficult enough to decide it *a posteriori,* as historians know. The statesman who tries to substitute abstract deductions for prudent judgment is not long for this world.

In fact, the rulers of the sixteenth and seventeenth centuries managed to survive reasonably well, and the most clever and resourceful of them prospered mightily. This was not because of anything they learned from their readings in the new "philosophy" of politics. They did what they thought was the sensible thing to do under the circumstances; and all that *raison d'état* constituted was the reassurance that whatever they did need not trouble their consciences. This perhaps made them a little more brutal than they might otherwise have been; but one can never be sure. As Machiavelli himself said, rulers had long practiced what he first preached.

3. *The democratic-enlightenment answer.* This has been by far the most influential of all, and it derives directly from the medical metaphor proposed by Bernardo di Giunta. Machiavelli is taken for an acute anatomist and diagnostician of political disorder, who has exposed the unscrupulousness of rulers in order to allow men to recover their political health in pure self-government, that is, popular government.

In its most extreme form, this view regards Machiavelli as a cunning satirist, and his *Prince* as a Swiftian, self-defeating "modest proposal." Though no less an authority on the Renaissance than Garrett Mattingly has recently restated this thesis, it is no more persuasive today than when it was first suggested by Alberico Gentile at the end of the sixteenth century. It involves, to begin with, a reading of the *Discourses* as a "republican" document that expresses Machiavelli's true convictions. Yet, as Macaulay pointed out in rejecting this possibility, all the "Machiavellian" sentiments of *The Prince* are also to be found scattered through the *Discourses.* There is also the fact that when *The*

*Prince* circulated in manuscript before Machiavelli's death in 1527, considerable odium was attached to it by the Florentine republicans, who saw it as a pro-Medici tract. Machiavelli, as we know from his play, *Mandragola,* was capable of first-rate satire; it is implausible that he would have so botched the job in *The Prince* as to make it produce an opposite effect to what was intended.

The main current of thought which takes Machiavelli as a precursor of "enlightenment" is content to see in him merely an honest man who exposed the trickery of princes. Trajano Boccalini, in his *News from Parnassus* (1612), recounts a tale in which Machiavelli, having been banished from Parnassus on pain of death, was found hidden in a friend's library. Before the court of Apollo, he enters the following plea in his self-defense:

> Lo hear, you Sovereign of Learning, this Nicolas Machiavel, who has been condemned for a seducer and corrupter of mankind, and for a disperser of scandalous political percepts. I intend not to defend my writings, I publicly accuse them, and condemn them as wicked and execrable documents for the government of a State. So if that which I have printed be a doctrine invented by me, or be any new precepts, I desire that the sentence given against me by the judges be put in execution. But if my writings contain nothing but such political precepts, such rules of State, as I have taken out of the actions of Princes, which (if your Majesty gives me leave) I am ready to name, whose lives are nothing but the doing and saying of evil things—then what reason is there that they who have invented the desperate policies described by me should be held for holy, and that I who am only the publisher of them should be esteemed a knave and an atheist? For I see not why an original should be held holy and the copy burnt as execrable. Nor do I see why I should be persecuted if the reading of history (which is not only permitted but is commended by all men) has the special virtue of turning as many as do read with a politic eye into so many Machiavels: for people are not so simple as many believe them to be (and have) the judgment to discover the true causes of all Prince's actions, though they be cleverly concealed.

The judges are so impressed by this logic that they are ready to release him, when the prosecuting attorney reminds them of their responsibility: "For he has been found by night amongst a flock of sheep whom he taught to put wolves' teeth in their mouths, thereby threatening the utter ruin of all shepherds." And for this, Machiavelli is duly burnt on Olympus.

He fared much better, however, down on earth, where shepherds were beginning to lose their good repute, as a preliminary to losing their heads. Harrington saw in Machiavelli the Hippocrates of the body politic; Spinoza praised him by name (a rare honor) as *prudentissimo;* Diderot flattered him in his encyclopedia; while Rousseau eulogized *The Prince* as *"le livre des republicains"* and its author as one who "pretending to give lessons to kings, gave some important ones to the people." Even John Adams admired him as a republican benefactor.

It is easy to see how Machiavelli's work of "enlightenment" suited the various thinkers of the Enlightenment. Their project was the discrediting of traditional political authority and the revelation to all of the *arcana imperii,* so that the rule of special privilege could be replaced by the sovereignty of the common good.* Machiavelli was all the more attractive in that his writings do contain several laudatory references to popular government, which seemed to give him a "democratic" bias. This was, of course, a misreading. Tyranny and democracy were not, for Machiavelli, exclusive conceptions; and his notion of popular government was sufficiently elastic to include the kind of rule projected by the popular leader of 1378, in the speech already quoted. But the men of the Enlightenment were not much worried about the future of popular morals; they took the moral instinct as natural, unless corrupted by government, and foresaw the progressive accommodation of human government to innate human goodness. The best state was the one that made its own existence as near to superfluous as possible; and any literature which cast obloquy on the medieval idea of the state as a coercive force necessary for man's mundane perfection was welcome.

4. *The "positivist" answer.* Like the nationalist answer, this is of more symbolic than practical significance, since it involves only the corruption of professors. It belongs to the twentieth century and most particularly to America, though it was first stated by Francis Bacon ("We are much beholden to Machiavel and others that wrote what men do, and not what they ought to do"), was revived for our time by Sir Frederic Pollock, and is now being promoted in Europe together with the rest of American "political science." According to this view, Machiavelli was a predecessor to Professor Harold Lasswell in trying to formulate an "objective" set of political generalizations derived from, and to be tested by, experience. His seeming amorality is nothing but the passionless curiosity of the scientific imagination.

It is obvious that this interpretation is incompatible with the medical metaphor, and with the idea that the political thinker is a physician to the state. Medicine, after all, is a normative and practical discipline,

---

*For the way in which this moral passion was inverted into a set of fanatical ideologies, see Michael Polanyi's Eddington lecture, *Beyond Nihilism,* (Cambridge: Cambridge University Press, 1960) (and *Encounter,* March 1960), as well as *The Logic of Personal Knowledge,* chapter 5.

in that it has an ideal of bodily health to which its activities are subordinated. Even medicine's allied sciences (anatomy, physiology, etc.) share this character: Structure is studied in terms of function, function in terms of structure, and the whole is related to an ideal human organism—"ideal" in the Aristotelian sense of most appropriately "according to nature." The "positivist" approach—I use quotation marks since the term itself is a source of contention—refers to physics as its model instead of to medicine. It proposes to establish demonstrative "truths" about men in politics that will be available to whatever set of "values" wishes to employ them.

Were this line of thought as fruitful as its proponents think it might be, it would itself pose a major political problem. No government could allow such potent truths to enter freely into political life—any more than it can permit the knowledge of how to make atom bombs to circulate freely. Political scientists who were not content to stick to general theory and academic publications, and who tried to apply their knowledge to specific problems, would have to obtain a security clearance and work under official supervision. Sometimes one gets the impression that the political scientist, in his envy of the intellectual authority of the physical scientist, would not in the least mind such flattering coercion. But, fortunately, the "demonstrable truths" of political science have so far been relatively trivial. And there are even many who think the whole enterprise is misconceived—that it is as senseless for "political scientists" to try to achieve an "objectivity" toward political man as it is for medical science to seek such objectivity toward the human body.

It is interesting, nevertheless, that the assertion should be made—that an influential and reputable group of scholars should insist that it is *right* for political knowledge to be divorced from moral knowledge. This goes a long step beyond the older *raison d'état,* which merely recognized, and took advantage of, their frequent incongruence. Machiavelli would have approved; though he would have been properly skeptical of the willingness of academic persons to carry this assertion through to its boldest implications.

There have been three major figures in the history of Western thought during the last five centuries who have rejected Christianity, not for its failure to live up to its values, but because they repudiated these values themselves. The three are Machiavelli, de Sade, and Nietzsche. A great part of the intellectual history of the modern era can be told in terms of the efforts of a civilization still Christian, to come to terms with Machiavelli in politics, de Sade in sex, Nietzsche in philosophy. These efforts have been ingenious, but hardly successful. The "slave morality" of Christianity is constantly in retreat before the revolt of "the masters," with every new *modus vivendi* an unstable armistice. Heidegger has even gone so far as to say that the struggle is over—that with Nietzsche the Christian epoch draws to a close. If this is so, then it can also be said that Machiavelli marks the beginning of this end.

1961

# IV

## THE POLITICAL
## ECONOMY OF
## NEOCONSERVATISM

# 12

## Adam Smith and the Spirit of Capitalism

THE founding text of modern capitalism, Adam Smith's *An Inquiry into the Nature and Causes of the Wealth of Nations,* was published in 1776, the same year that the Declaration of Independence founded the modern world's capitalist nation par excellence. This is one of those nice historical coincidences that seems to have a touch of the providential about it, especially since Adam Smith turned out to be sympathetic to the cause of the rebellious American colonies, while the Founding Fathers turned out to be followers of Adam Smith *avant la lettre*—that is, they subscribed to his doctrines before they had ever been promulgated. What Madison called the new "science of politics," as later enunciated in *The Federalist Papers* and as incarnated in the Constitution, is incomprehensible without an understanding of that new science of society which is animated by the spirit of modern capitalism and whose economic aspects are delineated in *The Wealth of Nations.* Not many of the Founding Fathers actually read the entire book, but they certainly read summaries of it, knew about it, and—most important—"understood" it thoroughly (in their bones, as it were) without having to read it. It is fair to say that the American democracy was born as a capitalist democracy, that the spirit of capitalism infuses our institutions and what has come to be known as the "American way of life," and that the destiny of this democracy as it enters its third century of existence is profoundly intertwined with the fate of modern capitalism.

Both this destiny and this fate seem, at the moment, to be highly dubious, and it is not an exaggeration to apply the term "crisis" to the events of recent decades. In such times of crisis, it is natural for all political communities to turn their attention back to their origins—perhaps in anticipation of finding grounds for hopeful reaffirmation, perhaps (and more probably) out of an acute need to answer the question "Where did we go wrong?" It turns out to be a fiendishly difficult question to answer, mainly because people who have been formed by a particular civilization—in this case a democratic-capitalist civilization—are least likely to have a true understanding of that civilization. Time breeds a kind of amnesia, so that one simply forgets, not the answers, but the original questions which gave birth to those answers. One takes things for granted which, at the beginnings, could not be and were not taken for granted. One has only the dimmest sense of the alternatives which were possible but which were rejected. One finds it very hard, above all, to keep vividly in mind the *problematics* of one's own civilization—the recurring costs which make all benefits possible and which, at the same time, make all benefits ambiguous. We are likely to think either that the benefits are intrinsic to "the system," whereas the costs are malevolently and contingently imposed from without, or that the founders, being circumscribed by the "climate of opinion" of their times, never really understood the implications of their ideas and intentions.

As concerns capitalism and democracy, we would be wrong on both counts. The founders understood reasonably well what they were doing—including the ultimate limitations of their accomplishments. They understood the alternatives at hand, because these were authentic alternatives, not academic ones. They were not prisoners of the "climate of opinion" prevailing in their era; on the contrary, it is we who are prisoners of the climate of opinion which they created for us to live in. In a sense, it is accurate to say that they understand us better than we understand them. Our task, therefore, is not to attempt a peremptory judgment upon them but rather to try to understand them as they understood themselves. If and when we have done that—assuming we ever do—we shall then be in a better position to understand ourselves and our predicaments.

## Adam Smith and the Spirit of Capitalism

In the case of the Founding Fathers, such an exploration into our origins is now well under way—though one must add that it still lacks much of the necessary philosophic rigor. The reason for this can be quite simply stated: The Founding Fathers understood that democracy is an inherently problematic regime—more problematic, indeed, than any other. They learned this from their reading of classical (i.e., premodern) political thought as well as from a casual glance at history, which revealed democratic regimes to be turbulent, short-lived, and generally less than admirable. *Our* difficulty is that we tend to regard democracy as the most "natural" as well as the best of all possible regimes, so that even our most critical scholars find it almost impossible to achieve a critical detachment from the democratic idea itself. Among our major historians, only Henry Adams was able to manage this—more than half a century ago.

In the case of capitalism, the situation is almost the reverse. We have become so acutely aware of the problematics of this economic and social system, so critically detached from it, that we find it difficult to perceive the *intentions* of this system—and, in the light of these intentions, its accomplishments. Even those who defend the intentions and the accomplishments usually misunderstand both. We overwhelm all discussions of capitalism with accusations of abstract possibilities unrealized—possibilities that the founders of capitalist thought specifically excluded from their perspective, as having "costs" that were unacceptable. Or else we constrict our discussions of capitalism by apologias that the founders would have found to be only marginally relevant —sometimes even directly contrary—to their purposes. Before one can address oneself to the question "Does capitalism work?" one must have a clear sense of what *working* means in this context. That is to say, one must have a sense of what kind of society capitalism is supposed to create. To learn that, there is no better way than to turn back to the writings of Adam Smith.

One cannot understand Adam Smith without knowing something about the intellectual movement out of which he emerged, and of which he may be said to be the culminating figure. That movement, the Anglo-Scottish Enlightenment, has remained in relative obscurity. It has received a fair degree of scholarly attention, to be sure, but usually in terms of one particular aspect or another—its relationship to the history of economic thought, to eighteenth-century English literature, or to modern British philosophy. It is rarely considered on its own as a major intellectual movement that had a decisive influence in shaping the world we live in, and also in shaping our ways of thinking about this world.

When university students today take a course on "the Enlightenment," their attention is almost invariably focused on the French Enlightenment. They are likely to be asked to read selections from Rousseau, or Voltaire, or Diderot, or Condorcet—or even from such relatively minor figures as d'Holbach or La Mettrie. They are less likely to be asked to read Locke, Hume, or Adam Smith as Enlightenment thinkers and will surely complete their course without ever having heard of Shaftesbury or Adam Ferguson. This posthumous victory of the French over the Anglo-Scottish Enlightenment is itself a major event in the intellectual history of the West—indeed, of the modern world—during the past two hundred years.

There is, of course, no denying the intellectual and literary brilliance of the major French thinkers of the eighteenth century. But this "brilliance" is not an independent or accidental factor. It is intimately connected with the *intentions* of the French Enlightenment. To say that these intentions were ambitious would be grossly to understate the case. They were nothing less than grand, even grandiose. The goal of the French Enlightenment was the "universal regeneration of mankind," to use a phrase that was commonplace among both the thinkers of the French Enlightenment and their nineteenth-century heirs. This grand and inspiriting and extreme intention gave rise to a grand and inspiriting and extreme event: the French Revolution, which has established itself for modernity as *the* paradigm of what a revolution is supposed to be like, and, above all, what it is supposed to aim at. We all today find it quite natural to think of Robespierre, Saint-Just, and Marat as prototypical "revolutionary heroes." We certainly do not perceive George Washington as a prototypical revolutionary hero. Earlier generations of Americans were able to do so—but that was before the intellectual currents of modernity washed over traditional American pieties.

In comparison with the French Revolution, the American Revolution has come to seem a parochial and rather dull event. This, despite the fact that the American Revolution was successful—realizing the purposes of the revolutionaries and establishing a durable political regime—while the French Revolution was a resounding failure, devouring its own children and leading to an imperial despotism followed by an eventual restoration of the monarchy. The explanation for this apparent paradox lies in the intellectual sources of the two revolutions and in the subsequent fate of those intellectual traditions.

Though the American Revolution was inspired by a rather casual intermingling of the two Enlightenments, it was the Anglo-Scottish Enlightenment that was, in the end, decisive. It was this heritage of the Anglo-Scottish Enlightenment that enabled the American Revolution to achieve its climax, not in a reign of terror, but in the Constitutional Convention. And it was this same heritage that made a George Washington, rather than a Robespierre or a Saint-Just, into the national revolutionary hero. For those who hold grand and utopian expectations of politics transforming the human condition, George Washington is a comparatively "dull" figure and the American Revolution a comparatively "dull" event. Such grand and utopian expectations were at the very heart of the French Revolution and have become exceedingly common in the course of the past two hundred years—with the consequence that the intellectual traditions of the Anglo-Scottish Enlightenment now fail to appease the feverish yearnings of an inflamed political imagination.

These traditions are melioristic rather than eschatological in intention: They aim at a gradual improvement of the human condition—a process, moreover, in which each individual bears his share of responsibility for a successful outcome, rather than salvation being provided "from above" by a ruling party or class. These same traditions are also skeptical in temper, hostile to all forms of enthusiasm (political, or religious, or whatever), disbelieving of all dogmatic certainties about human nature and the "meaning of history," and suspicious of either the ability or desire (or both) of those who wield political power to do good rather than harm. In short, these traditions place an immense burden on the individual for the achievement of personal happiness and social contentment, while in return promising (1) a gradual—that is, slow but, over the longer term, steady—improvement in his material conditions, and (2) a degree of individual liberty without precedent in the history of nations. That the terms of this transaction should appear unexciting today ought not to blind us to the fact that there was a time when they seemed positively exhilarating, and to the further fact that, out of the traditions of the Anglo-Scottish Enlightenment there merged a sociopolitical order that defines an important epoch in human history: the "bourgeois" epoch, in which we Americans, at any rate, still live, though with increasing unease.

The Anglo-Scottish Enlightenment was a kind of response—the French Enlightenment bing another—to the historical experience of Europe in the previous centuries. Two aspects of this experience were decisive: the wars of religion and the economic consequences of mercantilism.

Modern bourgeois society has, as its original traumatic memory, the successive spasms of butchery, persecution, and international turmoil experienced by Europe in the two centuries following the Reformation. These had the effect of bringing discredit upon traditional religious dogmas as well as upon the religious institutions that so stubbornly proclaimed them. A powerful yearning for a predominantly *civil* society developed, a society in which citizens, as individuals or as national collectivities, could live at peace with one another—or, at the very least, *not* battle over controversial questions of theology whose adjudication by force of arms was inherently absurd.

Both the French and Anglo-Scottish Enlightenments shared this aspiration toward a civil society, but there was a significant difference in emphasis between them. The French Enlightenment was shot through with romantic visions of a new political community in which all previous religions would be replaced by a new civic religion: the religion of rationalist humanism, in which the civic bonds themselves would constitute a kind of religious association. This vision was subsequently incorporated into the Socialist and Communist movements, becoming, as it were, their dogma, and at its extreme producing in our time the odd phenomenon of vast polities whose official religion is atheism.

The Anglo-Scottish Enlightenment dreamed more prosaic visions. It had no ambition to create a new religion of any kind. Instead, it aimed at the establishment of religious toleration, and its method of achieving this was to convert religion into a "private affair," the individual's "own business" (itself a revealing phrase), and thereby to absorb religion *into* civil society. In this view, a church becomes one form of private association among many, immune (under ordinary circumstances) to governmental interference. The government itself would be secular, but not at all hostile to the religions of its citizens. On the contrary: Though most thinkers of the Anglo-Scottish Enlightenment tended to be religious skeptics, and were at most vague deists, they conceded that organized religion was, for the average person, a necessary and desirable form of human association. It served the very important purposes of inculcating moral habits and, above all, of providing consolation and hope to those whose earthly lives were less than satisfying. Government, therefore, would be benevolently respectful of all religions, even helpful to all religions—but partial toward none. This was the original notion of the "separation of church and state" as inscribed, for instance, in the American Constitution.

It is important to note the kind of society in which this vision could be realized. To begin with, it was a society in which government was *limited,* in both authority and power, in regard to what was then thought of as the most critical social fact: the religious beliefs of the citizenry. And it was a society in which the individual was free of religious authority as well—*free* to choose those religious beliefs and those religious associations which suited him best, a freedom that had never before

been legitimated in the entire history of Western civilization. These notions, of *limited government* and *individual liberty,* were radically innovative
and were bound to have an impact on all spheres of life. One such
sphere was the economic.

The dominant economic philosophy against which the Enlightenment pitted itself was mercantilism. This economic philosophy was
never vigorously articulated, and its meanings are still being debated
by scholars. In large measure this was because it was never a "proper"
economic philosophy at all, but rather an ideological offshoot of the political system of absolute monarchy, which, by 1700, was the norm for
most of Europe (though, after 1688, not for Britain). As the late Professor Jacob Viner put it:

> What we call "mercantilism" consisted primarily of a body of doctrine ex-
> pounding and of practice employing ways and means whereby govern-
> ment could make private interest, when subjected to taxes, import and
> export duties and prohibitions, subsidies, and other regulatory and coer-
> cive measures, operate to augment national wealth and national power.[1]

In its crudest form, mercantilist doctrine demanded that a nation seek
to have a perpetually favorable balance of trade, with the "surplus" (in
the form of gold) being available for purposes (usually military) of
statecraft. From the point of view of modern economics this doctrine
makes no sense: Since every seller must have a buyer, and vice versa,
a perpetual imbalance in the terms of international trade will merely
lead to a collapse of the international market and a crisis in international
trade itself. But mercantilism did not look at things in terms of modern
economics. It was much more a political doctrine than an economic one
and was therefore ready to regard commerce as an *exploitative* affair, in
which there is a loser for every winner—not, as in later capitalist economics, an arrangement for mutual profit. Mercantilism was not interested in increasing the permanent wealth of the people, which was (and
is) the goal of capitalist economics, but rather in increasing the temporary wealth of the state, a wealth that could then be translated into international power.[2]

From the point of view of subsequent developments, there are two
other noteworthy aspects of the mercantilist mode of thinking. First,
it tended to regard man—most especially the man engaged in com-

---

[1]Jacob Viner, "The Intellectual History of Laissez-Faire," *Journal of Law and Economics*
3 (October 1960): 45–69.
[2]Those who, having taken a course in modern economic theory, still find this concept "irrational" and therefore incomprehensible might examine with profit the approach
to foreign trade of the Soviet Union and Communist China.

merce—as a creature of avarice, little more than a self-seeking and self-regarding animal whose selfish energies and purposes had to be directed toward the achievement of a larger national purpose. We usually associate this conception of man with the spirit of capitalism—but, as we shall soon see, that spirit was far more complex and ambiguous. The theory of capitalism, as adumbrated by Adam Smith and his circle, certainly was indebted to mercantilism for "clearing the ground," as it were, of classical-medieval political moralism, which insisted that an individual could be virtuous only to the degree that he renounced his selfish qualities and aimed directly at the common good. But the capitalist idea can be best understood as a reaction against *both* that classical-medieval moralism and the gross indifference of mercantilism to individual motives at all.

Second, mercantilism was in principle also indifferent to the condition of the laboring classes, and it was commonly argued that the majority of the people had to be kept poor so that the price of exports could be kept low and the nation (i.e., the government) thereby become rich. It was also generally agreed that just as merchants were naturally avaricious, so working people were naturally lazy and could be brought to labor only when they faced actual starvation as an alternative.

The developing spirit of capitalism, as finally embodied in *The Wealth of Nations,* flatly rejected both of these ideas. Indeed, the reason capitalism commended itself to the most generous and compassionate men of the eighteenth century, of whom Adam Smith was one, was precisely because it offered a cheerful alternative to the bleak mercantilist assumptions. It is true that nineteenth-century economic theory tended to return to those assumptions, but this fact ought to warn us not to identify the original spirit of capitalism with its later transmogrifications.

When one speaks of the "spirit of capitalism," one is bound to have in mind the Anglo-Scottish Enlightenment rather than the French. It is true that there was considerable mutual influence and that both joined in rejecting classical mercantilism. But the French reaction to mercantilism, as represented by the Physiocrats, was doomed to ineffectuality. While the Physiocrats formulated the slogan "laissez-faire, laissez-passer" in opposition to the mercantilist ethos, they were not much less hostile to the emerging commercial ethos. "Real" wealth, they insisted, derived from agricultural productivity, and *only* from agricultural activity. When, after the Revolution, French thinkers and economists turned their attention to the new socioeconomic order that had replaced the ancien régime, it was Adam Smith they looked to for instruction, not to their Physiocratic predecessors. To be sure, they did not always understand Adam Smith as he might have wished to be understood, but this was equally true in Britain as well—and is largely true, everywhere, even today.

The Anglo-Scottish Enlightenment was a revolutionary movement, and like all successful revolutions it did not try to impose a set of preconceived ideals on a recalcitrant reality. Again, like all successful revolutions, it did not merely destroy an old order but created a new and viable one. And it was able to do this because it responded to the "intimations" (to use Michael Oakeshott's marvelous term) of the new order that were massively present in the old. It would be an exaggeration to say that it ratified changes in the polity that had largely already happened but which had not achieved lucid and widespread self-consciousness. It would be an exaggeration—but not much of one.

The Anglo-Scottish Enlightenment, therefore, was an authentic response to the emergence of a bourgeois-capitalist Britain as well as the indispensable intellectual agent of this process. The ideas of the Anglo-Scottish Enlightenment not only were thinkable but were actually acceptable to significant portions of public opinion, because Britain was the kind of liberal (by the standards of its day) constitutional monarchy that it was, because the British aristocracy (unlike the French) was much more interested in money than in the purity of its bloodlines, and because the agricultural revolutions of the preceding two centuries (1550–1750) had so increased productivity as to disarm what later came to be known as the "Malthusian scissors." But if these were necessary conditions for the development of a capitalist Britain, they were not sufficient conditions. We have in our own time seen more than one instance of a nation which, according to the conventional socioeconomic indicators, "ought" to have followed the British precedent, ought to have "taken off" into capitalist growth, but did not—simply because the dominant ideas, the "culture," as we now say, of that nation inhibited or frustrated such a process. Ideas, if they are to be influential, need to be born into a certain kind of world, but any kind of world will always be susceptible to diverse intellectual influences, and, in the end, it is the various fates of these ideas that will decide the destiny of the world. In Britain it was the Anglo-Scottish Enlightenment, offering a coherent, persuasive, and intellectually powerful statement of what might be called the "bourgeois persuasion," that ultimately prevailed.

At the heart of this bourgeois persuasion there is a shift of focus from the community to the individual as the proper subject of moral and philosophical inquiry.[3] The classical-medieval world took as primary the question "What virtues does the individual have to possess in order for him to be a member of a good community in which he can lead a good life?" This question itself assumed that the proper subject of moral and philosophical inquiry was a "polity," not a "society." Society, as the classical-medieval world saw it, came into existence out of the self-preserving needs of the individual in a "state of nature." "Polity" or "community" emerged because man has a "higher" yet equally "natural" need, not merely to survive, and not even merely to survive prosperously, but to lead a good life that fulfills his true "nature" (defined metaphysically or religiously). For such a good life to exist, a good community must make it possible for it to exist. Obviously, there are very different versions of "the good community," depending on the variety of circumstances which humanity encounters. And it is also true that, for a tiny minority of "the best"—that is, philosophers and saints—the meaning of the appropriate "virtues" will not be quite the same as for the average person. But it is precisely questions such as these which engaged the moral and political philosopher, who regarded society—the aggregation of individuals for the purpose of self-preservation—as a prephilosophical subject, as it is a prepolitical condition.

The modern tradition of political thought, as established by the bourgeois persuasion, abolishes the distinction between polity and society and takes the individual in his state of nature as the proper point of departure for political speculation. It is this individual who then asks the new political question: "What must I do to survive—and, after survival is assured, what must I do to survive most comfortably and happily?" It is reasonable to assume that the eventual popularity of putting *the* political question in this way owes much to the fact that Protestantism had reformulated *the* religious question as "What should *I* do to be saved?" as well as to the revival of Stoic and Epicurean modes of thought in the Renaissance, with its own question: "How do I live nobly in an ignoble world?" But this should not detract in any way from the bold originality of modern political philosophy. For, quietly and ruthlessly, it dismissed as "scholastic nonsense" all notions of man as having "higher" needs—needs that, if frustrated, cast him into misery. With this dimension of humanity denied, political philosophy could become "political science" or, better yet, "social science," an objective, value-free discipline dealing with a human animal who, for all his extraordinary differences from other animals, remains fundamentally of

---

[3]Alasdair MacIntyre's *A Short History of Ethics* (New York: Macmillan, 1966) has an excellent discussion of this topic.

their kind: a creature of prescribed needs, desires, and appetites whose activities are directed to their appeasement.

This abstract, schematic description of the "modernist revolution" of the sixteenth to eighteenth centuries is true only abstractly and schematically. In the real and historical world, as distinct from the universe of pure ideas, the relation of modern thought to modern actuality was far more complex (and, one may venture to say, more interesting). Though the entire structure of classical political thought was dismissed as an irrelevant confusion between the way things are and the way things ought to be, the "ought" turned out to be not so easily severed from the "is." Men, when they contemplated their condition and their destiny in the light of the bourgeois persuasion, generally seemed to end up by thinking themselves out of this perspective—generally seemed to find that the idea of "happiness" was not self-sufficient but rather had to be compounded with some idea of "virtue" to become viable. Similarly, the primordial individualism of modern political and social thought generally culminated in some vision of a good community. How one got from the one to the other was, of course, an intellectual and practical problem of the utmost difficulty, and it is not much of an exaggeration to say that the better part of the intellectual and political history of the past two centuries consists of contentious solutions to this problem. Such solutions are various, but they basically fall into two categories.

The first, the eighteenth-century "French" solution (later incorporated into Marxist and other totalitarian solutions), was to preserve in its harsh purity the modern idea of man as a creature of appetite and circumstance, but then to reply upon the redeeming activism of a "virtuous" elite to manipulate men and circumstance in such a way as to create a good community. One may fairly call this the "managerial" solution. It did not assume that men had to become virtuous (in whatever sense) for a virtuous community to exist. Rather, it assumed that if a virtuous elite created—by coercion, if necessary—the circumstantial preconditions of a good community, men would then "naturally" adapt to virtue as they had previously adapted to vice. One may also fairly call this the "utopian" as well as the managerial solution: beginning with what is (by classical standards) a "low" conception of the nature of man, it ends with an effort to realize, in the here and now, a universal regeneration of humanity.

The second, the "bourgeois" solution to the problem posed by the bourgeois persuasion, is associated with the Anglo-Scottish Enlightenment and especially with Adam Smith (once that thinker is properly understood). This solution involved a modification of the modern idea of man so as to place an inclination toward virtue somewhere within him. It then sought to create a decent society which would have some of the aspects of a virtuous community but would make no serious attempt to realize any such ideal. In short, the bourgeois solution elevated (though only to a moderate degree) the "low" conception of human nature so characteristic of modern thought and limited its aspirations to a vision of society which, for all its merits, fell far short of anything one might wish to call an ideal and virtuous community. In only one respect was this bourgeois society deemed to be markedly superior to all ideal communities, past or future: This was the degree of individual liberty it ascribed to the average citizen. If one wishes to use modern economic jargon, one can say that the Anglo-Scottish solution "traded off" virtue for the sake of liberty, whereas the French solution did exactly the opposite.

It is worth lingering a bit on these two modes of thought, if only because the differences between them are crucial to an understanding of the ideological turmoil of the twentieth century. It is interesting to note, for instance, that one readily calls the thinkers of the French Enlightenment—such as Voltaire, Diderot, d'Alembert, Condorcet—"intellectuals," whereas one does not think to apply that term to the likes of Locke, Hume, Ferguson, and Smith. Similarly, one would find it unexceptionable to refer to these French writers as "brilliant," a word that does not come to mind as appropriate to the Anglo-Scottish, who impress us with their "sobriety." These differences are of great importance. They reflect, above all, the marginal situation of the French men of letters, at home in the Parisian salons but not in the society as a whole, whereas the Anglo-Scottish thinkers were respectable and respected members of the community, frequently holding high academic positions and at ease in the company of worldly men (whether it was the world of politics or commerce). The French intellectuals were an "alienated" class (as we would now say), with all the wit, verve, boldness of imagination, and blithe irresponsibility that such a class will often display. The Anglo-Scottish philosophers were a more mundane lot, both sociologically and intellectually; they were in a position where they might anticipate that their ideas could be effectual, would be taken seriously by those who exercised power and authority. Being more or less "at home" in their world, they were content with melioristic ambitions, whereas the French intellectuals were inclined to rage against things as they were in the name of what they might ideally be.

Nowhere is the difference between these two intellectual currents, both children of the Age of Reason, more striking than in what they made of the idea of progress, in which they shared a common belief. For the French intellectuals, a realization of all the promises of progress became a mission, and peculiarly *their* mission, to be achieved against the massive resistance of tradition, custom, habit, and all the institutions of the ancient régime. French rationalism thereby identified the condition of being progressive with the condition of being rebellious, for the spirit of progress demanded the rational reconstruction of the social order if it was to fulfill itself. It did not take long for this French idea of progress to become wedded to a rationalist political messianism that has, ever since, been a dominant characteristic of continental "progressive" thought (and has, in our own time, been taken to be the only legitimate form of progressive thought by most of the world).

The Anglo-Scottish Enlightenment was no less rationalist than the French, but it found its appropriate expression in a calm historical sociology rather than in a fervent political messianism. These thinkers were convinced that a great deal of progress had already taken place, that the inhabitants of the British Isles were already the happy beneficiaries of it, and that it required but some amendment of contemporary practices for it to continue on its incremental and inexorable way. Above all, they did not share the French "voluntaristic" notion that the idea of progress was a truth possessed by an enlightened elite who had to impress this truth on a recalcitrant reality. On the contrary: The Anglo-Scottish philosophers conceived of social progress—the rise of commerce, the gradual "refinement" of manners and morals, the increase in knowledge—as something that happened to men as they strove to "improve their condition," a striving they took to be utterly natural. Implicit in this perspective is the notion of a "hidden hand," but it is a sociological rather than a quasi-theological (or providential) notion. That the human race as a whole, or any single nation, should be creative in a way beyond the intentions or prevision of any single individual or class of individuals they took to be inevitable. As Adam Ferguson (who was Adam Smith's teacher) put it:

> Every step and every movement of the multitude, even in what are termed enlightened ages, are made with equal blindness to the future; and nations stumble upon establishments, which are indeed the result of human action but not the execution of human design.[4]

This almost proto-Darwinian conception of social evolution has a crucial corollary: For such progress to occur, a maximum of human liberty is necessary, because it is only through the exercise of such liberty that the serendipitous effects of social evolution can emerge. The

[4]Gladys Bryson, *Man and Society: The Scottish Inquiry of the Eighteenth Century* (Princeton: Princeton University Press, 1945), p. 49.

Anglo-Scottish Enlightenment, therefore, is emphatic in the value it places on individual freedom and a more "liberal" society. The French Enlightenment, in contrast, ends up emphasizing the importance of power rather than liberty: The rational understanding of progress is the intellectual property of an elite which, furthermore, acquires the talent of prevision through the exercise of such understanding—and given such foreknowledge of the future, human freedom becomes otiose or destructive. Anglo-Scottish rationalism asserts that the past can be understood only in retrospect, that the present can be understood as the product of its past, and that the future cannot be understood at all since it will be unwittingly created; it will be the consequence of human actions but not of any clear human intention. French rationalism claims to "understand" progress in a far more comprehensive way—claims for the mind of an "enlightened" man the ability to make congruent human intention and the consequences of human action; a society which can explain itself rationally only by way of recounting its history, rather than by its approximation to a prescribed design, is in its eyes an irrational society.

It is not unexpected, then, that French rationalism proved to be so contemptuous of traditional French institutions, whereas Anglo-Scottish rationalism was so respectful of traditional British institutions. This also explains what, to the modern eye, seems to be a riddle of intellectual history: that Adam Smith, the father of nineteenth-century liberalism, and Edmund Burke, the father of nineteenth-century conservatism, should have shared a mutual affection and admiration. Both of these thinkers saw no intrinsic difficulty in reconciling the commercial spirit, with its emphasis on individual liberty, to the prescriptive claims of traditional institutions and traditional modes of individual behavior. The reason we find this perplexing is that we have become, in the twentieth century, more the heirs to the French Enlightenment than to the Anglo-Scottish.

But if the Anglo-Scottish Enlightenment appears, when counterposed to the French, so homogeneous, there is nevertheless a significant heterogeneity within it. More than heterogeneity: There is contradiction. For while the bourgeois persuasion was unanimous in its belief that modern man had to be (and was in fact) animated by "a spirit of avarice and industry" (Hume), and that it was foolish to rely upon his direct, personal concern for the public good,[5] there was a sharp division of opinion over just how radically this proposition was to be interpreted. At the root of this quarrel within the bourgeois persuasion was a disagreement over the nature of human nature.

[5]David Hume, *A Treatise of Human Nature*, Book 2.

## Adam Smith and the Spirit of Capitalism

One school of thought, represented by Thomas Hobbes and Bernard de Mandeville, considered man to be by nature an antisocial animal, ruled exclusively by self-concern and self-interest. The question then became "How does one create a decent polity if it is to be inhabited by such creatures?" Hobbes's answer was the sovereignty of Leviathan, the relinquishment of all human rights to the guardian-state, which, while interfering as little as possible in the "private" (i.e., nonpolitical) affairs of the citizenry, would ensure the most important right of all: self-preservation. Though this political solution was discredited by the Glorious Revolution of 1688, its mode of thought was partially preserved in mercantilist economic philosophy, in which the "liberated" selfishness and avarice of the individual—as exemplified in his "microeconomic" activity—was "managed" at a distance by the state to achieve the "macroeconomic" goal of national wealth as well as such political aims as power and glory.

The most provocative statement of this point of view is to be found in Bernard de Mandeville's *Fable of the Bees* (1714), a work so frank and bold and even cheerful in its inversion of traditional (i.e., classical and Christian) moral values that scholars have ever since wondered to what degree its intention was satirical and to what degree its author literally meant what he said. This scholarly controversy need not detain us. Mandeville's contemporaries certainly took him at his word and were, for the most part, duly shocked. More important, his ideas took on a life of their own and gradually infused the political and economic philosophies even of those who, when put to the question, would have denounced him as perverse to the point of wickedness. Among these latter were the authors of *The Federalist* and the American Constitution, and Adam Smith—who explicitly rejected Mandeville's teachings but nevertheless did not escape their influence.

Mandeville's views were crisply summed up in the subtitle to his work: *Private Vices, Publick Benefits.* He blandly accepted—or seemed to accept—the traditional distinctions between vice and virtue, right and wrong, but then proceeded to declare them to be utopian and utterly useless as a guide to the real world. Men can never govern themselves, can never attain virtue by aiming directly at it, by the practice of self-denial, for example. Their selfish instincts are simply too strong for any such program to succeed in the large: The history of human affairs, as distinct from the history of human philosophy, testifies to the truth of this proposition. But, Mandeville went on to say, "Private vices by the dextrous Management of a skilful Politician may be turned into Publick Benefits." One must not understand this as asserting merely that, in this imperfect world, political philosophers should not conceive

*153*

of a good society that is too demanding of human nature. Mandeville went further, to argue that without those human vices a good society could not possibly exist:

> I flatter myself to have demonstrated that, neither the Friendly Qualities and kind Affections that are natural to Man, nor the real Virtues he is capable of acquiring by Reason and Self-Denial, are the Foundation of Society; but that what we call Evil in this World, Moral as well as Natural, is the grand Principle that makes us sociable Creatures, the solid Basis, the Life and Support of all Trades and Employments without Exception: That there we must look for the true Origin of all Arts and Sciences, and that the Moment Evil ceases, the Society must be spoiled, if not totally dissolved.

One can appreciate the revulsion such a teaching would arouse among Mandeville's contemporaries, most of whom conceived of themselves as being good Christians, and all of whom thought that, though Christian dogmas may not be beyond disputation, Christian morality most certainly was. Even those who agreed with his critique of premodern political thought were alarmed that Mandeville had gone too far in his positive praise of what were still universally deemed to be symptoms of human wickedness. Nevertheless, the Mandeville credo served the purpose of those who, while criticizing its "extremism," wished to see modern society arranged on a principle of official *indifference* to the moral qualities of the individual. Its success in helping to "liberate" economic and political thought from moral philosophy can be seen by the fact that Immanuel Kant, justly famed as a moral philosopher, could later state, in all equanimity: "Harsh as it might sound, the problem of establishing the just state is soluble even for a nation of devils, if they have sense." And this conception of the inevitable relation between a good society and the average, unreformed individual profoundly shaped both capitalist and anticapitalist thought in the nineteenth and twentieth centuries.

Traces of what seem to be Mandeville-ism also appear intermittently in Adam Smith's *Wealth of Nations.* But one has to approach them, and interpret them, with caution. For Adam Smith was a violent critic of both Hobbes and Mandeville and claimed as his heritage a quite contrary current of thought within the Scottish Enlightenment: the so-called Sentimental School of eighteenth-century philosophy. This school of thought, associated with the names of Lord Shaftesbury and Francis Hutcheson, was launched as a rejoinder to Hobbes, and it was against the teachings of this school that Mandeville had directed his own writings.

The Sentimental School, vaguely deist in theology but still Christian in morality, also placed great emphasis on the self-regarding desires and ambitions of men as the rock on which a better society could be built. In this sense, it too was distinctively "modern" and antitraditional. It was this school which ultimately, in the work of Adam Smith, laid the basis for modern economics by freeing it from the sovereignty of moral philosophy. But that freedom was not total and unlimited, nor was moral philosophy dismissed as irrelevant to the possibility of a good life in a good society.

Adam Smith certainly subscribed to what has become, perhaps, the most fundamental axiom of modern economics, that is, that human behavior can in large measure be explained as the rational pursuit of self-interest. But it is worth noting that he did *not* say, as a Mandevillean would have, that a rational person must always seek to *maximize* such behavior. For the Sentimental School assumed and asserted that there were natural and self-correcting limits to the pursuit of self-interest. Their "liberal" society was not liberated from the traditional moral virtues but was, in its own way, still rooted in them. As one scholar wrote half a century ago:

> It is true that seventeenth- and eighteenth-century liberals accorded to the self-regarding desires and ambitions of individual men a measure of moral approval which medieval Christians had denied to them. But it does not follow that they wished to discard all moral restraints that might protect the community against the overweening greed of individuals. The new leniency toward individual desires was closely connected with a new faith in the moral faculties of individuals, and in the goodness of normal human nature. Self-centered desires were trusted to promote the general welfare, because reason and the moral sense were trusted to restrain them wherever their indulgence would be inconsistent with that welfare.[6]

The existence of such a "moral sense," as an integral and ineradicable part of human nature, had been posited by John Locke, who further argued that moral certainties could be deduced from the axioms revealed to this moral sense. The Sentimental School—encouraged by the decline of the doctrine of original sin in the seventeenth century, and its gradual replacement by a belief (widespread even among Protestant divines) in the original goodness of human nature—proceeded to put this thesis to work and came up with an elaborate set of "benevolent affections" which were as natural to man as his self-centered appetites. This philosophical psychology has little academic standing today, at a time when psychology strives to be as "scientific" as possible. But if

6Overton H. Taylor, "Tawney's Religion and Capitalism, and Eighteenth-Century Liberalism," *Quarterly Journal of Economics* 41, no. 4 (August 1927): 718–31.

we merely dismiss it as a fashionable intellectual eccentricity of the eighteenth century, as most textbooks do, we shall miss its real significance. For it was this philosophical psychology that lay behind Adam Smith's version of capitalism—though to what degree is a matter of dispute—and it was Adam Smith who, in his *Theory of Moral Sentiments,* following the line of thought traced by Locke, Shaftesbury, and (to a lesser degree) Hume, provided that theory of human nature with its most extensive and persuasive rationale. The exact relationship between the earlier *Theory of Moral Sentiments* (1759) and the later *Wealth of Nations* (1776) is a subject of scholarly controversy and constitutes what the Germans have portentously called *Das Adam-Smith Probleme.* But if the controversy is academic, its significance is not. For what is involved is nothing less than the meaning of "capitalism" as Adam Smith understood it, and whether modern conceptions of capitalism are simply an elaboration of his teachings or rather a perversion of them.

For an understanding of the teachings of Adam Smith, a knowledge of his life and a study of his personality are singularly unhelpful. Though some enthusiastic (or desperate) "psycho-historian" will surely, one of these days, "explain" his thinking by reference to his father's death before Adam was born, his bachelor condition, his attachment to his mother, the sexual inhibitions in the Scottish Presbyterian milieu in which he was raised, or whatever, the plain fact is that he was a familiar type: a distinguished, absentminded scholar, unprepossessing, with a mumbling manner of speech, amiable but often sharp-tongued, easy to get along with but difficult to get close to, a respected teacher, a pleasant dinner guest, a good citizen of Glasgow. In short, he was a man whose habits and demeanor were utterly conventional and whose thinking achieved its influence by synthesizing current intellectual opinion rather than by confronting it. He was born into modest circumstances, won scholarships, became an impecunious professor, then a more affluent tutor in a noble household, finally obtained a sinecure in a civil service—a fairly common version of the Scottish success story. The only untoward event in his life was his being kidnapped, at the age of four, by a band of passing gypsies, who soon abandoned him by the woodside. They must have realized what an improbable recruit he would make.[7]

But if there is little that is enigmatic about Adam Smith as a person,

---

[7]An excellent short portrait of Adam Smith is to be found in Robert Heilbroner's *The Worldly Philosophers,* chap. 3, "The Wonderful World of Adam Smith" (New York: Simon and Schuster, 1972). See also Walter Bagehot's essay, "Adam Smith as a Person," in his *Biographical Studies,* ed. Richard Holt Hutton (1881; reprint, New York: AMS Press, 1970).

there is much that is puzzling about Adam Smith as the author of *The Wealth of Nations.* True, the argument itself is clear enough. It is a sustained brief for the "system of natural liberty," and the logic of this brief has been admirably summed up by Professor William Letwin:

> The proof proceeds in stately steps. In order to establish that the free private market gives good results, Smith showed first that it tends naturally to set the prices of goods at their proper levels (Book I), and to steer capital into the uses that are most beneficial to society (Book II). He then demonstrates that efforts of government to improve on the workings of the free market are injurious, whether they aim to stimulate commerce or manufacture or agriculture (Books III and IV). Then, as Natural Liberty is not to be equated with anarchy, he explains what things government must do because they must be done in a civilised community and cannot be done reliably by private persons responding to private incentives (Book V).[8]

This argument, extending over half-a-million words, constitutes the structure of *The Wealth of Nations.* It is a clean, coherent, and remarkably persuasive structure—but it is less than the whole book, when that book is closely read. For the texture of Smith's thinking is not entirely congruent with this structure, and this is where problems of interpretation arise.

*The Wealth of Nations,* though infinitely more readable than Karl Marx's *Capital,* has experienced a not dissimilar fate. Not many people read it carefully or even at all, but practically everyone seems to think he knows what it "essentially" says. Scholars, on the other hand, who study both of these texts, end up in a state of bafflement and disagreement among themselves. And just as the major topic of controversy among the students of Marx is the relation of the earlier neo-Hegelian Marx to the later "scientific" Marx, so students of Adam Smith are divided on the issue of the relation of the earlier Smith, author of the "sentimental" *Theory of Moral Sentiments,* to the later author of the "tough-minded" *Wealth of Nations.* Moreover, there is a sense in which the "Adam Smith problem" is more perplexing than the "Karl Marx problem." The later Marx did, after all, repudiate his earlier writings, so one has to argue for a connection in the face of Marx's own opinion. Adam Smith, however, never suggested or hinted that his two major works were in any way incongruent with one another. On the contrary, after publishing *The Wealth of Nations* he carefully "revised" *The Theory of Moral Sentiments,* but the new edition shows little significant change from the earlier one. So Adam Smith himself seems not to have perceived any contradiction between his two

---

[8]William Letwin, "Adam Smith: Re-reading the 'Wealth of Nations,'" *Encounter* (March 1976).

major works. Yet practically everyone else sees, if not an outright contradiction, at least a decided difference in tone, emphasis, and perspective. And this difference is not an illusion.

In tone, *The Theory of Moral Sentiments* is cheerful and benign; it is even in some ways an inspirational book. *The Wealth of Nations,* in contrast, tends to be more objective in its rhetorical mode and is not infrequently dour and acerbic—almost Veblenesque—in its judgments on all classes of humanity. To some extent, which we can only guess at, this may have something to do with changes in Smith's attitude toward religion over the years. Though he was never an orthodox Christian and made no secret of the fact that he had no high personal regard for organized religion in general—a contemporary quotes him as saying, "God made heaven and earth but man made Holland"—in his earlier book he is very much a conventional deist, after the fashion of his teachers. That is to say, he asserts (or assumes) a minimal theology, to the effect that there is a benevolent deity about whom we know, if we know nothing else, that he is the author and guide of nature. On these terms, the world is a place mankind can feel at home in, a place in which its ideals and finer feelings have an inner compatibility with the nature of things. In *The Wealth of Nations,* however, the world is a much bleaker place: That benevolent deity seems to have become a *deus absconditus*—he is barely mentioned—and there is a persistent undercurrent of doubt and anxiety about the possibility of human happiness, regardless of the material prosperity that a correct economic philosophy would provide.

It might be said—it has been said by some scholars—that one ought not to take this change in tone too seriously, that one should not expect too much continuity between a book on moral philosophy and a book on economics, and that since Adam Smith exhibited no unease or concern about the matter, neither should we. But against this argument is the fact that there is an obvious intellectual difference between the two works, a difference in their conception of human nature and of the principle that shapes human behavior.[9]

*The Theory of Moral Sentiments* sees as the mainspring of human motivation what Arthur O. Lovejoy calls "approbativeness."[10] Smith expresses that principle in these terms:

What are the advantages of that great purpose of human life which we call bettering our condition? To be observed, to be attended, to be taken

[9]These differences are nicely explored in Jacob Viner's essay "Adam Smith and Laissez-Faire," in *Adam Smith, 1776–1926* (Chicago: University of Chicago Press, 1928).
[10]Arthur O. Lovejoy, *Reflections on Human Nature* (Baltimore: Johns Hopkins Press, 1961).

notice of with sympathy, complacency, and approbation, are all the advantages we can propose to derive from it. [Pt. 1, sec. 2, chap. 2]

But, Smith says, in addition to being so attentive to the expressed opinion of the community, all human ambition and striving operates under a kind of "inner check" as well. This takes the form of an ideal "impartial spectator" who resides within each of us, and who internalizes the community's approbation and disapprobation. The impartial spectator—who very much resembles Freud's "superego" and is also a kind of vulgarized version of the Protestant idea of conscience—does his work in this way:

> We can never survey our own sentiments and motives, we can never form any judgment concerning them, unless we remove ourselves, as it were, from our natural station, and endeavor to view them as at a certain distance from us. But we can do this in no other way than by endeavoring to view them with the eyes of other people, or as other people are likely to view them. Whatever judgment we can form concerning them, accordingly, must always bear some secret reference, either to what are, or to what, upon a certain condition would be, or what we imagine ought to be, the judgment of others. We endeavor to examine our own conduct as we imagine any other fair and impartial spectator would view it. [Pt. 3, chap. 1]

From all of this it follows that, "to feel much for others, and little for ourselves, that to restrain our selfish, and to indulge our benevolent affections, constitutes the perfection of human nature."

Now, this last sentence is not the kind of thought we ordinarily associate with the founding father of capitalism—even though it is, in this same *Theory of Moral Sentiments,* carefully connected with "that great purpose of human life which we call bettering our condition," a purpose that is also central to *The Wealth of Nations.* The earlier Adam Smith seems to have had a keen sense of the importance of moral and political community, and of the need for each striving and achieving individual, as he "betters his condition," to affirm and strengthen the bonds of community. The individualism of *The Theory of Moral Sentiments* is distinctly "bourgeois," in that it has as its goal, not merely the happiness of the individual, but the creation of a more humane and elevated bourgeois community, one with powerful feelings of fraternity and fellowship. It is explicitly anti-Mandevillean, envisioning a society in which individual liberty is perfectly reconciled with the conventional bourgeois—Christian—virtues, and in which this reconciliation is a source of profound satisfaction to all.

It is perhaps worth remarking that the Adam Smith of *The Theory of Moral Sentiments* was a professor of moral philosophy. Economics, as an independent intellectual discipline, did not yet exist, while its im- mediate progenitor, the discipline of "political economy," was only just emerging. "Moral philosophy," as then conceived, comprehended all of the social sciences, as we now term them—plus psychology, which had the crucial role of replacing metaphysics and theology as the ultimate basis of morality. (Psychology fulfilled this role by dis- covering those qualities common to everyone—sensations and senti- ments—which could serve as the foundation for a more "realistic" definition of the good life and a more "realistic" foundation for a good society.) *The Theory of Moral Sentiments,* despite its immense and radical revision of the classical-Christian tradition, was still linked to this tra- dition by its inability or unwillingness to "think economically," to re- gard the economic sphere of men's activity as autonomous.[11] It was with *The Wealth of Nations* that such a mode of thinking was introduced to the world.

Whether it was Adam Smith's intention to accomplish this is, as has been indicated, a question that evades an authoritative answer. It is not difficult to show the many continuities between *The Theory of Moral Sentiments* and *The Wealth of Nations,* and a determined, ingenious reading of both texts can even come up with a final and utter reconciliation of the two. The most powerful argument along these lines has been con- structed by Joseph Cropsey in his *Polity and Economy: An Interpretation of the Principles of Adam Smith.* Professor Cropsey insists that Adam Smith's writings do constitute a whole, that they proposed a "system of natural liberty" (to use Smith's term) which was quite different from later con- ceptions of "capitalism" (a term not yet invented). As Cropsey puts it: "Smith advocated capitalism because it makes freedom possible—not because it *is* freedom."[12] Which is to say: Smith was not a "libertarian" who saw the chief blessing of liberal capitalism as leaving everyone free to become prosperous as he saw fit, but rather defined freedom in a way that retained a firm connection with an idea of virtue to which the free individual submitted. The individual, free to "better his condition," was freed *from* various traditional tyrannies, large and petty, and was free *to* participate in a bourgeois way of life whose ethos and institutions were taken for granted.

It is always dangerous to disagree with Professor Cropsey, and his analysis is both detailed and powerful. Still, his argument convinces

---

[11]The attitude of the premodern world toward economics and economic thinking is delineated in M. I. Finley's *The Ancient Economy* (Berkeley: University of California Press, 1973).

[12]Joseph Cropsey, *Polity and Economy: An Interpretation of the Principles of Adam Smith* (The Hague: M. Nijhoff, 1957), p. x.

only during the reading of it, and when one turns back to the two texts themselves, one is struck by the differences as much as by the connections between them. The mainspring of human action in *The Wealth of Nations* is simply the "self-interest" of the individual, and a market economy is a "natural" way of serving the self-interestedness of individuals because there is "a certain propensity in human nature" to "truck, barter, and exchange one thing for another." True, there is mention of an "invisible hand," which ultimately reconciles the multiplicity of self-interests—but this famous phrase appears only once in *The Wealth of Nations,* and then in the hypothetical mood. And almost nothing is said, anywhere in the book, to suggest that there is such a thing as the "perfection of human nature," much less that such perfection is achieved through the flowering of our "benevolent affections." The tenor of *The Wealth of Nations* is such as to suggest that human beings are, by nature, little more than self-seeking, acquisitive creatures, but that it is nevertheless possible through statecraft—the creation of a market economy—to construct a humane and prosperous society. There is not the faintest suggestion that any kind of human "perfection" is likely to emerge through the workings of the market.

Yet Smith would hardly have recommended his "system of natural liberty" if he did not believe that humanity would be the better for it (not merely better *off*). One may surmise an assumption on his part that the incessant mutuality and interdependency of commercial transactions would themselves constantly refine and enlarge the individual's sense of his own self-interest, so that in the end the kind of commercial society that was envisaged would be a relatively decent community. Such self-interest "rightly understood" (to use Tocqueville's famous formulation) might even approximate, in its consequences, the results to be expected from the operation within each individual of a principle of benevolence.

In *The Wealth of Nations* Smith still firmly rejects the tradition of Calvin, Hobbes, and Mandeville. Man's "natural" instincts and man's reason, if given their freedom, will in the end lead to decent rather than to vicious behavior. In this sense, *The Wealth of Nations* is decidedly an "optimistic" book and was interpreted by Smith's contemporaries in this light. But such decent behavior, apparently, is something that appears *in the end,* not at the beginning—it is something man inevitably learns through the discipline of freedom in a free economy. Man could not learn it if his nature were such as to make such learning impossible. Smith never succumbs to the paradox of "private vices, public benefits," even though isolated sentences in *The Wealth of Nations,* quoted out of context, can make it seem as if he did. He expects men, in a free market society, to improve their spiritual as well as their material condition—to better themselves entirely. Only he does not expect them to become *much* better, and he does not think their betterment will occur automatically and easily. Though *The Wealth of Nations* is pungent and pointed in its criticisms of almost all interference with the workings of the free market, it is remarkably lacking in unconstrained enthusiasm for the world that the free market will create, or in joyful admiration for the kinds of people who will inhabit it.

One class of people for whom almost no enthusiasm of any kind, and almost no respect, is expressed is the businessman. He is presented as a scheming, conniving, self-seeking, soulless person, always looking for ways to conspire with other businessmen to defeat the workings of the free market and thereby to make illegitimate profits. In many references (which critics of capitalism are fond of quoting), the businessman is casually described as an incipient profiteer, that is, someone who, dissatisfied with the mutual, and inevitably limited, benefits that arise from the exchange of goods and services, seeks to achieve a one-sided advantage by "rigging" the market. (And joint-stock companies, the forerunners of the modern corporation, are even more harshly judged.) Almost nowhere in *The Wealth of Nations* does the upright, honest, public-spirited bourgeois businessman make an appearance. And yet, oddly enough, the contemporary readers of *The Wealth of Nations* seemed not to notice this fact and took it as a vindication of that very same bourgeois entrepreneur. Did they understand Smith better than we do? Did they read *The Wealth of Nations* in a larger context—of Smith's other writings, of his known opinions, of the shared assumptions of the time—that it is difficult for us, who read it as an isolated work in "economics," to discern? That is a possible explanation, in some ways a plausible one, but one cannot claim it is immediately convincing. Like all great books, *The Wealth of Nations* does not yield up its deepest meanings easily and unequivocally; that is why, again like all great books, it needs to be reread as much as read. What is fairly clear, however, is that the idea of business as a morally indifferent activity, an idea utterly alien to *The Theory of Moral Sentiments* but seemingly insinuated in *The Wealth of Nations,* was to have a profound and enduring influence on later economic thought.

There is another class of people who, in *The Wealth of Nations,* do not appear to good advantage: the factory workers. This is the result of the division of labor, about which the book is surprisingly ambivalent. For Smith the division of labor is practically identical with capitalism itself, and the absolute precondition of progress—economic progress, to begin with. It is the division of labor which makes possible the increase in productivity which, in turn, makes it possible for *everyone* in a capitalist society gradually to better his condition. As Smith puts it in Book I of *The Wealth of Nations:* "It is the great multiplication of the productions of all the different arts, in consequence of the division of labour, which occasions, in a well-governed society, that universal opulence which extends itself to the lowest ranks of the people." Moreover, it is this same division of labor which, by reason of the increase it engenders in the material well-being of all, is a necessary condition for the "refinement of manners" and general cultural elevation which make a free commercial society more "progressive" and more "civilized" than its predecessors, and which consequently make *all* of its citizens more fully "human" (as well as humane) than was ever the case previously.

So *The Wealth of Nations* has, unsurprisingly, many commendatory statements about the division of labor and its consequences. The economically progressive commercial society is described by Smith as "the cheerful and the hearty state to all the different orders of the society" (Bk. I). Yet in Book V there appears a now-famous passage which presents the division of labor in quite a different light.

> In the progress of the division of labour, the employment of the far greater part of those who live by labour, that is, of the great body of the people, comes to be confined to a few very simple operations, frequently to one or two. But the understandings of the greater part of men are necessarily formed by their ordinary employments. The man whose whole life is spent in performing a few simple operations, of which the effects are perhaps always the same, or very nearly the same, has no occasion to exert his understanding or to exercise his invention in finding out expedients for removing difficulties which never occur. He naturally loses, therefore, the habit of such exertion, and generally becomes as stupid and ignorant as it is possible for a human creature to become. The torpor of his mind renders him not only incapable of relishing or bearing a part in any rational conversation, but of conceiving any generous, noble, or tender sentiment, and consequently of forming any just judgment concerning many even of the ordinary duties of private life.

This has come to be known as the notorious "alienation" passage,[13] since many scholars read it as an anticipation of Karl Marx's indictment of capitalism in *Capital.* It is a passage that does indeed consort oddly with the generally laudatory observations on the division of labor that Smith makes elsewhere. True, one of the original features of *The Wealth of Nations* is its emphasis on the importance of education for all citizens,

---

[13]For an excellent discussion of this topic, see E. G. West, "The Political Economy of Alienation: Karl Marx and Adam Smith," in *Oxford Economic Papers* (March 1969).

and it is not unreasonable to understand him as saying that the stultify-
ing effects of the division of labor can be overcome by education, which
both prepares the worker for upward mobility toward less monotonous
work and provides him with the inner resources necessary to prevent
that monotony from dehumanizing him. It is also true that such a critical
attitude toward the division of labor in the factory was fairly widespread among Smith's contemporaries, even those who were all in favor
of capitalist economic development, and may be viewed simply as a species of "cultural lag." This state of mind, moreover, would have been
encouraged by the wave of romanticism then beginning to pervade all
of society, a kind of bourgeois nostalgia for aspects of prebourgeois life
that were perceptibly vanishing from the world.[14]

But whatever the explanation, the fact remains that there are in *The
Wealth of Nations* all kinds of crosscurrents and even countercurrents to
the dominant flow of the argument.[15] Adam Smith as a moral philosopher and Adam Smith as the father of modern economic analysis are
not easily reconciled to one another, though the ultimate possibility of
such reconciliation must never be excluded if only because Adam Smith
himself seemed to take that possibility for granted. These crosscurrents
and countercurrents within *The Wealth of Nations,* together with the strikingly different conceptions of human motivation in *The Theory of Moral
Sentiments* (with its emphasis on a benevolence derived from an innate
conscience) and in *The Wealth of Nations* (with its emphasis on the bourgeois individual as a self-interested and self-seeking creature), ensure
that the task of understanding Adam Smith will occupy scholars for a
long time to come.

Still, when all is said and done, one has to return to the dominant
meanings of *The Wealth of Nations* as these were perceived by Smith's contemporaries, on whom the book had such an immense influence. And
there is no doubt whatsoever that the book was read, or was interpreted
without having been read, as containing an essentially optimistic message about the human condition and the future of humanity under capitalism. A clear distinction was seen between bourgeois "acquisi-

---

[14]A rather ingenious explanation of Smith's attitude toward the division of labor,
to the effect that he saw it as elevating the level of civilization of society as a whole, while
excluding the lowest class of industrial worker—a minority in Smith's time, it must be
remembered—from participating in that general improvement, is to be found in Nathan
Rosenberg, "Adam Smith on the Division of Labour: Two Views or One?" *Economica* 32
(May 1965): 127–39.

[15]A provocative discussion of other such "contradictions" in *The Wealth of Nations*
may be found in Robert Heilbroner, "The Paradox of Progress: Decline and Decay in *The
Wealth of Nations,"Journal of the History of Ideas* 34, no. 2 (April–June, 1973). Mr. Heilbroner
sees the ideal world of Adam Smith as having implicit in it, not only moral decay, but
eventual economic stagnation.

tiveness" and prebourgeois "avarice," the latter representing a sterile hoarding of wealth, the former contributing to the general welfare by the reinvestment of accumulated capital. Commercial exchange in a bourgeois society, precisely because it was so common—with so many people competitively involved in it, and with all the information necessary for rational decisions easily available to all—would be exchange for mutual benefit. Both buyer and seller would profit, and the more nearly perfect the competition and the more comprehensive the marketplace, the greater would be the probability of both profiting equally. Profits in a bourgeois-commercial society, therefore, would be something qualitatively different from profits in a society where commerce was only a marginal activity, involving only a tiny minority of the population. In that prebourgeois state profits were not easily distinguishable from the fruits of profiteering, that is, an unequal transaction in which one party was at a clear advantage over the other and used this advantage to exploit the other. It was an indispensable premise of Adam Smith's espousal of capitalism that it of necessity created conditions in which such profiteering and exploitation would become ever more difficult.

Bourgeois acquisitiveness, therefore, was both natural and good, arising not from the desire to gain at someone else's loss but from "the desire of bettering our condition"—a desire that is universal—and in fact contributing to the improvement of *everyone's* condition. That this process of improvement might not lead to a greater overall equality of wealth was not taken to be a fact of much significance. What *was* significant was the fact that a general improvement in everyone's standard of living would inevitably lead to a greater equality in the *necessities of life*—food, shelter, clothing—since any rich person could consume only so much of these necessities and would then spend his money on "superfluities" (i.e., luxuries) or would simply reinvest it. As a Scotsman, Adam Smith had a scarcely concealed contempt for such superfluities and did not see why their unequal distribution should be a matter of concern to a thoughtful and reasonable man.

And, perhaps most important of all, *The Wealth of Nations* promised an economic system that not only made possible political and religious liberty for the individual; it made a fair degree of such liberty practically inevitable. An individual who possesses property, and has the right to augment this property as best he can, has the basic means to withstand the pressures of even the most autocratic government. If such property is divided very unequally, then it is only a relatively small proportion of the population that can set limits to the power of government. But these limits are nonetheless real, and if they benefit immediately only the small class of property owners, they offer a kind of protective umbrella under which everyone can, in an emergency, find protection. Moreover, if the free market operates as it is supposed to, with everyone gradually bettering his condition, an ever-larger percentage of the population will come to own property of one kind or another. This, in turn, will represent an immense diffusion of economic power that will make tyrannical government more difficult.

It used to be said in the Middle Ages that "city air makes men free." What generated this relatively free atmosphere was the fact that cities were centers of commercial activity, populated by bourgeoisie who had earned their wealth and property in the marketplace rather than holding it on the sufferance of lords or kings or churchmen. Modern capitalism universalizes this phenomenon; it urbanizes the world, both in fact and in principle. This is not to assert that a capitalist society is incompatible with, say, racial or religious discrimination, or even oppression. The history of Negro slavery in the United States shows otherwise. But it is instructive to note that, to achieve this effect, bourgeois society has to violate its own principles, that is, prohibit Negroes from owning and acquiring property, from becoming bourgeois, in other words. It also is possible that bourgeois society might discriminate against some of its own bourgeois citizens—blacks, or Jews, or Orientals. But so long as this discrimination only hinders their ability to better their condition, without stifling it completely, such disadvantaged groups can create their own "space" in which they live as free individuals. And in the end, all the inequalities of bourgeois society must yield to the great dissolvent, money, which knows nothing of race or religion or ideology.

*The Wealth of Nations,* and the spirit of capitalism which found such full-bodied expression in it, was not at all naive about the propensity of men to mistreat one another for ideological reasons. Memories of the bloody religious conflicts of the sixteenth and seventeenth centuries were still fresh in everyone's minds. What made capitalism so attractive was not merely its promise of gradually achieving "opulence" for all. Even more important was the hope it offered of "de-ideologizing" human relationships by emphasizing their purely economic aspect. Later generations were to see in this transformation a source of "alienation" of man from man, and of all men from their political or ideological community. (Adam Smith's near-contemporary, Jean-Jacques Rousseau, who anchored modern radicalism in a nostalgia for precapitalist modes of human association, perceived this process of alienation clearly enough. So, indeed, did the Catholic Church.) The accusation is not without substance: Bourgeois society does tend to make all human relations "thinner" and more abstract than is the case with a noncapitalist order. But what the objection failed to take into account—still fails to take into account—is the fact that this condition is merely the obverse of a society that permits greater individual liberty than history has ever known. There are no benefits without costs in human affairs (though there are frequently costs without benefits). Capitalism has its costs, but to hope to eliminate all of these costs while preserving all its benefits is surely a utopian fantasy. It was, however, precisely this utopian fantasy which was to enchant socialist thinkers in the nineteenth century.

Not only is there is an organic connection—a connection in both theory and fact—between modern capitalism and liberal society; such a connection is also to be found between modern capitalism and modern democracy, especially American democracy. For the American system of government is based on the same premises as Adam Smith's vision of capitalism, and, not accidentally, it reveals the same tensions and ambivalences. Though, in the abstract, capitalism may be regarded as one thing and democracy as another, *modern* democracy—a democracy in which the individual is actually encouraged to satisfy his desires and appetites, even as he multiplies them—is incomprehensible without its capitalist underpinnings.

One says *modern* democracy, with such emphasis, because it is a special and historically unique version of the idea of popular self-government. That idea, in premodern times, would have been called the "republican" idea, since the term "democracy" then meant no more than the rule of the majority (i.e., of the poor), which could easily be tyrannical. A "republic," on the other hand, was the political system appropriate to self-government by a citizenry. It envisaged a small, self-governing community, bound together by a powerful and automatically coercive consensus on religious and moral and political values—such a consensus being necessary to ensure that each individual, as he participated in the tasks of self-government, would place the interests of the community before his own. It was, by our lights, an "elitist" idea, available only to some fortunate people at some lucky historical moment. It is the kind of community envisaged by Rousseau in *The Social Contract*—a community so "virtuous" that the love of self need never be sacrificed to the "general will" since there is simply no disjunction between the two. The Greek city-states, at their peaks of excellence, were thought to represent this classical idea of democracy. In our own time, we can best get a sense of it by looking at the Israeli kibbutz: a voluntary "commune" that is a stable and enduring self-governing polity. Or one can see a grotesque parody of it in the theory and practice of "people's democracy" in Communist countries, where perpetual terror strives to achieve the pretense of such a voluntary and "virtuous" community. Indeed, the world today, as capitalism comes more and more to be regarded as a retrograde system of human relations, is constantly spawning farcical and vicious simulacra of the premodern democratic idea—"reigns of virtue" which are in actuality secular pseudotheocracies, but which claim nevertheless to be democratic in some abstruse metaphysical sense.

Modern democracy, as it emerges from the thinking of such men as Locke, Montesquieu, Adam Smith, and the Founding Fathers, is a popular government made safe for a liberal and commercial world. It does assume a moral-religious-political consensus, of course—there is no political community without consensus—but it is a "weak" consensus, extending not to the definition of happiness but rather to the means whereby government makes it possible for individuals to *seek* their happiness. A modern democracy, in their conception of it, can therefore be a heterogeneous society, a tolerant society, in short a liberal society—a government of laws, not of virtue. It is also inevitably a commercial society, since individuals in pursuit of happiness will surely seek to better their condition by engaging in commercial transactions with one another. Virtue, like religion, now becomes a private affair, to be achieved through institutions in the private sector—churches, the family, all kinds of voluntary associations. As concerns the public sector, the only virtue needed is a minimum of public-spiritedness, and this, fortunately, is provided by human nature itself. That minimum of public-spiritedness was thought to be sufficient to sustain the minimal government that was envisaged.

To twentieth-century eyes, the founders may seem to have had too low an appreciation of men's capacity to behave decently in government, and too high an estimate of the likelihood of their behaving well in what we now call the "private sector." Whether they were right or wrong about government is one of those questions of political philosophy which will doubtless be debated forever, with recurrent alternating cycles of faith in, and skepticism about, politics as a means to a better life. (In this respect, the future of political philosophy will be a recapitulation of its past.) But as to the private sector, it must be remembered that the Founding Fathers and Adam Smith were able to take certain important things for granted, and did take them for granted, in a way that we are not able to do. Above all, they were able to take for granted a *coherence* in the private sector achieved through the influence of organized religion, traditional moral values, and the family. To put it another way: Their confidence in the ability of men and women to live together socially and civilly under capitalism was not a fantasy; it was based on a realistic enough vision of the real world, as it then existed. But that was before the modern world was touched by the breezes of nineteenth-century rationalist doctrine, and devastated by the hurricanes of twentieth-century nihilism. If we today have less confidence in "natural" human sociableness, it is not because we see things as they are, while the founders were utopian, but rather because the preconditions of social life, which they imagined to be immutable, have turned out to be fragile. The climate of opinion has changed with the changes which have occurred in the capitalist world itself since their time.

From the point of view of *The Wealth of Nations,* the most relevant and significant of these changes involve capitalism's own conception of itself. Since the history of economic thought in the nineteenth and twentieth centuries is invariably written by scholars who are much interested in economics but little concerned with problems of political philosophy, this history is generally recounted as the "progress" (irregular, but inexorable) of man's ability to think "scientifically" about economic matters. The immense increase in that ability is indisputable. Whether it is such a pure gain, however, is not. Adam Smith, for one, while he would certainly have been appreciative of the technical virtuosity of later economic thought, would also have been perplexed by its moral implications. He would have been most perplexed by the blithe disregard by modern economics, in its eagerness to become a rigorous science, of the fact that any system of economic theory *must* have moral implications—must have, at its base, moral presuppositions and therefore must be a kind of moral philosophy as well as a purely economic one. The bland disregard of such presuppositions might well tempt one to describe the history of modern economics as chapters in the "degradation of the capitalist dogma."

The first great alteration in capitalist economic thought began shortly after Adam Smith's death, with the publication of Malthus's *An Essay on the Principle of Population* (1798). This inaugurated the era, which would last for more than a century, in which economics became the "dismal science." That conception of economics was so overwhelmingly popular among bourgeois theorists that one is likely to forget (as they did, for the most part) that in the founding text of capitalist economics, *The Wealth of Nations,* economics is not really a dismal science at all. True, it has its dismal aspects, in that it is alert to the human costs of a liberal capitalist society as well as to its economic benefits. But *The Wealth of Nations* was, overall, an optimistic book in that it expected those benefits to be substantial. Smith believed, as did the Founding Fathers, that in a liberal capitalist society *everyone* would gradually improve his condition. It was precisely this optimistic and reassuring message that permitted the proponents of capitalism in his time to advocate its cause in good conscience and in a cheerful spirit.

After Malthus, all this changed. Malthus proposed the thesis that, even though society as a whole would increase its wealth under capitalism, the laboring classes would not participate in this increase since, with the slightest improvement in their condition, their rate of population growth would quickly absorb and then outstrip the income available to them. In short, capitalism was an economic system in which the bourgeois minority would become ever more affluent while the laboring classes, the bulk of the population, were doomed to perpetual misery. A dismal teaching indeed! And a most curious one: It is difficult to think of a comparable social doctrine ever having achieved such widespread acceptance, a doctrine whose "iron laws" of wages and population doomed most of mankind to a living hell, without any credible promise of redemption in this world or the next. Presumably mankind was supposed to accept this doctrine in a spirit of resignation, simply because the authority of economic "science" said it had to. To the degree that capitalism in the nineteenth century acquired an ever more tarnished reputation, this new and revised vision of capitalist economic theory bore much of the responsibility.[16]

The oddity of this whole phenomenon has not been sufficiently explored by intellectual or social historians. Not merely the strangeness of defending an economic system with an argument from misery, but the paradox of learned men proposing such an argument in the face of overwhelming and obvious contrary evidence is extraordinary. The original edition of Malthus's work was published at a time when it was generally believed that Britain's population was declining, not rising, a belief Malthus himself did not challenge. Later editions, it is true, added more and more "empirical" material, but as often as not the empirical data worked against his thesis rather than for it.[17] Nevertheless, Malthus's work made an immediate and profound impression upon his contemporaries, and his thesis became the "conventional wisdom" of economic science for later generations. Indeed, these generations continued to subscribe to Malthusian doctrine in face of the fact that the

---

[16]It is true that Malthus later did suggest that, if the masses exercised rigorous sexual self-restraint, their condition was not utterly hopeless. The masses refused to get excited by such glad tidings.

[17]For a penetrating analysis of Malthus's weakness as an economic demographer, and his importance as an ideologist, see Gertrude Himmelfarb's essay in *Victorian Minds* (New York: Alfred A. Knopf, 1968).

condition of the laboring classes in the nineteenth century continued to improve, as Adam Smith had predicted. This improvement was irregular—in cyclical spurts, as it were—but obvious enough. Nevertheless, even in the United States, which Malthus had conceded might be an exceptional case, where the possibility of bettering one's condition was indubitably real, and where popular opinion reflected this reality, learned men continued to pay their respects (if less dogmatically than elsewhere) to Malthus's teaching.

It is a most curious episode in intellectual history, this sovereignty of the dismal science during the heyday of capitalist growth and expansion. In the end, of course, ideology caught up with reality, and economics became less ideologically pessimistic, more scientifically optimistic. But, as we shall see, the versions of this new optimism were associated with profound problems of their own. And in the meantime, the prevalence of Malthusianism left the intellectual and emotional arena open for a utopian philosophy of hope, that is, socialism.

As the popularity of Malthusianism gradually waned, it was replaced (or supplemented) by a new doctrine which, while not disputing the Malthusian essentials, nevertheless absorbed them into a more "affirmative" vision. One has to use quotation marks in this case because the affirmation was of a very peculiar kind indeed. Basing itself on the Darwinian conception of the survival of the fittest, it conceived of capitalism as the economic and social system that gave most perfect expression to the constant "war of all against all," which was presumably the foundation of all human societies. It was during this period—approximately 1880–1914, and most especially in the United States—that the idea of capitalism as a system of "free enterprise" was born, the term itself having a connotation of successful aggression on the part of those who aspired to the rank of the fittest to survive.

This conception of capitalism went back beyond Mandeville to Hobbes. Mandeville, after all, with his formula of "private vices, public benefits," did maintain a traditional moral distinction (however sophistical) between vice and virtue. Social Darwinism, resting itself squarely on a mechanistic rather than a teleological biology, dispensed with the moral dimension entirely. Society was merely the arena in which men exercised their "natural right" to self-preservation and survival. This was exactly Hobbes's idea, of course, but Hobbes understood that a society so conceived needed a powerful sovereign ("Leviathan") to keep the struggle among men within bounds, to prevent society from being permanently involved in civil strife and self-destruction. The Social Darwinists, in contrast, were individualists *à outrance,* believed in only a minimal state, and were utterly confident that they could persuade their fellow citizens, regardless of their degree of "fitness," to accept the "natural law" of Social Darwinism in the same calm way they accepted the law of gravitation. The smug arrogance behind this belief was of near-pathological dimensions, encouraging otherwise intelligent and worldly men to believe what a momentary accession of common sense would have shown to be absurd. In the event, of course, the majority who were "unfit" began to have an adverse opinion of capitalism, to see it as a "dog-eat-dog" system in which a few canines devoured all the rest.

And so, for more than a century after Adam Smith, the prevailing ideologies of capitalism were of a kind to be offensive and repugnant to the overwhelming majority of the citizenry of a capitalist society. Indeed, they affronted that basic human impulse which Smith saw as the cornerstone of his "system of natural liberty," namely, the desire of every man to better his condition, in terms of both material comfort and social esteem. Such a situation could not last: Whatever the "contradictions" of capitalism posited by socialists, they were of little weight when compared with *this* contradiction which capitalist ideologists imposed upon the system they were presumably defending. And it did not last. In the twentieth century there developed a new conception of capitalism which represented, in good part, a return to Adam Smith. It is this conception that is at the root of the modern science of economics, and it has become the "conventional wisdom" with which capitalism is defended today.

This new-old idea of capitalism, flowing from the development of marginal utility analysis in the last decades of the nineteenth century, once again sees the free market as a creative and benign institution. Through it, individuals may engage in transactions as a result of which *everyone* is better off than was previously the case. The free market, therefore, not only is a wealth-creating mechanism; it is also a wealth-distributing mechanism. The pattern of distribution might be unequal—a fact which provokes socialists to indignation—but that is regarded as less important than the fact that (1) everyone does benefit, even if unequally, and (2) inequalities are likely to be temporary, in the sense that different people, at different times, will be the beneficiaries of such inequality. This last point is of crucial significance. It means that capitalism, through the dynamics of a free market, does not give birth to any kind of permanent oligarchy which would subvert that "free society" which it is capitalism's ultimate purpose to create and sustain. The rich will always be with us, but in the course of several generations the old rich will gradually be superseded by the new rich, since the ability to respond to market opportunities is not—nor has anyone ever claimed it to be—an inherited human characteristic.

This conception of capitalism is today incorporated in the science of economics to such a degree that most economists cannot even see that it is there. The image of man—an isolated individual with a set of "preference schedules," a creature of appetite and of self-defined "wants"—seems so "natural" as also to appear self-evidently valid. And, indeed, there is a considerable degree of truth in it; otherwise, economic theory would not have the kind of explanatory and (to a lesser degree) predictive power which it unquestionably does have. Man in modern economic theory is congruent with man in modern capitalist society, an ultimate atom with measurable desires. The interaction of these desires in the marketplace can be given expression in sophisticated mathematical formulas, and criteria of economic efficiency can be devised to analyze whether or not the "system is working." The most popular of such criteria is the "Pareto maximization rule," which defines an efficient transaction as one in which someone is made better off without anyone else's being made worse off. The very idea behind such a criterion—that it is possible for people to better their condition without this being disadvantageous to others—certainly represents a reversion to the original optimistic Smithian notion of capitalism, after a century of neo-Malthusian and neo-Darwinian heterodoxy.

But it is a reversion that is a vulgarization, despite—or perhaps because of—the mathematical power which modern economic theory unquestionably possesses. The "economic man" of modern economics is not quite the same creature as the "bourgeois man" of *The Theory of Moral Sentiments* or even *The Wealth of Nations.* They do overlap, to be sure, but less than completely. Smith never did reduce man, as modern economic thought does, to the status of a naked individual who was the sum of his individual appetites. *That* kind of reductionism is necessary if one aims at the kind of mathematical precision and rigor which is the mark (and, in all fairness, the glory) of modern economics. But Smith's economic abstractions were of a more homely, less ambitious kind. In all of his writings, the human beings who are also economic men remain recognizably human and therefore remain recognizably social and political and moral beings as well. Economics, for Smith, was not a substitute for moral and political philosophy.

Because of this, Smith was able to speak to a central economic question about which modern economic theory is so strikingly impotent, that is, the *causes* of the "wealth of nations." He was able to address himself to this question for the same reason that modern economics cannot: The causes of economic prosperity are not themselves economic phenomena. They are rather "cultural" in the largest sense of that term, involving a sense of self, and of the relation between oneself and others, which in turn generates attitudes and practices that are favorable or inimical to economic growth. For the past twenty-five years economists have been trying to explain "economic development" in purely economic terms, for example, in terms of the intensity of capital investment or as a function of international economic relations. The results have been so pitiful, in their lack of explanatory power, that economists have been forced to conscript some noneconomic factors and try to convert them into economic quantities, for example, "human capital" defined in terms of the average years of schooling in the population. This has not helped much; the perspective is still too limited. Everyone, whether economist or not, is quite certain that if India or Peru were inhabited by Swiss and Dutchmen, they would be fairly prosperous countries, not poor ones. But this knowledge cannot be reduced to terms that fit into modern economic theory.

Adam Smith would not have been so baffled. His conception of economic theory was still sufficiently close to commonsense observations, and sufficiently distant from the often misplaced precision of modern economics, to take account of factors that were real enough even if difficult to define and quantify. He understood that men were not just producers and consumers, and that their religious and political traditions were bound to affect, in a powerful and pervasive way, their economic performance. This is not to say that religious or political traditions are necessarily to be judged by their economic consequences; such a judgment has to be philosophical, not economic. But it does mean that economic development—either of a nation, or a particular class of citizens within the nation—is to be understood within the perspective of a broad historical sociology, a humanistic historical sociology, rather than a narrow economic theory. In short, the "causes" of both prosperity and poverty are to be understood in terms of the consequences for economics of noneconomic behavior by individuals or their institutions, including the institution of government.

But even more important than an understanding of the causes of economic prosperity is an understanding of its *consequences.* Or, to put it in terms that would have been more congenial to Adam Smith, of its *purposes.* For Smith did not think it possible to talk about the best economy without reference to the character of the people who were the end result of the economic process. As Joseph Cropsey has written: "When authors like Adam Smith advocated policies and institutions that promoted production and accumulation, they did so because the wealth-giving institutions had salutary noneconomic consequences of the highest importance." And Professor Cropsey goes on to complain that "in one way or another contemporary welfare economics has substituted the economy for the polity."[18]

The complaint is worth paying close attention to. It directs itself to one of the most puzzling features of the modern world, the fact that as societies become more affluent as a result of adhering to Smithian economics, they seem to breed all sorts of new social pathologies and discontents, so that the Smithian conception of the best economy no longer seems to have any connection, in the minds of the citizenry, with a best polity. Crime and all kinds of delinquency increase with increasing prosperity. Alcoholism and drug addiction also increase. Civic-mindedness and public-spiritedness are corroded by cynicism. The pursuit of happiness no longer is organically related to the instinct to better one's condition by diligent application. And, ironically, it is among the children of the affluent especially that these two activities now are seen to be in radical opposition to one another.

In a bourgeois, affluent society, happiness comes to mean little more than the sovereignty of self-centered hedonism. The emphasis is on the pleasures of consumption rather than on the virtues of work. The ability to defer gratification, which is a prerequisite for a gradual bettering of one's condition, is scorned; "fly now, pay later" becomes, not merely an advertising slogan, but also a popular philosophy of life.[19] And in the realm of politics, a similar kind of debasement—as Adam Smith would certainly have termed it—takes place. The purpose of politics becomes the maximum gratification of desires and appetites, and the successful politician is one who panders most skillfully to this "revolution of rising expectations," a revolution which affluent capitalism itself generates and before which the politics of bourgeois democracy prostrates itself. Inevitably, the democratic state becomes ever more powerful, and more willing to supersede the processes of the free market, as it strives to satisfy these inflated demands of both the economy and the polity. Equally inevitably, since the demands *are* inflated, the democratic state fails in this effort, and it becomes possible for a great many people to think that a nondemocratic state might do better. It will not, of course; unreasonable demands are by definition insatiable. But it is true that the nondemocratic state will have the power to curb and repress these demands, where it cannot satisfy them, whereas the bour-

---

[18]Joseph Cropsey, "What Is Welfare Economics?" *Ethics* 65, no. 2 (January 1955): 122.

[19]See Daniel Bell, *The Cultural Contradictions of Capitalism* (New York: Basic Books, 1976).

geois-democratic state can rely only on the self-discipline of the individual, which affluent capitalism itself subverts.

Adam Smith did not foresee this situation. In part, this was because his conception of the nature of human nature, as expressed in *The Theory of Moral Sentiments,* reassured him that the bonds of social solidarity in a bourgeois community were too strong to be disrupted by the acquisitive instincts. In part, too, it was because, as a Scotsman in the last half of the eighteenth century, he took for granted the restraining influence of a set of institutions—organized religions, the family, the educational system—which did not otherwise much interest him. In this respect, he was of one mind with the Founding Fathers, who also took the "wholesome" influence of these institutions for granted, without devoting much thought to them. But what they took for granted has, in the twentieth century, become unsettled, controversial, ineffectual. Bourgeois affluence has "liberated" men (and women) from these wholesome influences and has thereby reopened all the large questions of moral and political philosophy that Adam Smith and the Founding Fathers thought had been definitively answered by "modernity" itself. Which is not to exclude the possibility that we may yet conclude that their vision of the best society and polity is, indeed, the best available one. Only we can no longer support this conclusion by a mere recapitulation of their reasoning.

To put it another way: Though Adam Smith and the Founding Fathers might well have the right answers, more or less—and the history of the twentieth century does not suggest that other, better answers are close at hand—it could be that they did not, from our point of view, ask the right questions. After two hundred years, their "system of natural liberty" has, by its very success, reopened fundamental questions as to the good life and the good society, and the meaning of life itself, which they felt no need to address themselves to. We, who are the beneficiaries of their vision, are also in a better position to appreciate the limits of their vision. But first we must understand that vision, fairly and comprehensively, that is, as they understood it. Then, and only then, will we be truly free to modify or supplement it. And we ought always to remember what it is so very easy to forget: This very freedom of ours is a legacy from them.

1976

# 13

# *Rationalism*
# *in Economics*

Ⓘ**T** is widely conceded that something like a "crisis in economic theory" exists, but there is vehement disagreement about the extent and nature of this crisis. The more established and distinguished leaders of the so-called neoclassical school—the dominant school for almost half a century now—would assert that the "crisis" is nothing more than the kind of muddle that all scientific disciplines intermittently flounder in, as they try to probe more deeply into the mysteries of natural processes. Other critics assert that all of Keynesian macroeconomics—or even the very idea of macroeconomics itself, in any precise meaning of that term—is now being called seriously into question. Still others insist that we shall get nowhere in our understanding of either macro or microeconomics until we go back to the kind of fundamental conception of economics to be found in the marginalist school (circa 1870–1910), or in the writings of Karl Marx, or Ricardo, or Adam Smith. There are even some (and they are increasingly numerous) who would go further back and reestablish economics as a subordinate branch of political philosophy—though these, being economists by profession, are likely to describe their venture as the latest version of a "new economics."

What is most interesting and surely most revealing about these varieties of dissidence is the prevalence of what might be called the "reformationist" impulse—the impulse to "go back" to some original and purer source of economic understanding that has been obscured by the intellectual aberrations of later times. Now, we are familiar with this impulse in the history of religion, where the spirit of innovation almost always takes the form of a return to original truths that the existing religious establishment has perverted beyond recognition. But one does not usually find such an impulse in the sciences: Physicists do not try to cope with the riddles of subatomic particles by restudying and reinterpreting the work of earlier scientists. Indeed, most scientists are extraordinarily and quite blissfully ignorant of the history of their disciplines—and, on the whole, properly so. For it is the distinctive characteristic of the modern scientist that he "stands on the shoulders" of his predecessors, and can therefore see further than they could. This is inevitably the case in any discipline where knowledge is, in some crucial sense, *cumulative,* and one might even say that it is only this feature of the discipline that gives it its standing as a *science,* as distinct from all other areas toward which the human mind directs the power of rational inquiry.

In the social sciences, it is now clear, the situation is radically different from that in the natural sciences. In sociology, for instance, after almost two centuries, there simply does not exist a body of knowledge that permits sociologists to talk with more authority about society than someone who may never have received sociological training. There have been great sociologists with most interesting *insights* into man's social life, and these insights are often embedded in a fertile conceptual schema. Anyone can read their works with profit. But these insights do not have the status of scientific truths, nor can they be assembled into a body of scientific knowledge, if only because they are (more often than not) in disagreement with one another. Today only Marxist sociologists still talk in grand terms of a "science of society," and that is because they are Marxists, not because they are sociologists.

Where does that leave economics, generally acknowledged to be the most "scientific" of all the social sciences? Well, economics is certainly in better shape than sociology, since the discipline does present a coherent body of theory about economic processes which, once mastered, does provide an "expertise" that a noneconomist will not possess. On the other hand, the existence of a crisis in economic theory is attested to by the fact that this body of *undisputed* theory is shrinking before our very eyes, not growing. More and more of the intellectual energy of economists, these days, goes into the *dis*establishment of what our university textbooks still proclaim with serene confidence. Almost everything—almost every concept, every theorem, every methodology—in economics today has become fair game for controversy.

Where will it all end? Short of the dismantling of economic science altogether, one may fairly assume. But there can be little doubt that economics is on its way to becoming a much more modest science and will experience the loss of its more grandiose scientific pretensions. Indeed, the reformationist impulses at work strongly suggest that it was the luxuriant growth of these pretensions over many decades which is at the root of the present crisis. Those pretensions accumulated under the influence of a spirit of rationalism—a belief that a comprehensive understanding of all human affairs (i.e., of ourselves) can be achieved through the same methods, and with the same degree of success, as our understanding of physical processes in nature. It is what Hayek calls "scientism." In this sense, rationalism may be defined as a case of elephantiasis of the spirit of rational inquiry—a spirit that is in itself, of course, always unobjectionable in principle. Or, if one wishes to be theological about it, one might say that rationalism in the social sciences is a case of *hubris,* or *superbia,* of affliction with the sin of pride. To the extent that current "revisionist" critiques of economic science take hold, economics will not become less scientific. Indeed, as it sheds what are now seen to be its pseudoscientific aspects, and its scope shrinks correspondingly, it will be more genuinely scientific. Only it will be more scientific about less of the human world.

What is economics about, anyway? That question is a lot less banal than it seems, for the ways in which we answer it will profoundly affect the methodologies thought to be appropriate for economists to use.

One famous answer to this question was provided by Sir Dennis H. Robertson who, responding to the query "What do economists economize?," replied: "Love." This answer contains a terribly important truth, as well as some unfortunate ambiguities.

Economics, as an intellectual discipline, emerges in the course of the seventeenth and eighteenth centuries as an aspect of that philosophical revolution which created a distinctly "modern" world. It is, to put it bluntly, a world in which the economizing of Love is, in certain circumstances, morally permissible, instead of being—as the traditional teachings of Christianity would have it—morally reprehensible.* It is

---

*In this respect the traditional teachings of Judaism differ radically from those of Christianity. While emphasizing the importance of "fairness" and "just conduct" in all commercial relations, Judaism never perceived commercial relations as being, in and of themselves, inimical to the moral and spiritual life. Jews could never accept Carlyle's definition of economics as a "pig philosophy," since they have always regarded commerce

a world in which the injunction "Thou shalt love they neighbor as thyself," while never repudiated, is interpreted as being inapplicable to commercial activities. This liberation from theological contempt of self-interest as a motive for human action is a precondition, not only of a capitalist economy, but also of a liberal society and a liberal polity, as a reading of *The Federalist Papers* makes plain. It is *the* essential aspect of the process which sociologists call "modernization." Just how this process worked itself out, prior to the publication of *The Wealth of Nations*—how religion and the social ethos came to reconcile themselves to a commercial civilization—is still a matter of scholarly controversy (revolving mainly around Max Weber's conception of "the Protestant ethic"), but the results are clear enough: The Western world had ceased to be hostile—or at least had become much less hostile—to commercial transactions between consenting adults.

The significance and originality of Adam Smith's *Wealth of Nations* is that it offered a reasoned explanation of why the proliferation of such transactions was morally defensible. It was a very simple yet powerful explanation, its essential thesis being that the individual's pursuit of self-interest in the marketplace produces unintended consequences that are, on the whole and over time, beneficial to everyone. This is where the analogy of the "invisible hand" comes in—a literary analogy, not a kind of "mystical faith," as some critics claim. Smith perceived in the seeming chaos of the marketplace an always-emerging spontaneous order, an order generated through self-correcting actions (what we now call "feedbacks") by the participants. The net result of such action and reaction is that *everyone* ends up in a more "opulent" condition (to use Smith's own term). For the first time in the history of the human race it became possible to conceive of material progress, in which everyone improved his condition, however unequally or tardily, as a reality rather than a wish-fulfilling fantasy.

Smith's original insight that commercial relations are such that, as in the cosmos itself, the seemingly inchoate flux of phenomena and events can be explained in terms of an orderly disorder (so to speak)—that is the rock upon which economics is built. We might, without too much strain, call it the Law of the Conservation of Eco-

---

and business as perfectly kosher activities. The famous Talmudic statement of Rabbi Hillel goes: "If I am not for myself, who will be for me? If I am only for myself, what am I?" Christianity tries to ignore the first question and directs its attention exclusively to the second, so that the "self-interest" which is a source of moral (or a least morally neutral) activity in Judaism is never that for Christianity. It is reasonable to think that this initial predisposition in Judaism has something to do with the relative economic success of Jews in capitalist societies. It also helps explain why so many Christian thinkers have felt, intuitively, that there was something peculiarly "Jewish" about capitalism.

nomic Energy. It is an easy principle to learn, much less easy to keep steadily in mind, as any teacher of economics—or an economic advisor to politicians—soon discovers. Most of the serious errors in economic policy committed by governments throughout the ages, and most of the layman's errors in thinking about economic affairs, flow from a failure (sometimes useful, often not) to consider the second-order or third-order effects of policies over time. (Wage, price, and rent controls are the most obvious examples.) Prior to Adam Smith, it was not at all clear that there were such effects, or that they could be discerned by coherent reasoning. The relations between such interacting phenomena as supply and demand can today quickly become the intellectual property of any high school student, and in this respect he does indeed stand on the shoulders of Adam Smith (and therefore need never read him). Without such intellectual guidance, our understanding of economic affairs would be overpowered by emotional anthropomorphism (e.g., blaming high prices on wicked merchants), as has been true throughout most of human history, and as is still true for some of us all of the time and most of us some of the time.

That there are some psychological assumptions beneath this analysis of human behavior in the marketplace, and of the rationality of economic phenomena, is clear enough. Smith took it for granted that the human beings he was talking about were at least as much (or almost as much) interested in improving their material condition as in saving their souls—and much more interested in improving their material condition than in saving other people's souls. He also assumed, not that these people were always and everywhere utterly rational, but merely that they were rational enough to adapt their economic behavior to what they learned from economic experience—for example, to lower prices when demand falls, to raise them when demand increases. These are the distinguishing features of the so-called "economic man"—the kind of man who makes a market economy work. If you have a civilization where the people are convinced that it is hopeless to try to improve their material condition, or where the desire to improve their material condition is radically subordinated to other goals, or where the populace is coerced into such subordination, Adam Smith is of little use to you, since people's behavior in the marketplace will not then be "rational" in the sense that makes economic theory possible.

There are two important points to make about the economic man of capitalism, as Adam Smith conceived of him. First, he was never thought to be a whole man, only a man-in-the-marketplace. Smith never celebrated self-interest per se as a human motive, he merely pointed to its utility in a population that wished to improve its condition. (That he also believed this a normal and near-universal human desire, in all societies above the primitive level, is hardly to be taken as some kind of idiosyncrasy on his part.) Smith's larger view of human nature, as expressed in *The Theory of Moral Sentiments*, was basically that of the eighteenth-century Sentimental School, a secularized version of the Christian outlook which rooted its perspective in psychology rather than theology, and which proclaimed "sympathy" to be as natural a human instinct as self-interest, and on the whole more powerful. Insofar as morality was concerned, he had little trouble with the received code of the Judeo-Christian tradition.

The second point has to do with the relation of economic man to economic theory. Economic theory concerns itself with the interaction of economic men in a marketplace. *There is no noncapitalist economic theory.* * It is no accident that Aristotle did not write a book on classical economic theory, or St. Thomas on Christian economic theory, or Marx on socialist economic theory. In all of their ideal societies, there was surely a place for economic *wisdom*—the prudential management, based on experience, of economic affairs. But to have an economic theory, you need a market economy—just as, to have a scientific theory in physics, you need a universe in which order is always being created through action and reaction, not a universe where God prudentially manages all physical events.

It follows that people who, for whatever reason, dislike a commercial civilization will be utterly dissatisfied with what we now regard as traditional economic theory. And if such a person is an economist, he will invent a "new economics" that, while it may appeal to some economist forefathers (e.g., Marx or even Ricardo), frequently turns out to be in fact little more than a version of precapitalist thinking about economics, parading about in modern economic guise.

After Adam Smith, up to our day, the history of economic thought is the story of how economists went about making economics a more rigorously analytical science. Smith was a primitive Newtonian, one might say, in his conception of market phenomena as an aspect of human relations that possessed an inherent order, behind the apparent disorderliness. But he meant little more by this than that economic phenomena—that is, man's economic activities—are interrelated in such a

*Socialism, in its ideal state, is a political community "in which, while no one is poor, no one desires to be richer" (John Stuart Mill). In such a community, what we have ever since Adam Smith called economic theory is superfluous. One might even say that the goal of socialism is to make economic theory superfluous.

way that they can therefore be rationally explained. His successors, influenced by the success and prestige of the natural sciences, were understandably prompted to move on from there and try to structure such explanations as "objective laws" of the economic universe, laws most perfectly expressed when they could achieve a precise mathematical form.

In contrast to later economics, *The Wealth of Nations* is unabashedly "humanistic." Its vision of an economic universe is "Newtonian" only analogically and qualitatively, with no pretensions to quantitative precision. All of its economic causes and economic effects are purposive human actions and reactions that we, who are accustomed to self-interested activity in the marketplace, find utterly plausible. The aim of post-Smithian economics is gradually to rid the economic universe of purposive human activity altogether—to make this economic universe an abstract model of reality in the same way that physicists create an abstract model of physical reality, and from this model, based on the fewest possible axioms, deduce "laws" that "govern" the actual world we inhabit. One of the axioms of any such model is that economic *growth* is in principle no different from physical *change*. The economic perspective can now provide a series of static "snapshots" of a universe-in-change, not a discursive description of a dynamic marketplace in which men learn, innovate, and generate economic growth. Economic *states* become the focus of analysis as contrasted with the economic *process* that Smith rather casually (though brilliantly) analyzed. Inevitably, the question of the distribution of income among abstract "factors of production" achieves preeminence over the issue of economic growth, the ceaseless striving of human beings in the marketplace to "better their condition."

Along with this change in perspective, the whole climate of economic discussion moved from a buoyant optimism to a quite chilling pessimism. Malthus, of course, with his "law of population," took the first step in this direction, followed by Ricardo with his several "laws," so that by the mid-nineteenth century, economics was generally perceived, by both economists and laymen alike, as that science which discovered the "iron laws" that ruled the economic universe. Smith's "open" economic universe—one vast marketplace—was now replaced by a closed universe in which human activity could no more affect the governing laws than the activity of an atom could affect the laws of physics. Economics, which had breathed an expansive spirit in *The Wealth of Nations,* now seemed eager to inform people that the economic universe was frigid, deterministic, indifferent to human aspirations. It was, in fact, the Newtonian universe without God as creator, sustainer, or redeemer—and just as a vision of such a universe horrified Pascal, so economic science, up to and through John Stuart Mill, was perceived by people of religious or literary sensibility as a kind of enemy to humanity. There can be little doubt that this evolution of economic thought, under the influence of "scientism," did much to encourage socialist idealism, with its utopian goal of abolishing economic man altogether. By destroying the axioms of economic science, humanity would be liberated from its cold conclusions.

But it was not socialism that liberated humanity from the dismal science; it was the further evolution of that economic science itself. The "marginalist revolution" after 1870 directed attention away from the forbidding macro-model of the economic universe to a new complex model of the marketplace itself. The focus was now on satisfying the wants and desires of the individual-as-consumer—and this included producers as well, who "consumed" the factors of production—and on the way in which a utilitarian calculus, governing the individual's rational choices, caused a constant process of price adjustments, under circumstances of "perfect competition." This process pointed in turn to an ideal condition of "equilibrium," in which available resources are mobilized so as best to satisfy wants (expressed in money prices). What young European socialists today scornfully dismiss as the "pseudohappiness" of "the consumption society" became the substance of economics.

Moreover, this utilitarian calculus, given a few additional, simple axioms about the rationality of economic man—for example, transitivity of preferences, so that if you preferred A to B, and B to C, you then preferred A to C—permitted the economist to apply mathematics as both an analytic and a descriptive tool in his work, so that economics achieved an intellectual rigor that soon made it the envy of the other social sciences. In addition, this mathematicization of human choice, it became apparent, offered the possibility of explaining individual human behavior in general, not merely in the marketplace, so that "the economic point of view" was applied to all sorts of social and political processes or phenomena. The philosophy of this intellectual enterprise achieved its *summa* in the work of Lionel Robbins, *An Essay on the Nature and Significance of Economic Science* (1935). Economics is now defined as the rational allocation of scarce resources, and the economist is engaged in studying "the logic of choice" so as to come up with a "maximizing" strategy. It is this conception of economics that is today dominant in our textbooks.

The "Keynesian revolution" did not affect this basic conception of economics,* which is still today's orthodoxy in what is called "micro-economics." Keynes' originality lay in taking "wage stickiness" (the reluctance of the price of labor to fall when unemployment is widespread) as a permanent fact of a modern economy, and in further arguing that a money-and-credit economy was capable of giving false price signals to the businessman and the policymaker, resulting in a "general glut," or depression. This matter of a general glut has perplexed economists from the beginning, since in traditional economics—which gave no independent power to money or credit, and regarded all markets as essentially barter markets, "veiled over" by money prices—it was theoretically impossible. Keynes devised an explanation in terms of macro-aggregates which could interact in such a way as to achieve an equilibrium at a depressed level. The later incorporation of Keynesian insights into an elaborate, highly mathematical econometrics, in which elaborate correlations were sought among the macroeconomic aggregates, might well have dismayed him. But as the "neoclassical synthesis" emerged after World War II, this is the path that macroeconomics took, ending up in those "black boxes" attached to computers, which presumed to "model" the economy and predict its course. The very existence of an official governmental body called the Council of Economic Advisors would have been unthinkable and pointless without a high degree of faith in such a methodology.

The evident inadequacies of economic theory, most glaringly revealed in the policies derived from such theory, over the past fifteen years have given rise to much dissent within the profession. Three major dissenting movements have arisen. They are, reading from the ideological Right to the ideological Left: (1) the "neo-Austrian" school; (2) the "post-Keynesian" school; and (3) "radical-humanistic" economics.†

These dissenting movements have quite a bit in common. To begin with, they all reject conventional Keynesian macroeconomics in its

---

*Keynes himself, however, following Marshall, was highly skeptical of the mathematicization of economics: "Unlike physics, for example, such parts of the bare bones of economics as are expressible in mathematical form are extremely easy compared with the economic interpretation of the complex and incompletely known facts of experience, and lead one but a very little way towards establishing useful results." It is perhaps worth pointing out that some of the "mathematical economics" used by business management (e.g., linear programming for inventory control) represent instances of applied mathematics that have no organic connection with economic theory.

†It is fair in this connection to ignore the resurgence, among young economists, of an interest in Marxist economics. This belongs to the history of Marxism, not the history of economics. Its purpose is to validate Marxism as a world view, not to explain actual economic phenomena.

present form, and they do so on similar grounds. Essentially they argue that the prevalent econometric models of the economy are, in whole or in part, "scientistic" simplifications of economic reality that mislead rather than illuminate. Such "static" models are deficient in that their basic axiom of *ceteris paribus*—"other things being equal"—can never apply to the world of human action, human innovation, human willfulness, all of which can revise or upset previously established relationships and correlations that the economic theorist has come to take for granted. These models, so far from being truly scientific, are but a form of mathematical mimicry of the physical sciences, inappropriate for the understanding of human activity.

Emile Grunberg has made this point forcefully in his contrast between the subject matter of economics on the one hand, and the subject matter of the physical and biological sciences on the other.* Economics deals with "open systems," while the physical sciences deal with "closed systems." In an open system there are no real constants, no invariant relations, since everything is influenced, in no clearly determinate way, by everything else. A closed system is one in which certain relations are so much stronger than others that these others can be pretty much ignored. The solar system is an example of such a closed system, with the relations among the planets so much more powerful than relations between the solar system itself and the rest of the galaxy (or cosmos) that, whenever we analyze the solar system, we can dismiss these latter relations to the limbo where "other things are equal." Because the economic universe has no such closed systems, precise predictions of future economic states are impossible. What economic analysis does allow us to forecast—and it is no small thing—is the *general* consequences of current economic processes and policies, but with no exact time-coefficient or exact measurement of those consequences attached to such forecasts.

Where neo-Austrians and post-Keynesians disagree sharply is in their attitudes toward economic aggregates *tout simple*. The post-Keynesians believe that "dynamic models" based on such aggregates are possible, and would be of sufficient theoretical power to permit the economy as a whole to be "planned" and "managed" by (the right kind of) political economists. The neo-Austrians are, at the very least, highly skeptical of the meaningfulness of macroeconomic aggregates altogether, since their perspective on economic activity ("radical subjectivism") is one that distrusts all economic statements that do not refer

*Emile Grunberg, " 'Complexity' and 'Open Systems' in Economic Discourse," *Journal of Economic Issues* (September 1978).

to something that is occurring in the minds of, and affecting the intentions and plans of, actual human actors.

Both post-Keynesians and neo-Austrians also reject, though in very different ways and again for very different reasons, the conventional, abstract models of the microeconomic universe—one in which there is "perfect competition" between profit-maximizing units which confront scarce resources and make rational, allocative decisions. For the post-Keynesians, the Smithian free market has been completely replaced by corporate and trade-union oligopolies, so that the textbook views of "competition" are little more than anachronistic myths, which constitute a form of capitalist ideology. They therefore see the need for economic planning—with wage and price controls, and so forth—to give the market the coherence that economic teaching assumed it had (or still pretends it has).

The neo-Austrian critique of textbook microeconomics is more fundamental and more interesting. Its vision of the marketplace is not so much consumer-oriented as entrepreneur-oriented, and it gives the innovative entrepreneur a creative and dynamic role—someone who takes advantage of generally unperceived opportunities, rather than someone who, by referring back to a utilitarian calculus, maximizes satisfaction by choosing among known alternatives. Those opportunities are found—it is inappropriate to say they "exist"—because competition is indeed always and inherently *im*perfect. The kind of "perfect" competition that permits of mathematical treatment assumes that something called "equilibrium" is achieved by virtue of every person in the market knowing every other person's intentions (and his own as well, of course), so that a complete coordination of these plans ensues. For the neo-Austrians the market is not a series of equations but an actual *marketplace*—where no one knows beforehand what goods are "scarce," or even what goods are "good"; only experience in the marketplace teaches us that. In the same way, it is only in the course of human participation in the marketplace that we can know what "capital" or "resources" are. To think of their existing outside human intention or human ingenuity is to commit the sin of what Marx (after Hegel) called "reification"—taking abstract concepts for real entities. It is only in the marketplace that we discover the meaning of such concepts, just as it is only *im*perfect competition and *dis*equilibrium that permits the marketplace to function at all. It functions, not as a *mechanism,* but more like a self-correcting, perpetually learning *organism.* The order that emerges from the marketplace is part of a process of growth, not a state—a process of incessant adjustment and readjustment of plans, intentions, and expectations.

It should be noted, however, that though both post-Keynesians and neo-Austrians are highly critical of the scientistic pretensions of modern economics, each is in its own way thoroughly rationalist. The post-Keynesians might wish to replace the Newtonian-clockwork model by something they call a "cybernetic" model, which may be an improvement (if it could ever be devised), but a shift from mechanical statics to sophisticated mechanical dynamics is no radical conceptual revolution. Basically, post-Keynesians still see the economy as a system organized as natural systems are organized, one whose governing laws can be discerned by economists, who in turn therewith earn the credentials for operating this system in a rational (least-cost, most-benefit) way.

And neo-Austrians, too, are wedded to a rationalist view of the economic universe—though, once again, it is a more interesting version of rationalism. Their rationalism is located within the individual himself, not within something called "the economy." Their "methodological individualism" in economic reasoning is based on "the self-evident proposition, fully, clearly, and necessarily present in every human mind" (von Mises) that man acts purposefully, learns from such action, and that any existential disparity between intent and result flows from an error of knowledge. These purposeful actions, of course, flow from "self-interest," defined as whatever it is the individual is interested in. To the objection, "And what if the individual is not interested in improving his condition in the marketplace?" the reply is that this is the nature of human nature, and only the mentally ill would think or believe otherwise.

The neo-Austrians really are so much the true heirs of the eighteenth-century Anglo-Scottish liberal Enlightenment that one member of the school has actually written: "Modern Austrian economists view capitalism as the only social system compatible with the nature of man." What this means for the history of the human race is left unexplained—but, then, neo-Austrians are not much interested in history (or religion, or politics). The critiques leveled by neo-Austrians against the scientism that began to envelop economic theory after Adam Smith are often very trenchant. Their great merit is that they perceive Economic Man to be a willing, striving, learning human being, not a manipulable mathematical abstraction. Their limitation derives from their tendency to reduce human beings to Economic Men.

No such limitation is to be found among dissident "radical economists," for whom economic man is a modern, monstrous invention, and whose postmodern economics can best be understood as an effort to reestablish the premodern sovereignty of political, moral, and religious values over economic life. Since most of these economists have never studied premodern thought, they are content to think of their efforts at "reformation" as being definitely "progressive."

A particularly interesting specimen of this genre, recently published, is a textbook called *The Challenge of Humanistic Economics,* by Mark A. Lutz and Kenneth Lux. It is in many ways a most attractive book—high-spirited, well-written, cogently argued. Its most important service is to bring to the fore some serious criticisms of conventional economic analysis which have been for the most part blandly ignored. Some of these criticisms overlap with both the post-Keynesians' and neo-Austrians'—for example, the "tyranny of the correlation." This refers to all of these research efforts in which the most sophisticated mathematics "teases out" one correlation or another without ever attaining the kind of causal explanations that the physical sciences insist on. Thus, biochemists find a very strong correlation between smoking and lung cancer, so strong as to imply causality; but they will never rest until they have substituted a causal explanation for this correlation. In economics, the correlations are rarely so strong—they are, indeed, often merely the temporary fruits of research, soon subverted by further research—and anything resembling a satisfactory causal explanation is a rare event. Indeed, there are some economists who, misunderstanding the nature of the physical sciences, insist—in the name of something called "positive economics"—that correlations can substitute for causal explanations, so long as these correlations permit precise predictions of economic phenomena. But there are very, very few correlations—some scholars would say there are none—that permit any such predictions in economics.

But some of the criticisms of Lutz and Lux are far more radical in the sense of challenging prevailing economic concepts that most economists would regard as absolutely essential to their professional equipment. The transitivity of individual preferences in the marketplace, a sign of the "rationality" of individual choice, is one such concept. It is, the authors point out, a dubious concept when applied to commodities which, from a consumer's point of view, have more than one dimension of utility or satisfaction. Thus, homes and automobiles not only have use-value, they also have status-value. In a sense, therefore, these are all-in-one multiple commodities, and the "indifference curves" on which the economist tries to locate preferences for such commodities become quite meaningless—one never knows what the choice signifies, or what satisfactions are being maximized. True, this dilemma can be avoided by appealing to something called "revealed preference" theory, which asserts that any actual purchase, by definition, maximizes satisfaction and is therefore rational. But this is Hegelian metaphysics, or market research; it is not economic theory. It offers no intellectual guide to understanding, explanation, or prediction.

Similarly, they point out that the "Pareto optimum"—surely one of the key concepts in "welfare economics"—is a rather defective guide for anyone concerned with the general welfare, as this is commonly understood. That concept decrees that an economic condition is at its optimum if no change is possible which increases someone's welfare without decreasing someone (or everyone) else's. But this means that, if the rich get richer while the poor get no poorer, a Pareto improvement has occurred. In effect, as Messrs. Lutz and Lux emphasize, this also means that there is a different Pareto optimum for every initial distribution of income—this latter being a subject about which economists qua economists have nothing to say, since it is history, not economics, that determines any such initial distribution. But such a version of welfare economics profoundly violates our commonsense understanding of what welfare economics is supposed to be about. Some welfare economists do try to "correct" this situation by reverting to interpersonal comparisons of individual utility, according to which a marginal increase in the income of the rich represents less "satisfaction" than a comparable marginal increase to the income of the poor. This *does* correspond roughly to commonsense understanding—but all such interpersonal comparisons of utility have no scientific basis in economic theory, and we have to import a philosophical-egalitarian bias into economics to legitimate them. The sad truth is that economics today has become so rigorously "scientific" that the idea of "economic welfare," which Adam Smith thought we all understood well enough, has become vague, ambiguous, even protean.

But, having made a forceful critique of the efforts of contemporary economic theory to reduce human experience—collective and individual—to rationalist-utilitarian premises, Messrs. Lutz and Lux then proceed toward the opposite extreme, and try to base economic theory on rationalist-*utopian* premises. Theirs is a Platonic economics, but bereft of Platonic political wisdom. Plato (and Aristotle too, for that matter) would have agreed that "economics as a science should promote human welfare by recognizing and integrating the full range of basic human values." But the inference to be drawn from that proposition would have been evident to them: Economics is a subordinate branch of political philosophy, not an autonomous intellectual discipline. For economics as a distinctive mode of intellectual inquiry into human affairs can exist only to the extent that it does *not* recognize and integrate the full range of basic human values.

There is a powerful moral impulse behind the new radical economics, and an equally powerful moral revulsion against contemporary capitalist society and the kind of economic theory it produces. The radical economists point out, for instance, that if one performed an economic analysis of a prison or a concentration camp, one would never know, from a reading of that analysis, that it *was* a prison or a concentration camp. In short, economics tells you nothing about the moral and human quality of the "universe" it knows how to explain. Most economists would agree that this is so, but would point out that there are other forms of human inquiry—political philosophy, moral philosophy, theology—whose task it is to deal with such "normative" issues. The trouble with this rejoinder is that political philosophy and even moral philosophy have themselves, as academic disciplines, in recent decades become transformed into positivistic, "value-free," sciences, while theology has practically ceased to be a respectable form of intellectual activity. So the young economist with moral passions, having nowhere to go, turns upon economics itself and proceeds to devour its substance.

Above all, what radical economics attacks is the basic idea that self-interest, the key human motive in economics, is an inexpungible aspect of human nature—not necessarily to be admired, but always to be respected and ultimately to be channeled into constructive (or at least harmless) activity. Once you deny this premise, it is easy to dissolve economics into moral and political philosophy. The tactic used by Lutz and Lux is derived from the psychological theories of the late Abraham Maslow, who posited a universal hierarchy of natural human needs—not subjective wants, but objective needs—and perceived human development as a progressive process of "self-actualization," whereby human beings become "mature" and most "human" as they subordinate their particular selfish "wants" to deeper "needs" whose satisfaction produces a community of autonomous—but no longer self-regarding—persons.

Maslow's distinction between wants and needs—a distinction which no mere economist is in a position to make—frees economics from the tyranny of the consumer and gives it refuge under the benign sovereignty of the philosopher-king, now transmuted into a "humanistic economist." As Lutz and Lux put it:

> Humanistic economics is a scientific framework for the theoretical understanding of, *as well as the design of appropriate institutional arrangements pertaining to,* the processes of production, distribution, and consumption that will enable optimal satisfaction of the hierarchy of human needs. (Emphasis added.)

The Maslovian distinction between wants and needs is little more than a secularized and pseudoscientific version of the ancient distinction between our "higher" and "lower" selves—a distinction that is at the core of both classical philosophy and the Judeo-Christian moral tradition. It is a distinction that Adam Smith, author of *The Theory of Moral Sentiments,* would never have dreamed of repudiating. Nor would Ricardo, Malthus, Mill, Jevons, Walras, or Keynes. What they would have said (and did say) is that such a distinction is outside the scope of economics, which deals only with the "wants" of our "lower selves." The assumption of those economists was that it was utterly utopian to think that these lower parts of ourselves could ever be successfully repressed, or completely transcended, or utterly nullified, and that the virtue of free commercial transactions between consenting adults was that it willy-nilly directed our self-interested impulses toward a simple (but limited) common good: the general improvement of humanity's material condition. As for the preservation and cultivation of our "higher selves," economics leaves that to philosophy and religion.

The vision of radical economics today is that of a democratic equalitarian community in which individual self-interest would be rendered a negligible force through education, peer-group pressure, community festivals, and a constant flow of elevating rhetoric. It is a romantic-utopian vision in its substance, though scrupulously secular-rationalist in its articulation. It is, in truth, utopian socialism in modern academic dress. That it should find expression within the economics profession itself, instead of inciting a mass exodus from that profession, is but one more testimonial to the intellectual confusion of our age.

So economics today does seem to be at something like an impasse. The dominant scientistic model tends to drift ever further away from economic reality, so that inferences for economic policy are ever more ambiguous and baffling. But the three main schools of thought that have arisen through dissociation from this excessively rationalistic model are themselves infused with varieties of rationalism that lead to their own kinds of impasses. Their criticisms of the status quo in economic theory are often well-taken, but the alternatives they propose are unconvincing. There is not the slightest reason to think—and many reasons to doubt—that post-Keynesians, fiddling with their cybernetic model, can do any better than Keynesians with their Newtonian-mechanical model. The neo-Austrians end up insisting that the best of all possible worlds would be one populated by rationalist-utilitarian individuals whose pursuit of self-interest (as defined by the individuals themselves) would be left undisturbed by state or church or whatever—an anarchical (or libertarian) world that is, in its own way, a construct of a rationalist-utopian vision. And the radical economists have, as counterpart, their own rationalist-utopian dream of a world in which individuals have so transcended their self-interested inclinations that economics itself has vanished along with its detestable incarnation, the marketplace. It is a fair judgment that common to all three of these ways of thought is the impassioned hope (1) that economic theory can give us a more absolute understanding of reality than it possibly can, and/or (2) that economic reality can give us more by way of human "fulfillment" and happiness than *it* possibly can.

And yet economic theory lives on, surviving all the unreasonable or suprareasonable demands that are made on it. It survives because of that bedrock of truths about the human condition that were first comprehensively enunciated in *The Wealth of Nations.* Among these truths are: (1) The overwhelming majority of men and women are naturally and incorrigibly interested in improving their material conditions; (2) efforts to repress this natural desire lead only to coercive and impoverished polities; (3) when this natural desire is given sufficient latitude so that commercial transactions are not discouraged, economic growth does take place; (4) as a result of such growth, everyone does eventually indeed improve his condition, however unequally in extent or time; (5) such economic growth results in a huge expansion of the property-owning middle classes—a necessary (though not sufficient) condition for a liberal society in which individual rights are respected.

This is not all we need to know, but it is what we do know, and it is surely not asking too much of economic theory that in its passion for sophisticated methodology it not leave this knowledge behind.

1980

# 14

## Some Personal Reflections on Economic Well-Being and Income Distribution

IT is my understanding, from surveying various studies of trends in income distribution in the United States over the past three decades, that economists have found very little significant change to have taken place. There does seem to have been a slight increase in the proportion of national income received by the very poor, a slight decrease in the proportion received by the very rich. What goes on in between is such a complex muddle that economic analysis can tease few unquestionable inferences from the data. Moreover, the very methodology of studying income distribution has, over these decades, become ever more controversial. Just what is to be included in the concept of "income" becomes less clear every time a new governmental "entitlement" program is launched (whether it involves food, housing, medicine, or whatever). And it has become ever more apparent that in order to take account of normal age differentials in earnings, of changing demographies, and of economic mobility (both up and down), the distribution of "lifetime earnings" would give us a far more valid report than any cross-sectional survey at a moment in time. The trouble is that economists have not come up with any accepted procedure for measuring any such distribution of lifetime earnings, and there are even some grounds for thinking they never will.

Does it matter? What, precisely, is the point of all of these studies and of the interminable controversies they generate?

When one raises this issue among economists, one discovers that they tend to feel that, in some way or other, income inequalities *ought* to have a significant relation to other larger issues such as the rate of economic growth, economic stability or instability, social and historical stability or instability, or even that sense of well-being we vaguely call "happiness" or "contentment." And yet it is astonishing how little by way of any such relationships economic and social research has come up with. Increases and decreases in income inequalities, as convention-ally measured, appear to be indifferently compatible with social turbu-lence as with social stability, with economic decline as with economic growth, with political order as with political chaos, with an increase in individual and social pathologies (e.g., suicide, alcoholism, drug addic-tion, crime) as with a decrease. Inequality, one gets the impression, is an important issue for today's social scientists *despite* the fact that such importance escapes all empirical verification.

To complicate matters even further, any effort to relate income in-equality even to strictly economic well-being is plagued by the fact that the concept of economic well-being is itself not so unambiguous as some economists believe. An improvement in economic well-being can be quite rigorously defined as an increase in (actual or potential) pur-chasing power over the material goods of this world (i.e., the goods that money can buy). But this brute statistical fact is always "processed" through people's minds, and it is the ideas and attitudes in these minds that ultimately determine the meaning we give to any brute statistical fact. Fortunately for the science of economics, those ideas and attitudes are not utterly disparate, incoherent, and inconstant. One can therefore say, with some confidence, that most people, most of the time, and most anywhere, wish to see their purchasing power increase and are pleased when that occurs. Having said that, however, one must also go on to say that particular circumstances can modify or even overwhelm any purely statistical measure of economic well-being. Both poverty and af-fluence can have ambiguities that escape the strictly economic perspec-tive.

It is an observable fact that not all people who are statistically poor are everywhere equally miserable or have an equal sense of being "badly off." The past and the future always shape our sense of the present. So much, therefore, depends on the hopes one may have for one's children, the faith one may have in the ultimate benignity and "fairness" of Providence, on the assurance and solace one may derive from traditions. Poverty does not always dehumanize, and relative affluence can have its costs in human terms—costs that are actually, if often dimly, felt. Anyone who has seen *Fiddler on the Roof* and contrasted the lives portrayed there with the lives of Jews in Long Island's Great Neck today will appreciate the immense difficulties involved in disentangling economic well-being from other kinds of well-being.

Similarly, on the street where I lived until recently there was a Chinese family, recent immigrants, who ran a basement laundry. The parents and their five children shared the two tiny rooms at the back of the tiny store, and I shudder to think what this family did to our official poverty statistics. Still, those parents expressed great confidence that their children would "get ahead"—and, in fact, all five ended up as college graduates. Ought not one to incorporate that *prospect* in any estimate of the family's economic well-being? In contrast, on that same street there were several welfare families whose incomes, in cash and kind and services, may well have been larger than that of our Chinese family, but who were in various stages of a dependency-induced corruption, with little family stability and with the children involved in drugs and delinquency. Would an increase in their welfare receipts really have improved their economic well-being? If it had merely accelerated their demoralization, how would that relate to economic well-being?

Or, at the other extreme, take the case of a statistically affluent suburban child who has every advantage, as we say, but who comes to experience those advantages as bars in a "gilded cage," to use Max Weber's prescient phrase. He perceives the improbability of his surpassing his successful father in either economic or professional terms. He finds family and community life empty of meaning, and school a distracting bore. So he "drops out" of the world he was born into and becomes a "bohemian," a pseudobohemian, or a drifter, living—perhaps placidly, perhaps miserably—off handouts and odd jobs. What meaning are we to ascribe to the statistics of his economic well-being, before and after? When affluence can demoralize as vigorously as poverty, can we take the statistics on economic well-being with the solemnity that economists are naturally inclined to do?

And, of course, this matter becomes infinitely more complicated if we try somehow to incorporate the idea of economic equality into the idea of economic well-being, as so many economists think proper. Here, ordinary people seem to have an intuitive respect for existential complexities that economists often seem to lack. The intensity with which economists work out their Gini coefficients, and the subtlety with which they measure income trends in the quintiles or deciles of the population, is matched—so far as I can see—by the utter lack of interest of the average American in their findings. To some extent, perhaps, this is because those findings are never definitive—every piece of research seems to give rise to an exercise in counterresearch, and the arguments soon unravel into microdisputes. But mainly, I think, it is because the average person is far less interested in economic inequality—or is interested in it in quite a different way—than is the average social scientist.

Why? One reason, I would say, is that the social scientist links the issue of inequality to the issue of poverty more rigorously than does the average person. It is certainly true that as a society becomes more affluent, the "poverty line," as popularly perceived, will also move upward. Today, for example, no one would dispute the fact that the absence of private, indoor toilet facilities—an absence our grandparents would have found not at all shocking—is a sure sign of poverty. On the other hand, the average person feels free to distinguish between needs and wants in ways that the average economist, qua economist, is prohibited from doing. People who have what are perceived to be minimally adequate food, shelter, and clothing may be seen as poor, but not as *problematically* poor, regardless of how far down they are in the income distribution. And if one looks at poverty in this way, then the percentage of the American people who qualify as poor is small—well under 10 percent. A social scientist might retort that any such "absolute" definition of poverty is arbitrary, as compared with a definition in terms of relative income. But it is precisely this question to which economics can never hope to give an authoritative answer.

This popular perception of poverty is closely linked to a popular perception of opportunity—specifically, the opportunity to move out of poverty. To the degree that poverty is not viewed as a necessarily permanent condition, it will be of less concern. And the average American is strongly of the opinion that, leaving the physically handicapped (in which one would include the elderly) aside, there really is no reason for anyone in the lowest quintile of the income distribution to interpret his condition as permanent, since opportunities for "bettering one's condition" will and do exist. It may be recalled that Adam Smith had earlier suggested that the *modus operandi* of a market economy is such that economic mobility—and the eventual distribution of income as well—would of a certainty be less unequal than in any other kind of society. The reason for this is that the talents requisite for success in such an economy are so mundane, and the role of sheer luck is so great, that economic mobility should be greater, and eventual economic inequalities less significant, than in noncapitalist orders. Americans on the whole tend to accept this thesis as a fact of life. Social scientists, in contrast, think it important either to prove or disprove this thesis by research.

I carefully say "social scientists" because sociologists are perhaps even more prominent in this endeavor than economists. It is they who have created a sizable library of ever more technical literature on the question of "social mobility," of which income mobility is the major component. It is an open question whether this literature provides more enlightenment than obfuscation. We do know, without benefit of research, that if economic growth tends to create new and better-paying jobs and occupations and professions (as it does), then the statistics will obviously reveal considerable upward social and economic mobility (as they do). But what sociologists appear to be worried most about is whether everyone benefits *equally* from these changes, and they do seem to be especially concerned as to whether those who are already in the top decile manage to hang in there. The statistical procedures of sociologists are such that one begins with a rigorously egalitarian definition of social mobility, one in which the children of upper-class parents are downwardly mobile, while their places are taken by the upwardly mobile—a world turned upside-down indeed!—and then measures the actuality in the light of this "ideal." The fact that there has never been such a society, or that the very idea of such a society is inherently absurd, somehow is lost sight of.

It is sociologists, too, who have popularized the concept of "relative deprivation," which is supposed to explain why people's views of their own economic well-being are inextricably intertwined with the idea of equality. Now, there certainly is such a thing as a sense of relative deprivation, but it turns out to have only a limited connection with the larger idea of equality and to be more intimately related to the idea of justice or fairness ("to each his due"). Thus, there have been innumerable strikes in the United States over pay differentials among workers ("equal pay for equal work!"), yet I do not recall a case of there being a strike over the chief executive officer's very high salary. If sociologists tacitly assume—as practically all seem to do—that a more egalitarian society is (and will be perceived to be) a more just society, that is an assumption which derives from ideology, not from history or contemporary experience.

And much the same is true, I would say, for the way in which—and the intensity with which—economists study income inequalities. One begins blandly with the premise that absolute equality is the ideal state and then one measures degrees of departure from this ideal. Yes, I know, there is nothing "normative" about such a statistical procedure—it is merely a mathematical convenience that zero inequality is taken as the base for all measurements. But is it not odd that it is impossible to point to a study that breathes satisfaction (as distinct from *Schadenfreude*) at discovering an increase in economic inequality? This whole literature is as profoundly suffused with ideology as it is liberally bespattered with statistics.

What, really, is the point of this keen interest among economists and sociologists in the issue of inequality? There is precious little evidence to the effect that it responds to a widespread popular concern and much evidence to the contrary. Indeed, one gets the distinct impression that much of the research is directed toward "raising the consciousness" of the public about the issue—and that the rest of the research is directed toward rebutting such consciousness-raising efforts. It is hard to believe that even the most casual reader can fail to perceive the essentially ideological nature of this disputation.

My own view—admittedly a bit extreme—is that when you need an economist or a sociologist to bring you intelligence about inequalities of income or social class, that is in itself proof that neither issue is of serious concern to the citizenry. There are simply no "mysteries" to be elucidated about income inequality and social class, since there is no reason to think that common opinion, based on observation and experience and gossip, is likely to be self-deceiving about a matter of such interest to everyone. The very notion that such self-deception is probable derives from the Marxist idea—an ideological conception of the role of ideology—that bourgeois society is constantly at work instilling "false consciousness" into the populace.

At this point a social scientist might object that opinion poll data do reveal that people misconstrue the social and economic reality they inhabit—that, for instance, households with incomes of $100,000 a year blandly report themselves to be "middle class." To this objection, there are two rejoinders.

First, if a $100,000-a-year household thinks itself to be middle class, then it *is* middle class. And the same is true for a $10,000-a-year household. What on earth gives social scientists the authority to dismiss such "subjective" conceptions of class and to impose a presumably more "objective" one? Here again we are dealing with a Marxist derivative that has been unthinkingly adopted by modern social science. Class may (or may not) find phenomenological expression, but at root it is a mode of self-definition. There are aristocrats in England who are as poor as church mice but are definitely "upper class." And there are immigrants to the United States who are also as poor as church mice but are definitely "middle class" from the moment they set foot here. The very thought that there is someone ("up there?") who knows better than we do what class we are in is as breathtaking in its intellectual presumption as it is sterile for all serious purposes of social research.

Second, when poll data reveal vast, apparent misconceptions about *other people*—about how rich or poor they are, or how powerful or weak they are—such data ought not to be taken too seriously. No economic, social, or political system could function for a moment if people actually had wildly unrealistic notions of their economic, social, and political reality. The interesting question here for social research is why people express such opinions and beliefs to pollsters, not why they have them.

My own explanation for the keen interest of social scientists in the nonobvious issue of equality is that this is but one manifestation of how nineteenth-century ideologies—and most especially the socialist ideology—have so decisively shaped modern social science. Thus, it is my understanding that the National Bureau of Economic Research was itself originally founded, back in the 1920s, to take a serious look at the issue of economic inequality—an issue then posed by socialist, quasi-socialist, or "progressive" critics who maintained that, under capitalism, the rich were getting richer while the poor were getting poorer. It was they who defined the issue—and it is they who have been defining it ever since. It is fascinating to note the way in which research does *not* dispose of this issue. One might have thought, as the evidence accumulated to the effect that nothing very novel or exciting has happened to the distribution of income in recent decades—and there is even evidence to suggest that nothing very exciting has happened in the past century—that social scientists would simply lose interest in the question. They have not. Instead the studies become ever more sophisticated, ever more incomprehensible to the noninitiated, ever more "scholastic" in the pejorative sense of that term—and they still do not bring us tidings of significance. The impulse behind such studies can hardly be designated as routinely "scientific."

It can, however, be quite easily recognized as "ideological." The prominence of the issue of equality, I should say, reflects the degree to which egalitarian, quasi-socialist conceptions of justice have permeated our culture, including the thinking of many social scientists who do not regard themselves as in any way socialist but who, as a matter of course, use the ideal of a socialist society—classless and egalitarian—as a proper criterion for the judging of capitalist reality. Of all the social sciences, economics has been the least influenced by this ideological impulse, in part because the discipline of economics is truly more rigorous than the other social sciences; in part because a respect for market processes is indigenous to the methodology of this discipline. But economists are human, and it could not remain unaffected. One has only to recall the ingenuity and persistence with which distinguished professors of economics elaborated quite fanciful justifications for the progressive income tax—for which there is no *economic,* as distinct from moral or political justification, since it involves an interpersonal comparison of utilities which is beyond the scope of economics.

It is understandably irksome to many economists that the science of economics, strictly considered, should not offer answers to many important questions that *appear* to be economic in nature but in fact belong to moral and political theory. Indeed, we have witnessed recently a vigorous dissenting movement by advocates of something called "political economy"—sometimes "normative economics," sometimes simply "radical political economy"—who argue in favor of a candid union of economics with ideology. These are for the most part younger economists who are discontented with the limits of their social-scientific discipline and who wish to import into economics all of those intellectual and moral considerations that used to constitute the body of political philosophy when *that* discipline still flourished. (One such consideration is equality, as an ideal or nonideal for a good society.) One may sympathize with the moral and intellectual passions behind this movement while realizing they are destructive of the integrity of economics as a scientific discipline.

What it comes down to, in the end, is the need for economists to recognize their severe limitations qua economists. Economics has many useful and important things to tell us, but it really has nothing to say about the larger features of a good society, or about the status of equality or inequalities in such a society, and it only has something to say about "economic well-being" on a fairly narrow—though not unimportant—definition. Those economic statistics we are being deluged with do tell us something valid about the real world; but they often tell us less of the truth about the real world than economists are—by virtue of their *déformation professionelle*—inclined to think.

1980

# 15

# On Corporate Capitalism
# in America

THE United States is the capitalist nation par excellence. That is to say, it is not merely the case that capitalism has flourished here more vigorously than, for instance, in the nations of Western Europe. The point is, rather, that the founding fathers *intended* this nation to be capitalist and regarded it as the *only* set of economic arrangements consistent with the liberal democracy they had established. They did not use the term "capitalism," of course; but, then, neither did Adam Smith, whose *Wealth of Nations* was also published in 1776, and who spoke of "the system of natural liberty." That invidious word, "capitalism," was invented by European socialists about a half-century later—just as our other common expression, "free enterprise," was invented still later by antisocialists who saw no good reason for permitting their enemies to appropriate the vocabulary of public discourse. But words aside, it is a fact that capitalism in this country has a historical legitimacy that it does not possess elsewhere. In other lands, the nation and its fundamental institutions antedate the capitalist era; in the United States, where liberal democracy is not merely a form of government but also a "way of life," capitalism and democracy have been organically linked.

This fact, quite simply accepted until the 1930s—accepted by both radical critics and staunch defenders of the American regime—has been obscured in recent decades by the efforts of liberal scholars to create a respectable pedigree for the emerging "welfare state." The impetus behind this scholarship was justified, to a degree. It is true that the founding fathers were not dogmatic laissez-fairists, in a later neo-Darwinian or "libertarian" sense of the term. They were intensely suspicious of governmental power, but they never could have subscribed to the doctrine of "our enemy, the State." They believed there was room for some governmental intervention in economic affairs; and—what is less frequently remarked—they believed most firmly in the propriety of governmental intervention and regulation in the areas of public taste and public morality. But, when one has said this, one must add emphatically that there really is little doubt that the founders were convinced that economics was the sphere of human activity where government intervention was, as a general rule, least likely to be productive, and that "the system of natural liberty" in economic affairs was the complement to our system of constitutional liberty in political and civil affairs. They surely would have agreed with Hayek that the paternalistic government favored by modern liberalism led down the "road to serfdom."

But one must also concede that both the Founding Fathers and Adam Smith would have been perplexed by the kind of capitalism we have today. They could not have interpreted the domination of economic activity by large corporate bureaucracies as representing, in any sense, the working of a "system of natural liberty." Entrepreneurial capitalism, as they understood it, was mainly an individual—or at most, a family—affair. Such large organizations as might exist—joint stock companies, for example—were limited in purpose (e.g., building a canal or a railroad) and usually in duration as well. The large, publicly owned corporation of today which strives for immortality, which is committed to no line of business but rather (like an investment banker) seeks the best return on investment, which is governed by an anonymous oligarchy—such an institution would have troubled and puzzled them, just as it troubles and puzzles us. And they would have asked themselves the same questions we have been asking ourselves for almost a century now: Who "owns" this new Leviathan? Who governs it—and by what right, and according to what principles?

To understand the history of corporate capitalism in America, it is important to realize in what sense it may be fairly described as an "accidental institution." Not in the economic sense, of course. In the latter part of the last century, in all industrialized nations, the large corporation was born out of both economic necessity and economic opportunity: the necessity of large pools of capital and of a variety of technical expertise to exploit the emerging technologies, and the opportunity for economies of scale in production, marketing, and service in a rapidly urbanizing society. It all happened so quickly that the term "corporate revolution" is not inappropriate. In 1870, the United States was a land of small family-owned business. By 1905, the large, publicly owned corporation dominated the economic scene.

But the corporate revolution was always, during that period, an unpopular revolution. It was seen by most Americans as an accident of economic circumstance—something that happened to them rather than something they had created. They had not foreseen it; they did not understand it—in no way did it seem to "fit" into the accepted ideology of the American democracy. No other institution in American history—not even slavery—has ever been so consistently unpopular as has the large corporation with the American public. It was controversial from the outset, and it has remained controversial to this day.

This is something the current crop of corporate executives find very difficult to appreciate. Most of them reached maturity during the postwar period, 1945–1960. As it happens, this was—with the possible exception of the 1920s—just about the only period when public opinion was, on the whole, well-disposed to the large corporation. After fifteen years of depression and war, the American people wanted houses, consumer goods, and relative security of employment—all the things that the modern corporation is so good at supplying. The typical corporate executive of today, in his fifties or sixties, was led to think that such popular acceptance was "normal," and is therefore inclined to believe that there are novel and specific forces behind the upsurge of anticorporate sentiment in the past decade. As a matter of fact, he is partly right: There *is* something significantly new about the hostility to the large corporation in our day. But there is also something very old, something coeval with the very existence of the large corporation itself. And it is the interaction of the old hostility with the new which has put the modern corporation in the critical condition that we find it in today.

The old hostility is based on what we familiarly call "populism." This is a sentiment basic to any democracy—indispensable to its establishment but also, ironically, inimical to its survival. Populism is the constant fear and suspicion that power and/or authority, whether in government or out, is being used to frustrate "the will of the people." It is a spirit that intimidates authority and provides the popular energy to curb and resist it. The very possibility of a democratic society—as distinct from the forms of representative government, which are its political expression—is derived from, and is constantly renewed by, the populist temper. The Constitution endows the United States with a republican form of government, in which the free and explicit consent of the people must ultimately ratify the actions of those in authority. But the populist spirit, which both antedated and survived the Constitutional Convention, made the United States a democratic nation as well as a republican one—committed to "the democratic way of life" as well as to the proprieties of constitutional government. It is precisely the strength of that commitment which has always made the American democracy somehow different from the democracies of Western Europe—a difference which every European observer has been quick to remark.

But populism is, at the same time, an eternal problem for the American democratic republic. It incarnates an antinomian impulse, a Jacobin contempt for the "mere" forms of law and order and civility. It also engenders an impulse toward a rather infantile political utopianism, on the premise that nothing is too good for "the people." Above all, it is a temper and state of mind which too easily degenerates into political paranoia, with "enemies of the people" being constantly discovered and exorcised and convulsively purged. Populist paranoia is always busy subverting the very institutions and authorities that the democratic republic laboriously creates for the purpose of orderly self-government.

In the case of the large corporation, we see a healthy populism and a feverish paranoia simultaneously being provoked by its sudden and dramatic appearance. The paranoia takes the form of an instinctive readiness to believe anything reprehensible, no matter how incredible, about the machinations of "big business." That species of journalism and scholarship which we call "muckraking" has made this kind of populist paranoia a permanent feature of American intellectual and public life. Though the businessman per se has never been a fictional hero of bourgeois society (as Stendhal observed, a merchant may be honorable but there is nothing heroic about him), it is only after the rise of "big business" that the businessman becomes the natural and predestined villain of the novel, the drama, the cinema, and, more recently, television. By now most Americans are utterly convinced that all big business owes its existence to the original depredations of "robber barons"—a myth which never really was plausible, which more recent scholarship by economic historians has thoroughly discredited, but which probably forever will have a secure hold on the American political imagination. Similarly, most Americans are now quick to believe that big business conspires secretly but most effectively to manipulate the economic and political system—an enterprise which, in prosaic fact, corporate executives are too distracted and too unimaginative even to contemplate.

Along with this kind of paranoia, however, populist hostility toward the large corporation derives from an authentic bewilderment and concern about the place of this new institution in American life. In its concentration of assets and power—power to make economic decisions affecting the lives of tens of thousands of citizens—it seemed to create a dangerous disharmony between the economic system and the political. In the America of the 1890s, even government did not have, and did not claim, such power (except in wartime). *No one* was supposed to have such power—it was, indeed, a radical diffusion of power that was thought to be an essential characteristic of democratic capitalism. The rebellion of Jacksonian democracy against the Bank of the United States had been directed precisely against such an "improper" concentration of power. A comparable rebellion now took place against big business.

It was not, however, a rebellion against capitalism as such. On the contrary, popular hostility to the large corporation reflected the fear that this new institution was subverting capitalism as Americans then understood (and, for the most part, still understand) it. This understanding was phrased in individualistic terms. The entrepreneur was conceived of as a real person, not as a legal fiction. The "firm" was identified with such a real person (or a family of real persons) who took personal risks, reaped personal rewards, and assumed personal responsibility for his actions. One of the consequences of the victorious revolt against the Bank of the United States had been to make the chartering of corporations—legal "persons" with limited liability —under state law a routine and easy thing, the assumption being that this would lead to a proliferation of small corporations, still easily identifiable with the flesh-and-blood entrepreneurs who founded them. The rise of big business frustrated such expectations.

Moreover, the large corporation not only seemed to be but actually was a significant deviation from traditional capitalism. One of the features of the large corporation—though more a consequence of its existence than its cause—was its need for, and its ability to create, "orderly markets." What businessmen disparagingly call "cutthroat competition," with its wild swings in price, its large fluctuations in employment, its unpredictable effects upon profits—all this violates the very *raison d'être* of a large corporation, with its need for relative stability so that its long-range investment decisions can be rationally calculated. The modern corporation always looks to the largest and most powerful firm in the industry to establish "market leadership" in price, after which competition will concentrate on quality, service, and the introduction of new products. One should not exaggerate the degree to which the large corporation is successful in these efforts. John Kenneth Galbraith's notion that the large corporation simply manipulates its market through the power of advertising and fixes the price level with sovereign authority is a wild exaggeration. This is what all corporations *try* to do; it is what a few corporations, in some industries, sometimes succeed in doing. Still, there is little doubt that the idea of a "free market," in the era of large corporations, is not quite the original capitalist idea.

The populist response to the transformation of capitalism by the large corporation was, and is: "Break it up!" Antitrust and antimonopoly legislation was the consequence. Such legislation is still enacted and reenacted, and antitrust prosecutions still make headlines. But the effort is by now routine, random, and largely pointless. There may be a few lawyers left in the Justice Department or the Federal Trade Commission who sincerely believe that such laws, if stringently enforced, could restore capitalism to something like its pristine individualist form. But it is much more probable that the lawyers who staff such government agencies launch these intermittent crusades against "monopoly" and "oligopoly"—terms that are distressingly vague and inadequate when applied to the real world—because they prefer such activity to mere idleness, and because they anticipate that a successful prosecution will enhance their professional reputations. No one expects them to be effectual, whether the government wins or loses. Just how much difference, after all, would it make if AT&T were forced to spin off its Western Electric manufacturing subsidiary, or if IBM were divided into three different computer companies? All that would be accomplished is a slight increase in the number of large corporations, with very little consequence for the shape of the economy or the society as a whole.

True, one could imagine—in the abstract—a much more radical effort to break up big business. But there are good reasons why, though many talk solemnly about this possibility, no one does anything about it. The costs would simply be too high. The economic costs, most obviously: an adverse effect on productivity, on capital investment, on our balance of payments, and so forth. But the social and political costs would be even more intolerable. Our major trade unions, having after many years succeeded in establishing collective bargaining on a national level with the large corporation, are not about to sit back and watch their power disintegrate for the sake of an ideal such as "decentralization." And the nation's pension funds are not about to permit the assets of the corporations in which they have invested to be dispersed, and the security of their pension payments correspondingly threatened.

One suspects that even popular opinion, receptive in principle to the diminution of big business, would in actuality find the process too painful to tolerate. For the plain fact is that, despite much academic agitation about the horrors of being an "organization man," the majority of those who now work for a living, of whatever class, have learned to prefer the security, the finely calibrated opportunities for advancement, the fringe benefits, and the paternalism of a large corporation to the presumed advantages of employment in smaller firms. It is not only corporate executives who are fearful of "cutthroat competition"; most of us, however firmly we declare our faith in capitalism and free enterprise, are sufficiently conservative in our instincts to wish to avoid all such capitalist rigors. Even radical professors, who in their books find large bureaucratic corporations "dehumanizing," are notoriously reluctant to give up tenured appointments in large bureaucratic universities for riskier opportunities elsewhere.

So the populist temper and the large corporation coexist uneasily in America today, in what can only be called a marriage of convenience. There is little affection, much nagging and backbiting and whining on all sides, but it endures—"for the sake of the children," as it were. Not too long ago, there was reason to hope that, out of the habit of coexistence, there would emerge something like a philosophy of coexistence: a mutual adaptation of the democratic-individualist-capitalist ideal and the bureaucratic-corporate reality, sanctioned by a new revised version of the theory of democracy and capitalism—a new political and social philosophy, in short, which extended the reach of traditional views without repudiating them. But that possibility, if it was ever more than a fancy, has been effectively canceled by the rise, over the past decade, of an anticapitalist ethos which has completely transformed the very definition of the problem.

This ethos, in its American form, is not *explicitly* anticapitalistic, and this obscures our perception and understanding of it. It has its roots in the tradition of "Progressive-reform," a tradition which slightly antedated the corporate revolution but which was immensely stimulated by it. In contrast to populism, this was (and is) an upper-middle-class tradition—an "elitist" tradition, as one would now say. Though it absorbed a great many socialist and neosocialist and quasi-socialist ideas, it was too American—too habituated to the rhetoric of individualism, and even in some measure to its reality—to embrace easily a synoptic, collectivist vision of the future as enunciated in socialist dogmas. It was willing to contemplate "public ownership" (i.e., ownership by the political authorities) of *some* of the "means of production," but on the whole it preferred to think in terms of *regulating* the large corporation rather than nationalizing it or breaking it up. It is fair to call it an indigenous and peculiarly American counterpart to European socialism—addressing itself to the same problems defined in much the same way, motivated by the same ideological impulse, but assuming an adversary posture toward big business specifically rather than toward capitalism in general.

At least, that is what Progressive-reform used to be. In the past decade, however, it has experienced a transmutation of ideological substance while preserving most of the traditional rhetorical wrappings. That is because it embraced, during these years, a couple of other political traditions, European in origin, so that what we still call "liberalism" in the United States is now something quite different from the liberalism of the older Progressive-reform impulse. It is so different, indeed, as to have created a cleavage between those who think of themselves as "old liberals"—and are now often redesignated as "neoconservatives"—and the new liberals who are in truth men and women of "the Left," in the European sense of that term. This is an important point, worthy of some elaboration and clarification—especially since the new liberalism is not usually very candid about the matter.*

The Left in Europe, whether "totalitarian" or "democratic," has consistently been antiliberal. That is to say, it vigorously repudiates the intellectual traditions of liberalism—as expressed, say, by Locke, Montesquieu, Adam Smith, and Tocqueville—and with equal vigor rejects the key institution of liberalism: the (relatively) free market (which necessarily implies limited government). The Left emerges out of a rebellion against the "anarchy" and "vulgarity" of a civilization that is shaped by individuals engaged in market transactions. The anarchy to which it refers is the absence of any transcending goal or purpose which society is constrained to pursue—and which socialists, with their superior understanding of history, feel obligated to prescribe. Such a prescription, when fulfilled, will supposedly reestablish a humane "order." The vulgarity to which it refers is the fact that a free market responds—or tries to respond—to the appetites and preferences of common men and women, whose use of their purchasing power determines the shape of the civilization. Since common men and women are likely

*It must be said, however, that even when it is candid, no one seems to pay attention. John Kenneth Galbraith has recently publicly defined himself as a "socialist," and asserts that he has been one—whether wittingly or unwittingly, it is not clear—for many years. But the media still consistently identify him as a "liberal," and he is so generally regarded. Whether this is mere habit or instinctive protective coloration—for the media are a crucial wing of the "new liberalism"—it is hard to say.

to have "common" preferences, tastes, and aspirations, the society they create—the "consumption society," as it is now called—will be regarded by some critics as short-sightedly "materialistic." People will seek to acquire what they want (e.g., automobiles), not what they "need" (e.g., mass transit). Socialists are persuaded that they have a superior understanding of people's true needs, and that the people will be more truly happy in a society where socialists have the authority to define those needs, officially and unequivocally.

Obviously, socialism is an "elitist" movement, and in its beginnings—with Saint-Simon and Auguste Comte—was frankly conceived of as such. Its appeal has always been to "intellectuals" (who feel dispossessed by and alienated from a society in which they are merely one species of common man) and members of the upper-middle class who, having reaped the benefits of capitalism, are now in a position to see its costs. (It must be said that these costs are not imaginary: Socialism would not have such widespread appeal if its critique of liberal capitalism were entirely without substance.) But all social movements in the modern world must define themselves as "democratic," since democratic legitimacy is the only kind of legitimacy we recognize. So "totalitarian" socialism insists that it is a "people's democracy," in which the "will of the people" is mystically incarnated in the ruling party. "Democratic socialism," on the other hand, would like to think that it can "socialize" the economic sector while leaving the rest of society "liberal." As Robert Nozick puts it, democratic socialists want to proscribe only "*capitalist* transactions between consenting adults."

The trouble with the latter approach is that democratic socialists, when elected to office, discover that to collectivize economic life you have to coerce all sorts of other institutions (e.g., the trade unions, the media, the educational system) and limit individual freedom in all sorts of ways (e.g., freedom to travel, freedom to "drop out" from the world of work, freedom to choose the kind of education one prefers) if a "planned society" is to function efficiently. When democratic socialist governments show reluctance to take such actions, they are pushed into doing so by the "left wings" of their "movements," who feel betrayed by the distance that still exists between the reality they experience and the socialist ideal which enchants them. Something like this is now happening in all the European social-democratic parties and in a country like India.

The United States never really had any such movement of the Left, at least not to any significant degree. It was regarded as an "un-American" thing, as indeed it was. True, the movement of Progressive-reform was elitist both in its social composition and its social aims: It, too, was distressed by the anarchy and vulgarity of capitalist civilization. But in the main it accepted as a fact the proposition that capitalism and liberalism were organically connected, and it proposed to itself the goal of "mitigating the evils of capitalism," rather than abolishing liberal capitalism and replacing it with "a new social order" in which a whole new set of human relationships would be established. It was an authentic *reformist* movement. It wanted to regulate the large corporations so that this concentration of private power could not develop into an oligarchical threat to democratic-liberal-capitalism. It was ready to interfere with the free market so that the instabilities generated by capitalism—above all, instability of employment—would be less costly in human terms. It was even willing to tamper occasionally with the consumer's freedom of choice where there was a clear consensus that the microdecisions of the marketplace added up to macroconsequences that were felt to be unacceptable. And it hoped to correct the vulgarity of capitalist civilization by educating the people so that their "preference schedules" (as economists would say) would be, in traditional terms, more elevated, more appreciative of "the finer things in life."

Ironically, it was the extraordinary increase in mass higher education after World War II that, perhaps more than anything else, infused the traditional movement for Progressive-reform with various impulses derived from the European left. The earlier movement had been elitist in fact as well as in intention—that is, it was sufficiently small so that, even while influential, it could hardly contemplate the possibility of actually exercising "power." Mass higher education has converted this movement into something like a mass movement proper, capable of driving a president from office (1968) and nominating its own candidate (1972). The intentions remain elitist, of course; but the movement, under the banner of "the New Politics," now encompasses some millions of people. These are the people whom liberal capitalism had sent to college in order to help manage its affluent, highly technological, mildly paternalistic, "postindustrial" society.

This "new class" consists of scientists, lawyers, city planners, social workers, educators, criminologists, sociologists, public health doctors, and so forth—a substantial number of whom find their careers in the expanding public sector rather than the private. The public sector, indeed, is where they prefer to be. They are, as one says, "idealistic"—that is, far less interested in individual financial rewards than in the corporate power of their class. Though they continue to speak the language of Progressive-reform, in actuality they are acting upon a hidden agenda: to propel the nation from that modified version of capitalism we call "the welfare state" toward an economic system so stringently regulated in detail as to fulfill many of the traditional anticapitalist aspirations of the Left.

The exact nature of what has been happening is obscured by the fact that this new class is not merely liberal but truly "libertarian" in its approach to all areas of life—except economics. It celebrates individual liberty of speech and expression and action to an unprecedented degree, so that at times it seems almost anarchistic in its conception of the good life. But this joyful individualism always stops short of the border where economics—that is, capitalism—begins. The new class is surely sincere in such a contradictory commitment to a maximum of individual freedom in a society where economic life becomes less free with every passing year. But it is instructive to note that these same people, who are irked and inflamed by the slightest noneconomic restriction in the United States, are quite admiring of Maoist China and not in the least appalled by the total collectivization of life—and the total destruction of liberty—there. They see this regime as "progressive," not "reactionary." And, in this perception, they unwittingly tell us much about their deepest fantasies and the respective quality of their political imagination.

Meanwhile, the transformation of American capitalism proceeds apace. Under the guise of coping with nasty "externalities"—air pollution, water pollution, noise pollution, traffic pollution, health pollution, or what have you—more and more of the basic economic decisions are being removed from the marketplace and transferred to the "public"—that is, political—sector, where the new class, by virtue of its expertise and skills, is so well represented. This movement is naturally applauded by the media, which are also for the most part populated by members of this new class who believe—as the Left has always believed—it is government's responsibility to cure all the ills of the human condition, and who ridicule those politicians who deny the possibility (and therefore the propriety) of government doing any such ambitious thing. And, inevitably, more explicitly socialist and neosocialist themes are beginning boldly to emerge from the protective shell of Reformist-liberal rhetoric. The need for some kind of "national economic plan" is now being discussed seriously in congressional circles; the desirability of "public"—that is, political—appointees to the boards of directors of the largest corporations is becoming more apparent to more politicians and journalists with every passing day; the utter "reasonableness," in principle, of price and wage controls is no longer even a matter for argument, but is subject only to circumstantial and prudential considerations. Gradually, the traditions of the Left are being absorbed into the agenda of Progressive-reform, and the structure of American society is being radically, if discreetly, altered.

One of the reasons this process is so powerful, and meets only relatively feeble resistance, is that it has a continuing source of energy within the capitalist system itself. That source is not the "inequalities" or "injustices" of capitalism, as various ideologies of the Left insist. These may represent foci around which dissent is occasionally and skillfully mobilized. But the most striking fact about anticapitalism is the degree to which it is *not* a spontaneous working-class phenomenon. Capitalism, like all economic and social systems, breeds its own peculiar discontents—but the discontents of the working class are, in and of themselves, not one of its major problems. Yes, there is class conflict in capitalism; there is always class conflict, and the very notion of a possible society without class conflict is one of socialism's most bizarre fantasies. (Indeed, it is this fantasy that is socialism's original contribution to modern political theory; the importance of class conflict itself was expounded by Aristotle and was never doubted by anyone who ever bothered to look at the real world.) But there is no case, in any country that can reasonably be called "capitalist," of such class conflict leading to a proletarian revolution. Capitalism, precisely because its aim is the satisfaction of "common" appetites and aspirations, can adequately cope with its own class conflicts, through economic growth primarily and some version of the welfare state secondarily. It can do so, however, only if it is permitted to—a permission which the anticapitalist spirit is loath to concede. This spirit *wants* to see capitalism falter and fail.

The essence of this spirit is to be found, not in *The Communist Manifesto,* but rather in the young Marx who wrote: "The enemy of being is having." This sums up neatly the animus which intellectuals from the beginning, and "the new class" in our own day, have felt toward the system of liberal capitalism. This system is in truth "an acquisitive society," by traditional standards. Not that men and women under capitalism are "greedier" than under feudalism or socialism or whatever. Almost all people, almost all of the time, want more than they have. But capitalism is unique among social and economic systems in being organized for the overriding purpose of giving them more than they have. And here is where it runs into trouble: Those who benefit most from capitalism—and their children, especially—experience a withering away of the acquisitive impulse. Or, to put it more accurately: They cease to think of acquiring money and begin to think of acquiring power so as to improve the "quality of life," and to give *being* priority over *having.* That is the meaning of the well-known statement by a student radical of the 1960s: "You don't know what hell is like unless you were raised in Scarsdale." Since it is the ambition of capitalism to enable everyone to live in Scarsdale or its equivalent, this challenge is far more fundamental than the orthodox Marxist one, which says—against all the evidence—that capitalism will fail because it *cannot* get everyone to live in Scarsdale.

Against this new kind of attack, any version of capitalism would be vulnerable. But the version of corporate capitalism under which we live is not merely vulnerable; it is practically defenseless. It is not really hard to make a decent case, on a pragmatic level, for liberal capitalism today—especially since the anticapitalist societies the twentieth century has given birth to are, even by their own standards, monstrous abortions and "betrayals" of their originating ideals. And corporate capitalism does have the great merit of being willing to provide a milieu of comfortable liberty—in universities, for example—for those who prefer *being* to *having*. But the trouble with the large corporation today is that it does not possess a clear theoretical—that is, ideological—legitimacy within the framework of liberal capitalism itself. Consequently the gradual usurpation of managerial authority by the new class—mainly through the transfer of this authority to the new breed of regulatory officials (who are the very prototype of the class)—is almost irresistible.

So long as business was an activity carried on by real individuals who "owned" the property they managed, the politicians, the courts, and public opinion were all reasonably respectful of the capitalist properties. Not only was the businessman no threat to liberal democracy; he was, on the contrary, the very epitome of the bourgeois liberal-democratic ethos—the man who succeeded by diligence, enterprise, sobriety, and all those other virtues that Benjamin Franklin cataloged for us, and which we loosely call "the Protestant ethic."*

On the whole, even today, politicians and public opinion are inclined to look with some benevolence on "small business," and no one seems to be interested in leading a crusade against it. But the professionally managed large corporation is another matter entirely. The top executives of these enormous bureaucratic institutions are utterly sincere when they claim fealty to "free enterprise," and they even have a point: Managing a business corporation, as distinct from a government agency, does require a substantial degree of entrepreneurial risk taking and entrepreneurial skill. But it is also the case that they are as much function-

*I say "loosely call" because, as a Jew, I was raised to think that this was an ancient "Hebrew ethic," and some Chinese scholars I have spoken to feel that it could appropriately be called "The Confucian ethic."

aries as entrepreneurs, and rather anonymous functionaries at that. Not only do we not know who the chairman of General Motors is; we know so little about the kind of person who holds such a position that we have not the faintest idea as to whether or not we want our children to grow up like him. Horatio Alger, writing in the era of precorporate capitalism, had no such problems. And there is something decidedly odd about a society in which a whole class of Very Important People is not automatically held up as one possible model of emulation for the young—and cannot be so held up because they are, as persons, close to invisible.

Nor is it at all clear whose interests these entrepreneur-functionaries are serving. In theory, they are elected representatives of the stockholder-"owners." But stockholder elections are almost invariably routine affirmations of management's will, because management will have previously secured the support of the largest stockholders; and for a long while now stockholders have essentially regarded themselves, and are regarded by management, as little more than possessors of a variable-income security. A stock certificate has become a lien against the company's earnings and assets—a subordinated lien, in both law and fact—rather than a charter of "citizenship" within a corporate community. And though management will talk piously, when it serves its purposes, about its obligations to the stockholders, the truth is that it prefers to have as little to do with them as possible, since their immediate demands are only too likely to conflict with management's long-term corporate plans.

It is interesting to note that when such an organization of business executives as the Committee for Economic Development drew up a kind of official declaration of the responsibilities of management a few years ago, it conceived of the professional manager as "a trustee balancing the interests of many diverse participants and constituents in the enterprise," and then enumerated these participants and constituents: employees, customers, suppliers, stockholders, government—that is, practically everyone. Such a declaration serves only to ratify an accomplished fact: The large corporation has ceased being a species of private property, and is now a "quasi-public" institution. But if it is a quasi-public institution, some novel questions may be properly addressed to it: By what right does the self-perpetuating oligarchy that constitutes "management" exercise its powers? On what principles does it do so? To these essentially political questions management can only respond with the weak economic answer that its legitimacy derives from the superior efficiency with which it responds to signals from the free market. But such an argument from efficiency is not compelling when offered by a quasi-public institution. In a democratic republic such as ours, public and quasi-public institutions are not supposed simply to be efficient at responding to people's transient desires, are not supposed to be simply *pandering* institutions—but are rather supposed to help shape the people's wishes, and ultimately, the people's character, according to some version—accepted by the people itself—of the public good and public interest. This latter task the new class feels itself supremely qualified to perform, leaving corporate management in the position of arguing that it is improper for this quasi-public institution to do more than give the people what they want—a debased version of the democratic idea which has some temporary demagogic appeal but no permanent force.

Whether for good or evil—and one can leave this for future historians to debate—the large corporation has gone quasi-public, that is, it now straddles, uncomfortably and uncertainly, both the private and public sectors of our "mixed economy." In a sense one can say that the modern large corporation stands to the bourgeois-individualist capitalism of yesteryear as the "imperial" American polity stands to the isolated republic from which it emerged: Such a development may or may not represent "progress," but there is no turning back.

The danger which this situation poses for the American democracy is not the tantalizing ambiguities inherent in such a condition—it is the genius of a pluralist democracy to convert such ambiguities into possible sources of institutional creativity and to avoid "solving" them, as a Jacobin democracy would, with one swift stroke of the sword. The danger is rather that the large corporation will be thoroughly integrated into the public sector, and lose its private character altogether. The transformation of American capitalism that *this* would represent—a radical departure from the quasi-bourgeois "mixed economy" to a system that could be fairly described as kind of "state capitalism"—does constitute a huge potential threat to the individual liberties Americans have traditionally enjoyed.

One need not, therefore, be an admirer of the large corporation to be concerned about its future. One might even regard its "bureaucratic-acquisitive" ethos, in contrast to the older "bourgeois-moralistic" ethos, as a sign of cultural decadence—and still be concerned about its future. In our pluralistic society we frequently find ourselves defending specific concentrations of power, about which we might otherwise have the most mixed feelings, on the grounds that they contribute to a general diffusion of power, a diffusion which creates the "space" in which individual liberty can survive and prosper. This is certainly our experience vis-à-vis certain religious organizations—for example, the Catholic Church, the Mormons—whose structure and values are, in some respects at least, at variance with our common democratic beliefs, and yet whose existence serves to preserve our democracy as a free and liberal society. The general principle of checks and balances, and of decentralized authority too, is as crucial to the social and economic structures of a liberal democracy as to its political structure.

Nevertheless, it seems clear that the large corporation is not going to be able to withstand those forces pulling and pushing it into the political sector unless it confronts the reality of its predicament and adapts itself to this reality in a self-preserving way. There is bound to be disagreement as to the forms such adaptation should take, some favoring institutional changes that emphasize and clarify the corporation's "public" nature, others insisting that its "private" character must be stressed anew. Probably a mixture of both strategies would be most effective. If large corporations are to avoid having government-appointed directors on their boards, they will have to take the initiative and try to preempt that possibility by themselves appointing distinguished "outside" directors—directors from outside the business community. At the same time, if corporations are going to be able to resist the total usurpation of their decision-making powers by government, they must create a constituency—of their stockholders, above all—which will candidly intervene in the "political game" of interest-group politics, an intervention fully in accord with the principles of our democratic system.

In both cases, the first step will have to be to persuade corporate management that some such change is necessary. This will be difficult: Corporate managers are (and enjoy being) essentially economic-decision-making animals, and they are profoundly resentful of the "distractions" which "outside interference" of any kind will impose on them. After all, most chief executives have a tenure of about six years, and they all wish to establish the best possible track record, in terms of "bottom line" results, during that period. Very few are in a position to, and even fewer have an inclination to, take a long and larger view of the corporation and its institutional problems.

At the same time, the crusade against the corporations continues, with the new class successfully appealing to populist anxieties, seeking to run the country in the "right" way, and to reshape our civilization along lines superior to those established by the marketplace. Like all crusades, it engenders an enthusiastic paranoia about the nature of the Enemy and the deviousness of His operations. Thus, the *New Yorker,* which has become the liberal-chic organ of the new class, has discovered the maleficent potential of the multinational corporation at exactly the time when the multinational corporation is in full retreat before the forces of nationalism everywhere. And the fact that American corporations sometimes have to bribe foreign politicians—for whom bribery is a way of life—is inflated into a rabid indictment of the personal morals of corporate executives. (That such bribery is also inherent in government-aid programs to the underdeveloped countries is, on the other hand, *never* taken to reflect on those—for example, the World Bank—who institute and run such programs, and is thought to be irrelevant to the desirability or success of the program themselves.) So far, this crusade has been immensely effective. It will continue to be effective until the corporation has decided what kind of institution it is in today's world, and what kinds of reforms are a necessary precondition to a vigorous defense—not of its every action but of its very survival as a quasi-public institution as distinct from a completely politicized institution.

It is no exaggeration to say that the future of liberal democracy in America is intimately involved with such prospects for survival—the survival of an institution which liberal democracy never envisaged, whose birth and existence have been exceedingly troublesome to it, and whose legitimacy it has always found dubious. One can, if one wishes, call this a paradox. Or one can simply say that everything, including liberal democracy, is what it naturally becomes—is what it naturally evolves into—and our problem derives from a reluctance to revise yesteryear's beliefs in the light of today's realities.

1976

# 16

## Business Ethics
## and Economic Man

THE *PROGRESSIVE,* a left-of-center monthly, has been restrained by the courts from publishing an article which provides useful instructions on how to construct a hydrogen bomb. The media, in reporting the event, have solemnly discussed the case in terms of the First Amendment and the prerogatives of government vis-à-vis that amendment. Of "journalistic ethics" or "journalistic social responsibility" there has been scarcely a mention. Yet these same media seem to be passionately concerned with "business ethics," and would surely have had a moralistic tantrum if an effort had been made to publish that same article in, let us say, one of General Electric's corporate publications.

All of which suggests that, in the current furor over business ethics, not everything is what it appears to be. That it is a hot new issue, in the sense in which Wall Street uses the term, is undeniable—there is clearly active promotion of, and a keen speculative interest in, an issue whose intrinsic merits are anything but obvious. Moreover, a great many "insiders" stand to profit handsomely from going public with this issue. Professors—who regard any code of academic ethics as an infringement on academic freedom—have new courses to offer, new research to be funded, new moral authority to be acquired. Journalists—who regard any code of journalistic ethics as a violation of free speech—have a new field for muckraking. Government bureaucrats—who regard the very idea of a bureaucratic code of ethics as preposterous—have a wider scope for their exercise of power.

So one has the right to be very skeptical about the authenticity of this moralistic fervor, and to suspect its intentions and motives. Much of it—most of it, I would go so far as to say—represents nothing more than an improvised assault against the legitimacy of business enterprise itself, one in which sanctimonious self-righteousness and crude self-interest are neatly wedded. And it has, of course, been enormously successful. Note how "lack of due diligence" by a corporate executive is now legally defined by the SEC [Securities and Exchange Commission] and the courts as a species of "fraud," whereas the same lack of due diligence by a newspaper editor provides no ground whatsoever even for private legal action. Apparently, we are all to be terribly sensitive to any "chilling effect" on journalistic activity, but utterly indifferent to chilling effects on business activity. The fact that journalistic activity is, as often as not, itself a form of business activity is conveniently ignored. The upshot is that a presumption that all businessmen would be crooks, did not the media and the bureaucracy keep them honest, is now so widespread that it has become practically impossible even to debate the matter.

Still, after all this has been said and noted, it remains true that there really is such a thing as business ethics, and that business activity does sometimes involve a confrontation with moral dilemmas. (Since business is a human activity, it would be indeed astonishing if this were not the case!) And it is also true that, over these past decades, the business community has not been particularly attentive to, or even interested in, questions of business ethics, blithely leaving such questions to be settled in negotiation between their lawyers and the government's lawyers. But lawyers are just about the last class of people one wants to see involved in these matters, since for a lawyer (and rightly so) the ethical is simply identical with the legal. Unfortunately, this is also precisely the point of view most congenial to politicians and bureaucrats, who then proceed to regulate business activity with enthusiasm.

Business ethics, in any civilization, is properly defined by moral and religious traditions, and it is a confession of moral bankruptcy to assert that what the law does not explicitly prohibit is therefore morally permissible. Yet, curiously enough, this is what businessmen often seem to be saying—therewith inevitably inviting government to expand its code of prohibitions. And the reason this has happened is that business-men have come to think that the conduct of business is a purely "eco-nomic" activity, to be judged only by economic criteria, and that moral and religious traditions exist in a world apart, to be visited on Sundays perhaps.

Such a state of affairs is anything but "natural." After all, business is not a new or peculiarly modern phenomenon. Commercial transac-tions—like sexual transactions and political transactions—have always been among the most common and important experiences of everyday life. And around that experience there has, over the centuries, grown a huge library of moral commentaries and moral casuistry, in all the world's religions. That businessmen should be unmindful of this tradi-tion is understandable, since the current crop of theologians is, for the most part, itself quite ignorant of it, much preferring superficial "trendi-ness" to sober learning. Still, it is businessmen who suffer more from this deprivation, since they are likely to be the objects rather than the subjects of moral discourse.

The value and importance of these forgotten ethical traditions is their subtlety and complexity. They apply general rules of moral con-duct in the context of circumstances that are always novel in some spe-cific and vital respect. They give no easy answers, because moral practice (as distinct from moral theory) poses no easy questions. We can all eas-ily agree that businessmen should not be dishonest or untrustworthy, on the simple grounds that no one can claim a right to be dishonest or untrustworthy. But nothing is ever simple in the moral life, and an actual businessman will often find himself confronted by perplexing dilemmas.

If the bribing of officials is a common and widespread practice in a foreign nation, should an American corporation participate in such a practice? Only a simpleminded moral absolutist would (as our govern-ment has) answer instantly in the negative, and such absolut-ists—disdaining all casuistry—are of little use when it comes to practical moral problems. A sage moralist would have to take into account the conflict of public interests that are involved. After all, if British and Ger-man corporations are free to bribe, while American corporations are not, then American jobs are lost and the American economy as a whole is adversely affected. It is always nice to strike the correct moral pos-ture—but if such posturing is totally ineffectual or very costly, then we are talking about a kind of "conscientious objection" that, in the real world, is not always the most productive kind of moral behavior. This is one of those cases where the general rule is clear enough—bribery is bad and to be discouraged—but where it is not all that easy to come up with specific guidelines appropriate to the specific situation. Priests and rabbis engaged in moral counseling encounter exactly such problems more often than not.

They also frequently encounter problems involving a conflict, not of public interests, but between public morality and private. It is easy to assert glibly that each of us has a moral as well as legal obligation to convey knowledge of any and all illicit activities ("blow the whistle") to the proper authorities. But what if the illicit activity is minor or transient and is committed by a lifelong friend? Or an amiable colleague who has become a close friend? Does that make a difference? Of course it makes a difference. The bonds of friendship are *moral* bonds, and personal loyalty to a friend—or even to an institution one is part of—is a moral sentiment. Here, as elsewhere, the really difficult moral issues arise, not from a confrontation of good and evil, but from a collision between two goods. That is what makes the moral life so intensely interesting—and so eternally perplexing. But one would not know of such perplexities from the quick and easy rhetoric about business ethics that is so popular today.

It is not surprising, therefore, that the solution of our popular moralists to issues of business ethics should be just about the worst of all possible solutions. It involves what can fairly be called the "bureaucratization of ethics," with an array of lofty and contemptuous Sanhedrins (the SEC, the FTC [Federal Trade Commission], the FCC [Federal Communications Commission], and all the rest) issuing moral directives that veer between the dogmatically simpleminded and the incomprehensibly ambiguous. No other group in American life is subject to such mindless, pettifogging tyranny, nor can any reasonable person truly believe that this could possibly result in an elevation of morality, public or private, individual or corporate.

To the degree that the business community protests against this situation, it is in terms of an abuse of power. It is indeed an abuse of power—but power will, in the end, always rush in to fill any available moral vacuum. It is that vacuum which is at the root of the problem. The business community should itself get interested, in a serious way, an intellectually thoughtful way, in the issue of business ethics. There are some, if not many, theologians and philosophers who have no particular animus against business and who have worthwhile things to say on the matter. But the business community, for the most part, does not know who they are—or even that they exist.

Once again, modern business is paying the price for conceiving of itself as representing an abstract species of "economic man," rather than as men and women engaged in a fully human activity. It is this self-delusion that has helped so significantly to create the divorce between the business communities and academic-intellectual communities—a divorce that leaves the business community so defenseless when ideas (about morality or anything else) are used unscrupulously as weapons against it.

1979

# V

# NEOCONSERVATISM
# AND
# FOREIGN POLICY

# 17

## Diplomacy vs. Foreign Policy in the United States

Every secretary of state soon finds himself threading his way through pools of quicksand. In no time at all he comes to feel that merely keeping his footing denotes a successful conduct of foreign policy. In the meantime, he has completely forgotten where he was supposed to be going and why.

Those pools of quicksand represent the innumerable treaties, conventions, and alliances we have blandly committed ourselves to over the past four decades, under the illusion that we were moving toward an eventual "world community." In such a world, foreign policy—the defense of one's national interests—would cease to exist, having been completely replaced by a diplomacy aiming to reconcile the interests of all. Our State Department acts most of the time as if that world were already at hand, as if diplomacy were no longer the handmaiden of foreign policy but its master.

So it is that we now have the spectacle of our secretary of state mediating a dispute between Britain and Argentina, while informing us that he is steering a middle course between these two "allies." I cannot be the only American to have been astonished by the discovery that Argentina—an official member of the "nonaligned" (i.e., anti-American) bloc of nations—is our ally in the same sense that Britain is. When did that happen? Well, according to the State Department, it all goes back to something called the Rio Treaty.

The existence of such a treaty was news to me as well, and so I scurried to the *Columbia Encyclopedia.* There I discovered that, back in 1947, we signed the Inter-American Treaty of Reciprocal Assistance, a treaty then ratified by all twenty-one American republics. According to the terms of this "Rio Treaty," as recounted in my indispensable encyclopedia, "an armed attack or threat of aggression against a signatory nation, whether by a member nation or by some other power, will be considered an attack against all." Moreover, "it is provided that no member can use force without the unanimous consent of the other signatories."

So much for any thought of military intervention by the United States anywhere in South or Central America. It seems that, years ago, we gave our "allies" a veto over any such action, regardless of provocation or circumstance.

I put the term "allies" in quotation marks because I was not aware we had so many allies south of the border, and still find it less than believable. As best I can make out, many of them, much of the time, do not sound like allies or act like allies.

An alliance, according to my dictionary—another indispensable tool in this Orwellian age—is "an association or union formed for the furtherance of the common interests and aims of the members." But what are the common interests and aims of the United States and the nations of Central and Latin America, nations whose chronic political instability is matched only by their economic irresponsibility? We doubtless have common interests and goals with some of them, some of the time. But with all of them, all of the time? With Bolivia? Peru? Ecuador? Panama?

How on earth did we ever come to sign such an absurd treaty? And why do we persist in remaining a signatory to it? To put it bluntly: What national interest of ours is served by this treaty?

In fact, we get nothing out of this treaty, but even to ask such a question is to shake the State Department to its foundations. For it challenges the department's basic assumption: that we live in a world in which foreign policy (the expression of national interest) is "progressively" being superseded by the "rule of law" in international relations—a lovely goal but unattainable short of a Second Coming. It is in pursuit of this goal that we get a Rio Treaty, or the establishment of the Organization of American States (1948), a kind of mini-United Nations where we can be voted down in only three languages, thereby saving translators' fees.

It is in pursuit of this same utopian goal that we permit our foreign policy and our national interests to be regularly savaged at the United Nations. Make no mistake about it: Serious things *do* happen at the UN, serious commitments *are* entered into there. The proceedings have the air of comic opera, but those same absurd proceedings end up in treaties or resolutions whose authority we recognize.

It is all the more important, therefore, that we realize that the UN, as it has developed, is an entity hostile to American interests. It is the UN which has created the "Third World"—a coalition of nations with no real common interests except the political capital to be gained domestically by striking anti-American, anti-Western, anti-"colonialist" postures. If the UN did not exist, the Third World would not exist. There would be no forum where these nations are compelled, for internal reasons, to define their foreign policy in such an ideological way.

A good part of the time, our ambassador to the UN is listening to explanations from Third World representatives as to why their votes against us do not really reflect their true sentiments and why, therefore, we should not take them too seriously. Incredibly enough, the State Department—though not our [current ambassador] to the UN—tends to find such "explanations" persuasive.

But though votes at the UN may not have consequences for those nations that blandly vote against us, therewith providing them with no incentives to act otherwise, they do have consequences for us. We cannot, like the Soviet Union, ignore them when it suits our convenience. We like to think of ourselves as a law-abiding nation in international affairs. Being a democratic capitalist nation, we like to take contracts seriously. The upshot is that we find ourselves implicated in endless negotiations—over the Law of the Sea, international communications, multilateral foreign aid programs, environmental and safety regulations—in a setting where we are habitually being outvoted by nations that have no material interest in these issues. It is inevitable that the "compromises" we end up with always signify our giving away something in return for nothing.

There can be no question that such issues would be settled to our better advantage if we were to negotiate privately, bilaterally or multilaterally, with the nations directly involved. And if such negotiations were fruitless—well, presumably that would be to our advantage too.

There are many occasions when no settlement of disputes is preferable to a settlement on poor terms. This is definitely the case when one of the parties of the negotiations is a large, powerful and affluent nation like the United States, which can almost always seek other options. But at the UN, all nations are equal, and all negotiations begin with a list of outrageous demands upon us—demands which we then try to whittle down, with every shaving seen by our State Department as a triumph of diplomacy.

On the most serious and sensitive issues, too, the UN is a place that provokes, not consensus, but—in the words of Ambassador Jeane Kirkpatrick—"conflict extension, exacerbation, and polarization." The situation in the Middle East would be much less explosive than it is, and negotiations among interested parties would be more serious than they are, did the UN not exist. The nations of Latin America would not then be selling their votes to the highest bidder, which is their custom. The nations of Africa would not be tempted to meddle in world politics instead of solving their desperate domestic problems. All parties with authentic, material interests in the Israeli-Arab conflict would have more "space" for maneuver, did not the UN create a spurious "world opinion" that constricts such flexibility.

Since all of this is obvious, one would think that our State Department would be giving some thought to it. But it firmly resists any such invitation. Rethinking our membership in the UN is simply out of bounds. Even the prospect of relocating the UN, and thereby weakening its influence, is out of bounds.

It would definitely be to our advantage if some other nation, far away, were to have the honor of providing hospitality to the UN for the next decade or so. Why not give Lagos a chance? Or Kuala Lumpur? One can understand the reluctance of the UN bureaucracy, or of foreign diplomats, or of the KGB, to entertain such a suggestion. But if our State Department were really interested in foreign policy, it would not be so averse to floating the idea.

Our State Department, however, is not interested in foreign policy, only in its own version of diplomacy. And it just does not seem to matter who is president or who is secretary of state. The department, in the end, always manages to prevail.

1982

# 18

## Our Incoherent Foreign Policy

IN a recent issue of *Time* magazine, the veteran Washington journalist High Sidey wrote sadly:

> We no longer seem sure what our interests in the world are or how to pursue them realistically. There is no overall view of the world and what our role should be that is held by a majority of the men and women in the federal government, a theme that gives direction and coherence to the way we build and deploy our military forces, use our Foreign Service and encourage our private traders.

He is, alas, only too right, and the signs of our disarray are too numerous to count. Thus, if you do not have a foreign policy, you are likely to rely on diplomacy—a "dialogue" at the United Nations, for instance—to fill the vacuum. But diplomacy is only a useful, even indispensable adjunct to foreign policy, not a possible replacement for it. If you enter into negotiations without a clear understanding of what the power relations are, how negotiations might affect them, what your goals are, what the other party's goals are, what an acceptable settlement would look like from your point of view, you will always leave the table a loser. That is what has happened at the SALT [Strategic Arms Limitation Talks] negotiations, the Law of the Sea negotiations, the International Monetary Fund negotiations, and just about every other such proceeding.

If you do not have a foreign policy, you are easily tempted to engage in symbolic actions that are ultimately self-defeating. President Carter's embargo on grain exports to the USSR, after the Soviet invasion of Afghanistan, was a perfect illustration of such an action—or, perhaps one should say, reaction. Economic sanctions of this kind never have worked. They did not work against Italy in the 1930s, they did not work against Rhodesia yesterday, they do not work against South Africa today. The Soviet Union is getting its grain, if at a slightly higher cost. Meanwhile, the embargo has become an albatross around our own neck. Lifting that embargo now means, in effect, legitimizing the Soviet occupation of Afghanistan. But surely we are not going to try to enforce it forever? There is no way we can come out of this situation without humiliation.

Why do we not have a foreign policy worthy of the name? The reason, put bluntly, is that for too long we have had a foreign policy unworthy of the name. That is to say, we have had—and, on the whole, still have—a foreign policy based on all sorts of illusions as to the kind of world we live in.

For the sake of convenience, and at the risk of some simplification, these illusions can be divided into two major categories: illusions about the Soviet Union and illusions about the so-called Third World. At bottom both of these illusions flow from a common source—the one grand illusion that the world of nations is so constituted that liberal pieties and liberal aspirations must be congruent with the nature of things, must eventually be ratified by history.

Of these two illusions, I would say that, oddly enough, it is the Soviet illusion which is the lesser danger to us. The reason is that it is continually self-correcting, in the sense that the Soviet Union regularly and determinedly will move to disabuse us of it. Every time a Secretary Vance leaves a meeting with the Russians to assure us cheerfully that Mr. Brezhnev and Mr. Carter share the same aspirations for mankind, the Soviet government will quickly act so as to reveal the inanity of such an assertion. To be sure, by that time the Soviets will have taken advantage of our self-deception to gain an advantage over us, and the cumulative effect can be very dangerous indeed—as our present situation of military and strategic inferiority makes clear enough. But the United States is inherently a far more powerful nation than the USSR, and we usually have the time to move forcefully to restore an equilibrium in world power politics.

One of these days, of course, we may find that we do not have the time, and those who eloquently describe "the present danger," and who remind us that the cold war is an article of Soviet faith, not a figment of our fevered imagination, therefore play an invaluable role. But the Soviets, though strong militarily, are weak politically—witness recent events in Poland—and do not find it all that easy to exploit their seeming advantages.

In any case, the most important point to be made about this situation is that, while the State Department or the White House may have illusions about Soviet intentions, the American people do not—and never have. It is relatively painless for any administration to mobilize popular and congressional opinion against a manifestation of Soviet hostility. Certainly a Reagan administration would have little difficulty in gaining support for a foreign policy that takes the Soviet threat seriously. Even in many liberal and left-wing circles there is less of a predisposition to give the Soviet Union the benefit of any doubt, since most of these people have by now transported their illusions elsewhere.

Elsewhere, in this case, means the nations of the Third World, and it is in regard to these nations that our foreign policy stumbles into profound intellectual difficulties.

There are some who try to simplify the problem by insisting (or assuming) that our problems with the Third World arise from Soviet meddling or Soviet instigation or Soviet conspiracy, and that a more realistic policy toward the Soviets is somehow a comprehensive answer to all our foreign policy perplexities. Unfortunately, that is not the case. Yes, the Soviet Union does all it can to encourage left-wing anti-American movements or regimes in the Third World. But these movements and regimes represent a powerful autonomous impulse, and are not mere contrivances of Soviet cunning. Indeed, the Third World can often be as much of a headache for the Soviets as it is for us.

Third World is one of those political terms whose meaning is far less obvious than current and casual usage would suggest. The ambiguities in such usage are revealed when we ask the simple question: What kind of nation qualifies for membership in this category?

Originally, the answer seemed clear enough. Nations which were "neutralist" in foreign policy as between the United States and the USSR, and which were economically underdeveloped as compared with either, had a sufficient commonality of interests to constitute a Third World. But with the passing of time that definition has undergone a radical transformation. Thus, Cuba, not at all "neutralist," is officially recognized as a Third World nation, but South Korea, also not "neutralist," is not. At the same time, Saudi Arabia, Kuwait, and Libya, now incredibly rich, retain their Third World status, while affluent Singapore does not.

As one studies the picture, the pattern becomes clear. In order to be a Third World nation, one has to be anti-American, in word if not always in deed. (This distinction permits Saudi Arabia to retain membership.) One does not have to be pro-Russian, but one must not be explicitly and overtly anti-Russian. One must not be a constitutional democracy—India barely qualifies as an exception that proves the rule—though the modes of authoritarian government are various. One is usually self-designated as "Marxist" or "Socialist" in political philosophy but in any case one cannot be explicitly procapitalist. A willingness to denounce "Western imperialism" and "Western colonialism" as the root of the world's evils is taken for granted as an attribute of membership.

The hostility may fluctuate in vehemence, the entity itself may change its shape as members move in or out. But the Third World will continue to confront us.

Only we are not confronting it. The idea that we should be is rejected even by many of those who understand the need to confront the Soviet Union when it becomes overly aggressive. Somehow we cling desperately to the notion that these nations are going through a troublesome adolescence as they proceed ineluctably toward a "mature" involvement in a "community of nations," as this is defined by traditional liberal ideals. We actually manage to convince ourselves that we ought to feel guilty about their poverty—see the Brandt Commission report or Mr. McNamara's farewell address to the World Bank—even though it is their own governments which work to frustrate their economic growth and are largely responsible for the economic chaos that deprives their peoples of life, liberty, and the pursuit of happiness. In forum after forum, we speak in placatory or apologetic accents, in response to their absurd or venomous accusations. In negotiation after negotiation, we make concession after concession to their unreasonable demands.

All to no avail, inevitably. The radical-nationalist ideologies of these nations, so far from being a prelude to the liberal-constitutionalism we revere, are a kind of epilogue. They—or at least their ruling elites—have seen our present and reject it as their future. So long as we refuse to confront this reality, we do not have a clear vision of the world the United States inhabits. And so long as there is no such clear vision, there can be no coherent foreign policy.

Mind you, confronting reality is not the same thing as engaging in a perpetual politics of confrontation. The truth is that, once it is perceived that our vision is unblurred by illusions, such confrontation will be less probable. We are a strong nation, and they will respect our strength, as well as our loyalty to our own political and social ideals, when we behave in a self-respecting way. Then, and only then, can there emerge a coherent and effective American foreign policy.

1980

# 19

# *Does NATO Exist?*

I HAVE NOT chosen this title out of intellectual perversity or a willful desire to shock or provoke. It is a question that many Americans are only too likely to ask in the course of the 1980s. True, at the moment the opinion polls show that NATO [North Atlantic Treaty Organization] is quite popular among Americans. But this positive response is little more than a vague benevolence toward nations that are understood to be our allies. As the nature and depth of this alliance is put to the test, however, those attitudes will surely change.

Indeed, by putting the title in the form of a question I believe that, in a spirit of moderation, I am giving NATO the benefit of the doubt. For in a very real sense the NATO alliance has already been tested—and has been found wanting. It is my own sad conviction that, after an initial decade of quite vigorous existence, NATO ceased to be a living reality some years ago. I also anticipate that, sometime in the not too distant future, the appropriate formal funeral services will occur.

In retrospect, one can see that NATO was programmed to self-destruct. As the late Martin Wight acutely remarked: "It may be noted, as a melancholy law of coalitions, that they are designed to avert the last war." NATO was designed to avert World War II, the only difference being that (1) it was now the Soviet Union rather than Germany which was to be deterred from aggression against its European neighbors, and (2) the United States was now, from the beginning, a full part-

ner in this coalition. The lessons of the 1930s were well learned, if somewhat belatedly, and were applied to the 1950s. And because there were
genuine resemblances between the situation of Western Europe in the
1930s and 1950s—but only to the degree that there were such resemblances—this response was quite effective.

It is important, however, to note one crucial difference between the
hypothetical coalition of the 1930s and the actual coalition of the
post–World War II period. This difference involves the nature of the
military deterrent. While deterrence in the 1930s involved what we now
call "conventional" weaponry, NATO was originally entirely depen-
dent on the strategic nuclear "umbrella" of the United States. This umbrella, of course, was only aggression-proof to the extent that the
United States had a clear superiority over the Soviet Union in strategic
nuclear weaponry. The retaliatory threat was simple: If Soviet troops
were overtly to move against Western Europe, the Soviet Union would
be annihilated. That is "deterrence" with a vengeance.

But as the Soviet Union gradually acquired its own strategic nuclear
capability, this mode of deterrence became less and less credible. It then
became reasonable to wonder just how much destruction and loss of
life the United States would be willing to accept on behalf of Western
Europe, in a massive nuclear exchange. And as the Soviet Union moved
inexorably toward something approaching strategic nuclear equiva-
lence—in short, as the terms of the equation became steadily less favorable to the United States—the very notion of such deterrence became
ever more preposterous. In the 1980s, according to practically all military analysts, the strategic nuclear balance will actually have tilted
somewhat in favor of the Soviet Union. Under these circumstances, the
idea of strategic deterrence will have slid from the merely preposterous
to the patently absurd.

It is still the official military doctrine of the United States and
NATO that the use of strategic nuclear weapons is not excluded, in a
case of Soviet aggression with conventional military forces—or, *a fortiori,*
using tactical nuclear weapons—against Western Europe. There may
even be American and NATO generals who believe this is so. They, and
anyone else who believes it, are living in a world of fantasy. Under no
conceivable circumstances—I repeat: under *no* conceivable circumstances—will an American government respond to such Soviet aggression in Western Europe by initiating a strategic nuclear exchange. *That*
deterrence has ceased to exist, whatever some military men or politicians may officially say. The function of America's strategic nuclear
weaponry today is to deter a Soviet first strike against the United States
itself—that and nothing but that.

Indeed, it was in implicit recognition of this fact that NATO, in the course of the 1950s and 1960s, began to place an ever-greater reliance on *tactical* nuclear weapons. These could inflict such enormous losses on Soviet troops that, even though NATO troops (and civilians) were suffering comparable losses from Soviet tactical nuclear weapons, there would be a genuine deterrent effect. This is certainly a far more credible deterrent than the (by now) empty threat of a strategic nuclear exchange. But one wonders: Just how credible *in fact* is it, now that the Soviets have effective parity (at the least) in such weapons? Here again, the official point of view is so insistent, even adamant, that one suffers twinges of conscience in engaging in private, skeptical speculation. Still, one cannot help but wonder . . .

Let us assume the following, perfectly plausible, scenario: Soviet troops, together with East German troops, move massively against West Germany on several fronts. Given their clear superiority in numbers, as well as in tanks, artillery, and so forth, they will certainly achieve some breakthroughs. The NATO troops will then, presumably, duly employ their tactical nuclear weapons, inflicting substantial casualties on the enemy. The enemy replies in kind, inflicting large casualties in turn—not only against NATO troops but, inevitably, against some of NATO's urban centers and their civilian population. What then? Will the governments and peoples of Western Europe grit their teeth, fighting on tenaciously in the face of huge casualties and mass suffering, until the Soviets agree to withdraw? Will the NATO nations of Western Europe accept the devastation of their own lands in stoical, heroic, and perhaps ultimately successful resistance to Soviet domination?

The official doctrine is that they will. I, for one, do not believe it, and I have met precious few observers of the European scene who do believe it. It seems clear to me that, as things stand today, such a martial spirit, a spirit of patriotic self-sacrifice, does not exist in any European country (with the possible exception of Switzerland). Yes, initial resistance there certainly would be—this is practically built into the present military structure of NATO, is well-nigh automatic—and the enemy would doubtless suffer many casualties. But after that initial response? After some NATO divisions have been decimated and some NATO cities ruined? Then, I think, the spirit of resistance will quickly give way to a spirit of negotiation and accommodation. Whereas in the 1930s resistance followed appeasement, in Europe today it is likely to be the other way around.

The reasons why the governments and peoples of Western Europe can, in my opinion, be expected to react in this way has to do with their political experience and formation since World War II. Perhaps one can sum it up, roughly and vaguely, by saying that, in the intervening three decades, the social-democratic temper, the inward-turning politics of compassionate reform has largely replaced the patriotic temper, the politics of national self-assertion. I shall enlarge on this theme in a moment, but would like first to address myself to the obvious question: If strategic nuclear weapons are no longer a credible deterrent, and if tactical nuclear weapons are a less than convincing deterrent, what *does* deter the Soviet Union from a takeover of Western Europe?*

One possible answer is that the Soviet Union simply does not realize how feeble a deterrence they are confronted with; they apparently at least half-believe the solemn, official declarations as to our resolute will to resist at any cost. There may be some truth in this. It is possible that the Soviet leaders really do believe that there are "ruling circles" in the West who will fight to the death to maintain their power and prerogatives. (If this is the case, it would be nice to figure out a way to keep this illusion alive.) But it seems to me that there are three better explanations for Soviet behavior, explanations which give more credit to Soviet realism than to Soviet self-deception.

There is, to begin with, the factor of unpredictability. Once any kind of nuclear conflict begins, no one can be absolutely sure how it will evolve. It just might end up with nuclear holocaust. And it just might provoke new and devastating tensions within the Soviet system itself. The Soviet leadership has generally revealed itself to be cautious and prudent (if persistent) in its aggressiveness. There would seem to be no reason, under the circumstances existing today, for it to engage in the kind of desperate action that overt military aggression in Europe would represent. It may, at some point, feel forced to such action should this appear necessary to preserve the regime. It is hard to imagine it taking such action, however, simply because cold-blooded military calculations imply a favorable outcome.

Perhaps more important is the fact that the Soviet leadership may actually not be much interested in achieving a Soviet-occupied Western Europe. Whatever the paranoid fears of a rearmed and aggressive Germany which once existed, these have surely been dispelled by the progress of Soviet nuclear capability over the past fifteen years. And the satellite nations of Eastern Europe, after all, are not exactly secure and

---

*The United States is now trying to persuade its NATO allies to participate in a Theatre Nuclear Force (TNF)—i.e., missiles whose capability lies somewhere between the tactical and the strategic. As of this writing, the nations of Western Europe are demonstrating a great reluctance to permit any such force to be located on their territories. This suggests to me that a TNF will be but another fictitious deterrent, born of the union of two older fictitious deterrents.

profitable assets—one doubts very much that the Soviet leadership is eager to expand this portion of their portfolio. To be sure, it would like to see something approaching the "Finlandization" of Western Europe. But it has many reasons to think that, with patience, this goal can be achieved without resorting to armed conflict. After all, the very existence of Soviet military superiority at all levels, with its prospects for intimidation, is itself a long step in that direction.

A third reason—in my opinion the most important—is that Western Europe itself is no longer so central to the foreign policy of either of the two superpowers. Other areas of the world—the Middle East and Latin America especially—are of at least equal importance to those foreign policies. Some kind of armed confrontation between the United States and the Soviet Union in the Persian Gulf is far more probable than such a confrontation in Central Europe. It would be a wild exaggeration to say that Western Europe has shrunk to insignificance on the world scale where foreign policies are weighed and measured. But what *is* true is that the nations of Western Europe who are America's NATO allies have, since World War II, become increasingly "isolationist." They have no coherent foreign policy that looks beyond the geographical confines of Western Europe. To an ever-increasing degree the foreign policies of the United States and the Soviet Union, as these great powers maneuver for position and advantage, can and do ignore Western Europe as a factor in their reckonings. Western Europe, in turn, seems perfectly content that this should be the case.

And it is this situation, I believe, that will guarantee the eventual demise of NATO. Not only are the *military* assumptions on which NATO is based highly problematic today. But the key *foreign policy* assumption—that Western Europe is, as it were, the "world's cockpit," the critical locus of world conflict—is rapidly being emptied of substance. These two assumptions remain as *fables convenus,* duly reiterated by the NATO governments. But no one outside the diplomatic corps takes them seriously anymore. And in this context, a growing divergence between the United States and its NATO allies is inevitable. For the United States is and will—despite the current disarray in Washington—remain a great power, profoundly enmeshed in world politics. The nations of Western Europe, in contrast, seem to have opted out of the strenuous game of world politics in order to pursue the comforts of domestic life.

One might say, in retrospect, that NATO at birth was predestined to suffer such a dissolution. A purely defensive coalition, having neither the intention nor the will to defeat the enemy in case of conflict, nor to achieve larger goals of its own, but only successfully to resist overt military aggression, has assumed a posture which, sooner or later, will give rise to acute tensions and strains. But it is also true that when NATO was formed, it was widely hoped that something more than a contingent, purely defensive coalition had taken shape. There was the thought that the nations of Western Europe together with the United States would develop a "foreign policy for the Free World." That thought has all but vanished from memory.

To a considerable degree, the United States must bear a large share of the responsibility for the way things turned out. We still do not have (in my opinion) an adequate intellectual history of American foreign policy in the postwar world, and it is not entirely clear just how we Americans ended up being so besotted with callow, even childish, notions of what foreign policy is all about. But it is clear that our State Department, over these years, blandly forgot the first principles of foreign policy as these pertain to a great power. Above all it forgot that, to quote Martin Wight once again, "a Foreign Minister is chosen and paid to look after the interests of his country, and not be a delegate for the human race." To put it another way: What one might call "the global point of view" is appropriate enough for the scholar and philosopher, or even for the statesman who is out of office—but not for the statesman in office. Nevertheless, it is this global point of view, the legacy of a debased and vulgarized Wilsonianism, which to this day permeates our foreign policy establishment, and leads to a posture and actions in foreign affairs which future scholars will have difficulty taking at face value. But, alas, they will be wrong, for in this case, face value conceals nothing more substantial.

One clear sign of this global point of view is the way in which the United States has retained a solemn commitment to the United Nations as an international institution, long after it became clear that the majority of the UN's members were and would remain hostile to the basic purposes of American foreign policy. Indeed, it is not too much to say that the idea of NATO having any kind of foreign policy for the free world, while its members are loyal members of the United Nations, has become a flat contradiction. This would not be the case if the nations of NATO were disloyal members of the UN, using that institution cynically where and if this served their purposes. This, of course, is exactly the way Communist nations or Third World nations use the UN. But they can only do this precisely because the NATO nations, and most especially the United States, do *not* behave with a corresponding cynicism. Were everyone to be purely manipulative of the UN, it would soon cease to exist. That prospect, oddly enough, is regarded as alarming, even unthinkable, by the American foreign policy establishment, which is firmly committed to a global point of view, to the utopian notion that the ultimate and governing purpose of American foreign policy is to establish a world community of nations all living amiably under the rule of law.

It may be difficult for Europeans, with their long and disenchanting experience in foreign affairs, to believe that our State Department is actually intoxicated with this vision. They are likely to think that it is little more than sanctimonious, self-serving rhetoric. They are quite wrong to think this. Sanctimonious it may be, self-serving it is not. Indeed, all too often it is self-destructive.

Nothing exemplifies this better than the Suez imbroglio of 1956, when the United States, having to choose between the ideals of the United Nations and the reality of NATO, firmly and disastrously chose the former. I am convinced that this incident was the turning point in the history of NATO, and perhaps even a watershed in the diplomatic history of this century. Until that point, it was possible to think that NATO, for all the original flaws in its conception, might yet develop into an authentic force in world affairs. After the event, that prospect could not seriously be entertained.

Obviously one cannot know with any assurance what the world would be like today if the United States had not frustrated the Anglo-French occupation of the Suez Canal. Perhaps such an occupation could not have endured for long, in any case. Or perhaps it could have—and we might have been spared the 1967 Israeli-Arab conflict, OPEC [Organization of Petroleum Exporting Countries], and sundry other unfortunate happenings. But one thing is clear: After Suez, the idea of a NATO foreign policy, one applicable to troubled areas of the world as well as to the defense of Western Europe, had vanished from the realm of possibility. What survived is the actuality of today: an American foreign policy that tries to cope, on its own, with noxious eruptions all over the globe, and a Western Europe only too anxious to avoid overseas responsibilities or even involvement, whose foreign policy has degenerated into a desperate reliance on the "NATO shield" to protect it against the Soviet Union, while moving toward nervous appeasement of all other enemies everywhere else. I note that the Atlantic Institute has called for a "new partnership" between NATO and OPEC—one hardly knows whether to laugh or cry at such hypocrisy.

It may be that this decline of Western Europe as a force in world affairs, even if the United States had not provided such adequate leadership, was inevitable—and there are doubtless numerous observers who, without hesitation, would be happy to give us an appropriate philosophic explanation for the "decline of the West." The trouble with such explanations, however, is that they mystify more than they explain. Anyone who, looking at Western Europe after World War II, could be impressed mainly by signs of decline would have to be working with a very peculiar notion of "decline." Never had Western Europe shown more rapid economic growth accompanied by significant population growth—the two indicators one ordinarily looks at first when discussing national decline. Even today, Western Europe as a whole possesses the economic and demographic preconditions for matching the Soviet Union in conventional military strength, thereby placing on the latter the risk of first use of nuclear weapons—a risk it is not likely to underestimate. These same preconditions make it possible for Europe as a whole, in the abstract, to rank as a great power. What is lacking is, quite simply, the motivation.

I have already referred to the "social-democratization" of Western Europe—and to a far lesser degree, of the United States as well—as explaining the absence of a will to self-assertion. By this I mean the increasingly intense focus on satisfying the demands of a "risk-aversive" society, demands which in themselves are natural enough but which are magnified many times over by the politics that inflames them even as it seeks to satisfy them. More and more, the politics of Western European nations centers on the provision of more complex and expensive social services, more complex and expensive subsidies to practically every group and subgroup, not merely to those whom we have conventionally deemed to be "needy." All political parties, and not only those which designate themselves as social-democratic, seem to be captive (in varying degrees) to this conception of what national politics is all about. Among contemporary European leaders, only Charles de Gaulle had a vision that rose above this level of prosaic domesticity—the nation as one vast household, whose daily problems have now been transformed into the stuff of politics. But he, most unfortunately, thought that France alone, not Western Europe in coalition, could reemerge as a major power. This was and is a chimera. Had he been able to think in European terms, had he been able to bring himself to imagine a strong NATO consisting of European powers alone, his anti-Americanism would have served a positive end—one, indeed, that would have suited American ends (in spite of American objections) better than the NATO that survives today. His legacy, however, is merely a France which indulges in the rhetoric of national pride and power, but which in international affairs engages mainly in independent strategies of appeasement.

One hears it said that this social-democratization of politics—the movement from a mere welfare state to a truly paternalistic (or maternalistic?) state—is an inevitable end product of democracy itself, and that it would have been futile to contemplate any other destiny for the Western democracies. Perhaps. Or perhaps this is a rationale for ideologists whose utopian vision of a good society has no place for foreign policy, with all its moral ambiguities. (It is surely no accident that one cannot even mention a socialist work on foreign policy worth the reading. Socialism in any community is supposed to conquer the hearts and minds of men, everywhere, simply by its inspiring example.) Or perhaps it is our democratic politicians, as distinct from our democratic peoples, who prefer this type of political order, since it offers seemingly endless opportunities for quarrelsome self-advancement. I myself think there is much to be said in favor of this last thesis. After all, at the time of Suez it was not the British or French people who suffered a failure of nerve, but their political establishments. And while it is often said that a democratic people will almost always incline toward a higher budget for social services and a lower budget for military expenditures, it is remarkable how infrequently they are ever candidly offered such a choice. Of course, no one will vote for higher military expenditures unless he perceives ways in which these expenditures are likely to be put to productive use. It may well be that, so far from an acceptable level of military expenditures defining one's foreign policy, it is the nature of one's foreign policy that sets limits to the acceptable level of military expenditures.

In any case, there can be little question that the democracies of Western Europe seem today to be far more interested in relatively marginal increments in "welfare" than in playing any significant role in world affairs. The impulse toward the welfare state, in its origins very naturally and properly seeking a program of collective insurance for all citizens in a dynamic, often turbulent, if affluent society, has degenerated into a fierce internal struggle between proliferating interest groups for particular advantage, a struggle usually fought under the banner of "equality." The economic consequences are already highly visible: a rate of taxation that frustrates economic incentives, and an inexorable decline in productivity and economic growth—the same thing, really—so that each new generous gesture can be financed only by inflation. This, in turn, results in collective impoverishment which eventually makes every particular gain more and more illusory. It is not the case, as some lament, that this kind of "welfare-state politics" transforms life in a liberal democracy from a game in which, in the longer run, everyone (as a consequence of economic growth) wins (if to unequal degrees), to a zero-sum game in which there are arrogant winners and embittered losers. It transforms liberal democracy into a process of conflict in which everyone loses, although unequally.

And the political consequences are predictable. So far from achieving greater social and political stability, accompanied by more universal tranquillity, social-democratization generates discontent, cynicism, and "alienation" among the citizenry. Those of us of a certain age can easily remember the hopes, which we may have shared, for a new and better world that accompanied the impulse to reform after World War II. The reforms have been effected, and the reality is disillusioning. This has a terribly important implication which we are only now beginning to perceive: *Modern social democracy is an inherently unstable system.* It generates a momentum for equality—in the bizarre sense of special privileges for all—which, unless firmly controlled, creates an overbearing, bureaucratic state confronting a restless and "ungrateful" citizenry. And such firm control appears extraordinarily difficult to attain, except intermittently for relatively brief periods.

So the nations of NATO and Western Europe—social-democracies all, in their different ways—are at the point of realizing that they will have to drift either to the Left or to the Right (to use the conventional terminology which is as indispensable as it can be confusing). This realization has already spread so rapidly in the leading NATO nation, the United States, that even the American government of today, which when elected two years ago had expected to proceed along familiar social-democratic lines, finds itself out of phase with a popular opinion that is moving massively to the Right. It is trying somewhat desperately (if most reluctantly and ineffectually) to catch up.

As it pertains to foreign policy, I would say that this shift of American opinion represents the initial stages in the burgeoning of a new American nationalism. It is "new" in a crucial respect: It is in the process of transcending the older isolationist-internationalist polarity that has hitherto established the parameters for all controversies over foreign policy. Oddly enough—odd certainly by European standards—it is the isolationist current of thought that has always been nationalistic in temper, while the internationalists have always operated with the global point of view. The new nationalism, however, is based on the proposition that the United States should be *the* major and most influential world power, and as it gathers ideological momentum—some would say *if*, I venture to say *as*—it is going to place a strain on NATO which it can hardly cope with.

Thus, the United States is not only now increasing its military budget (over the objections of an administration which hangs grimly on to an enfeebled version of the older "internationalist" conception of America's role in the world), it is also now forming, at the insistence of Congress and the military, something called a "unilateral force"—a small army of 100,000 rigorously trained men with a "logistics tail" that will permit it to operate anywhere in the world *independently* of support from any existing ally. One would have to be maddened with optimism to think that no occasion will arise—in the Middle East, the Indian Ocean, Africa, perhaps South America, perhaps even Southern Europe—for this force to be used. And what happens to NATO when it is used, when it is engaged in combat somewhere, with someone? If, as now seems most probable, our European allies simply stay aloof, discreetly approving or sullenly disapproving, what will the consequences be? One certain consequence, I predict, would be overwhelming support in Congress and in public opinion for the removal of American troops from Western Europe. Such a movement of opinion could already be discerned during the Vietnam War. Another such situation and it will be irresistible. Indeed, NATO officials are already quietly discussing the mechanisms whereby the United States may be given "permission" to withdraw its troops "temporarily," in case of need. But no one is going to be asking their permission.

The message for Western Europe is clear: *il faut choisir.* If American military operations abroad are executed entirely by a unilateral force, a corresponding unilateral foreign policy will emerge. From having been the centerpiece of American foreign policy, NATO will become an afterthought, and then a mere memory. Not that the United States will ever repudiate a very keen interest in the defense of Western Europe. But the European partners in NATO will discover the partnership to have been dissolved, and that they are now allies of convenience—"client states"—on the order of South Korea, let us say. And unless they sharply increase their own defense expenditures and efforts—again, let us say, to the South Korean level—they could end up as allies of inconvenience. It is also worth noting that, though the United States is committed in a general way to the defense of South Korea against aggression from the North, it is most definitely *not* committed to the initial use of nuclear weapons in such a defense. Presumably that would also hold true in the case of Western Europe. There are some who would claim that, de facto, it already holds true.

I should like to make it clear that I am *not* saying that Western Europe faces the choice between becoming client states of the United States or of the Soviet Union. There is indeed a third alternative: for Western Europe to begin thinking of itself as a world power in its own right, and to take the painful steps necessary to make that thought a reality. The first such step is to move toward parity with the Soviet Union in conventional military strength. The second is to begin thinking (once again) in terms of world power and world politics, as against merely Western European power and politics. It is possible that such a new "great power" will so define its interests, and conduct its foreign policy, in a way that occasionally makes the United States unhappy. *Tant pis.* The world, in my opinion, would still be much better off if Western Europe were to become an independent and effectual force in world affairs. For these nations share a legacy of civilization that, however shaky it may be at the moment, the world very much needs.

1979

# 20

# *Exorcising the Nuclear Nightmare*

FOR more than thirty-five years, ever since the explosions at Hiroshima and Nagasaki, I have favored a doctrine of non-first-use of nuclear weapons by the United States. Since I am generally—and correctly—regarded as a "hawk" on foreign policy, this view has puzzled and irritated many of my political associates. They have tended to regard it as an inexplicable aberration. Today, with the rise of a powerful, popular antinuclear movement, they may wish to reconsider the issue.

The arguments in favor of non-first-use are, as they always have been, threefold: moral, psychological, and strategic.

The moral issue is clear enough. A just war loses its moral legitimacy if it is unjustly conducted—that is, if the destruction of life and property is markedly and obviously disproportionate either to the occasion of the conflict or the war aims that are being pursued. Nuclear weapons are so indiscriminately destructive, and on such a relatively large scale, that their use is morally justified only in the most extreme conditions.

In fact, ever since the end of World War II our Pentagon and State

Department have always had an intuitive, commonsense perception of this truth, though pretending it does not exist. For instance, can anyone imagine a circumstance in which the United States will use nuclear weapons against a nonnuclear power? We did not use them in Vietnam and, had we gone to war with Iran over the hostages, we would not have used them there either. Nor is it conceivable that we should use them against Cuba or Nicaragua. The foreseeable revulsion of public opinion, both at home and abroad, excludes any such possibility.

So why does not the Pentagon at least openly say that we will not use nuclear weapons against nonnuclear nations? Why does it bridle at any such suggestion? Why does it persist in the pretense that nuclear weapons differ only quantitatively, not qualitatively, from more conventional weapons?

The answer from military officials is that it is to our advantage to keep those nations uncertain with regard to our possible use of nuclear weapons—the assumption being that, in such a state, they will behave more circumspectly toward us. But is there the slightest shred of evidence that Iran or Cuba has been in any way intimidated by our nuclear arsenal? Is there even any hint of uncertainty in their actions? They *know* we are not going to use nuclear weapons against them. The Pentagon, deep down, knows it too. The only ones who are intimidated by our present posture are the American people and our allied populations, who keep fearfully wondering whether the Pentagon, in a moment of pique or panic, might actually do the unthinkable.

The psychological argument in favor of a doctrine of non-first-use points to the corrupting effects of the illusion of military security that nuclear weapons create. Neither the United States nor our NATO allies have been willing to make the necessary sacrifices, in money and manpower, so that we can effectively cope with the inevitable crises in a decaying world order. The United States does not even have the conventional strength to confront Cuba in a convincing way. As for our European allies, they have become utterly insular—citizens of a "little Europe."

This situation has come about not only because nuclear weapons are seemingly so powerful as to provide an invincible "deterrent," but because they are so much cheaper than conventional armies, navies, and armaments. As a consequence, politicians in the free world inevitably gravitate toward a policy of steadily diminishing *usable* military strength while investing in nuclear arms to protect "national security," defined in the most limited and parochial way. Any such policy will gradually but surely produce a weakening in the military ethos and, indeed, a decline in patriotic spirit. We have seen this happening in the Western world, and the proper term for it is decadence.

The strategic argument in favor of a doctrine of non-first-use derives from the parity of nuclear power that now exists as between the United States and the Soviet Union. That such a parity would one day exist was predicted. But the implications of parity are only beginning to dawn upon us. Those implications now threaten an imminent collapse of the NATO alliance and are also visible in the growing popularity of an antinuclear campaign in Western Europe and the United States.

In the years shortly after World War II, when Western Europe was disarmed, when we were "bringing the boys home" while the Soviet military remained near full strength—at that time the idea of an American nuclear response to Soviet aggression in Western Europe may have made temporary strategic sense. It really did provide the nations of Western Europe with an "umbrella" under which they could rebuild their economies and reconstruct their military establishments.

Shortly thereafter, when the Soviet Union developed its first atomic bombs, the umbrella was perceived to have a hole in it. The United States, for obvious reasons, became a lot less enthusiastic about the prospect of an automatic, immediate nuclear response to Soviet aggression. And so NATO was invented.

From the outset, the military philosophy behind NATO was ambiguous. The United States saw NATO as eventually becoming a military force powerful enough to repel a Soviet onslaught—all at the conventional level, of course. To that end we stationed some 350,000 U.S. soldiers in Europe. The Europeans saw NATO's eventual capability as being sufficient merely to "check" and slow down any Soviet movement across NATO's borders, providing time for the Soviets to contemplate the inevitable consequence of continued action. That consequence was an American nuclear attack on the Soviet Union. Those American troops in Europe were a "tripwire"—hostages, really—to make this consequence both credible and inevitable.

Note how attractive this situation was at the time, from the European point of view. Should a full-scale war actually take place, the Soviet Union would be annihilated, the United States would suffer a fair degree of devastation from Soviet nuclear retaliation, while Western Europe would experience only minimal or moderate damage.

Alas, this agreeable prospect was not to endure. By the 1960s, it became clear that the nations of Western Europe preferred to expand their welfare states rather than their military establishments, even while the Soviets were closing their "missile gap." The umbrella was looking a bit porous. So tactical nuclear weapons were inserted into the NATO arsenal. This did not alarm the Europeans too much, since it was assumed their use on European soil would be limited and short-lived. They would "signal" the Soviets that an act of aggression had passed the nuclear threshold. If the Soviets then persisted, an American-Soviet nuclear exchange would occur—over the heads of Europeans, as it were.

The 1970s witnessed the emergence of U.S.-USSR parity at the nuclear level, and of Soviet superiority vis-à-vis Western Europe at all levels. The Soviets now had at least as many tactical nuclear weapons as NATO. They had, moreover, a new arsenal of intermediate-range missiles, pointing to all major European cities. At that point we and our European allies, reacting like automatons, decided that NATO too needed such intermediate-range missiles on European soil. And that is when the current crisis broke out and the antinuclear movement assumed mass proportions.

Behind this crisis in NATO is the recognition of two facts. First, the American umbrella is now purely imaginary. It is always possible that, if the Soviets overrun Western Europe, an American president will press the button that will bring about the mutual, assured destruction of both the United States and the Soviet Union. It is possible—but how likely? What would be the sense of such an action? The people of Western Europe have perceived that any such reaction by any U.S. president is very, very unlikely—would, indeed, be stupid. Their governments continue to say otherwise, but they are speaking into the wind, with hollow voices.

The second fact is that any Soviet aggression against Western Europe will now mean that Western Europe becomes a nuclear battlefield, as NATO's "unbroken spectrum" of weaponry, from conventional to nuclear, unfolds. In short, NATO has now maneuvered itself into a position where Western Europe is doomed to near-annihilation if it resists—however successfully or unsuccessfully, whatever that means—a Russian attack! Is it any wonder that a spirit of defeatism is beginning to pervade the political atmosphere in Europe? And, of course, various left-wing groups are only too eager to turn this spirit into an active policy of appeasement—which they are doing, with much success.

The root cause of this disaster in foreign policy has been our failure, and the failure of our European allies, to insist on a clear line of demarcation between the use of conventional weapons and nuclear weapons. Such an insistence would be possible only if we were fully prepared to be a match for the Soviets at the conventional level, just as they have shown themselves prepared to make the sacrifices necessary to match us at the nuclear level. With such matching strength, it might be possible to negotiate a reduction in nuclear armaments. But without it, there is a mismatch that can result only in a tilt of world power toward the Soviets.

A doctrine of non-first-use would reassure the American people and the world that we are doing our best to avoid a nuclear holocaust, large or small. It would also place upon the Americans and their allies the burden of large, expensive, conventional military establishments, so that we can meet our responsibilities without always and immediately raising the specter of nuclear disaster.

If we and they are unwilling to shoulder that burden, then we are simply unworthy of the liberties we seek to preserve. A nation or an alliance that prefers mass annihilation to higher taxes or a diminution of social services will, when the crunch comes, surely decide that appeasement is preferable to both.

1982

# 21

# *The Key Question:*
# *Who Owns the Future?*

W E live in an ideological age
—that is to say, an age in which human passions and frustrations
find expression in politics rather than, as was once the case, in religion.
We may deplore this phenomenon, wish it were otherwise, and hope
it will eventually pass. But that we live in such an age is a fact, as it
is a fact that, in such an age, the key political question is: Who owns
the future?

It is not a question conservatives, who have always based their
claim to political authority on ownership of the past, are comfortable
with. This, in turn, explains why conservative parties in all countries
have been, for these last decades, so inarticulate when in opposition,
so inept when in office.

In contrast, modern left-wing movements—whether communist,
socialist, or liberal (i.e., social-democratic)—have the immense advantages of being ideological in their essence. They own the future, or they
own nothing. Their politics, as a consequence, tend to be bold, energetic,
often reckless, sometimes ruthless. As against such a political style, conservative prudence is seen as timidity, conservative caution as feeble-
ness of the imagination, conservative government as a tedious if

necessary interregnum during which the excesses of the Left are tidied up. This is the basic rhythm of politics in all democratic societies, and it is a rhythm that inexorably moves these societies leftward.

But the ideological politics of the Left suffers from a mortal flaw, one that is becoming ever more apparent. Its ideology is, in varying degrees, utopian. The future it actually shapes is never anything like the future that was envisioned or hoped for. Most often it is a grotesque caricature. And the more rigorous and extreme the ideological effort, the more perverted the actual result.

The events in Poland are only the most recent and dramatic evidence to this effect. Even now the significance of those events is not fully appreciated. It is not simply that the Polish working class is in rebellion against a "dictatorship of the proletariat." Every decade since World War II has seen such a rebellion in Eastern Europe. What is truly significant in today's Poland is that, in order to restore order, the rule of the army has replaced—probably forever—the rule of the utterly discredited Communist party. Poland has ceased being a nation with even a pretense of Communist rule, a rule that is legitimated by Marxist ideology.

The consequences of this transformation will very likely be enormous. If it is Poland today, will it not be Rumania tomorrow? And Czechoslovakia too? And what about the implications for the Soviet Union itself, governed by a corrupt, inefficient, and coarse bureaucracy whose Marxist-Leninist creed is a subject of ridicule for its citizenry? Cannot one now foresee the inevitability of naked military rule once this bureaucracy begins to crumble—as soon it must?

For many years, left-wing theoreticians of a purist cast of mind have expressed solemn anxiety over the possibility of a "Thermidor" in the Soviet Union—that is, of the military inheriting a decadent revolutionary authority, just as Bonaparte inherited it from Robespierre. Well, it has happened in Poland and, with this precedent established, it has ceased being an academic possibility for the entire Soviet empire. The odds are that such a Thermidor is now the shape of the empire's future, and a not-too-distant future at that.

But it is not only within the Soviet empire that the ideology of the Left shows unmistakable signs of frustration. In Africa, Asia, and Latin America, nation after nation with "planned economies" and socialist or quasi-socialist political mythologies see their economic conditions inexorably deteriorating while political chaos ferments beneath the repressive surface of authoritarian rule. Even the "intellectuals" in these countries, always the last to recognize the reality principle, are by now cynical, corrupt, or in prison.

And in the Western democracies too, the Left shows clear signs of ideological exhaustion. It can still win elections—because conservatives are still so good at losing them—but it cannot govern. It has no credible agenda any longer, its economic policies are invariably counterproductive, its ruling parties are constantly fragmenting into warring sects. That the Left no longer securely owns the future is becoming ever more apparent, every day, to everyone.

But do conservatives now own it? Alas, most conservatives do not even think in terms that are relevant to this question. They assume, simply and naively, that trouble for the Left means comfort and reassurance for the Right. It often does mean that—temporarily. In the longer run, however, unless conservatives can legitimate their claim to office with a persuasive assertion of a claim to the future, theirs is a lost cause. As between no claim to the future and a fraudulent claim, the latter will always prevail in an ideological age.

One has the clear impression that Ronald Reagan understands this, at least in part, and intuitively if not abstractly. Indeed, he often seems to be just about the only conservative in his administration who appreciates the full ideological significance of his economic policy, as distinct from its more narrow practical implications. Mr. Reagan, with his massive tax cuts, has put the welfare state in a moderately tight straitjacket for the rest of this decade at least. And he has done this by being bold enough to create a conservative deficit (one resulting from tax cuts) as a counterweight to liberal deficits (resulting from increased government expenditures).

It is evident that many congressional conservatives, probably a majority, are uncomfortable with this kind of boldness. It is even more evident that such boldness is alien to the spirit and substance of this administration's foreign policy. It is a conservative foreign policy all right—prudent, defensive, and lacking in ideological self-assurance or ideological direction.

The position of the United States in the world today is paradoxical to an extreme. The majority of the world's population, and most especially the peoples of "socialist" countries, would be thrilled if offered the opportunity to emigrate here. They perceive the reality clearly enough: that life here is better, whatever its problems. Nevertheless, not many even of these people find it easy to articulate a good opinion of the United States, and the media in most lands can fairly be described as anti-American.

The reason for this paradox is that we are simply not a sufficiently active presence in the world, at either the politico-military level or the ideological. The two do go together—otherwise, one's claim to the future is empty rhetoric. We permit our European allies to circumscribe our policy in Eastern Europe; we permit our foreign economic policies to be shaped by the United Nations; we permit Mexico to veto any vigorous response to Cuba's intervention in Central America and Africa; we tongue-tie our president, our secretary of state, and our ambassador to the UN when confronting Third World impudence and insult; we are blackmailed so successfully, by friend and foe alike, that we habitually pay up in advance.

What single bold action has this administration taken in foreign affairs? None. What single bold ideological affirmation has this administration uttered in foreign affairs? President Reagan occasionally says something that approximates such an affirmation, but the State Department quickly blankets it with an obfuscatory "explanation." Diplomacy becomes a substitute for, rather than a tool of, foreign policy.

Most American conservatives, and most Republican leaders, equate conservatism with a desperate, defensive commitment to the status quo, not with staking a claim on the world's future. They are risk-aversive, in both temperament and policy. And in an era of ideological politics, the risk-aversive most emphatically do not inherit the earth.

1982

# 22

# *A Letter to*
# *the Pentagon*

The Hon. Caspar Weinberger
Secretary of Defense
The Pentagon
Dear Mr. Secretary,

THERE is a matter that I must raise with you. It concerns the state of our armed forces. It has nothing to do with strategic or tactical armaments, global strategies, or other such arcane matters. Not being even an amateur military analyst, I am content to leave such issues in the hands of you and your experts. But there is a problematic dimension to our military condition that has nothing to do with expertise—indeed, one might say it is to a considerable degree created by an emphasis on such expertise at the expense of more mundane matters. Among these latter are the levels of morale, discipline, and plain competence of our fighting men in the field.

One reads, for instance, about the enormous drug problem in our forces, especially among soldiers stationed abroad. The European press is liberally sprinkled with spectacular incidents of crime, violence, and insubordination, linked to drugs, among our NATO soldiers. I realize that this is not a problem unique to the military. Many of our schools are in the same situation. On the other hand, not all schools are. Those schools that have firm discipline and high educational morale have been able to cope quite well with this problem. Why are our armed forces so ineffectual by comparison?

Could it be that military discipline has been allowed to become only a shadow of its former self? One suspects so. Only a couple of months ago, the press reported that sailors at a midwestern training facility were refusing to stand at attention when the national anthem was played at the base theater. The commandant solved this little problem by ceasing to have the national anthem played! Did this create a storm in the Pentagon? Was exemplary action taken? If so, the world knows nothing of it.

And there can be little doubt, for anyone with the slightest military experience, that such indiscipline must affect military efficiency in the field. I call your attention to the horrifying report, by Arthur T. Hadley in the *Boston Globe* last October 19, of the miserable performance of our forces during the autumn NATO maneuvers—a performance that caused the Dutch to snicker contemptuously.

There will be some who say that all this is a function of a volunteer army with poor pay, which brings us the "wrong kind" of recruits. While I agree that pay should be substantially increased, I find this explanation implausible. Britain, after all, also has a volunteer army with even more niggardly pay schedules, but without such gross symptoms of demoralization. No, I think the problem goes deeper than that—or perhaps I should say higher than that, for I suspect it emanates from a lack of attention in the uppermost levels of the Pentagon.

A major reason for this disarray, I would suggest to you, has been the dominance within the Pentagon itself—ever since World War II and especially since the McNamara period—of what may be fairly described as a technocratic-bureaucratic ethos. There has been an overwhelming emphasis on strategic and tactical analysis, with men regarded merely as constituting the "firepower" necessary to solve the appropriate military equation. Never has the level of abstract thought in our Defense Department been so high, so sophisticated, so recondite even. And never have the brute realities of men in arms been so minimized, neglected even. Surely it was the disjunction between sophisticated military analysis and battlefield realities that was, in good part, responsible for our Vietnam debacle—a war which we kept winning on paper and losing in actuality?

Would you not agree that the whole idea of military management exemplified by the McNamara approach—an extraordinary conflation of academic subtlety, intellectual arrogance, and inattention to human realities—has been discredited? Perhaps you do agree, but I have seen no signs from the Pentagon to show it. There, today as before, all the emphasis seems to be on the *management* of men and matériel, not on military leadership, and certainly not on military pride and morale.

On this last point, I would like to ask you: Why, oh why, did not the Pentagon take the occasion of the return of the hostages from Iran to pay formal and public homage to the eight men who died in that abortive rescue attempt? If this is the unsoldierly regard in which top military men hold their dead comrades in arms, is it astonishing that so many of our enlisted men and officers have come to feel that no one gives a damn about them, dead or alive?

But in addition to the technocratic-bureaucratic ethos, our military has suffered the pernicious intrusion of the liberal ethos, especially during the past four years. The Carter administration seemed unable (and, I think, unwilling) to distinguish between the Army and the CETA [Comprehensive Employment and Training Act] program. The armed forces recruiting ads have emphasized exclusively how wonderful a place the service is in which to learn a skilled trade. Fighting, apparently, would be an anachronistic interruption of this education process. Military discipline itself was interpreted as a menace to civil liberties. At West Point, I am authoritatively told, courses in military history are no longer prescribed, only elective—the idea, presumably, being to make West Point less "militaristic," more like any other college campus. The effort seems to have been successful.

And then there have been the absurd attempts to fully "integrate" women into our services, so as to please the more militant and more radical women's libbers. There certainly are many parts of the armed forces where women can contribute to our military efficiency—but mainly at home, and certainly nowhere near a possible combat zone. Despite all the propaganda about male-female differences being cultural, not biological, the fact remains that 15 percent of our woman soldiers became pregnant last year—and pregnancy is no longer a permissible cause of discharge. About 7 percent of our NATO soldiers are single women with children who live on the base. The notion of "fighting women" is bad enough. (The Israelis tried it and quickly gave up.) But fighting *mothers?*

So, Mr. Secretary, you have a serious problem on your hands—but one, I fear, you are only too likely to overlook from the high position you occupy. Attention must be paid at ground level. Our battered military ethos must be restored to health. And even a moderate injection of the older-fashioned martial ethos would be appropriate, in view of the fact that, in the decade ahead and as the world is going, our soldiers and sailors and Marines are all too likely to be called on to be fighting men, not students at Vocational High.

In this connection, Sir, may I recommend that on Memorial Day next you reinstitute the tradition of proper military parades? A small matter, but of some symbolic significance. There is nothing like a parade to elicit respect for the military from the populace, just as there is nothing like a parade to instill self-respect and pride among the military. I could weep every Memorial Day when I watch those high-school bands go by, led by nubile versions of the Dallas Cowboys cheerleaders, the spectators few and only casually interested.

Military parades are not going to solve the problems of an indisciplined, sullen soldiery, but they at least will send out a signal that someone up there really cares. I shall be looking for such a signal.

1981

# 23

# "Moral Dilemmas" in Foreign Policy

IT WAS George Orwell who once said: "We have now sunk to a depth at which the re-statement of the obvious is the first duty of intelligent men." This, it seems to me, is our situation with respect to the "moral dilemmas" of American foreign policy today—except that any such restatement of the obvious is likely to be regarded as unthinkable by most of our intelligent men.

Take the case of the Shah [Reza Shah Pahlevi] whose "crimes" will soon be exposed by an ad hoc international commission, established with our approval. The rank hypocrisy of such an exercise in political theater is instantly nauseating—two of the nations represented on that commission (Syria and Algeria) have records on human rights far more illiberal than the Shah's. Moreover, we know beforehand exactly what the findings of this commission will have to be. They will be to the effect that the Shah restricted political rights, imprisoned or exiled his opponents, appropriated a portion of the nation's income for his family's personal use, permitted (or ordered) his secret police to torture some hundreds of his opponents, and so forth.

We also know beforehand what such a commission will not say. It will not point out that all of these wickednesses of the Shah have also characterized every government the Iranian people have known since time immemorial, and usually to a greater degree. Nor will it point out that the Shah instituted a land reform in which vast areas belonging to the crown and clergy were distributed to the peasantry. (It was, incidentally, this land reform which brought him the hatred of all those ayatollahs.) Or that he strove energetically, and with considerable success, to use Iran's wealth from oil to modernize the Iranian economy. Or that he tried to modernize the Islamic culture of Iran, giving women greater individual freedom and the universities greater academic freedom than they had ever possessed. Or that during his reign, foreign periodicals, scholars, and journalists were free to circulate in Iran to a degree not known before, or since. Or that his regime actually sent to Europe and America, on government subsidy, more than one hundred thousand college students, to acquire skills and knowledge essential to the modernization of their country. Or that, on the whole, his despotism compared quite favorably with the despotic rule that now prevails in such other countries as Algeria, Syria, Iraq, Saudi Arabia, or our latest ally, Pakistan.

Even to suggest that such discriminating judgments, however valid, are appropriate in the case of the Shah is bound to make us feel uncomfortable and to invite opprobrium. Is it not a betrayal of the democratic idea to imply that some dictatorships are better than others—that some dictatorships may claim a degree of political legitimacy that even liberal democrats ought to respect? We really do not know how to cope with such a question. Our common sense tells us that it would be more than a little absurd—and in any case highly impractical—to declare that all of the world's undemocratic regimes are equally anathema to us. That would be like saying that we Americans are just too good for this world, so that any foreign policy would represent an expense of spirit in a waste of shame. On the other hand, how do we go about making the necessary distinctions between nonliberal and undemocratic regimes with which we might, in relatively good conscience, have amicable relations, and others which, at best, might be allies of convenience but nothing more?

Interestingly enough, prior to World War I the way in which this question should be answered was quite obvious. That answer was provided by the traditions of liberal constitutionalism. To the degree that any authoritarian regime was "enlightened"—that is, to the degree that it could be judged to be creating economic, political, and cultural preconditions for possible self-government by the people—it was worthy of cautious respect. If it displayed no such enlightened intentions, it was "benighted."

The disappearance from our thinking of these old-fashioned categories has created an intellectual vacuum. As a result, we simply cannot bring ourselves to say—or even think—what is clear to any candid observer of the world scene: that there are significant differences among regimes loosely classified as "authoritarian," and that in many countries, where a liberal constitutional regime can only be a more or less distant ideal, politics necessarily revolves around a choice of authoritarian rule. Moreover, it is a real choice. Some authoritarian governments exhibit at least a halfway respect for the rule of law, others do not. Some govern in a way that is respectful of any potential for eventual self-government, others are petty, personal, narrow-visioned, indifferent to the nation's future. (Somoza in Nicaragua exemplified this latter type.)

And there are still others, increasing in number, who are hostile in principle to the very idea of liberal constitutionalism—the Communist regimes are of this type, and so, of course, is the present "Islamic-Marxist" regime in Iran. These latter, indeed, ought not to be classified as "authoritarian" at all, but can fairly be described as "totalitarian," since they represent a principled antithesis to constitutional democracy.

It is the fundamental fallacy of American foreign policy to believe, in face of the evidence, that all peoples, everywhere, are immediately "entitled" to a liberal constitutional government—and a thoroughly democratic one at that. It is because of this assumption that our discussions of foreign policy, along with our policy itself, are constantly being tormented by moral dilemmas, as we find ourselves allied to nonliberal and nondemocratic regimes. These dilemmas are guilt-inducing mechanisms which cripple policy—an attitude that no nation can sustain for long—or else we take flight into sweeping crusades for "human rights," which quickly brings us up short before intractable realities.

Now, there is nothing inevitable about this state of affairs. As a matter of fact, it is only since World War I—a war fought under the Wilsonian slogans of "self-determination for all nations" and "make the world safe for democracy"—that American foreign policy began to disregard the obvious for the sake of the quixotic pursuit of impossible ideals. Before World War I, intelligent men took it for granted that not all peoples, everywhere, at all times, could be expected to replicate a Western constitutional democracy. This was a point of view, incidentally, shared more or less equally by conservatives, liberals, and socialists.

It was only with World War I and its aftermath that thinking about foreign policy lost its moorings in the real world and became utterly ideologized. For socialists, this transition was accomplished by the transformation of liberal-democratic socialism into totalitarian communism, a form of government that, while relying on sophisticated modes of coercion, is yet so primitive in its political substance—so tribal, one might say—that it is in truth a possibility for all nations, at all times. It is a possibility, of course, purchased at the cost of the liberal, the democratic, and the socialist ideals themselves, but the prospect of immediate power has persuaded socialists throughout the world that this is a profitable trade-off.

For Americans, the transition occurred via the utopian enthusiasm of Woodrow Wilson, preaching "self-determination," "human rights," "one man, one vote," "a world without war" as if these were in fact unproblematic possibilities. The consequence has been a foreign policy that is intellectually disarmed before all those cases where a government is neither totalitarian nor democratic, but authoritarian in one way or another, to one degree or another. We could, if we were sensible, calmly accept this basic reality of world politics, while using our influence to edge unenlightened despotisms toward more enlightened behavior, or enlightened despotisms toward more liberal and humane behavior. Instead, we end up in either an unstable, guilt-ridden and seemingly "immoral" alliance with them or displaying a haughty censoriousness that helps "destabilize" them.

Such instability and such diplomatic destabilization offer the totalitarian opponents of these authoritarian regimes wonderful opportunities, which they are quick to take advantage of. And, as our illusions, along with our waverings of purpose, breed defeat after defeat, we come to believe that it is, after all, totalitarianism that today has the Mandate of Heaven, or at least the Mandate of History. We come to believe—what is fast becoming an article of liberal faith—that totalitarianism, which effectively represses dissent, is actually a more legitimate form of government than the older types of authoritarianism, which repress dissent less effectively, and that it is positively immoral to support the latter as against the former. Note with what good conscience we embraced Mao's China as an ally, while uneasily chastising the government of Taiwan for violations of political liberties.

The abstract slogans of the cold war, which President Carter and others are in the process of refurbishing, are an improvement over the abstract slogans of "detente" and "swords into ploughshares," since they at least take account of the totalitarian reality. But this will not help our situation all that much. For it is not a question of our mouthing the wrong abstract slogans but of trying to base a foreign policy on abstract slogans in the first place. The world is heterogeneous and complex—and until we learn to cope with this complexity, and rid ourselves of a guilt complex engendered by our refusal to confront this very complexity, we shall never have a foreign policy worthy of the name.

1980

# 24

# The "Human Rights" Muddle

Having pressed the "human rights" issue so vigorously during the 1976 campaign, and then having so vociferously reiterated it in the early months of his administration, President Carter is now stuck with it. Obviously, and predictably, the whole business now makes him very uncomfortable and he rather wishes it would go away.

I doubt that Mr. Carter ever gave any serious thought to what he meant by human rights. To some degree, surely, he merely seized the issue as a way of mobilizing, in an America thirsty for self-affirmation, the latent electoral appeal of Wilsonian idealism against Henry Kissinger's version of *Realpolitik*. The younger and more "liberal" members of his staff, on the other hand, who believe that left-wing authoritarian regimes are by definition more "humane" than right-wing ones, saw it as offering pleasing possibilities for disrupting relations with the likes of Chile, Argentina, the Philippines, and so forth. It was, therefore, an issue with an ambiguous attractiveness both to anticommunist sentiments, troubled by "detente," and to left-wing opinion. One may safely assume that it lost Mr. Carter no votes.

But the election is over; the inaugural rhetoric has been dissipated, while the serious job of conducting a foreign policy remains. And, quite suddenly, this issue of human rights seems to plague the administration at every turn. That it complicates our relations with our enemies is surely less important than the fact that it even more severely complicates our relations with many friendly governments. (This is so, in part, because Congress, taking the administration at its word, has demanded that the State Department publish "evaluations" of human rights in all countries which receive American military or financial assistance.) We seem to be heading toward a posture of moralistic isolationism while simultaneously being irretrievably involved in the brute actualities of world politics, that is, power politics. No wonder the rest of the world is at a loss to figure out the relation of what we say to what we mean to what we might in fact do.

The trouble, of course, begins with that phrase and concept, "human rights." It is not that the idea behind this phrase is meaningless. On the contrary, it has too many meanings—and we have, sometimes mindlessly, sometimes with premeditation, made an incoherent jumble of them.

The concept of human rights really includes four very different political ideas. Not necessarily incompatible, one hastens to add, and in practice always overlapping—but nevertheless very different. I would put these four meanings of human rights as follows:

*Human rights proper.* This is the least political of the four meanings, since it applies equally to all governments, regardless of their political structure. It refers to those practices of government which, in the perspective of our Judeo-Christian civilization, can flatly be called abominations—that is, where questions of degree are irrelevant. Genocide, whether on a large scale or small, is such an abomination. So is torture. And so are restrictions on the right to emigrate.

Though the United States since World War II has been properly outspoken on the issue of genocide and torture, it has avoided making any fuss about the right to emigrate. The reason, to put it bluntly, was fear of offending the Soviet and other Communist governments. The Carter administration seems willing to continue this particular policy of "moral detente"—on the one moral issue which most directly affects the lives of tens of millions of people.

*Civil rights.* These are the rights of an individual vis-à-vis his government, and are summed up in the phrase "the rule of law," to which even government is subject. It is important to emphasize, since we Americans have so parochial and impoverished a sense of history, that such civil rights can exist even in nonliberal or nondemocratic societies.

In both Tudor England and Tsarist Russia, it was not uncommon for people to be arrested, tried—and acquitted by judge or jury. Neither Henry VIII nor Tsar Nicholas I ever presumed to think he had the kind of arbitrary power which many member governments of the United Nations exercise today as a matter of course.

Naturally, we Americans prefer to see the scope of civil rights, everywhere, defined as broadly as possible; and it would be absurd if our government did not publicly affirm this basic principle of our polity.

But, as Robert Goldwin recently emphasized, we seem to have forgotten that our own broad definition is rooted in our political and economic structure—in federalism, the separation of powers, judicial review, the diffusion of property in a private sector. In short, our civil rights derive from the theory and practice of limited government.

But our political leaders, when they come to praise civil rights in one world forum or another, do not argue in favor of limited government—perhaps because they no longer really believe in it. They always talk as if their mission is to persuade authoritarian or totalitarian governments to make a gift of civil rights to their people. Not only is this a silly and fruitless exercise; it also suggests that our leaders have quite forgotten the relation of civil rights to limited government, and seem to believe that the people's civil rights are distributed by a paternalistic government as part of a general welfare program.

*Political rights.* These are the rights to participate, in one degree or another, in government. Again, and properly, we Americans cherish such rights. But only if one has a kind of mystic belief in "the people" (like the "proletariat" in Marxist mythology) as a redeeming force in history will one be inclined to give political rights priority over, or even equality with, civil rights or human rights proper. One person, one vote is indeed a constitutional principle by which a people may govern itself. But it is not the sole such principle, and only a dogmatist would insist that it is, everywhere and always, the best principle. Even the United States, after all, for most of its history has not been governed by this principle.

The proper extent of political rights in any nation is not something our State Department can have a meaningful opinion about. It can only be determined by the people of that nation, who will draw on their own political and cultural backgrounds in arriving at a suitable disposition of this matter. We can try to set them a good example by making our democratic republic as admirable as possible—as our Founding Fathers urged. But that is about all we can do—as our Founding Fathers recognized.

*Socioeconomic rights.* These were inscribed in the United Nations

Charter, and the United States, in its folly, has duly subscribed to the principle behind them. The principle is that a welfare state is always and everywhere better than a non–welfare state; that the more comprehensive a welfare state, the better; and that the right to a broad range of government services is absolute, whether the nation can afford them or not, and whether the people want them or not. A particular and debatable version of twentieth-century liberalism is suddenly presented to us as a universal human right. Since, at this late date, it might be difficult to repudiate this absurd principle outright, we ought to ignore it as much as possible.

These four aspects of human rights are more closely intertwined in the real world than I have suggested. And, taken together, they will naturally and inevitably help shape our foreign policy. Under ordinary circumstances, our closest allies will always be those nations which share our basic political values, since they will also share with us a common vision of a desirable (or even tolerable) world order. But there will also be circumstances in which considerations of strategic interest—of who is friend, who is foe, for whatever reason on whatever occasion—must enter into the making of foreign policy. It would therefore be nice if the United States were less vaguely moralistic in its pronouncements, more specifically moral when it can properly be—and, above all, more candid with itself and its citizenry as to the limited if real role which, under conditions prevailing at the moment, the pursuit of human rights will play in the conduct of our foreign affairs.

It would also be nice if the Carter administration would disengage itself from the double standard, whereby left-wing governments are given the benefit of every doubt as concerns human rights while right-wing regimes are continually indicted. Nothing could more effectively make a mockery of the whole issue.

1978

# 25

## *Understanding the Soviet Mafia*

THE death of Brezhnev and the accession of Andropov have loosed the usual torrent of speculation. There are those who point to Andropov's knowledge of English and his supposed taste for Scotch whiskey and American popular music as signs of hope for an easing of tensions. This is puzzling, since these observers are, for the most part, the same persons who criticize Mr. Reagan for being overly belligerent, despite the fact that he too knows English and has been seen to sip an occasional Scotch while listening to American popular music.

Others view with alarm the fact that Andropov, for fifteen years, headed the dreaded KGB, which in turn has close ties to the armed forces. This makes more sense, but not much. Khrushchev, after all, was one of Stalin's closest henchmen with an unmatched reputation for ferocity, yet he significantly moderated the degree of terror that the Soviet state directed against its people.

The plain fact is that we do not know and have no way of knowing what changes in emphasis or leadership style, if any, Mr. Andropov will inaugurate. It is altogether likely that he himself does not yet know. The real danger, however, is that such speculations will distract us from what we do know about the nature of the Soviet leadership—and we know a great deal.

We know that the Soviet leaders are—to borrow Ben Wattenberg's pellucid phrase—"liars and thugs." We know this from firsthand accounts of East European leaders now in exile, men who, over many years, had intimate relations with top Soviet officials. Their accounts are depressingly uniform and strongly suggest that, if you wish to understand the Soviet political system and the people who inhabit it, you could make an excellent beginning by going to the movies and seeing *The Godfather* and *The Godfather, Part II.* The Soviet system since Stalin may be usefully regarded as a regime of mafioso types who, incredibly, have become the political establishment.

This is not an accusation but a fair description-by-analogy. Obviously, there are individual variations among the membership, at all levels. But if you are in the unhappy position of having to do business with the Mafia, you learn very quickly that such variations in the type do not count for much. They are, in truth, far more important to the membership than to the world outside.

This Soviet mafia is, of course, a very special kind of mafia. It is an official, bureaucratized mafia by now; so that all the tensions and conflicts inherent in any such organization are obscured to us by the fact that, instead of straightforward shoot-outs, one witnesses a lot of shuffling and reshuffling at all bureaucratic levels. Our Kremlinologists make a valiant effort to keep a scorecard on who has gone up or down, in or out, and we are in their debt for such dogged detective work. But there is always the danger of reading too much political significance into such data. The struggle is always for power, and for the perquisites of power (of which political survival is the main one). Policy differences are used in this struggle, and may even become focal points of conflict, but are always transient rationalizations, never serious causes. There is no established "peace party" or "war party," liberal wing or conservative wing, in the Soviet leadership. There are only the ins and outs.

In addition to being official and bureaucratic, the Soviet leadership is a Communist mafia. Much ink has been wasted in trying to figure out in what sense, or to what degree, Soviet leaders "believe" in Marxist-Leninist doctrine. But the current Soviet leaders, unlike the Bolshevik founding fathers, are not intellectuals or Marxist theoreticians. They do not even bother to quote Marx or Lenin any more, except on special occasions. Soviet leaders "believe" in Marxist-Leninism the way our own mafia "believes" in God and free enterprise—there are no atheists in *The Godfather,* and no socialists either. Marxist-Leninism is the political faith of the Soviet leaders, one that legitimates their very existence as a leadership. They know no other set of beliefs, are hostile to other beliefs, and see the world through the most primitive kind of Marxist-Leninist spectacles.

Along with being bureaucratic and communist, the Soviet leadership is intensely nationalistic. Nationalistic, not just patriotic. This nationalism is extreme to the point of being pathological. Official Soviet textbooks and encyclopedias engage in wholesale fabrication—not just exaggeration—in order to emphasize Russian priority in scientific invention and artistic distinction. Soviet history textbooks not only faithfully echo Marxist-Leninist dogma, but blandly promulgate the most blatant falsehoods about the past to emphasize the role of the Russian people as the predestined saviors of the human race.

So there we have the Soviet leadership: an official bureaucratized mafia, Communist and nationalist. *That* we know.

We also know that it is a leadership that is inefficient, unpopular, and in total, ruthless control of the country. Its inefficiency is most evident in the economy, which is a hopeless mess, hopeless because any major economic reforms would subvert the political system. The unpopularity can be confirmed by conversations with Soviet émigrés, and can also be inferred from the fact that the ideology of Marxist-Leninism, while it may flourish in some Western intellectual circles, is so atrophied in the Soviet Union that there has not been a single interesting work on Marxist-Leninism, of either Russian or Western origin, published there during the past fifty years. The totalitarian control of the regime over every aspect of life needs no description.

What does one make of all this so far as Soviet intentions are concerned? And what are its implications for our foreign policy?

We know a great deal about Soviet intentions—as much, perhaps, as we can know. One of the problems that plagues this whole issue is the absurd insistence by demagogic congressmen, assisted by the media, that American intelligence services ought to be able to forecast every turn or twist of the Soviet internal power struggle as well as every discrete foreign adventure a particular gang of leaders may engage in. That is a preposterous expectation. The Soviet leaders themselves cannot make such forecasts, and we cannot know the minds of Soviet leaders better than they do.

But if we cannot know the dominant intentions at any moment, present or future, we certainly do know the general thrust of Soviet policy. It is a policy that regards the international status quo as unacceptable, even intolerable. In part, this is because the leadership is communist and believes with an utter and awful simplicity that there is an ineradicable conflict between communism and capitalism. In part, too, it is because this leadership is rabidly nationalist and believes that Russia does not yet have its duly recognized place—which is the first place—under the sun. And, in part, it is because this leadership is radically insecure and bereft of popular support; and an insecure mafia is always an aggressive mafia.

Since we really know all this, certain conclusions seem to follow. One is the hopelessness of trying to affect Soviet intentions—to move the regime toward "liberalization," say—by benevolent economic transactions and a gentle diplomacy. No such movement by the Soviet leaders, of an extent that would alter the basic nature of the system, is possible or imaginable. Not because they are wicked men or monstrous creatures, but simply because they are what they are, where they are: a bureaucratic, Communist, nationalist, mafia, ineffectual at governing except by coercion, and with no popular roots in the Soviet Union or in any of the nations they now occupy.

Another conclusion that seems to follow is that this is a peculiarly vulnerable regime—armor-plated, to be sure, but with a brittleness that cannot withstand too many shocks. A Western foreign policy that is not merely reactive, that does not rely only on Soviet stupidity or bad luck for its own successes, could find many opportunities to test that regime's metal.

Is it thinkable that the United States could ever have such a foreign policy? One would like to think so. But what is certain is that we shall never get there if we persist in thinking that time is on our side, that somehow or other the Soviet regime will evolve and "progress" into something other and nicer than what it is. For the Soviet leaders are utterly convinced that time—that is, history—is on their side. And so far there is precious little evidence to prove them wrong.

1982

# VI

## RELIGION AND
## THE JEWS

# 26

# *Is Jewish Humor Dead?*

IT is known that the surest way of killing a joke is to explain it, and humor has, in self-defense, made an especially comic figure of the man who would earnestly analyze it. Thus humor and seriousness contest the field, with all arbitration or appeasement ruled out, and with the possibility of rising above the battle simply unimaginable; one rises above the battle either through seriousness or humor—and then one is right back in the fight. It is an unequal struggle: Humor is more aggressive, more mobile, and has the more penetrating weapons. But in the end, humor loses and seriousness wins. Humorists die and dead men tell no jokes, and this, it must be admitted, is a serious matter.

Jewish humor died with its humorists when the Nazis killed off the Jews of Eastern Europe, though it seems likely that even without the intervention of Hitler this humor would not long have survived the disintegration of the ghetto community from which it drew its inspiration. This opinion is certain to be challenged, especially by those who, though willing to concede that persecution can wound the flesh, are reluctant to believe that it can murder the spirit or that the spirit can, by the erosion of time, simply wither and die. They will ask: Does not this humor still flourish in the Jewish communities of America and Israel? is not Jewish humor a treasure in the perpetual custody of the Jewish people? The answer to both questions is, I think, no, and in the course of this essay I hope to show why. But first I would like to illustrate the defeat of humor with an anecdote that some will find amusing but that is really not a Jewish joke so much as the dying echo of one.

A group of Jewish refugees from Poland, recently arrived in the United States, visited one evening with their American-born relatives. One of the latter thought to lighten the conversation by telling an old Jewish joke:

A Jew in czarist Russia wished to buy a ticket that would permit him to enter the platform of a railroad station, and he was referred to a vending machine where such tickets were sold at ten kopecks each. The Jew eyed the machine curiously and mused, "Maybe you'll take five kopecks?" He inserted five kopecks and pressed the lever. No ticket came out. The Jew shrugged his shoulders and said, "Well, there was no harm in trying." He inserted another five kopecks, and pulled the lever. Nothing happened. As he stood there, bewildered, a Cossack brushed past him, inserted ten kopecks into the machine, pulled the lever, and got his ticket. The Jew flew into a rage, spat at the machine, and yelled: "Filthy anti-Semite! For a Cossack you give tickets, but for a Jew's ten kopecks you don't bother!"

To the narrator's pleasure, the newcomers laughed heartily at the joke though it is but an inferior specimen of the familiar genre of Jewish humor that pokes fun at the Jews for their propensity to gloss over their own shortcomings and blame the always available anti-Semite for their misfortunes.

Some weeks later there was another family gathering, this time to welcome some still newer arrivals from the DP [displaced person] camps. One of the refugees who had been present at the earlier meeting volunteered to tell the "very funny joke" that the *Amerikaner* had related. He told it as follows:

A Jew in czarist Russia wished to buy a ticket that would permit him to enter the platform of a railroad station, and he was referred to a vending machine where such tickets were sold at ten kopecks each. The Jew inserted his ten kopecks, but nothing happened. As he stood there, bewildered, a Cossack brushed past him, inserted ten kopecks into the machine, pulled the lever, and got his ticket. The Jew flew into a rage, spat at the machine, and yelled: "Filthy anti-Semite! For a Cossack you give tickets, but for a Jew's ten kopecks you don't bother!"

The laughter was every bit as hearty at this version of the joke, though the original point had been blunted and what had been a joke had really become a parable. Actually, these Jews from Poland were not laughing at any joke at all, but only at the way the story summarized their sense of a senseless persecution. The seriousness of the concentration camps had conquered.

It is true that in my telling of this incident the original point has been in part regained, for the butts of my story are Jews so sensitive to anti-Semitism that they have lost the detachment that is at the root of true humor. But it is a point that barely reaches the mark, and whatever smile it arouses is the mere shadow of a shadow. Too many corpses obstruct the comic perspective.

One recent anthologist of Jewish humor, doubtless expressing the sentiments of many, sees in the Jewish joke a victory gained by the Jewish spirit over centuries of adversity, an exultant defiance of persecution and harassment, an affirmation of the will to survival in the face of an ever-impending doom. It would surely be to the glory of the entire human race, and of the Jews in particular, if this were the case. And it is agreeable to note that there is some truth in this description. But not the whole truth.

Though the records are scanty, it seems safe to assert that the kind of humor we know came late to Jewish history, gaining ground in the seventeenth and eighteenth centuries and reaching its apogee in the nineteenth and early twentieth centuries. It is, then, a preeminently *modern* phenomenon. The Jews of an earlier day were rich in proverbs (some of them witty), parables, moralistic anecdotes—but not, it seems, in humor. This fact is no occasion for surprise if we cast a glance at the development of humor in the various Western Christian nations of the Middle Ages. There we see that humor could exist only in the interstices of a religious civilization (just as the Purim parodies existed within orthodox Judaism), that the religious authorities frowned upon it, and that it won popular affection to the extent that the dominion of religion became questionable, and that, indeed, one of its functions was to challenge this dominion. Humor needs to breathe the air of skepticism, and prior to the modern epoch the Jews were men of faith, piety, and hence sobriety. When one believes that this life on earth is implicated in eternal salvation or eternal damnation, there is little motive for levity.

Take, for example, the matter of *Galgenhumor* (gallows humor), which was elevated to such a fine art in the writings of the man who gaily signed himself Sholom Aleichem. Here is how Sholom Aleichem has one of his characters, Yisrolik of Kishenev, write to his friend Yankel in America after the Kishenev pogrom of 1903 (I use the version given by Maurice Samuel in his fine book, *The World of Sholom Aleichem*):

Dear Yankel: You ask me to write at length, and I'd like to oblige, but there's really nothing to write about. The rich are still rich and the poor are dying of hunger, as they always do. What's new about that? And as far as the pogroms are concerned, thank God we have nothing more to fear, as we've already had ours—two of them, in fact, and a third wouldn't be worth while. . . . All our family got through it safely, except for Lippi, who was killed with his two sons, Noah and Mordecai; first-class artisans, all three of them. Oh yes, and except Hersh. Perel was found dead in the cellar together with the baby at her breast. But as Getzi used to say: "It might have been worse; don't think of the better, because there's no limit to that." You ask about Heshel. He's been out of work now for over half a year. The fact is they won't let him work in prison. . . . Mendel did a clever thing; he up and died. Some say of hunger, others of consumption. Personally, I think he died of both. I really don't know what else there is to write about, except the cholera, which is going great guns.

This is Sholom Aleichem at his best, which means that it is at the top rung of the world's literature of irony. Yet it is most improbable that a pious Jew who had, say, undergone the expulsion from Spain in 1492 would have found this letter as entertaining as did his descendants, or that he would have found it as "cathartic" as his own Cabalistic speculations. For him, death at the hands of persecutors was *kiddush ha-shem,* the sanctification of the Name. It was an affair in the realm of the sacred, and jesting was unthinkable. But for Sholom Aleichem death in a pogrom was a somewhat more ambiguous event. It might be *kiddush ha-shem* —Sholom Aleichem nowhere states that it is not. Or it might be nothing but bad luck ornamented with a high-sounding title. In this equivocation between the sacred and the profane, the eternal and the finite, the spark of humor is fanned.

It is interesting to note that fifty Jews were killed in the Kishenev pogrom and that the civilized world was shocked and horrified. Sholom Aleichem's irony was a harmonic counterpoint to this shock and horror. But when some six million Jews were slaughtered during World War II, the world was numbed by the enormity of the crime, and the victims themselves could not respond with the aesthetic freedom of Sholom Aleichem. The kinds of jokes that Jews brought forth from the concentration camps were mainly bitter thrusts at the idiocy of their oppressors. For just as humor cannot mature in a life of utter religious faith, so it cannot survive a life of sheer nihilism.

No pranks, no slapstick, no practical jokes—nothing that reduces the spiritual and human to the mechanical. Jewish Humor is a humor of the spirit, not against the spirit.

What we call Jewish humor is Yiddish humor. It is the humor that was conceived and expressed in the Yiddish language, in a secular language of the marketplace that had as part of its everyday idiom a multitude of Hebrew phrases having to do with modes of Talmudic exegesis or with such nonsecular affairs as the world-to-come, the afterlife, and reincarnation; a language full of the chanting and inflections that accompanied the translation of holy texts and their memorization: a "knowing language," in Maurice Samuel's phrase, full of internal hints and esoteric references. It is the humor of a folk community of garrulous intellectuals and hair-splitters cut off from nature and animal life, intrigued only by the oddities of the human and the divine, taking as its frame of reference the complex structure of ghetto society, ghetto life, and Jewish tradition. It is, supremely, the humor of an intelligence running amok in the household of the gods without ever daring, or wanting, to set foot outside the open door.

Many of the specific jokes, of course, were borrowed from other peoples and other tongues, and have since been reclaimed with interest. Others have survived the long voyage to America or Israel and translation into English or modern Hebrew. But, with the wiping out of the Yiddish-speaking communities, the creative source of this humor is gone. To the extent that old habits and folk ways persist among Jews in America, Europe, and Israel—especially insofar as they involve the family and the hazards of earning a living—slices of Yiddish humor will be appreciated (mother-in-law jokes, marriage-broker jokes, *luftmentsh* jokes). However, it is clear that a good part of the pleasure these jokes provide results from the warm nostalgia of merely hearing them. The old folkways are disappearing and Yiddish itself is on its way to becoming a dead language. The Jews of Israel prefer not to think of the ghetto, and their humor seems to be content with variations on Viennese café wit. (Example: Ben Gurion offers a friend the post of minister of colonies. "But we have no colonies," the friend protests. "So what?" replies Ben Gurion. "Isn't Kaplan minister of finance?") American Jews are not so pressed to forget the ghetto, and Yiddish humor has for them a sentimental as well as comic value. But, though parts of the body have been preserved, even adorned and dressed as new, the soul is gone. The Jewish joke is no longer *important*. We are no longer in that world, and of that epoch, where the greatest of all Jewish writers was—one can even say, had to be—a humorist.

The "Jewish situation" that brought forth a humor unique in man's history has altered. What was that situation?

Stated briefly, the situation was one of God-forsaken religiosity. And the humor of this situation is a humor of pious blasphemy, in which the religious emotion is siphoned off into explosive wit.

In one of Sholom Aleichem's stories, Tevyeh the dairyman, riding home hungry after a day's work, with one ruble in his pocket with which to sustain his nagging wife and seven thriving daughters, addresses God as follows:

"Thou hast made us a little lower than the angels. It depends upon what you call a little, isn't it? Lord, what is life, and what are we, and to what may a man be likened? A man may be likened to a carpenter; for a carpenter lives, and lives and lives, and finally dies. And so does a man."

The form of this speech is that of an edifying rabbinic discourse. The content is impudent and sophistical. But—and this is what is most significant—Sholom Aleichem is loyal at one and the same time to both the form and the content that controverts it. The Jews in their ages of faith had experienced the contradictions of life and the cosmos as revelation, as theophany; now they are only contradictions, existing side by side with a faith that cannot comprehend them.

The conflict between form and content can be seen in innumerable jokes, of which the following is a rather good representative:

If I have the right to take money out of my pocket, from which the other man has no right to take money, then is not my right all the greater to take money from *his* pocket, from which even he has the right to take money?

This "joke" is chanted in the melody usually reserved for Talmudic study, and the parody is further stressed by the fact that in the original Yiddish the two clauses are joined by the technical Hebrew phrase, which is the Talmudic counterpart to the logician's *a fortiori*. Indeed, the form is impeccably orthodox; only the content negates the purpose of this form, which in the Talmud aims at establishing the immutable principles of justice and piety. But though the form is negated it is not denied, for the jokester—assuming him to have been an average ghetto Jew—had no intention of substituting other and novel laws of thought: These laws were as good as any, it just happened that reality made an absurdity of them, and that was what was funny.

Ernst Simon has shown how the method of argument in the Talmud, and the singsong incantation of the unpunctuated text, lent itself to the uses of humor.* But before such use could be made, a measure of detachment had to be gained; the mind had to be able to stand apart from the sacred text, and to see itself as standing apart. The affective power of faith had to be stilled, replaced by what Bergson has called "a momentary anesthesia of the heart," and the world given over to

---

*In his article "Notes on Jewish Wit," in the *Jewish Frontier* (October 1948).

pure intelligence. The life of faith is then seen as something absurd.

But, after that, Jewish humor takes another bold step: The world of nonfaith, of pure intelligence, is seen to be equally absurd.

Jewish humor is the humor of a rebellious rationalism. It is also the *reductio ad absurdum* of rationalism. Thus there is produced a distinctive quality of Jewish wit: its circularity.

Immanuel Olsvanger has recorded three versions—Arabic, Russian, and Jewish—of the same joke, which purports to reveal the "secret of Telegraphy":

Arabic—"Imagine a huge dog having its head in Beirut and its tail in Damascus. Pull the dog's tail in Damascus and the bark will be heard in Beirut."

Russian—First Russian: "Imagine a horse, its head in Moscow and its tail in Tula. Pinch the horse's nose in Moscow and it will wag its tail in Tula. And so it is with telegraphy." Second Russian: "Yes, but how do they telegraph from Tula to Moscow?"

Jewish—First Jew: "Imagine, instead of the wire, a dog, whose head is in Kovno and whose tail is in Vilna. Pull the tail in Vilna and the bark will be heard in Kovno." Second Jew: "But how does wireless telegraphy work?" First Jew: "The very same way but without the dog."

Here, rational explanation ends up by being identical with the original confession of ignorance, yet is offered as a proof. Now this circularity is partly a sardonic and sophisticated mimicry of the naive circularity that is intrinsic to religious faith and that, for instance, permits the pious commentator to prove that Abraham wore a hat when he invited the angels into his tent—for would the patriarch Abraham *not* wear a hat? In the nineteenth century this mimicry was directed in particular against the "wonder-working" rabbis of Hasidism, as in the following:

Rabbi A., in Cracow, while praying, saw in a vision that Rabbi B., in Lemberg, had just died. He and his congregation went into mourning. Later, travelers from Lemberg reported that Rabbi B. was still alive and in good health. The critics of Rabbi A. took this opportunity to scoff at his supposed supernatural powers. To these the disciples of Rabbi A. retorted: "And isn't it miracle enough for you that our rabbi could see all the way from Cracow to Lemberg?"*

But if the reasoning of the devout is absurd, it is not ridiculous, for there is always one bit of evidence that makes sense out of the nonsense of faith: the pious man, who by his presence converts what is ra-

*This is taken from Freud's *Jokes and Their Relation to the Unconscious,* which is still one of the best books on Jewish humor ever written.

tionally absurd into something real. One must bear in mind to what extent the fullness of Jewish life was, for almost two millennia, devoted to what is rationally absurd, to what extent it was a dream-life, a sane type of madness. Jewish existence was grounded in a series of fantastic "make-believes." The Jews, seemingly the lowliest of the low, were God's chosen people. The Temple was destroyed but the routine of sacrifice was studied. On the last day of the Feast of Booths all Jews prayed for rain so that the nonexistent crops of Palestine's nonexistent Jewish settlements might prosper.

And here the Jewish jokester is in a dilemma. He is the child of a later age, and he believes that what is rationally absurd should be really absurd. He is, however, also close enough to the vitality of Jewish faith to be profoundly aware that the absurd can, through faith, become real. He *knows,* uncontrollably, and in every fiber of his being, that the Jew is the son of the covenant, even if such an idea is an outrage to enlightened intelligence. He becomes the victim of an exhilarating paranoia. Truth and reality diverge: What is true is rational, but what is real is the absurd. His reason finds itself impotent, and in the circular joke it proceeds to outwit itself.

A Jew, whose life had been one long trial and who was sustained only by the hope of compensation in the afterlife, lay dying. With his remaining breath he told his children, assembled round his bed, how he had suffered and with what joy he looked forward to the world-to-come. "But," he concluded, "what a joke it would be if there were nothing over there!"

The joke comes about if one ardently believes in a God who does not—and one secretly fears it—exist.

Jewish humor dances along a knife-edge that separates religious faith from sheer nihilism. It "knows" that the material world is the only true reality, but it also finds that this world makes no sense in its own terms and is impossible to live in, while the absurd world of Jewish faith, the one into which it was born and whose air it is accustomed to breathe, is no longer true. The intensity of Jewish humor derives from this double loyalty to incompatibles, to the sacred and the profane. Bergson has said that "a situation is invariably comic when it belongs simultaneously to two altogether independent series of events and is capable of being interpreted in two entirely different meanings at the same time." So it is that the European Jew, achieving self-consciousness in the Enlightenment, found himself at the point of intersection of faith and reason, in a comic situation he could master only with a joke.

Jewish humor is, consequently, also nostalgic. It looks backward to a state where the Jew did not know the comic, was incapable of wit, and did not need humor to make him laugh. Occasionally, its nostalgia is so acute that, as Theodor Reik has demonstrated, Jewish humor, especially in its self-aggression, strongly resembles psychopathic melancholia.

What is this but to say that Jewish humor is of the essence of modernity? Sholom Aleichem is a truly modern writer in the same sense that Dostoevski and Nietzsche are modern writers. He has eaten of the fruit of the tree of rational knowledge but he hungers for the fruit of the tree of religious life. And Sholom Aleichem's true heir is Franz Kafka, who used to laugh until the tears came to his eyes when he read his work aloud to friends. But Kafka does not make *us* laugh. That is a measure of the extent to which the modern situation, dissolving into murderous nihilism, robs Jewish humor of its victory.

1951

# 27

# God and
the Psychoanalysts

*My courage fails me, therefore, at the thought of
rising up as a prophet before my fellow-men, and I
bow to the reproach that I have no consolation to
offer them; for at bottom that is what they all
demand—the frenzied revolutionary as passionately
as the most pious believer.*

—Sigmund Freud

PSYCHOANALYSIS was from its
very beginnings disrespectful, when not positively hostile, toward all
existing religious creeds and institutions. Naturally, the religious rheto-
ricians replied with heat, though, it must be said, with unequal light.
The contest was not exactly an exciting one, if only because few people
could get enthusiastic about God, one way or the other. The psychoanalysts found it sufficient to explain with supreme objectivity just how
it was that this mountain of nonsense and error came to rest on human
shoulders. The preachers retorted with anathemas or plaints of misrep-
resentation. The general conviction of the century was that the analysts
were going to unnecessary extremes of detail to dissect a patient ripe
for the grave, and that the patient was showing a lack of taste in hanging
on so grimly to a life that held no future for him.

But then the contest was transplanted to the melting pot of America, with astonishing consequences. In America all races and creeds live
and work peacefully side by side—why should not ideas do likewise?
For the ancient habit of supposing that an idea was true or false, there

286

was substituted the more "democratic" way of regarding all ideas as aspects of a universal Truth which, if all of it were known, would offend no one and satisfy all. It is under such favorable circumstances, and in such a benign climate of opinion, that the current love affair between psychoanalysis and religion has been, time and again, consummated. There have been bickerings and quarrels, of course, and the Catholic Church has shown itself to be a rather frigid partner. But, all in all, things have gone well, and the occasional Catholic reserve has been more than made up for by Protestant acquiescence and Jewish ardor.

Where once a Judaism liberated from the ghetto fled into the arms of a universal Pure Reason (which did, after all, proclaim honorable intentions), now a Judaism liberated from just about everything religious embraces psychoanalysis without a first thought as to the propriety of the liaison. So we read of a speech by the dean of Hebrew Union College, calling for a reexamination of religious teachings to determine whether "they strengthen or weaken the mental and emotional health of the common man"—the assumption obviously being that God is a fiction anyhow and He may as well make Himself useful. Another distinguished professor at Hebrew Union College is on record with this "tip" for alert investors: "The person who will contribute money for religio-psychoanalytic inquiry will have entered upon the way of all ways in which religion can be furthered by money." And two bright young rabbis have proposed to a conference of Jewish chaplains that the prayer books for hospitalized Jewish veterans be "screened" by psychiatrists to eliminate "any mystic elements from religion." Everyone knows how toxic mysticism is.

The monument to this tendency is, of course, the late Joshua Loth Liebman's *Peace of Mind*. This book informs us quite simply that "psychological discoveries about conduct and motive are really the most recent syllables of the divine"; that "men who are inwardly tormented and emotionally unhappy can never be good partners of God"; that the Decalogue was, for its time, rather sensible: "In the stages of human development from infancy to adolescence, it is quite proper to present rules of moral behavior as categorical commandments"; that atheism is the result of a child's being rejected by its parents; that "businessmen attacking the administration, grumbling about taxes, or worrying about our relations with Russia" ignore the fact that "the true root of their anxiety lies deep within themselves"; that "a wise religion" [no mention is made of a true one] "is indispensable to peace of mind"; that self-confident Americans who regard themselves as "responsible co-workers with God" can have no use for all those religious notions which arose out of the "helpless, poverty-stricken, powerless motifs in

European culture." The book closes with a list of "commandments of a new morality," the first of which is: "Thou shalt not be afraid of thy hidden impulses."

In an attempt to dispel the impression that *Peace of Mind* made upon many—that today no one is so sick as our spiritual healers—Fulton J. Sheen has written a Catholic *Peace of Soul.* Monsignor Sheen makes it clear that it is only with the greatest of distaste that he has written this book, and that it is to be taken as a concession to modern man's moral disorder. He is repelled by the "scum and sediment" of the unconscious and feels sure that ecclesiastical dogma would prefer that the unconscious not exist. But since it reputedly does, Monsignor Sheen sets out to purge psychoanalysis of its impurities, absorb it into the Catholic intellectual hierarchy, and leave it to perish there of boredom. These impurities are attributed to a misemphasis on "sex analysis" (Freudianism), which Monsignor Sheen accuses of undermining the moral order and defying the prerogatives of religion and church. Specifically, he dislikes the fact that psychoanalytical patients spend so much time on their backs, a posture which invites the devil; he wishes to save "sin" as a reality born of a defective will and not let it be dismissed as a neurotic fancy; and he would like to mark out the boundaries between the confessional and psychoanalysis, leaving for the latter only those situations where the emotional derangement could have had no moral (or immoral) antecedents—which would leave it with very little at all. He is especially friendly to self-analysis because the intimacy between patient and analysis is a sore temptation as well as a trespass on the clerical province.

All this indicates that Monsignor Sheen is considerably more zealous than was Rabbi Liebman in asserting the priority of morality and the Church over psychoanalysis. Yet they have more in common than would appear at first sight, even more than their literary ties to the fraternity of vulgar journalism (Monsignor Sheen writes: "Nine months later the Eternal established its beachhead in Bethlehem."). Both would like to be of assistance to those modern psychoanalysts who would "revise" or emasculate Freud to make him palatable, or even useful, to the *ecclesia.* Though Monsignor Sheen, unlike Rabbi Liebman, gives a positive religious status to anxiety—as a necessary quality of man who is a fallen creature, and as a spur to seeking God—he is just as eager for this anxiety not to be taken too much to heart: Monsignor Sheen promises peace of soul inside the Catholic Church as glibly as Rabbi Liebman promises peace of mind outside it. Where for Rabbi Liebman an excess of anxiety is "unhealthy," for Monsignor Sheen it is—unless it is quickly dissolved into Catholic "peace of soul"—a possible prelude to heresy and a certain sign of deficient faith. For neither of these two cler- ics is the existence of God, and man's relation with Him, a problem which should worry men to morbid excess. And both join their voices in eagerly quoting from psychiatrists' testimonials concerning the be- neficent influence of religion on mental health.

But, most of all, what Monsignor Sheen and Rabbi Liebman and their numerous Protestant counterparts share is a disinclination, or in- ability, to take Freud seriously, to take his challenge to religion serious- ly, and in the end, to take religion itself seriously.

What is remarkable in all current demonstrations of how well reli- gion and psychoanalysis supplement each other is that the question of truth—whether we live under God or entirely in the realm of nature—is ignored. Most clerics and analysts blithely agree that religion and psy- choanalysis have at heart the same intention: to help men "adjust," to cure them of their vexatious and wasteful psychic habits (lasting despair and anxiety), to make them happy or virtuous or productive. Insofar as religion and psychoanalysis succeed in this aim, they are "true." But against this stands the overwhelming objection of Nietzsche: "Nobody will very readily regard a doctrine as true merely because it makes peo- ple happy or virtuous. . . . A thing could be *true*, although it were in the highest degree injurious and dangerous; indeed the fundamental constitution of existence might be such that one succumbed by a full knowledge of it."

And Moses and Freud are in agreement with at least the first part of Nietzsche's statement; they came to speak the truth about the funda- mental constitution of existence and not to sow propaganda which would lead men to feel themselves happy or virtuous. Moses did not promise the Jews "happiness," nor did he say they should walk in the path of the Law because he thought it a virtuous law. The Law was true because it was divine—it was God's Law, a revelation of man's place in the fundamental constitution of existence. Though men suffer and die in the following of it, yet it is the truth, and men's true happiness and virtue are in adhering to this truth—because it is true; any other kind of pretended happiness is but mere euphoria. Freud, in turn, did not assert that religion made men "unhappy,"* but that it was based

---

*That religion could claim a "therapeutic" value, Freud understood very well in his own way: "The true believer is in a high degree protected against the danger of certain neurotic afflictions; by accepting the universal neurosis he is spared the task of forming a personal neurosis"; and further: "At such a cost—by the forcible imposition of mental infantilism and inducing a mass delusion—religion succeeds in saving many people from individual neuroses."

on an illusion about the fundamental constitution of existence. Freud, like Moses, could not conceive of authentic happiness as something separate from truth. In his eyes, religion was a mass obsessional neurosis, and all attempts to enlist psychoanalysis in its support were dementedly clever stratagems whereby the neurotic incorporated a new experience into a larger obsessional pattern. Even if it could be proved that men could not live without religion, that "they succumbed by a full knowledge" of reality, this showed only that man was a creature who could not live in the truth.

The truths of religion and psychoanalysis, it should be clear, lay mutually exclusive claims upon the individual; their understanding of "the fundamental constitution of existence" is antithetical.

For religion, we live under the jurisdiction of the past. The truth is in the revelation on Sinai, and in Scripture, which fully comprehends us while we are powerless to fully comprehend it. God's word, spoken in the remote past and now hardly audible, is ever more true than the persistent chatter of men. Religion informs us that our ancestors were wiser and holier than we; that they were therefore more normal because they lived by divine Law, while our laws are driftwood in the stream of time; that no matter how mightily we strive we shall probably never see with their clarity into the fundamental constitution of existence and shall always be of little worth compared with them; and that, indeed, the virtue we inherit by reason of being descendants of Abraham, Isaac, and Jacob is far greater than any we can hope to claim to have merited. "What are we? What is our life? What is our piety? . . . Nevertheless we are Thy people, the children of Thy covenant, the children of Abraham."

Psychoanalysis, on the other hand, must repeat Freud's words: "But these ancestors of ours were far more ignorant than we." Psychoanalysis insists that it understands the past better than the past understood itself. Since all men have been driven by unconscious motivations which only we moderns really understand, and of which past generations were for the most part ignorant, a Freud of the twentieth century, or, presumably, one of his competent pupils, equipped with the tools of psychoanalysis, can know Moses, Da Vinci, Michelangelo, and Dostoevski better than they knew themselves. At most we can say of certain great minds of the past that they had an intuitive and premature inkling of the true constitution of human nature and existence which is now known (or will soon be known) in its fullness. The history of the human race is a tale of growth from primitive times—when men were as children—to the present age of adulthood, when man finally understands himself and his history.

## God and the Psychoanalysts

There is a crucial disagreement here, which can never be mediated, as to what is the true and the real. Psychoanalysis explains religion; it describes how and why religion came into being, how and why what we clearly see to be irrational was accepted as superrationally true, and how and why that which we know to be a product of the human fancy came to be regarded as an existing, supernatural being.* To this, religion answers that the understanding of psychoanalysis is only a dismal, sophisticated misunderstanding, that human reason is inferior to divine reason, that the very existence of psychoanalysis is a symptom of gross spiritual distress, and that religion understands the psychoanalyst better than the psychoanalyst understands himself.

In this dialogue between psychoanalysis and religion, it is to be expected that psychoanalysis would try to establish its position behind the starched apron of science. What is surprising is that the religionists should be so eager to assist it—until we remember that in the long, grueling warfare between science and organized religion, the latter received valuable instruction in tactics. Abandoning the frontal attack, the pastors were successfully able to persuade the scientists that science was not at all atheistic, as some brash people claimed, but that its sphere of activity was quite a different one from that of religion, that it dealt with an "abstract" reality and not the "real" reality, that its arid language was inadequate to religious statement, that it operated on another "level of meaning," and so on. In the same way today, pacific priests and analysts are eager that psychoanalysis should renounce its wild and Freudian past and become a medical science; for the more medicinal it is, the smaller is the danger that it will seem to say anything about the fundamental constitution of existence, the less does it encroach upon religion, and the greater is the mutual security of religious and psychoanalytic institutions; psychoanalysis would deal only with "health" and never with "truth." The result is a revision and "correction" of Freud—especially in America—which tends to make of psychoanalysts mental counselors, in no necessary conflict with religion, "adjusting" patients to their infirmities, their limitations of talent, their jobs (or else the analyst serves as a vocational guide), their bad luck, their wives, their children, and, in the armed forces, to their officers. Some analysts even send their patients to church, as a therapy.

Psychoanalysis, then, would seem to be on its way to becoming simply the medical treatment of the psyche, cohabiting with religion

*The psychoanalytical theories of Jung, which accept the subjective religious experience as something ultimate, are an interesting deviation from this line. But Jung never commits himself as to whether God *is*, and therefore cannot genuinely decide whether the religious experience is normal or abnormal.

in all amiability. But on this way it stumbles and falls. For if psychoanalysis is disloyal to the implications of its method—to what this
method assumes as the fundamental constitution of existence, as enunciated by Freud—it sinks into a realm of relativism in which the human
intellect circles upon itself like a dog chasing its tail.

Psychoanalysis is unlike traditional medicine in that nature does
not so readily supply us with a working definition of the psychically
"normal." Our definition of physical normality ("health") is not something we have strenuously to imagine or blindly to postulate, and there
are obvious and sharp limits to possible disagreement; it is simply given
to us because we are what we are. But psychoanalysis is in a more ambiguous position. Its definition of mental health has to be in good measure "thought up," and it must be done by men whose ideas are
influenced by their lives and times. Psychoanalysis is always open to
the accusation that its criteria of "neurosis" and "mental health" and
"adjustment" have a cultural bias, and are influenced by political ideologies, national prejudices, and personal whims. To take the accusation
in its most general form: Any psychoanalytical approach which, out of
diplomatic cordiality toward religion, renounces its claim to an objective
knowledge of human nature or to a lasting, true insight into the fundamental constitution of existence must admit that it is historically and
socially conditioned. And once there is no objectively *true* human nature
which is taken as the norm, there is no possibility of general agreement
on what it means to be "sick" and what it means to be "cured." We
can then have communist analysts, Nazi analysts, democratic analysts,
anarchist analysts, all with irreconcilable criteria of mental health.

Actually, the dilemma of the "revisionist" schools of psychoanalysis arises from their reluctance to abandon—at the same time that they
drop all Freudian "metaphysics"—either of the two branches of psychoanalysis joined by Freud: the pathological and the general psychological. (This distinction is very lucidly made by Theodor Reik in
*Listening with the Third Ear.*) Pathological psychology seems to have some
intimate relation with the organic, intimate enough, in any case, for it
to be a (still largely unexplored) subbranch of medicine. But in this field,
psychoanalysis has to compete with formal psychiatry and neurology,
both of which are closer to what is universally deemed medical science:
Psychoanalysis can "explain" more than psychiatry only because it is
less rigorously scientific. To be sure, psychoanalysis has effected cures
of pathological cases. But cures have also been reached by treatments
which have nothing to do with psychoanalysis, nor can psychoanalysis
claim greater efficiency, greater rapidity, or any other advantage. Moreover, psychoanalysis is splintered into various schools, all of which

claim to cure, and no way exists of deciding for or against any one of them, or of finding out whether they may work for reasons quite different from those given by all of them. In pathology, psychoanalysis stands to the ideal of medical science as the herb-doctor (whose herbs work too sometimes, and not entirely by chance) to a diagnostician.

Yet when psychoanalysis turns to nonpathological cases, and tries to fall back upon general psychology, upon its theory of human nature, for a warrant of competence, then it has to say what human nature rightfully *is;* it has to be explicit as to whether man prays to God or is trapped in an obsessional neurosis, it has to decide the question of truth before it dares raise the question of therapy. And this would involve it in those discussions about man and his place in the universe which would be fatal to its ambitions to live at peace with religion.

Freud, too, was faced with the problem that before one could aim at healing human nature it was necessary to decide what human nature in its undamaged state is, and in his analysis of dreams he stepped unhesitatingly from pathology to depth (general) psychology. The pathological and the abnormal were points of departure for the determination of the "really" normal, and Freud ceased to be a doctor and became a thinker. Truth precedes healing—Freud's own italicized definition of the task of psychoanalysis was *"education to reality."* Where in all of his past history man had achieved only a self-deceptive self-consciousness, riddled with mythical projections of the unconscious, now man has acquired the ability to see the human situation as it really is.

Perhaps because of the verbal resonance of such terms as the "unconscious" and the "libido," and certainly because of his own harsh comments on various facile and optimistic beliefs, Freud is often viewed as a reaction to the nineteenth century's certainty that man was master of his fate and to its adoration of the goddess Reason. Freud himself, in certain passages, seemed to encourage this interpretation, as when he noted the three wounds inflicted by science on humanity's self-love: the cosmological blow of the Copernican revolution, the biological blow of Darwinian evolution, and the psychological blow of Freudianism. But such an interpretation of Freud would be erroneous, and Freud's remarks seeming to support it must be understood mainly as a not unflattering explanation of the hostility which his contemporaries directed at him.

Copernicus, Darwin, and Freud did not attack *man's* self-love, but only the *religious man's* self-respect. They diminished God (though, except for Freud, without intention) and aggrandized man as the rational animal. They did not undermine man's reason, but enthroned it, at the expense of the religious authority. Freud did not come to proclaim the law of Reason at an end—he came to fulfill it, at the same time explaining how previous efforts at fulfillment had been overly glib and superficial. Man, by virtue of Freud's work, was not less than he had been; he was infinitely more, facing for the first time the prospect of an authentic self-consciousness and self-control which would make him the true measure of all things. Though Freud, in comparison with his contemporaries, complicated human nature, it was the kind of theoretical complication (like Einsteinian physics) which makes possible the lucid solution of hitherto baffling problems; it is a gain for Reason, not a loss.

Freudianism was a legitimate son of nineteenth-century philosophy (Marxism was another) which declared that in all previous world history the human mind had not been free but had been enslaved to nature or society, and that now life according to true Reason (not ideological or neurotic rationalization) was within men's reach. The epoch of human history in which man's mind had been "alienated" from reality was approaching its end. And Freud was supremely a man of the nineteenth century in his idea of history as the development of the human race from infancy to adulthood, in his conceiving of the biography of humanity as entirely analogous to the biography of the individual, with religion as a childlike obsessional neurosis which the child had failed to outgrow and which the doctor was now hurrying to cure, so as to secure, in his own words, "the psychological ideal, the primacy of the intelligence."

Freud is of one mind with Spinoza, that to have a rational understanding of what our instincts (Spinoza called them passions) are up to is to make us master of them. The purpose of psychoanalysis is to redeem the ego from compulsive irrationality (neurosis) and to place the instinctual libido in the service of a rational ego, for it is not the instinctual unconscious itself which resists psychoanalytical treatment—its goal is to be discharged, into consciousness or action—but the irrational ego, the ego that has "solved" its problems by a nonrational adjustment (neurosis) and that desperately defends its precarious solution. This redemption of the rational ego is achieved in the three steps of the psychoanalytical treatment: (1) the "recall" of the repressed—a conscious awareness of what is behind the particular neurosis; (2) transference, or redirection of the libidinal force to the analyst, which gives the ego a chance to wrestle openly, through a transference neurosis, with the material raised from the unconscious; (3) mastery of the instinctual urges by the rational ego.

It is clear from this how absurd is the charge against Freud of being the high priest of the irrational, goading the instincts, especially the sexual instincts, into a coup d'état. (Monsignor Sheen seems to be of this opinion.) It would be more accurate to say that Freud was a supreme puritan. The tenor of Freud's writings is that the present sexual standards of respectability are maliciously provocative of nervous disorder. His plea for greater sexual freedom is the plea of a wise and experienced statesman, not the appeal of an irresponsible radical. For Freud, sex is the blind, powerful, and eternally rebellious subject of the legitimate despot Reason. Revolt means calamity: At the least, the established order is forced to share power with new tribunes, in an uneasy compromise; at the most, sheer anarchy prevails. It is because of his fear of the herd of sexual instincts that Freud would concede so much to them, would abrogate the existing sexual morality in favor of a less provocative one, would assure a free genital sexuality in order to provide protection to all those other zones threatened with erotic invasion. The localization in the genitals of the sexual urge is the necessary condition for the natural reign of Reason. The greater the liberty of the genitalia in satisfying this urge, the greater the security of the Rational state.

There are two fairly distinct trends in Freud's analysis of religion, both of them hostile, but corresponding, respectively, to his earlier mood of moderate hope and his later mood of only faintly relieved gloom. The second is more important in what it tells us about the ultimate destiny of psychoanalysis. The first is important too, however, in that it provided a crucial supplement to the rationalist refutation of religion. Though rationalists of the eighteenth and nineteenth centuries spoke of the slow education of human reason from superstition upward, from credulousness and helplessness to manly independence of spirit, it was Freud who came to show the psychological necessity of this evolutionary process. Freud's attack on religion cut more deeply than even that of Voltaire or Marx, for while Voltaire could expose the unreasonableness of religious dogmas, and Marx could show how religion mirrored the inauthenticity of man in the precommunist era, neither could satisfactorily explain the psychological mechanism by which human beings came to be so duped in the first place and why it lasted as long as it did.

According to Freud, religion is the price paid for the *blind* renunciation of inherent instincts. Religious prohibitions deprive sexuality of its due at the same time that religious creeds leave reason defenseless and feeble, so that sexuality is able to reappear in the disguise of neurotic behavior such as prayer, pilgrimage, theological speculation, and the like. Religions owe their obsessive character to "important happenings in the primeval history of the human family" and "derive their effect on mankind from the historical truth they contain"—a truth imprinted on the racial memory of every newborn child. The "happening" from which religion grew was the slaying and communal eating, in the primal horde, of the primal father by his sons, who had joined together in order to share the father's sexual prerogatives—the original Oedipal revolt, and one which each individual recapitulates in his own mental experience. But the victorious sons were tormented by anxiety about their portentous deed, and by fear of continual, bloody sexual rivalry. So there came into being, in these "ages of ignorance and intellectual weakness," the sense of guilt and sin, as well as moral codes and religious catechisms, to repress all sexual rivalry with the fathers, to appease the memory of the primal father who had been transformed into God, and to guarantee the existence of an orderly community. And each individual not only "remembers" the historic past, but in his own lifetime has to make some sort of adjustment to his own Oedipus complex, his impotence as a child to challenge the father for the mother's favors, his jealousy, and the anxious repression of it.

The history of religion is analogical to the history of neurosis in the growing child, its strength gathered from childhood anxieties and frustrations, and this strength dissipated with natural growth into adult rationality. The history of humanity, like the life-history of every one of its members, is a process of maturation in which the instinctual renunciations necessary for the stability of the community are rationally comprehended and lose their malevolent potential. Freud writes:

"We know that the human child cannot well complete its development towards culture without passing through a more or less distinct phase of neurosis. This is because the child is unable to suppress by rational mental effort so many of those instinctual impulsions which cannot later be turned into account, but has to check them by acts of repression, behind which there stands as a rule an anxiety motive. Most of these child neuroses are overcome spontaneously as one grows up, and especially is this the fate of the obsessional neuroses of childhood. The remainder can be cleared up later by psychoanalytical treatment." And in the same volume (*The Future of an Illusion*): "One might prophesy that the abandoning of religion must take place with the fateful inexorability of growth, and that we are just now in the middle of this phase of development."

By virtue of science and psychoanalysis, mankind begins to see the approaches to the Kingdom of Reason. The false knowledge of a supernatural Other, which was only an evasion of true self-knowledge, will be sloughed off like an outworn garment, and God, together with bibles, saints, and churches, will be consigned to the museum of human infancy.

What can religion reply to this? It is impossible to ask what *does* religion reply to this, for religion in our time for the most part does not reply at all. It either gives up the ghost and tries to show its social and psychological utility in an imperfect world where the triumph of Reason is not yet complete; or it utters grave twaddle about incorporating "the enduring insights" of psychoanalysis in a "larger perspective," as if its perspective were infinitely elastic. Religion is uncertain, does not know whether we were really on Sinai or whether it was only a dream.

Yet there are certain lines of argument, it seems to me, which religious thought, because it is religious, must take. Religion must agree with psychoanalysis that the world in which we live is sick, but where psychoanalysis asserts that religion is a symptom of this illness, religion must cling to its own diagnosis and see psychoanalysis itself as a symptom of a mind diseased. Religion has to deny the thesis of progressive human evolution, and must explain psychoanalysis, must explain it away, by tracing its genesis and showing that the error in which it is involved points to the truth which it denies.

Psychoanalysis, in the eyes of religion, is a historical passion of men obsessed with the death of God. Nietzsche proclaimed that God was dead, Freud followed with the news that we had eaten and devoured His human archetype, and that His spiritual existence had always been an illusion. Both were right, for the nineteenth and twentieth centuries have regarded God as a corpse whose essence has been appropriated by man—the so-called divine attributes have been made over into human possibilities. Yet in this era of humanism and godlessness, man found himself more than ever alienated: His flight from God has also been a flight from his true self, which had been made in His image. So it was that Freud could build a theory of human nature on the basis of his experience with hysterics and neurotics, a unique and strange achievement which testifies to our modern psychic equilibrium, whose fulcrum is at the edge of an abyss.

Religion cannot deny that psychoanalysis has discovered the unconscious. It can only say that the unconscious as such is a new phenomenon, the toll paid to God and nature for the presumptive effort to have man's conscious rationality prevail over all of existing reality—including divine reality; in the days when God's face was turned to man, the unconscious was integrated with consciousness and did not whirl madly free through psychic space. The age of Reason, through a series of strenuous introjections, has attempted to press all of religious reality into the rational intellect and to imprison God, cowering and sullen, behind the forehead. The reward of this effort is psychic fragmentation, for divine reality is not within the rational mind of man but outside it, and the mind which would encompass it bursts. Instead of a divine reality that was a great chain of being, there is now, for each man, only a hall of mirrors. Since man has cut all ties with divine reality, has indeed denied to it reality, his psyche has been sentenced to follow upon itself in a dark and unending maze.

Psychoanalysis, religion might say, comes not to remove insanity, but to inaugurate it.

It would seem that this debate between psychoanalysis and religion can continue indefinitely, until it is terminated by God speaking unequivocally or the Kingdom of Reason being attained. And since God is silent and the Kingdom of Reason unborn, the debate goes on, important but nonetheless wearisome. But it is not a debate without end—for that we have Freud's word. Freud's final and tragic message is that the truth is with Reason and against God, but it is a truth in which man probably cannot live. Rational self-consciousness is the avenue to perfect wisdom, which leads in most men to perfect despair. Though Reason still has the task of "reconciling men to civilization," it is an authority entirely vitiated by the fact that "man is a creature of weak intelligence who is governed by his instinctual needs."

This message is found in Freud's later "metapsychological" works, such as *Beyond the Pleasure Principle* and *Civilization* and *Its Discontents.* Many contemporary psychoanalysts, exercising the privilege of little minds to "revise" greater ones, casually dismiss these writings as deviations from the pure principles of science. But Freud was no eccentric, and if he went beyond the conventional limits of psychological science in his later works (just as he did, incidentally, in his earlier ones), he must have been of the serious opinion that the limits were too confining for the truth as he then saw it. In a letter to Einstein in 1932, in which he outlined his theory of the death instinct as the cause of war, Freud wrote: "All this may give you the impression that our theories amount to a species of mythology, and a gloomy one at that! But does not every natural science lead ultimately to this—a sort of mythology?"

Freud's final "mythology" involves a modification of the earlier postulated contradiction between sexual instincts and ego instincts into one between Eros and Thanatos, the life instinct and the death instinct. The concept of instinct is redefined as "a tendency innate in living organic matter impelling it towards the reinstatement of an earlier condition." What is this earlier condition? "It must be an ancient starting point, which the living being left long ago, and to which it harks back again by all the circuitous paths of development. If we may assume as an experience admitting of no exception that everything living dies from causes within itself, and returns to the inorganic, we can only say 'The goal of all life is death.' . . ." This drive toward extinction is countered by the sexual and reproductive instincts, which are the only ones which do not have as their aim the reinstatement of a previous condition, and which push to life, its extension and unification.*

Instead of being the evolution of Reason and its eventual enthronement, history is blind and its contradictions unresolvable: "And now, it seems to me, the meaning of the evolution of culture is no longer a riddle to us. It must present to us the struggle between Eros and Death, between the instincts of life and the instincts of destruction, as it works itself out in the human species." The death instinct, under the influence of Eros, is extraverted and becomes aggression. Civilization is a huge detour constructed by Eros so as to make the death instinct take the long way home.

Civilization tries to disarm the aggressive instinct by directing it against the ego, by making it over into the "superego" whose aggression against the ego takes the form of "conscience." This tension between the ego and the superego results in the sense of guilt, which while possibly neurotic by the absolute standard of Rational Man, is a normal quality of the human animal in the state of civilization. "The price of progress in civilization is paid in forfeiting happiness through the heightening of the sense of guilt."

Men who are loyal to the truths of Reason are doomed by their very natures to unhappiness. Happiness (but not *true* happiness, not happiness in the *truth*) is available only to those—the immense majority—who cannot face the truth of man's condition, who live with and by illusions, illusions of God, salvation, and the world to come. Freud's metapsychology concedes no more truth to religion than did his psychology. His "mythology" is a rational one. It is a mythology of rational despair.

The present attempts to wed a vulgarized psychoanalysis to a vulgarized religiosity are certain to fail: Between the two parties is stretched the sword of truth, and both are pledged to keep their backs to it. Sooner or later, the world will perceive the lineaments of frustration and will know that the union was never fully consummated. But this marital ca-

---

*There are important variations in Freud's formulations of his metapsychology. Thus, he seems to say at times that the sexual instinct too is conservative, and that it too aims at death. In *Beyond the Pleasure Principle* he makes use of the myth in Plato's *Symposium* of an original hermaphroditic nature which split into male and female, so that living matter, through sex, seeks a primordial unity.

tastrophe is not inevitable—all the mates have to do is, acting together in full consciousness, stealthily to remove the sword of truth and hide it under the bed.

Oddly enough, it is only on the late-Freudian foundation of rational despair that psychoanalysis can be "reconciled" with religion—but at a price, a price that Freud, with his intense personal loyalty to the truth, could never pay. For there are a few men, very few, who are willing to look at life boldly as a bleak prelude to death, and at civilization as an enormous distraction from self-extinction. These men submit to the truths of Reason, because in them Reason is the master of the instincts and not its slave. But in the great mass of men, it is the opposite: Reason is the toy of instinct and happiness in untruth is preferred to truth.

If God does not exist, and if religion is an illusion that the majority of men cannot live without, then psychoanalysis and religion can be reconciled—if that is what one wishes—by the simple expedient of a double standard of truth. Let men believe in the lies of religion since they cannot do without them, and let the handful of sages, who know the truth and can live with it, keep it among themselves. Men are then divided into the wise and the foolish, the philosphers and the common men, and atheism becomes a guarded, esoteric doctrine—for if the illusions of religion were to be discredited, there is no telling with what madness men would be seized, with what uncontrollable anguish. It would indeed become the duty of the wise publicly to defend and support religion, even to call the police power to its aid, while reserving the truth for themselves and their chosen disciples.

Psychoanalysis itself, which assumes religion to be an illusion, would become a form of esoteric wisdom, and the psychoanalyst would, with regard to dreams, agree with Maimonides: "Persons whose mental capacity is not fully developed, and who have not attained intellectual perfection, must not take any notice of them."

Such a program is bound to sound unpleasant in the ears of twentieth-century Americans, though it does have the advantage of enabling many to do what they seem to want to do: to drive in two directions at once, in pursuit of peace of mind at any cost and in pursuit of rational truth. But, of course, there is always the further possibility that the truth is not with Freud and Reason, but with God, and that men *can* live in this truth and find their happiness—simply living in it, though it be a scandal to Reason. "Because the foolishness of God is wiser than men."

1949

# 28

# Einstein: The Passion of Pure Reason

*Arrows of hate have been shot at me too; but they never hit me, because somehow they belonged to another world, with which I have no connection whatsoever.*

—ALBERT EINSTEIN

IN Philipp Frank's biography, *Einstein: His Life and Times,* we read the following anecdote:

"Einstein was once told that a physicist whose intellectual capacities were rather mediocre had been run over by a bus and killed. He remarked sympathetically: 'Too bad about his body!'"

Of course it is probable that Einstein was having his own quiet little joke, making a gesture to the public image of himself as an abstracted, bloodless intellect floating languidly in the stellar spaces. And indeed, according to Einstein's way of thinking, body is body and mind is mind, and it is hard to think of a logical reason why one should have anything to do with the other. The body grows old, but that is hardly worth a thought: Einstein believes birthday celebrations are for children. The body perishes and is buried—of what interest is this to a mature mind? ("Attending funerals is something one does to please the people around us. In itself it is meaningless.") Men are prone to make spectacles of themselves, watching the calendar, meditating on their imminent dissolution into dust, but "the true value of a human being is determined primarily by the measure and the sense in which he has attained liberation from the self."

A volume recently published in Einstein's honor* contains an auto-biographical sketch he wrote four years ago. It opens with the naked sentence: "Here I sit in order to write, at the age of sixty-seven, some-thing like my own obituary." Then, with a few personal asides, there follow forty-five pages of physics and equations. The asides, to be sure, are illuminating. We learn that: "Even when I was a precocious quite young man I became vividly aware of the nothingness of the hopes and strivings that chase most men restlessly through life." Einstein's reac-tion to this discovery was a deep religiosity that ended abruptly at the age of twelve, giving way to a passion for science, which seemed more capable of freeing him from "the chains of the 'merely personal,' from an existence which is dominated by wishes, hopes, and primitive feel-ings." We are told all this briefly, in a few paragraphs quickly sub-merged in pages of technical discussion. But, on page 33, Einstein pulls himself up short, to dispel once and for all any confusion in the mind of the reader:

" 'Is this supposed to be an obituary?' the astonished reader will likely ask. I would like to reply: essentially yes. For the essential in the being of a man of my type lies precisely in what he thinks and *how* he thinks, not in what he does or suffers."

This, then, is how Einstein would like to see himself: no mournful pilgrim on earth, but the spirit of Pure Reason; not an anguished voice calling futilely from the depths, but a creative spirit hovering over the world of chaos; not a suffering creature, but a thinking creator, whose science is "the attempt at the posterior reconstruction of reality by the process of conceptualization," and whose duty it is "to arrive at those universal elementary laws from which the cosmos can be built up by pure deduction."

What is the path which the spirit must take to this "posterior re-construction of reality"? On this point, Einstein is unequivocal: The path is through mathematics. And if one can "reconstruct" reality with the aid of mathematics, then it is clear that the original creation must have been according to formula. God is a mathematician, and mathe-matics is *imitatio Dei*. Of course, God is an exceptional mathematician and his creation is an exceptionally "well-designed puzzle." But not an

*Einstein: Philosopher-Scientist, ed. Paul Arthur Schilpp (Evanston, Illinois: The Library of Living Philosophers, 1949). This collection of essays by outstanding philosophers and physicists is most valuable for an understanding of Einstein. It can be read in conjunction with a collection of Einstein's more recent essays and addresses, *Out of My Later Years* (New York: Philosophical Library, 1950), and Leopold Infeld's *Albert Einstein* (New York: Scrib-ner's, 1950); as well as Philipp Frank's biography, *Einstein: His Life and Times,* trans. George Rosen (New York: Knopf, 1947).

insoluble puzzle, for God is just. *"Raffiniert is der Herrgott, aber boshaft ist er nicht"* ("God is subtle, but he is not malicious")—with such words Einstein consoles and encourages Princeton's mathematicians when they lounge in Fine Hall and read the inscription over the fireplace. God is not only not malicious, he is also divinely simple: "Our experience . . . justifies us in believing that nature is the realization of the simplest conceivable mathematical ideas."

And if one should inquisitively demand why God is, after all, a mathematician? Ah, that is the mystery, that "pure thought is competent to comprehend the real," that nature is intelligible.

Einstein is not involved in what have been, at different times, designated as the two major scandals of philosophy: the first, that philosophers have not yet been able to prove the existence of the external world; the second, that philosophers should ever have presumed to believe this to be their business. For Einstein, the real world simply is. *Simply—is.* For if its existence is not to be questioned by serious men, neither is its simplicity. This simplicity may not be apparent to those who are prisoners of their senses and have not been able to make the leap from the kingdom of the bodily self to the kingdom of selfless mind, which is the realm of mathematics and necessity. The world of the body's sense perception is real—but the realer world, the world of order behind the confusion of perceived existence, is the one which is also rational, that is, mathematical. When Einstein refers to the world that is both real and rational he uses the phrase "Physical Reality."

The way to physical reality is through the mathematical imagination, through an exercise of "musicality in the sphere of thought." Such exercises, giving birth to formulas, need to be verified by experiment in order to sift the true from the false; but this does not affect the fact that "the creative principle resides in mathematics." Sense experience is, in itself, chaotic; order is of the mind. "A theory can be tested by experience, but there is no way from experience to the setting up of a theory." The "fateful" error is to entertain the belief that scientific concepts can be abstracted out of experience. They are "free inventions of the human mind." Fortunately for us, these free inventions of the human mind are found to be congruent with those free inventions of the divine mind which make up the real and rational world of Physical Reality.

One may well ask: What manner of scientist is this? He does not fit the popular image of a white-frocked manipulator of test tubes, or speak with the familiar accents of an apostle of "scientific method." He is, for instance, flatly in disagreement with the positivist Philipp Frank, who expresses what is probably the majority opinion of philosophers of science when he writes that "science cannot discover what actually happens in the world, but can only describe and combine the results of different observations." Einstein is old-fashioned, agreeing with most classical metaphysicians, and incidentally with the man in the street, that science aims to find out what *really* happens beyond the veil of appearance. Is Einstein a crank, his head filled with anachronistic jargon about God and physical reality, who by sheer luck stumbled upon some useful equations? Or is the inadequacy with a misinterpretation of scientific method?

If we examine the phrase "scientific method," we see that there is a studied ambiguity between a "method" of discovery and a "method" of verification, with "scientific method" presumably uniting the two. But, as Morris Raphael Cohen properly emphasized many years ago: "Science knows of methods of verification, but there are no methods of discovery. If there were such, all we need would be discovered, and we would not have to wait for rare men of genius." The universe of scientific discovery is ruled by an aristocracy of talent, not a democracy of method. All theories are in principle equal before the bar of verification, but only a few can gain seats in the house of truth, and there is no way of determining beforehand which these shall be. Genius is not reducible—to method or to anything else—and its very essence is to be uncommon, even exotic.

It is to be expected that men will be resentful of this state of affairs and attempt to circumvent it. The rise of modern science has been accompanied by an insistent philosophic effort at "the taming of the mind." Bacon set up his inductive method, whereby a scrupulous attention to the facts and the relation between facts would make an intelligent man a scientist; Descartes proposed his analytic method, by which "all those who observe its rules exactly would never suppose what is false to be true, and would come—without fatiguing themselves needlessly but in progressively furthering their science—to the true knowledge of all that can be known"; Dewey has sought to make science's "method of inquiry" a human habit, to divert men from "meaningless" metaphysical questions, and to encourage them to good works; and, most recently, logical positivism announced that science cannot hope to plumb the nature of things, but "can only describe and combine the results of different observations," a task for which genius is dispensable, though not entirely useless.

Yet in the actual history of science, discoveries have not been the offspring of any omnipotent "method." As often as not, private fancies have been more productive than the staid virtues of sobriety and skepticism. Men of genius—Galileo, Kepler, Newton, Einstein—have stubbornly gone their own way, possessed by metaphysical ideas of God and reality, perversely trying to plumb the depths of nature, passionate to the point of extravagance in their speculations. Descartes himself could be so certain of his method—and could make his mathematical contributions—only because he was convinced that the book of nature was in the script of geometry. The record of scientific thought gives us leave to say of science what Goethe said of poetry, that it "presupposes in the man who is to make it a certain good-natured simple-mindedness, in love with the Real as the hiding place of the Absolute."

So intimate has been the relation between scientific creativity and metaphysical (and theological) speculation that even so astringent a thinker as Bertrand Russell has wondered at the possibility of the wellsprings of science drying up in an era which deprecates metaphysical curiosity. Positivists, early in this century, were too well versed in scientific method to believe that atoms were "real," that they were more than a convenient intellectual construct by which one could "describe and combine the results of different observations"; but the atom was split nevertheless. Afterward, of course, the revelation of genius is taken as testimony to the virtue of scientific method, for it is not difficult to show—after the event—that by a proper extension of scientific method we could have known what we did not know, and to forget that we did not know it.

To this it might be retorted: What is of importance is the *result* of Einstein's work, not the idiosyncrasies that spurred him on to the job. Science is interested in what Einstein *does,* not in what he says.

If this were so, then Science would be an extremely discourteous mistress—as she has indeed often appeared to be. In actual fact, the relation between what Einstein says and what Einstein does is not so easily severed. It is true that *after* Einstein has done something, his work can be repeated by other physicists and mathematicians who will have no truck with anything called physical reality. The General Theory of Relativity can be used by anyone; it has no metaphysical patent any more than had Kepler's laws of planetary motion (which were also born of some very private fancies). It is also true, however, that it was Einstein who formulated the theory, and had he had none of these private fancies about physical reality there would not have been a General Theory of Relativity.

That it was Einstein who developed the Special Theory of Relativity in 1905 may be classified as an "accident." Physics was suffering a crisis in its foundations, experimental data refused to conform to prevailing theories, and a drastic revision of the Newtonian mechanical world view was clearly in the offing. If there had been no Einstein, someone else probably would have thought up something similar to the special theory—though precious and painful years might have been wasted. But if Einstein had not devised the General Theory of Relativity, there is a good chance that it might never have been formulated at all. For the general theory was not needed by science to explain any baffling facts. It was needed by Einstein—and by him alone—to unite the basic concepts of inertia and gravitation in one formula, in order to approximate more closely to the divine mathematical simplicity of the universe.

This intimacy between Einstein's private metaphysics and his public science is dramatically revealed in his lonely position in contemporary quantum physics. Despite the fact that his early work on photoelectric phenomena (1905)—for which he won the Nobel prize—has been extremely important in the development of quantum theory, Einstein is today an isolated and somewhat embittered figure among physicists. He believes that quantum physics has gone off the right track and has deviated from "the programmatic aim of all physics," which is the description of any situation as it really is, regardless of the act of observation. For his own part, he toiled stubbornly during the past decades to construct his recently published Unified Field Theory, which covers electromagnetic as well as gravitational fields, and which would establish—in a nearly final form—the programmatic aim of physics. Never, perhaps, has any theory by so eminent a scientist been so thoroughly ignored by his colleagues. His Unified Field Theory is not even a subject for polemic—evoking only indifference. The newspapers, of course, gave it a big play. In the laboratories, it was a topic for wisecracks. The quantum physicists feel that Einstein is exactly where he charges them with being: in a blind alley.

Einstein's reproach against quantum physics is similar—at least superficially—to that which the Catholic Church leveled against Copernicus's theory, or the conservative physicists against relativity: It is mathematically useful but not really, that is, metaphysically, true. Einstein sees the similarity but insists that the present situation is truly unique. For while the Copernican and Newtonian revolutions radically revised man's image of nature, and the relativity theory helped to substitute a mathematical model of nature for a mechanical one, the principles of quantum physics rule out the possibility of a model altogether. And this, Einstein believes, is the suicide of physics. His theory of relativity, he says, "teaches us the connection between different descriptions of one and the same reality." But the reality is there, and *physics must describe it.*

In a letter to the physicist Max Born, in 1944, Einstein wrote: "In our scientific expectation we have grown antipodes. You believe in God casting dice and I in perfect laws in the world of things existing as real objects, which I try to grasp in a wildly speculative way."

"God casting dice" is a picturesque but not inaccurate representation of how quantum physics conceives of physical reality. The statistical probability laws of quantum mechanics are not the kind of statistical laws one meets in actuarial work, for instance. In the latter, each individual event has its cause, even if statistics gives us only an average report. In quantum physics a detailed causal analysis of atomic phenomena is not only renounced for convenience' sake, but is excluded in principle. The very idea of causality does not pertain; all we know is the probability of the results of measurement at a given time.

Einstein concedes that quantum physics has made great progress with the aid of its probability statistics, but he will not admit that the present state of quantum theory is more than a stopgap. His aim is still a theory that represents "events themselves and not merely the probability of their occurrence"; he will not give up the principle of causality: He is convinced that the laws of the microscopic universe and of the macroscopic universe are continuous—nature is of one piece.

Obviously, science itself will ultimately decide whether Einstein's Unified Field Theory is relevant to the problems of modern physics—whether God casts dice or is subtle but still rational. The point here is that between Einstein as scientist and Einstein as thinker the relation is closer than some overly glib enthusiasts of scientific method consider decent.

Recently, the British positivist A. J. Ayer wrote (in *Partisan Review*) rather contemptuously of present-day intellectuals who turn to religion: "They want a form of explanation which will say something more than merely that this is how the world works. They have to be given a reason for its working as it does. . . . It is not enough to state what happens to be true; it has to be shown that it is necessarily true."

This may be taken as a fair summary of Einstein's philosophy of science. For Einstein is one of those—again in Ayer's words—"to whom it is intolerable that facts should be contingent, that things should just happen to be as they are."

Indeed, it can be said that it is not only Einstein's philosophy of science that Ayer has described, but the philosophy of science itself. For if it were not intolerable "that facts should be contingent, that things should just happen to be as they are," why should science ever have been born? In our epoch of technology, we tend to view the aim of science as prediction and control. But this is a modern belief that would have horrified the Greeks, Copernicus, Kepler, Descartes, and Newton, and which has been alien to the temper of Planck, Eddington, and Einstein, to name only a few contemporaries. For them, science has meant a passion for the rational truth which lies concealed behind all sense experience. Science in the West has been, and is, based on the assumption that what is factual and contingent has to be explained by what is rational and necessary, that statements of fact must be deduced from statements of mathematics, that matter is to be illuminated by Reason. Einstein is, par excellence, the scientist of the Western world, wedded to the belief that behind the particular and contingent there is the general and rational. The goal of science is a formula from which everything that ever happens can be logically and rigorously derived. Behind the All there is the One.

If we press further, and ask why Reason should have any success in comprehending physical reality, then, according to Einstein, we burst through science and philosophy together, and arrive at religion: "To the sphere of religion belongs the faith that the regulations valid for the world of existence are rational." This faith is not something tranquil and final; it is restless and perpetually dissatisfied, always goading Reason to convert it into a rational certitude.

God wills that the scientist—who is Reason incarnate—shall dissolve Him into demonstrable theorems. Probably the dissolution will never be final, and Einstein has uttered some forlorn sentiments on the mystery of existence. But, as Henry Margenau has acutely pointed out, in the case of Einstein "a certain pathos for the unknown, though often displayed, always intimates the ultimately knowable character of existence, knowable in scientific terms." For God may be subtle but he does not deceive.

There are, according to Einstein, three ascending stages in the development of religion: the religion of fear, the religion of morality, and the religion of the cosmos.

The religion of fear is the product of primitive, self-centered, unenlightened men, of the kind we meet in the Pentateuch. These men believed in a personal God who was involved in their destinies, who rewarded and punished his creatures. The religion of fear not only did not free men from their bodily concerns and egocentric anxieties—it made these very concerns and anxieties an occasion for God's intervention in the workings of the world.

The religion of fear is superseded by the religion of morality, as embodied in some of the Jewish prophets and elaborated by the New Testament. Knowledge itself provides only the means, not the ends of life; religion—acting through the intuition of great teachers and radiant personalities—sets up the ultimate goals of life and provides the emotional context in which they can influence the individual. Men, left to shift for themselves, would see the ends of life to be ease and happiness; such a selfish ethic, dominated by elementary instincts, is "more proper for a herd of swine." A genuinely religious person is one who has "liberated himself from the fetters of his selfish desires and is preoccupied with thoughts, feelings, and aspirations to which he clings because of their super-personal value."

The religion of morality is the highest that the great mass of men can aspire to, and it is sufficient to tame their animal spirits. But for a select few there is something finer and more noble: the religion of the cosmos. For the wise man—and this is the very definition of his wisdom—ethical behavior needs no religious sanction; sympathy and love of humanity he finds to be sufficient unto themselves. His religion, as distinct from his morality, is the result of a unique religious event, the mystical experience of the rationality of the cosmos, in which the individual is annihilated. Of this experience Einstein writes: "The individual feels the nothingness of human desires and aims and the sublimity and marvelous order which reveal themselves both in nature and the world of thought. He looks upon individual existence as a sort of prison and wants to experience the universe as a single significant whole."

This experience is not reached by any Cabalistic practices. On the contrary: The *via mystica* is nothing other than the *via scientiae*. Science, at its greatest, is identical with religion, at its most sublime. Science provokes a "profound reverence for the rationality made manifest in existence." The scientist "achieves a far-reaching emancipation from the shackles of personal hopes and desires, and thereby attains that humble attitude of mind towards the grandeur of reason incarnate in existence." And just as science leads us to true religiosity, so does true religiosity lead us to science:

> The cosmic religious experience is the strongest and the noblest, driving scientific research from behind. No one who does not appreciate the terrific exertions, the devotion without which pioneer creation in scientific thought cannot come into being can judge the strength of the feeling out of which alone such work, turned away as it is from immediate practical life, can grow.
>
> What deep faith in the rationality of the structure of the world, what a longing to understand even a small glimpse of the reason revealed in the world, there must have been in Kepler and Newton.

When a Boston Catholic priest took it upon himself in 1929 to warn Americans of Einstein's "atheism," Rabbi Herbert S. Goldstein cabled Einstein: "Do you believe in God?" Einstein cabled back: "I believe in Spinoza's God, who reveals himself in the harmony of all Being, not in God who concerns himself with the fate and actions of men"—a statement which so affected Rabbi Goldstein as to make him predict hopefully that Einstein "would bring mankind a scientific formula for monotheism."

Instead of the worship of the God of Abraham, Isaac, and Jacob, we have—in the tradition of Maimonides, Spinoza, and Hermann Cohen—the *amor Dei intellectualis*. Instead of the Lord of Hosts, we have the God of the philosophers—the Logos, the Reason which governs the universe, the incorporeal meaning behind the chaos of concreteness.

Reason, which worships the God of Spinoza, begins with the *proposition* "all men are mortal," and is most interested in the immortal truth of this and other propositions. Biblical faith, which worships the God of Abraham, begins with the *fact* that "all men are mortal." The truths of Reason are true even if man does not exist; they are true, as Husserl remarked, for "men, angels, monsters, and gods." Faith is less concerned with the truths of Reason than with the fate of man—the mortal, finite creature who cannot volatilize himself into Reason. Reason is what we have gained by the eating of the Tree of Knowledge: We are like unto gods, sharing in divine omniscience. Faith is the human condition experiencing itself in its most naked actuality, for with the eating of the apple there goes the Fall, and we must surely die.

The struggle between the God of Abraham and the God of Spinoza is the central theme of the spiritual history of the Western world. Out of it there comes the Old Testament and the New, Greek philosophy and Gnosticism, medieval Scholasticism and Renaissance science, German Idealism and modern atheism.

And in this conflict the Jew is tensed and sundered. For he is of the Covenant of Abraham, whom God commanded; and he has also prominently been of the opinion of Philo and Spinoza, to whom the world is the garment of Reason.

Einstein was born in 1879 into a German-Jewish family whose Judaism had been pretty well eroded by the tide of assimilation. He was sent to a Catholic elementary school in Munich, and even here the fact of his being a Jew was in no way impressed on him. We are told in his autobiographical sketch about a preadolescent religious fervor, but it seems to have been in no way Jewish. At the Gymnasium, at the age of fourteen, he was instructed in the elements of Judaism; he was attracted to what he regarded as its elevated morality, repelled by its ritual codification. When Einstein was sixteen, his family moved to Milan from Munich for financial reasons; after six months, unable to bear the rigid discipline of the Gymnasium, Einstein joined them. In Milan he renounced both his German citizenship—becoming stateless—and his membership in the Jewish community; only by such a double renunciation could the rational young man show his contempt for the idols of the herd.

Einstein formally became a Jew once again in 1910 when he accepted the chair of theoretical physics at the German University in Prague. Emperor Francis Joseph believed that only members of a recognized religious denomination were qualified to teach there, so Einstein had to register as a follower of the "Mosaic creed." More than half the German-speaking population of Prague were Jews, and the city at that time was witnessing, under the general influence of Martin Buber, a Jewish intellectual renaissance. Einstein came to know and be friendly with the active leaders in this movement, especially Hugo Bergmann and Max Brod. (He met Franz Kafka, too—one wonders what they had to say to each other.) But Einstein still refused to take being a Jew seriously.

In 1921, however, Einstein publicly declared himself to be a Zionist—to everyone's surprise and the consternation of not a few. The man who was known to despise nationalism as an excrescence of the herd mentality praised Zionism as "the embodiment of the reawakening corporate spirit of the Jewish nation." What happened to bring this "conversion" about? Nothing singular or dramatic so far as we know. Indeed, it is best understood as not a conversion at all, but as a relapse—from the religion of the cosmos to the religion of morality. It was apparently not possible to sustain forever the ecstasy of Reason; one had to return to the realm of matter and men, and there the best of all possible demeanors was an exalted, abstract morality. Einstein was able to announce that he found in Judaism an admirable ethical sensibility that demanded not faith but "the sanctification of life in a suprapersonal sense." Jewish morality, like Reason (though not so nobly), turned man from himself to the sanctification of life in general. He liked to quote Rathenau to the effect that "when a Jew says he's going hunting to amuse himself, he lies."

More to the point, one feels, is the tone and inflection with which he writes of his generations of ancestors, the ghetto Jews: "These obscure humble people had one great advantage over us; each of them belonged in every fiber of his being to a community in which he was completely absorbed."

Einstein's new Jewishness was not the result of his discovering a hidden Jewish self. It was, on the contrary, a new means of escaping from his self. The flight to Reason from the chaos of existence, which seemed to have succeeded so well, was now acknowledged to have been, at least in part, a failure. Something ponderable and indissoluble had been left behind: the flesh-and-blood Jew born of woman, the specific presence of the absentminded professor. And Einstein once again fled—into community, the ghetto, the warm mass of Jewry. What could not be transmuted into Reason would be absorbed into "the Jew."

And what could not be absorbed into the Jew would be once more etherealized—this time into the "world citizen."

Einstein's political and social opinions—so naive, so superficial, so bizarre—have baffled and disturbed his many admirers. They have usually sought to explain these opinions away with the statement that there is apparently no correlation between scientific and political intelligence. But this does less than justice to Einstein, who certainly would not concede the point. Moreover, it is possible to show that Einstein's political views are closely related to his entire outlook. He has applied to society that same rage for simplicity and love for the abstract that accomplished so much in his theoretical physics. But men cannot be so profitably transformed into clear and logical abstractions. The result of such an effort is confusion, contradiction, and, inevitably, an unpleasant impatience on the part of the thinker.

Thus, Einstein has always been a pacifist. His pacifism is bred of an intense hatred of the military, which he regards as the bestialization of man. But in so selfless a devotion to "Humanity" as Einstein's, strange things happen in one's relations to men. Sometimes, indeed, one cannot see men for Humanity. So it happened that Einstein not only vigorously supported the Second World War; he also defended the indiscriminate bombing of German cities as "morally justified," and urged that the Germans be "punished as a people" for their "collective guilt."

Einstein despises capitalism because it presupposes the existence of discrete, free, and autonomous selves in competition and even conflict. The individual's position in our society is such that "the egotistical drives in his make-up are constantly being accentuated, while his social drives, which are by nature weaker, progressively deteriorate. . . . Unknowingly prisoners of their own egotism, they [individuals] feel insecure, lonely, and deprived of the naive, simple, and unsophisticated enjoyment of life." Such a simple celebration of life can only come about when men have transcended their selves into Humanity, and the chaos of existing societies has been stilled into Community. Rejecting the idea of capitalism, Einstein elects for the idea of socialism.

The ideal community is the antithesis of the self-centered individual, and the perfect community, like the purified self, can only be won through Reason. But Reason has a way of discovering the "laws of society," the observance of which constitutes freedom. So there is the not uncommon sight of the radical rationalist—for example, George Bernard Shaw or the Webbs—who is favorably disposed to a society that suppresses the "self-seeking ego" (that is, the individual) in the name of a selfless *raison d'état.* Einstein's habit of sending messages to Communist-controlled "congresses of intellectuals" does not represent any sympathy for Russian totalitarianism—which he detests—but is rather a genuflection before the socialist idea, and an act of homage to those of vigorous intellect "who get things done," especially when they wish to "do things" for "peace." An international organization of the intellectual elite influencing the policies of nations has always been one of Einstein's fondest dreams.

The escape from the self into the Jew and Humanity, however, like the flight into Reason, has failed Einstein. Though he still signs petitions and sends encouraging communications, there is abundant evidence that his heart is not in them. Einstein's melancholic loneliness is the salient feature of his personality, as it is of his face.

> My passionate sense of social justice and social responsibility has always contrasted oddly with my pronounced freedom from the need for direct contact with other human beings and human communities. I have gone my own way and have never belonged to my country, my home, my friends, or even my immediate family, with my whole heart; in the face of all these ties I have never lost an obstinate sense of detachment.

Philipp Frank comments further: "He always has a certain feeling of being a stranger, and even a desire to be isolated. On the other hand, however, he has a great curiosity about everything human and a great sense of humor, with which he is able to derive a certain, perhaps artistic pleasure from everything that is strange and even unpleasant."

And: "His attitude in intercourse with other people, consequently, was on the whole one of amusement. He saw everyday matters in a somewhat comical light.... The laughter that welled up from the depths of his being was one of his characteristics that immediately attracted one's attention."

Einstein has not succeeded in becoming pure spirit or pure citizen or the selfless member of an organic community. He has ended up as simply more himself, laughing at his own presumption, though not for that the more content with man's condition and man's fate.

Einstein's gaiety, his informality of dress and manner, his quick sympathy—they [are] of that humanism which springs, not from love of fellowmen, but from compassion at the brutal fact that men exist at all. Perhaps if Einstein and Kafka—whose earthly self was amiable too, and from the same cause—had talked a while, they would have found more in common than one might expect! The Jew as Pure Reason and the Jew as Pure Alienation might have sensed in each other a kinship—perhaps even a secret identity, for the Kingdom of Reason can be as cold and infinitely empty as K.'s Kingdom of Nothingness; and both are as uninhabitable as the illusory world of the average sensual man. They might have smiled with a common irony at the world of matter and men, so complacent and blind in the ignorance of its own essential unreality. And they might have sighed, too, at being forever excluded from it.

1950

# 29

# Christianity, Judaism, and Socialism

I WANT to say first what a privilege it is to have the opportunity to deliver a sermon to theologians, aspiring theologians, and theologians *manqués.* * This is not the first time I have performed that function. I can think of three occasions in the past five years when I have spoken to large bodies of "concerned clergy" in various American cities. I always say the same thing. I tell them to stop being so interested in politics, and I ask them why they don't take an interest in religion instead. Invariably, they are disinclined to take my advice.

I have been called a neoconservative—never mind precisely what that means, the term does suggest the general ideological posture from which I speak. I should make it clear that I also speak as a neo-orthodox Jew, in belief at least. That is, I am nonpracticing—or nonobservant as we say—but, in principle, very sympathetic to the spirit of orthodoxy. When I talk about religion, I talk as an insider, but when I talk about Christianity, I think it will be very clear that I talk as an outsider. When

*This is the slightly revised text of a talk to professors and students of divinity, given on July 9, 1978 at a conference sponsored by the American Enterprise Institute.

I say I am not a Christian, I do not say it polemically, of course. But whether one is Jewish or Christian does, it seems to me, affect one's attitude toward capitalism.

Orthodox Jews never have despised business; Christians have. The act of commerce, the existence of a commercial society, has always been a problem for Christians. Commerce has never been much of a problem for Jews. I have never met an Orthodox Jew who despised business—though I have met some Reformed Jews who are businessmen and despise business.

Getting rich has never been regarded as being in any way sinful, degrading, or morally dubious within the Jewish religion, so long as such wealth is acquired legally and used responsibly. I was raised in a fairly Orthodox Jewish home, and everyone I knew was in business, including most of the rabbis. No one could make a living in those days as a rabbi, so rabbis ran shops, or their wives ran shops for them. It was generally assumed that the spirit of commerce is perfectly compatible with full religious faith and full religious practice. I think this is true in Islam as well, but it is not true in Christianity. The difference is that both Islam and Judaism are religions of the Law, and Christianity is a religion that has repealed the Law. This difference gives Christianity certain immense advantages over both Judaism and Islam in terms of spiritual energy; but in its application to the practical world, it creates enormous problems.

A year or so ago, I was chatting with a prominent rabbi, an old friend who heads a major institution of Jewish learning. He had just returned, sweating and angry, from a meeting with some of the faculty at Union Theological Seminary. He said he could not understand why they would talk about nothing but "prophetic Judaism" and "prophetic Christianity." At the end of the meeting, he told them that he was a rabbi, and asked why they would not talk about rabbinic Judaism, or rabbinic Christianity—to coin a phrase. They did not understand what he meant, or were not much interested in what he meant.

Now this dichotomy, this antagonism, I think, is absolutely crucial to an understanding of the relationship between any religion and the real world—the real world of politics, the real world of social life. The terms "prophetic" and "rabbinic," which come, of course, from the Jewish tradition, indicate the two poles within which the Jewish tradition operates. They are not two equal poles: The rabbinic is the stronger pole, always. In an Orthodox Hebrew school, the prophets are read only by those who are far advanced. The rest of the students read the first five books of the Bible, and no more. They learn the Law. The prophets are only for people who are advanced in their learning and not likely to be misled by prophetic fervor.

These two poles, of whatever different intensities, are present in all religions, so far as I have been able to determine. One may, adapting the concepts of Eric Voegelin, call the one pole orthodoxy and the other pole gnosticism. I think these are quite useful categories. I assume the tension between the prophetic and the rabbinic—or the orthodox and the gnostic—to be eternal.

We are talking about an eternal debate about the nature of reality, about the nature of human authenticity. When are human beings most perfectly human? When are they fulfilling their human potential to the utmost? The gnostic tends to say that the proper and truly authentic human response to a world of multiplicity, division, conflict, suffering, and death is some kind of indignant metaphysical rebellion, a rebellion that will liberate us from the prison of this world.

That thrust, that tendency, exists within Judaism, within Christianity, within Islam. It seems to be a natural human response to reality, because in some respects this world we live in is, in fact, a hell. Little children, as Dostoevski pointed out, suffer hideous pain—innocent little children die of cancer, of ghastly diseases. Is it not proper, then, for us to be indignant at the world and desire either to escape from it or to reconstruct it radically in some way?

This is the gnostic reaction to the existential reality in which we all have to live. The word "prophetic" may be misleading; in traditional Judaism, prophetic is not really the same as gnostic, since the ancient Prophets were law-observers, not law-repealers. But in recent decades the term "prophetic" has come to allude to a similar spiritual impulse.

These gnostic movements tend to be antinomian—that is, they tend to be hostile to all existing laws and to all existing institutions. They tend to engender a millenarian temper, to insist that this hell in which we live, this "unfair" world, can be radically corrected.

Orthodoxy, on the other hand, has a very different view of how human beings achieve their full human authenticity. The function of orthodoxy in all religions is to sanctify daily life and to urge us to achieve our fullest human potential through virtuous practice in our daily life, whether it be the fulfillment of the law in Judaism or Islam or *imitatio Christi* in Christianity.

Orthodoxy, in other words, naturally engenders a somewhat stoical temper toward the evils of the world. It says that evils exist, that we don't know why they exist, and that we have to have faith that, in some larger sense, they contribute to the glory of the world. Orthodoxy seriously concerns itself with the spiritual governance of human beings who have to live in this world and whose faith is being tested and tried every day. Orthodoxy has to do its best to give answers to questions that are unanswerable, that is, questions of why we live in a world that is "unfair," to use a term that has recently entered political discourse.

Christianity emerged out of a Jewish rebellion within Judaism. Christianity emerged out of what, I think, can fairly be called a Jewish gnostic movement. We know very little about it, but it seems evident that in the decades prior to the appearance of Jesus, there were all sorts of gnostic millenarian bubblings within Judaism. There were sects that were resentful of the Law, resentful of the world, promising to—or attempting to—achieve a radical reconstruction of reality, and a redemption of human beings from a condition that they perceived to be inhuman.

The trouble with gnosticism, however, is that it cannot ultimately win, because such radical reconstructions never do occur. Human nature and human reality are never transformed, so whether gnostic movements seem to win or lose, they always lose in a sense. The very different ways in which they lose, however, are terribly important. They can lose destructively, or they can lose constructively. A gnostic movement can mature into an orthodoxy, which from the gnostic point of view is a loss. From the world's point of view, however, a new orthodoxy is a good thing, if it is a genuine orthodoxy, one that people freely consent to. A gnostic rebellion can also spend itself, of course, in futile dissent, in revolution and blood baths, or whatnot.

For the first two centuries of the Christian era, the church fathers had to cope with precisely this problem: namely, how to take the gnostic temper of Christianity—so evident in the New Testament, as contrasted with the Old—and convert it into an orthodoxy. They had to convert it into a doctrine for the daily living of people, into something by which an institution could spiritually govern the people. I find it interesting to note that one of the ways the church fathers did this—and they did it in many ways—was by incorporating into Christian scripture the Old Testament.

I remember reading many years ago about the Marcionite heresy, the fearful dispute over whether or not the Old Testament should be included as part of Christian scripture. Marcion, who eventually lost, had a very good argument—why include the Old Testament when the New Testament transcends and repeals it? That seemed reasonable to me. Since the books did not say why the church fathers thought otherwise, why they insisted on including the Old Testament into Christian scripture, I did some desultory reading on the matter. It became clear that the church fathers needed the Old Testament to help convert what was originally a gnostic movement into a new creative orthodoxy, which they did brilliantly. They needed the Old Testament for certain key statements that are not found in the New Testament, or at least are not found there in an emphatic way, such as that when God created the world, he saw that "it was good." That is an Old Testament doctrine. It became a Christian doctrine, and it is crucial to any orthodoxy, in contrast to gnosticism, which says that no one knows who created the world—a demiurge or whatever—but that the world is certainly bad.

Another key statement needed for a new orthodoxy was the injunction to be fruitful and multiply, which is an Old Testament, not a New Testament, injunction. Again, this is crucial to any orthodoxy, any institutionalized religion that spiritually governs human beings and helps them cope with their inevitable and irresolvable existential problems. It affirms the goodness of life, in addition to the goodness of Being.

The reason why Christianity and Judaism both take the same controversial view toward homosexuality is not because they are narrow-minded, but because legitimization of homosexuality flouts the injunction to be fruitful and multiply. As a matter of fact, a gnostic movement can always be recognized by its reaction to that commandment. Gnostics are always interested in sex, since it is such a dominant human passion. Sometimes they become orgiastic; sometimes they become ascetic—the monastic movement was a form of gnostic asceticism that was co-opted by the church. It simply told the monks they could be ascetic so long as they did not go around teaching that everyone should be ascetic. But whether orgiastic or ascetic, gnostic sexuality rejects the injunction "be fruitful and multiply." In gnostic sexuality it is obscene for a woman to become pregnant in an orgy. Homosexuality contradicts that principle too, as does abortion at will.

The modern secular world, as it emerged after the Renaissance and the Reformation, is shot through with gnostic elements. Since the dissolution of the great Roman Catholic orthodoxy of medieval Europe, the modern world has oriented itself toward beliefs that premodern theologians, Christian or Jewish, would have quickly identified as heresy. In fact, the Catholic church, almost until yesterday, did regard them as heresy. I used to require my graduate class to read Pius IX's *Syllabus of Errors,* a wonderful statement of the credo of modernity. Pope Pius IX issued it in 1870 as a list of what it is anathema to believe, and he included just about everything that every one of my graduate students believes. They believe it all implicitly, as if it were natural and unarguable.

The Catholic church probably would not say quite the same things today. The *Syllabus* represents the premodern view. The modern view, to which the church increasingly leans, is much more gnostic in its lack of calm acceptance of the world. And, in its political versions, gnosticism takes the form of utopianism.

Modern thought has two characteristics not to be found in classical Christian thought or in classical Jewish thought. One is the absence of the idea, in any version, of original sin. This is crucial because a belief in progress, in the sense in which modernity believes in progress, is incompatible with a belief in original sin. (One must remember that a belief in the advancement of certain fine arts or technical arts is not quite the same as a secular faith in progress.) The modern way of thinking did not emerge fully until the doctrine of original sin—or whatever its counterpart would be in Judaism (and there is a counterpart)—had been abolished in favor of a doctrine of original innocence. The doctrine of original innocence meant that the potential for human transformation here on this earth was infinite, which is, of course, the basic gnostic hope.

The second element that made the modern secular world so gnostic-utopian by classical standards was the rise of science and technology, with the promise it gave of man's potential mastery over nature, and over human nature through something called the social sciences. The modern world, in its modes of thinking, has become so utopian that we do not even know when we are utopian or to what degree we are utopian. We utter utopian clichés in politics as if they really were clichés—for example, "a world without war." What would happen if a president of the United States said to us tomorrow: "I understand that previous presidents have told you that one of the aims of our foreign policy is to create a world without war. Well, let's face it, there will never be a world without war. Human beings have fought ever since the beginning of time, and human beings as we know them will not cease fighting. I will give you a world in which we will try to avoid war; if we get into war, we will try to limit the war; and if we get deeply into war, we will try to win the war. But I cannot promise you a world without war."

Can you imagine a president of the United States saying such a thing on television? Yet, everything that is said in that imaginary speech is true. The very notion of a world without war is fantastic. The lion shall lie down with the lamb, but not until the Second Coming.

The opening sentence of a very good book, *Political Messianism,* by J. L. Talmon, reads: "The present inquiry is concerned with the expectations of universal regeneration which animates men and movements in the first half of the nineteenth century." After I first looked at that, I asked the author whether his allusion to "expectations of universal regeneration" was meant to be ironic. He responded that this was a fair description of much of political thought in the first half of the nineteenth century—the thoughts of Saint-Simon, Comte, Fourier, Marx. Prior to the eighteenth century, anyone enunciating the notion that politics—politics, not religion—is concerned with the expectation of a universal regeneration of humanity, of the world, would have been regarded as mad. Regardless of political views, no one ever thought that politics could offer any such ambitious promise. It is only in our era that this conception begins to prevail. We even teach the Utopian Socialists in our history courses as if they were political philosophers, instead of religious fanatics of a peculiarly modern kind.

The major form which the expectation of universal regeneration takes is socialism. Modern political messianism or utopianism eventuates in the socialist movements of the last century and a half. These movements have been increasingly attractive to Christians and to Jews. The Jews who have played a prominent role in them are, on the whole, those who believe in what they call "prophetic" Judaism. These are Jews who rebel against rabbinic Judaism as something stale and decadent. They feel they have a historic mission to fulfill and then proceed to engage in the cardinal sin known to both Judaism and Christianity as "the hastening of the end"—the ushering in of the Messianic Age or the Second Coming through magic, or politics, or some other human contrivance.

Socialism also has a natural attraction to both Jews and Christians because of its emphasis on community, as distinct from a liberal society's emphasis on individualism. In an individualistic society, voluntary communities can be created and sustained only with great difficulty. Indeed, an individualist society is constantly subverting the voluntary communities the individuals themselves establish. This has been our own past experience in the last hundred years with voluntary institutions, including churches. Individual initiative, simply on its own and without official support, cannot satisfy the natural desire for community among human beings. This happens to be one of the crucial weaknesses of the individualistic, liberal, capitalist society of the modern era.

I think the attraction of socialism also has something to do with the decline of certain "primitive" aspects of both Christianity and Judaism. Above all, there has been a decline in the belief in an afterlife in whatever form—the belief that, somehow or other, the "unfairness" of this life in this world is somewhere remedied and that accounts are made even. As more and more people cease to believe any such thing, they demand that the injustice and unfairness of life be coped with here and now. Inevitably this must be done by the government, since no one else can claim a comparable power.

Capitalism and modern secular society encourage a rationalist way of looking at the world that renders incredible any notion of an afterlife, of eternity, or of a supernatural redress of experienced injustice. To the degree that capitalism does this, it generates an avalanche of ever greater expectations directed to the temporal power—demands which no socio-economic or political system can in fact meet. The consequence is that even a victorious socialist politics, arising out of these urgent demands, can only survive by repressing them.

These seemingly inherent weaknesses of liberal capitalism unquestionably encourage people to turn toward socialism. But there is a way in which socialism is peculiarly attractive on its own merits to Christians, or people who have what are thought to be Christian impulses. The root of all socialist economics is the separation of the distribution of wealth from the production of wealth. Socialist economics assumes that there is no problem of production, only a problem of distribution. This appeals to Christians, or to people of Christian impulses, because Christianity, as a religion, fares much better in a static society and in a static economy than in a dynamic one. Moreover, socialist redistribution bears some resemblance to Christian charity.

Now, it is true that, if there is no economic growth, and if distribution can be separated from production, then the question of distribution becomes an overwhelming moral issue. In my opinion, it is a trivial moral issue in our world because economic growth solves the problem—the problem of poverty—toward which redistribution aims. But Christianity has never much liked a commercial society that produces economic growth, a dynamic society in which everyone improves his condition. It prefers a static society in which Christian virtues are practiced, and the merits of that are not to be sneezed at. They have been eloquently expressed by T. S. Eliot in his *Idea of a Christian Society.*

The trouble, however, is that socialism offers a redistribution that only looks like Christian charity, and that socialist societies, when they come into being, are but grotesque parodies of a Christian community. One major reason why this is so is that the socialist promise is not truly a Christian promise. It offers redistribution *and* abundance—and on this promise it simply cannot deliver.

There is another reason why people who are experiencing a Christian impulse, an impulse toward the *imitatio Christi,* would lean naturally toward socialism, and that is the attitude of Christianity toward the poor. And here, again, I have to speak as a Jew. Traditional Judaism does not have Christianity's attitude toward the poor.

I know of no sacred Jewish writing that says it is particularly difficult for a rich man to get into heaven; it is just not in our tradition. But Christianity does begin, as I said, as a gnostic movement with the attitude that there is something especially good about poor people, that they are holy in a sense. They are God's children, in some special way, even though their poverty is not voluntary (one could understand voluntary poverty being regarded as such).

The result is interesting to watch today in our political attitudes toward poor people and toward movements that either speak in the name of the poor or, for that matter, may actually be representative of the poor. Let us imagine there is a revolution in Mexico in the name of poor people, one that may even be genuinely supported by them. I am giving myself the hardest possible case. Poor people, in fact, never make revolutions. They are made by professors and students and intellectuals in the name of the poor. But let us assume a case where it is really the poor who are making the revolution. We know, as students of political theory and history, that this revolution will only end in tyranny, in the ruin of the economy, and in a situation in which the poor themselves will be worse off than before, with the destruction of whatever liberties may have been provided by tradition, if not by liberal legislation.

If we know that, would we call this an unjust revolution? How many of us would really put ourselves flatly in opposition to a revolution of poor people, even if we had good reason to think that this revolution would lead to disastrous results? Not many, I think. And I believe the Christian attitude about the presumed special quality of poor people is part of the reason. One feels, somehow, that if the poor act this way, they must be doing it for good reason and we must respect that reason, even if it seems to us not really reasonable.

One of the difficulties of American foreign policy today in coping with so-called socialist and communist countries is the claim of those countries to represent the poor, and the claim of revolutionary movements in the so-called Third World to represent the poor. The claim is usually false, but it might in some instances be true. In my view, it would not matter whether it were true or false. But I suspect it would matter very much to most people, who would be most uncomfortable to find themselves opposing a majority composed of poor people. In terms of political philosophy, however, there is no reason why one should feel uncomfortable opposing a majority of poor people. There is no reason to think that poor people are wiser or nicer than any other people, or that they have an inherent sense of justice which other people do not have.

In the churches today, there is an attitude toward poor people that derives from Christianity, though it is in its profoundest sense anti-Christian. In Dostoevski's novel, *The Brothers Karamazov,* the Grand Inquisitor says that when the Antichrist comes, his message will be first to feed the people of the world, and then to ask of them virtue. But is that not the message that most Christian churches today preach?

Again, Judaism differs in this respect from Christianity. Judaism gives no exceptional status to the poor. Charity is a primary virtue, to be sure—Judaism is certainly not neglectful of the poor, as anyone who knows anything about Jewish communal life will agree. But no one can claim any exemption from any of the Jewish laws because he is poor. In contrast, the conventional Christian wisdom of today is that the poor—what we call underprivileged people—need not be expected to behave virtuously until their material situation has been remedied.

Socialism being an inherently gnostic movement—that is, trying to achieve the impossible in this world—always fails. The world remains unredeemed under socialism, as much as it was unredeemed under capitalism.

One can even see why and how the failure is inevitable. Socialism, like all gnostic movements, has a morphological structure. There is a group at the top—the "perfect" is the gnostic way of describing them. According to Marxist-Leninist dogma, this group would be the party leadership. Below that are the believers—the party; and below that the masses. All gnostic movements have this structure, and anyone with political experience would know that this structure must lead to a government of the perfect over the believers and the masses. And, since the believers and masses are not perfect, the perfect will have to coerce them in order to make them perfect. Our experience with human nature throughout history shows they will fail to make them perfect and that the coercion will, therefore, be permanent.

Even granting all conceivable good intentions to the communist movements of the Soviet Union, Eastern Europe, and China, that is precisely what has happened. A movement has to be led by a small group of people because they are the only ones who have *gnosis,* the arcane knowledge of how to reorganize the world, so as to make it a perfect place. And those high ideals then sanction the most Machiavellian means.

All of modern socialism is a movement that says it will create a good society, which will then create good people. I can think of no political doctrine more contemptuous of both the Jewish and Christian traditions, which say that there cannot be a good society unless there are good people.

It is true that a good government can improve the people somewhat, with difficulty. But the notion that a handful of true believers can, by manipulating the mass of the people, create a good society inhabited by good people is pernicious nonsense. All such movements end the same way, coercing people "for their own good" until, at a certain point, the people who are doing the coercing forget why they are doing it and come to regard the coercion, in and of itself, as legitimate.

Socialism today is a gnostic movement that has been unable to transform itself into an orthodoxy. It could not create a new orthodoxy, as Christianity did in its day through the creative brilliance of the church fathers who added a new dimension to man's religious experience. Socialism evidently cannot do anything like that. What interesting socialist book has come out of the Soviet Union in sixty years? There has not even been a decent biography of Karl Marx. There is no hagiography coming out of the Soviet Union, because no one wants to write it or read it. To discuss Marxism, go to Berlin, or to Paris, or to Rome, or to Berkeley, but not to Moscow, where no one is interested in discussing Marxism. The doctrines of socialism are dead within the socialist world, as the Russian dissidents are showing us. There are no church fathers in modern socialist thought. There are some who tried to be, but they all ended up being denounced as heretics and driven from the fold.

In the area where it promised so much, namely economics, socialism has been a calamitous failure. That failure is due to its basic conception that production can be separated from distribution, that is, that production can be organized according to the dictates of whoever is running the state, and that distribution is a separate process also at the command of the state. But it turns out that there is a link between production and distribution, the link called human incentives. In order to distribute, there must be something to distribute. Production is not autonomous, and distribution is not autonomous. Human incentives are what create wealth, and to create affluence, as socialism promises, an economy must be respectful of human incentives.

Socialism says that we do not need that human incentive we call self-interest, that we can rely on altruism, on the pure spirit of fraternity. The experience of the world says, no—not in large societies. In the Israeli kibbutz, a self-selected elite may work altruistically for the common good for a generation or two. But this is not possible in a large

325

heterogeneous society. It is not only impossible; it is inherently absurd. To increase wealth, production must be increased through the use of materialistic incentives. Without those materialistic incentives, there will be less and less to distribute, and any redistribution will become less effective in bettering the material condition of human beings than was the capitalist system it replaced. Again, I think this is quite evident in the economies of all the socialist nations.

It is ironic to watch the churches, including large sections of my own religion, surrendering to the spirit of modernity at the very moment when modernity itself is undergoing a kind of spiritual collapse. If I may speak bluntly about the Catholic church, for which I have enormous respect, it is traumatic for someone who wishes that church well to see it modernize itself at this moment. Young people do not want to hear that the church is becoming modern. Go tell the young people that the message of the church is to wear sackcloth and ashes and to walk on nails to Rome, and they would do it. The church turned the wrong way. It went to modernity at the very moment when modernity was being challenged, when the secular gnostic impulse was already in the process of dissolution. Young people, especially, are looking for religion so desperately that they are inventing new ones. They should not have to invent new ones; the old religions are pretty good. New ones are being invented because the churches capitulated to modernity at the very moment when the rebellious, gnostic, self-confident spirit of modernity was entering a major crisis and was moving toward its own discreditation.

It is all very sad.

1979

# ACKNOWLEDGMENTS

The material in this book originally appeared in the following publications:

"Memoirs of a Trotskyist" in *The New York Times Magazine* (January 23, 1977). © 1977 by The New York Times Company. Reprinted by permission.

"Memoirs of a 'Cold Warrior' " in *The New York Times Magazine* (February 11, 1968). © 1968 by the New York Times Company. Reprinted by permission.

"The Adversary Culture of Intellectuals" in *Encounter* (October 1979). Copyright 1979 by *Encounter*.

"Pornography, Obscenity, and the Case for Censorship" in *The New York Times Magazine* (March 28, 1971). Reprinted in *On the Democratic Idea in America* by Irving Kristol (New York: Harper & Row, 1972).

"Confessions of a True, Self-Confessed—Perhaps the Only—'Neoconservative' " in *Public Opinion* (October/November 1979). Copyright © 1979 by the American Enterprise Institute.

"The American Revolution as a Successful Revolution" from *America's Continuing Revolution: An Act of Conservation*. Copyright © 1975 American Enterprise Institute.

"American Historians and the Democratic Idea" in *The American Scholar* (Winter 1969–70).

"Socialism: An Obituary for an Idea" in *The Alternative* (October 1976). Copyright *The Alternative* (*The American Spectator*) 1976.

"Machiavelli and the Profanation of Politics" from *The Logic of Personal Knowledge: Essays by Various Contributors Presented to Michael Polanyi on his Seventieth Birthday* (London: Routledge and Kegan Paul, 1961).

"Adam Smith and the Spirit of Capitalism," which appeared originally in *The Great Ideas Today* (1976), is reprinted with permission of that publication and of Encyclopedia Britannica, Inc.

"Rationalism in Economics" from *The Crisis in Economic Theory*, ed. Daniel Bell and Irving Kristol. Copyright © 1981 by Basic Books, Inc. Reprinted by permission.

"Some Personal Reflections on Economic Well-Being and Income Distribution" from *The American Economy in Transition*, ed. Martin Feldstein (Chicago: University of Chicago Press, 1980). Copyright © 1980 by National Bureau of Economic Research. All Rights Reserved.

"On Corporate Capitalism in America" from *The American Commonwealth—1976*, ed. Nathan Glazer and Irving Kristol (New York: Basic Books, 1976). Copyright 1976 by National Affairs, Inc.

"Does NATO Exist?," in *The Washington Quarterly* (Autumn 1979).

"Christianity, Judaism, and Socialism" from *Capitalism and Socialism: A Theological Inquiry*, ed. Michael Novak. Copyright © 1979 American Enterprise Institute.

The following material originally appeared in the *Wall Street Journal:*
"The Emergence of Two Republican Parties" (January 4, 1983)
"Business Ethics and Economic Man" (March 20, 1979)
"Diplomacy vs. Foreign Policy in the United States" (April 15, 1982)
"Our Incoherent Foreign Policy" (October 15, 1980)
"Exorcising the Nuclear Nightmare" (March 12, 1980)
"The Key Question: Who Owns the Future?" (January 11, 1982)
"A Letter to the Pentagon" (February 20, 1981)
"Moral Dilemmas in Foreign Policy" (February 28, 1980)
"The 'Human Rights' Muddle" (March 20, 1978)
"Understanding the Soviet Mafia" (November 18, 1982)

The following material originally appeared in *Commentary:*
"Urban Civilization and Its Discontents" (July 1970)
"Is Jewish Humor Dead?" (September 1950)
"God and the Psychoanalysts" (November 1949)
"Einstein: The Passion of Pure Reason" (September 1950)

*327*

# INDEX

Abortion, 319
Abraham, 290
Absolute monarchies, 130, 145
Academic freedom, 219
Adams, Henry, 98, 141
Adams, John, 86, 133
Adler, Mortimer J., 11
Adversary culture, 27–42, 66–67
Advertising: power of, 45; regulation of, 51
Affluence, morality and, xi
Afghanistan, 232
Afterlife, 321–22
Aggression, 299
Agrarian bias, 56
Alcohol, 67–68, 175; prohibition of, 51, 68
Aleichem, Sholom, see Rabinowitz, Solomon
Alembert, Jean d', 150
Alienation, 5, 166; Smith on, 163, 166
American colonies, charters of, 87
American Jewish Committee, 16–17
American Revolution, x, 78–94, 142–43
Andropov, Yuri, 270–71
Anglo–Scottish Enlightenment, x, xi, 141, 142–43, 144, 146–47, 149–56
Anti–anticommunists, 20–21
Anti–capitalism, 114
Antichrist, 91, 324
Anticommunism, 20–22
Antinomianism, xi, 317
Anti–Semitism, 278
Antitrust legislation, 207
Anxiety, 288, 296
Arab nations, 230, 242
Arendt, Hannah, 80, 84, 88
"Aristocratic Opinions of Democracy," 103
Aristotle, 58, 76, 123
Armed forces: discipline, 258–60; drug abuse in, 257–58
Arms control, 231
Arnold, Matthew, 99
Arrow, Kenneth, 10
Art of War, 128
Arts: modernism in, 35–36; religion and, 36
Asceticism, 319
Atheism, 144, 300
Atlantic Institute, 242
Austen, Jane, 31, 37, 40
Authoritarian regimes, 263, 264
Ayer, A.J., 307

Bacon, Francis, 133, 304
Bacon, Roger, 123
Bailyn, Bernard, 80
Balance of trade, 145
Bancroft, George, 100
Banfield, Edward, 74
Bank of the United States, 206
Bearbaiting, 45
Beard, Charles A., 102, 104
Bell, Daniel, 9–10, 20, 35, 74, 76

Bellow, Saul, 11
Bellush, Bernard, 10
Berger, Morroe, 10
Bergmann, Hugo, 311
Bergson, Henri, 282, 284
Berns, Walter, 45
Beyond Culture, 38
Beyond the Pleasure Principle, 298
Blacks, 111, 166
Boccaccio, Giovanni, 52
Boccalini, Trajano, 132
Bohemianism, 35
Books, 44; censorship of, 44, 45, 52–53
Boorstin, Daniel, 105, 106
Boston Globe, 258
Bourgeois populism, xiv
Bourgeois society, 28–33, 37–38, 40, 143, 165–66, 175–76; broadening base of, 65–66; family in, 46; intellectuals and, 32; limitations of, 116–17; neoconservatism and, 76
Brecht, Bertolt, 32, 116
Brezhnev, Leonid, 270
Bribery, 218, 221–22
Brod, Max, 311
Brothers Karamazov, The, 91, 324
Brown, Norman O., 49
Buber, Martin, 311
Bureaucracy, 120, 121, 122; corporate, 122; in USSR, 271–72, 273
Burke, Edmund, xi, 105, 152
Burnham, James, 11, 12
Business ethics, 219–22

Calvin, John, 161
Camp, George Sidney, 101
Capital, 157
Capital punishment, 47
Capitalism, 40–41, 116–17, 200, 202–3, 322; Christianity and, 179–80, 192, 316; corporate, 203–18; democracy and, 202–3; Founding Fathers and, 136–46, 176, 202–3; Judaism and, 180n, 316, 318–19; liberal, 77; neo–Austrian view, 188; social Darwinism, 171–72; Smith and, 139–40, 146, 156–67, 169, 172; State, 232, 264, 266
Carter, Jimmy, 232, 264, 266
Carter administration, 266–69
Castro, Fidel, 24
Catholic Church, see Roman Catholic Church
Causality, 307
CCNY., see City College of New York
Censorship, 43–44, 51–54; of books, 44, 45, 52–53; civil liberties and, 43, 52; of drama, 52; of libraries, 52
Central America, 228
Central Intelligence Agency (CIA), 14–19, 24
CETA (Comprehensive Employment and Training Act), 259
Challenge of Humanistic Economics, 189
Charters of American Colonies, 87

329

# Index

# Index

Egalitarianism, *xiv*, 102–3, 121, 196–97, 198–200, 244–45

Ego, 299

Einstein, Albert, 301–14; political views of, 312–13; religion and, 301–2, 308, 310–12; *see also* Relativity, theory of

Eisenhower, Dwight D., 73–74, 111

Eliot, T.S., 130, 322

Elitism, *xiv*, 33, 149, 167, 208, 211; socialism as, 210

Elkins, Stanley, 104

Embargo, grain, 232

Emigration, right of, 267

*Encounter* (periodical), 10, 15, 16–17, 19, 22, 23

Enlightenment: Anglo–Scottish, *x*, *xi*, 141, 142–43, 144, 146–47, 149–56, 188; French–Continental, *xii–xiii*, 142, 143, 144, 130–32; Machiavelli and, 133

Ennui, 40

Environmentalism, 33, 212

Erasmus, Desiderius, 125

*Essay on the Nature and Significance of Economic Science, An,* 184

*Essay on the Principle of Population, An,* 169, 170

Ethics: economics and, 179n–80n, 181–82, 219–22; journalistic, 219–20; in Judaism, 179n, 192, 214n; legal, 220; media, 219–20; *see also* Morality

Ethnic voters, 111

Europe, 249–51; NATO and, 236–47

Europe, Eastern, 324

Evolution: of human race, 297; social, 151

Excellence, pursuit of, 28–29

Executives, corporate, 204

Existence, reality of, 303

Experience, significance of, 303

*Fable of the Bees,* 153

Faith, 289; humor and, 279, 280, 281, 282, 283; reason and, 310; *see also* Religion

Family, 77, 168, 176

*Fanny Hill,* 53

Fanon, Frantz, 23

Farfield Foundation, 15–16

Fathers of the Church, 116, 318, 325

*Federalist, The,* 57, 81, 88, 92, 98, 139, 153, 180

*Federalist Papers, The, see Federalist, The*

Ferguson, Adam, 142, 150, 151

*Fiddler on the Roof,* 196

Fiedler, Leslie, 11, 20

Fielding, Henry, 40, 45

First Amendment, 144, 219

Fleischmann, Julius (Junky), 15–16

*Florentine History,* 128

Ford, Gerald, 111

Foreign policy, 231–35, 255, 272–73, 323; diplomacy and, 227–30, 256; human rights and, 267–69; NATO and, 236–47; non-democratic governments and, 262–64, 272–73; nuclear weapons and, 248–52

Founding fathers, 80–81, 83, 87–88, 90, 92, 93, 97, 98–100, 268; capitalism and, 129–46, 176, 202–03; cities and, 56–57, 58, 62, 64–65; democracy and, 57, 140–41, 168

Fourier, Charles, 321

France, 243

Francis Joseph I (Emperor of Austria), 311

Frank, Philipp, 303–4, 313

Franklin, Benjamin, 214

French Revolution, *xii*, 80, 84, 86, 89, 142

Freud, Sigmund, 283n, 286, 288–90, 292–99

Freudianism, 288

Friedman, Milton, *xii*, 76

Frontier experience, 102

Fundamentalists, 112

Future, 253–56

*Future of an Illusion, The,* 296

Gaddi, Giovanni, 129

Gaitskell, Hugh, 22

Galbraith, John Kenneth, 207, 209n

Galileo, 305

Gallows humor, 279

Genocide, 267

Gentile, Alberico, 131

Germany, 238

Ghettos, humor of, 277–78, 281

Gilbert, Allen, 124

Giunta, Bernardo di, 129, 131

Glazer, Nathan, 10, 20, 74

Gnosticism, 318, 319–20, 324–25; arts and, 35–36; as rebellion, 317

*Godfather, The* (film), 271

Godkin, E.L., 65, 98, 103–4

Goethe, Johann Wolfgang, 305

Goldstein, Herbert S., 310

Goldwin, Robert, 268

Goodman, Paul, 12

Government: authoritarian regimes, 263, 264; decentralization, 59–60; dictatorships, 262; local, 87, 90; reactionary regimes, *x*; republican, 167; state constitutions, 87; *see also* Democracy

*Graduate, The* (film), 67

Grain embargo, 232

Greenberg, Clement, 12

Grunberg, Emile, 186

Guevara, Ernesto ("Che"), 23, 24

Guilt, sense of, 299

Hadley, Arthur T., 258

Harrington, Michael, *ix*, 74, 132

Hartz, Louis, 105–06

Hasidism, 283

Hayek, Friedrich, *xii*, 76, 179, 203

Healey, Denis, 22

Hebrew Union College, 287

Hegel, Georg Wilhelm Friedrich, 41, 187

Heidegger, Martin, 135

Herder, Johann, 129

Heresy, 289

Hillel, Rabbi, 180n

*History of the Formation of the Constitution,* 100

Hobbes, Thomas, 153, 161, 171

Hofstadter, Richard, 98, 104

Homosexuality, 24, 139

Hook, Sidney, 12, 20

House of Representatives, 112

Howe, Irving, 9

Human rights, 266–69

Humanism, 144, 297

# Index

Marcuse, Herbert, 23, 49
Market economy, 29, 76, 182; economic growth and, xii
Market research, 190
Marlowe, Christopher, 127
Marshak, Robert, 4
Marx, Karl, 41, 77, 157, 177, 187, 213, 321; religion and, 295
Marxism, xi, 11–12, 28, 33–34, 116, 119–20, 254, 294, 325
Marxist–Leninism, 271–72, 324
Maslow, Abraham, 191–92
Mathematics, 301–3, 308
Mattingly, Garrett, 131
*Mayflower* Compact, 87, 89
Media: ethics of, 219–20; political bias of, 212, 255
Meinecke, Friederich, 130
Melman, Seymour, 10
Memorial Day, 260
Mercantilism, 143, 145–46, 153
Meyer, Marvin, 104
Microeconomics, 177, 185, 187
Middle America, 61–62, 66
Middle East, 230, 240
Military Academy, U.S., 259
Military morale, 259–60
Mill, John Stuart, 182n, 184, 193
Millenarianism, 86, 317, 318
Mises, Ludwig von, 188
Mobilization of society, 34
Mobs, 64–66; revolutionary, 84, 85
Modernism, 35–36, 39, 40
Montesquieu, Charles de Secondat, 58, 168, 209
Moral philosophy, 191
Morale, military, 259–60
Morality: xi, xii; affluence and, xii; business ethics, 219–22; Christian, 153–55; democracy and, 168; religion and, 220; republican, 51, 57, 62–68; sexuality and, 319; urbanization and, 61–62; see also Ethics
More, Paul Elmer, 98
Morgan, Edmund S., 80
Mormon Church, 217
Morgenau, Henry, 308
Moses, 289–90
Moynihan, Daniel Patrick, 74
Muckraking, 205
Muggeridge, Malcolm, 16, 17
Mussolini, Benito, 130
Mystical experience, 309

*Nation* (periodical), 65
National Bureau of Economic Research, 200
Nationalism, xiii; and Union of Soviet Socialist Republics, 272, 273; and United States, 245
Nationalization of industry, 121
NATO (North Atlantic Treaty Organization), 236–47, 250–51
Nazism, 277
Neo–Austrian economics, 185, 186–88, 192–93
Neo–Castroism, 23
Neoconservatism, xii, 73–77; conservatism and, xiii
*Neoconservatives: The Men Who Are Changing America's Politics, The,* 74
Neurology, 292

Neurosis, religion as, 289n, 291, 294
"New class," 211, 216, 217
*New International* (journal), 11–12
*New Leader* (journal), 19
*New York Review of Books,* 18, 23
*New York Times,* 48
*New Yorker* (journal), 217
Newman, Cardinal John Henry, 122
*News from Parnassus,* 132
Newton, Isaac, 305, 306, 308, 309
Nietzsche, Friedrich, 49, 134–35, 285, 289, 297
Nihilism, 117, 126, 127, 169; humor and, 280, 284
Nisbet, Robert, 74
Nixon, Richard, 111
North Atlantic Treaty Organization, *see* NATO
Novels, 28, 31
Nozick, Robert, 210
Nuclear deterrence, 237–38
Nuclear weapons, 237–38, 248–52; tactical, 251

Oakeshott, Michael, x, 90, 147
O'Brien, Conor Cruise, 23
Obscenity, 45–47, 51, 52–54; *see also* Pornography
Oedipal revolt, 296
Old Testament, 29, 41, 316
Olsvanger, Immanuel, 283
*On Revolution,* 80
OPEC (Organization of Petroleum Exporting Countries), 242
Organization of American States, 229
Organized crime, leadership of, 271, 273
Organized labor, 121, 207, 210
Original sin, doctrine of, 155, 320
Ortega y Gasset, José, 108
Orthodoxy, 317–19, 325
Orwell, George, 261

Pacifism, 312
Pahlevi, *see* Reza Shah Pahlevi
Parables, 279
Parades, 260
"Pareto maximization rule," 173, 190
Paine, Thomas, 87
Parkman, Francis, 101–2
*Partisan Review* (journal), 11, 12, 20
Paternalism, xii
Pathological psychology, 292
Patriotism, 57
Pay differentials, 198
*Peace of Mind,* 287–88
*Peace of Soul,* 288
Pension funds, 207
Pentateuch, 308
Perfectibility of humanity, 320
Phillips, William, 12
Philo of Alexandria, 310
Philosophy, 40; science of, 307; traditions, xii
Physics, 304–7
Physiocrats, 146
Picasso, Pablo, 116
Pilgrims, 86
Pius IX, 319
Planck, Max, 308
Planning, economic, 187

# Index

Plato, 58
Podhoretz, Norman, 74
Poetry, 28
Pogo, 69
Pogroms, 279, 280
Poland, 233, 254
Polanyi, Michael, 34
Political machines, 59
*Political Messianism*, 320
Political parties, changes in, 109–10; *see also specific party*
Political philosophy, 97; economics as, 177, 190–91, 201
Political rights, 268
Political science, 124
Politics: definitions, *x*; ideologies and, *ix–x*; pornography and, 49–50; religion and, *x*; terminology, *ix*
*Polity and Economy: An Interpretation of the Principles of Adam Smith*, 160
Pollock, Sir Frederic, 133
Popular culture, 28–31, 37
Populism, *xiii–xv*, 204–6, 217
Pornography, 24, 44–45, 47–48, 52–54, 126–28; *see also* Obscenity
Post–Christian thinking, 125–26
Post–Keynesian economics, 185, 186–88, 192
Positivism, 304–05
Poverty, 195–96, 322–23; revolution and, 89; self-government and, 90; Third World, 234
*Preuves*, 16
Price controls, 212
*Prince, The*, 124, 125–34
Printed word, power of, 44
Privacy, 46
Probability statistics, 307
Profiteering, 162, 165
Progress, concept of, 150–51
*Progressive*, 219
Progressive–reform movements, 208
Prohibition of alcohol, 51, 68
Promiscuity, 35
Property, ownership of, 165–66
Prophets, 316–17
Protestant ethic, 180, 214
Proverbs, 279
Psychiatry, 292
Psychoanalysis: religion and, 286–300; schools of, 292–93
Psychology, pathological, 292
Public opinion, 53–54; democracy and, 51

Quantum physics, 306–7

Rabbis, 316
Rabelais, François, 52
Rabinowitz, Solomon, 279–80, 282, 285
Racial discrimination, 166
Radical–humanistic economics, 185, 188–91
Rahv, Philip, 12
*Ramparts*, 18
Rational behavior, 181
Rationalism, 169; economics and, 179; utopian, 39
Reactionary regimes, *x*
Reagan, Ronald, 110, 111–12, 255, 256

Reason: faith and, 310; religion and, 293, 294
Rebellion: gnosticism as, 317; vs. revolution, 84–85, 88
Referenda, 96, 97
Reformation, 41, 143
Redistribution, economic, 322
Reification, 187
Reik, Theodor, 285, 292
Relativity, theory of, 305
Religion, 176, 301–2, 308; arts and, 36; decline of, 122; democracy and, 168; economics and, 117–18, 174; humor and, 279–83; innovation as return, 178; Karl Marx and, 295; law and, 316; morality and, 220; neoconservative view of, 77; as neurosis, 289n, 291, 294; politics and, *x*, 168; psychoanalysis and, 286–300; reason and, 293, 294; science and, 307–09; transcendence, 67; *see also* Christianity, Judaism
Religion of fear, 308
Religion of morality, 308–09
Religion of the cosmos, 309
Religious toleration, 144–45, 168
Religious wars, post–Reformation, 143–44
Representation, nature of, 91–92
Republican government, 167
Republican morality, 51, 57, 62–65; mobs and, 64–66; substance abuse and, 67–68
Republican party, 110–11
Republican virtues, 81, 86
Republics, 85–86, 92–93
Revolutionary mobs, 84, 85
Revolutions, 232; American, *x*, 78–92, 142–43; French, *x*, 80, 84, 86, 89, 142; Russian, 84
Reza Shah Pahlevi, 261–62
Ricardo, David, 177, 183, 192
Richardson, Samuel, 37, 40
Right, ideology and, *ix*
Rio Treaty, *see* Inter–American Treaty of Reciprocal Assistance
Robbins, Caroline, 80
Robbins, Lionel, 184
Robertson, Sir Dennis H., 179
Robespierre, Maximilien, *xi*, 142, 143
Roman Catholic Church, 217, 326; alienation and, 166; Fathers of, 318, 325; psychoanalysis and, 287, 288, 295; science and, 305, 306; sexuality and, 319; voters in, 111
Romanticism, 30, 33; neoconservative opposition to, 76; utopian, 39
Roosevelt, Franklin D., 109
Roosevelt, Theodore, 110–11, 113
Rosenberg, Harold, 12
Rosenfeld, Isaac, 11
Rossi, Peter, 10
Rousseau, Jean Jacques, 33, 133, 166
Russia, *see* Union of Soviet Socialist Republics

Sacks, I. Milton, 10
Sade, Marquis de (Donatien Alphonse François de), 45, 53, 126, 134
Sadism, 48
Saint–Just, Louis Antoine Lēon de, 142, 143
Saint–Simon, Claude Henri de Rouvroy, *xi*, 36, 41, 117, 210, 321
SALT negotiations, 231
Samuel, Maurice, 279, 281

# Index